Archives 101

ABOUT THE SERIES

The American Association for State and Local History Book Series addresses issues critical to the field of state and local history through interpretive, intellectual, scholarly, and educational texts. To submit a proposal or manuscript to the series, please request proposal guidelines from AASLH headquarters: AASLH Editorial Board, 2021 21st Ave. South, Suite 320, Nashville, Tennessee 37212. Telephone: (615) 320-3203. Website: www.aaslh.org.

ABOUT THE ORGANIZATION

The American Association for State and Local History (AASLH) is a national history membership association headquartered in Nashville, Tennessee, that provides leadership and support for its members who preserve and interpret state and local history in order to make the past more meaningful to all people. AASLH members are leaders in preserving, researching, and interpreting traces of the American past to connect the people, thoughts, and events of yesterday with the creative memories and abiding concerns of people, communities, and our nation today. In addition to sponsorship of this book series, AASLH publishes *History News* magazine, a newsletter, technical leaflets and reports, and other materials; confers prizes and awards in recognition of outstanding achievement in the field; supports a broad education program and other activities designed to help members work more effectively; and advocates on behalf of the discipline of history. To join AASLH, go to www.aaslh.org or contact Membership Services, AASLH, 2021 21st Ave. South, Suite 320, Nashville, TN 37212.

Archives 101

Lois Hamill

ROWMAN & LITTLEFIELD
Lanham • Boulder • New York • London

Published by Rowman & Littlefield
An imprint of The Rowman & Littlefield Publishing Group, Inc.
4501 Forbes Boulevard, Suite 200, Lanham, Maryland 20706
www.rowman.com

6 Tinworth Street, London SE11 5AL, United Kingdom

British Library Cataloguing in Publication Information Available

Library of Congress Cataloging-in-Publication Data
Names: Hamill, Lois, 1957– author.
Title: Archives 101 / Lois Hamill.
Description: Revised and expanded edition. | Lanham : Rowman & Littlefield, [2021] | Series: American Association for State and Local History book series | Includes bibliographical references and index.
Identifiers: LCCN 2020049949 (print) | LCCN 2020049950 (ebook) | ISBN 9781538133002 (cloth) | ISBN 9781538133019 (paperback) | ISBN 9781538133026 (epub)
Subjects: LCSH: Archives—Handbooks, manuals, etc. | Archives—Administration—Handbooks, manuals, etc. | Archival materials—Management—Handbooks, manuals, etc.
Classification: LCC CD971 .H356 2021 (print) | LCC CD971 (ebook) | DDC 027—dc23
LC record available at https://lccn.loc.gov/2020049949
LC ebook record available at https://lccn.loc.gov/2020049950

♾️™ The paper used in this publication meets the minimum requirements of American National Standard for Information Sciences—Permanence of Paper for Printed Library Materials, ANSI/NISO Z39.48-1992.

Contents

Figures, Tables, and Textboxes

Figures

Tables

Textboxes

Preface

Many cultural organizations are small, have limited resources, or both. Whether the organization has paid staff members or relies entirely on volunteers, the number of personnel dedicated to the management and care of the cultural collections may be as few as one person, who may or may not be professionally trained.

The collections themselves may consist mainly of a single format or include varying quantities of archival manuscripts, photographs, books, audio or video recordings, art, or objects. Each of these types of materials has its own separate profession or even specialists within a larger field: archivist, manuscript curator, photograph curator, digital archivist, librarian, rare book librarian, film archivist, sound technician, digital librarian, painting curator, or museum curator. Many cultural organizations cannot afford one of these specialists, much less a separate specialist to care for each of these material types.

Just as there are separate specialties for the care and management of these materials, the books about these materials also tend to be specialized. The volunteer or a professional educated in just one of these specialties does not necessarily have the time or training to comprehend narrowly focused books about a single aspect from any of the other specialties.

This practical guide will explain the basics for performing the most common functions for managing collections in small cultural organizations. It will address how to manage archival manuscripts (paper records), photographs, audio and video material, books, and, to a lesser degree, art and objects. Basic concepts and vocabulary are defined to establish a minimum foundation from which to proceed. Specific examples are given that the reader may copy or modify and adopt. Policies and guidelines for the basic management of cultural collections are addressed. The reader will come away with a solidly grounded, practical overview for the most typical duties. This will prepare the reader with the basics. If a more specialized or exceptional situation should occur, more specialized research or consultation with a trained professional of the appropriate specialty should be sought.

Many functions will be easier to perform with the minimum of a computer with word processing and spreadsheet software. PastPerfect museum collection management software is widely used by museums, local historical societies, and smaller archives. This manual explains how to integrate PastPerfect software with archival practice. For example, the archival inventory or finding aid is presented as the primary method for describing archival records, but for those readers using PastPerfect, guidance is given on the use of specific components of the software to build on what a finding aid does. An integrated blend of both plays to the strength of each without unnecessarily reentering information from the finding aid into PastPerfect. Those who are only interested in how the software functions are referred to the user's guide. When discussing PastPerfect, bolded words indicate terms, forms, or functions specifically referenced in the user's guide.

This book is intended for those cultural organizations with a small staff who manage a diverse collection. Local historical societies, local history rooms in public libraries, or historical properties that also hold an assortment of historical papers, photographs, and objects are prime examples, but this does not exclude churches and cultural or civic organizations. Staff members may be paid or volunteer and may be professionally trained but not as archivists. They may be entry-level professionals who find themselves working without the guidance of a more experienced professional or librarians or art or object curators who have responsibilities for materials outside their specialty. Faculty teaching courses to prepare students to work in or manage cultural or nonprofit organizations in archival programs, library schools, public history programs, or possibly even museum studies or integrative studies may find this text helpful.

Throughout the text, the terms *institution* or *organization* are used for convenience instead of writing an inclusive list each time, but they include local historical societies, the local history room of the public library, historical properties that also have small quantities of archival material, museums, churches, cultural or civic organizations, the town clerk's office—whoever is responsible for archival material but lacks the appropriate professional training.

In the same vein, the term *staff* is used inclusively to refer to all who manage or care for historical collections regardless of whether they are paid, volunteer, part-time, full-time, or temporary.

The term *archival*, as in *archival boxes or folders*, implies that they are *acid free*. *Acid free* will not be repeated each time. Many of these supplies are also lignin free and buffered. Assume supplies are acid free, lignin free, and buffered unless otherwise stated.

Some terms are defined in chapter 1 to explain the difference between some of the more specialized kinds of archives and the material they collect; thereafter the terms *records* or *materials* are used inclusively rather than continually listing all record types or formats.

Photograph or *photographic materials* is understood to include prints, slides, and negatives instead of repeatedly listing all formats. Although the text discusses analog photographic formats heavily, much of the information is also applicable to digital photo files.

PastPerfect software is specifically mentioned, but other collection management software is available. These products tend to be more specialized, just for museum collections, just for books, or just for archival records. They require extensive advanced education (a master's degree) in book cataloging or archival description and knowledge and application of numerous standards. The software is more expensive because it is intended for larger institutions and includes options not required by those who would use PastPerfect. Some professional institutions have looked to open-source software because of issues, including cost, with proprietary software. However, these often require high levels of computer skills to support their use.

PastPerfect is written to describe museum objects, books, and archival records. Photographs are a subset or type of archival record. It also integrates scans of photographs or documents or photographs of objects with their record. It is the only collection management software I am aware of that manages all these formats at a price affordable to a smaller institution. The needs and resources of smaller institutions are different from larger ones. PastPerfect provides for the description of diverse formats in a single unified catalog, works with optional modules to provide web access or create exhibits, and manages to be affordable for its target audience. Further, the software can be used by people without professional training or advanced computer software skills. It is efficacious and is a good fit for its audience, which is the same audience for whom I have written this book. For these reasons, I mention it.

It's impossible to predict all the possible variations for the circumstances in any given situation. My goal is to present the most significant questions or issues to consider, or the most common variations in a situation. By providing the thinking behind a situation, I hope to empower this book's readers with the ability to modify best practices and professional experience, while still respecting them, to fit the specifics of their situation. There is no single right way to perform archival work, but some are better than others. May you find the best path.

—Lois Hamill
Covington, Kentucky

Acknowledgments

As historians and people who value the past, we work to preserve the records in our custody. Not everyone who protects and manages historical records is professionally trained for this work. Although well intentioned, they can unknowingly cause damage for lack of appropriate training. I hope that this volume will help those who read it to at least cause no irreversible damage. I am hopeful, however, that they will go beyond that and do good.

I would like to thank Jim O'Toole, who taught me the questions to ask, and Don Corey of the Bedford (Massachusetts) Historical Society for the many pleasant hours I spent working there. Special thanks go to Lisa Perna, Patrick Diesman, and Kiki for their support and encouragement. Thanks to my colleague John Schlipp for updates on copyright and intellectual property and my supervisor Lois Schultz for release time.

Thank you, Rick Hilton and Brian Gomez of PastPerfect Software, Inc., for allowing me to test the latest version of their software and for the honor of being the first person outside the company to have a copy of the newest user guide.

Thanks to my editor Charles Harmon for the opportunity to work with him again.

1

Basic Definitions and Concepts

This manual focuses on those types of materials that might typically be found in a local historical society, the local history room of the public library, a historical property, or a small cultural organization: paper archival records or manuscripts, photographs, audio and video material, books, art, and objects. Most of these types are found to varying degrees in archives. In order to establish a common starting point, we will start with some terms as they are most often defined by archivists.

The word *archives* has three meanings. Archives can be the records that are collected, the physical space that houses the archival records, or the department or unit that manages the archival records. The context should indicate which meaning is intended. The word *archives* is the broadest, most general and inclusive term used to describe archival records.

What is a *record*? "Any type of recorded information, regardless of physical form or characteristics, created, received, or maintained by a person, institution or organization." According to archival educator and author Bruce W. Dearstyne, "A record is unique, one of a kind." Former archival educator James M. O'Toole says that "what makes the records 'archives' is neither age nor appearance, but rather content, meaning and usefulness."[1] Correspondence, reports, diaries, journals, ledgers, deeds, agreements, photographs, maps, blueprints, and drawings are all examples of archival records. A record is defined by its information content, not its physical *format*. A record can exist in many diverse formats: paper; microfilm; audiocassette tape; videotape or digital film; computer disks, tapes, flash, thumb, or hard drives including external hard drives; and CDs or DVDs. The distinction between the content and the carrier or format is particularly important in the case of electronic records.

The quality of uniqueness is an important part of the definition of a record. A record can be reproduced. Copies of modern meeting minutes are often distributed to all attendees. The first or original copy produced by the person or office responsible for creation of the minutes is the official copy or *record copy*. All others are duplicates. Limited quantities of a record can be produced without losing its status as a record, but when it is published en masse, it crosses the line from record to book, newspaper, report, or other published item. Archival records are primary sources while published materials are secondary sources. Each is organized and managed differently from the other. Newspapers can be good research sources and are frequently found in archives, but they are not archival records.

Government, private businesses, and organizations create documents while conducting their normal daily business, frequently as a result of documenting transactions. Many of the documents are kept and organized in some manner so that they can be found and used until they are no longer needed. They may document the history of a decision, set policy, or be required for legal reasons. The body of records produced by the federal, state, or local government can also be called *public archives*. Records created by businesses, organizations, and institutions can also be called *institutional archives* because the records are created by the institution about itself, its activities, and its transactions.

Papers created by private individuals are different from public or institutional archives. Public and institutional archives usually document transactions and have an official nature. They normally consist of a group of documents that, when examined, together provide a more complete record of a transaction than one individual document. Papers created by private individuals lack an official nature. They normally do not document transactions. They may consist of one document. The reason for their existence may be conscious intent. Papers created by individuals during the course of their lives (as opposed to during "official" hours when they are employed by someone) are called *manuscripts* or *personal papers*. Historical manuscripts usually have historical or literary value or significance. Noted archival leader Solon J. Buck says that historical manuscripts have "value because of their association with significant events or personages of the past" or present, or as useful sources of information about the past or present.[2] In the past, some historians felt that personal papers would express the personal biases of their author and provide less reliable or accurate historical accounts than public archives.

After varying periods of time, records are no longer actively used. When they reach the inactive stage, those with permanent historical value may go to an archives. Federal government records are preserved, as are many state government records. Not all states have public records laws. Unfortunately, preservation of most other records of historical value may depend on chance. Institutions that preserve nongovernment records can be broadly divided into two categories. First are the private businesses and institutions that care for the records they themselves have created. These records are managed in their own institutional archives. The second category includes organizations that collect records that others have created. These organizations are called *manuscript repositories*. Manuscript repositories may collect records created by businesses, religious or civic organizations, private groups, personal papers, or any combination of these. State and local historical societies are examples of manuscript repositories. Both institutional archives and manuscript repositories can be referred to by the broader collective term of archives.[3]

Some institutions maintain an institutional archives of their own records and also collect the same type of materials as a manuscript repository. In this case, the term *Special Collections* is used to simultaneously describe their manuscript *holdings* while contrasting them from their institutional records. Colleges and universities are the most common examples of institutions that also have Special Collections. They recognize the value of historical records for research conducted by their students, faculty, and others.

Additional Reading/Resources

O'Toole, James M. *Understanding Archives and Manuscripts*. Archival Fundamentals Series. Chicago: Society of American Archivists, 1990. This is a good basic introduction to archives for a novice.

O'Toole, James M., and Richard Cox. *Understanding Archives and Manuscripts*. Archival Fundamentals Series II. Chicago: Society of American Archivists, 2006. This is the updated version of O'Toole's earlier edition.

Pearce-Moses, Richard. *A Glossary of Archival and Records Terminology*. Archival Fundamentals Series II. Chicago: Society of American Archivists, 2005. Note that a free online version of *A Glossary of Archival and Records Terminology* is available online from the Society of American Archivists at https://www2.archivists.org/glossary. This is a good source for terminology and explanations. Try the online version first. This was written for professionals and may be confusing to a novice.

Notes

1. Richard Pearce-Moses, *A Glossary of Archival and Records Terminology*, Archival Fundamentals Series II (Chicago: Society of American Archivists, 2005), s.v. "record"; Bruce W. Dearstyne, *Managing Historical Records Programs: A Guide for Historical Agencies* (Walnut Creek, CA: AltaMira Press, 2000), 1; James M. O'Toole, *Understanding Archives and Manuscripts*, Archival Fundamentals Series (Chicago: Society of American Archivists, 1990), 3.

2. Lewis J. Bellardo and Lynn Lady Bellardo, comps., *A Glossary for Archivists, Manuscript Curators, and Records Managers*, Archival Fundamentals Series (Chicago: Society of American Archivists, 1992), 22, 25; Solon J. Buck, "Essentials in Training for Work with Public Archives and Historical Manuscript Collections," in *Archives and Libraries*, ed. A. F. Kuhlman (Chicago: American Library Association, 1940), 114.

3. Lois D. Hamill, "Provenance and Original Order: The Evolution of Their Acceptance as Principles of Arrangement and Description" (master's thesis, University of Massachusetts–Boston, 1997), 6. Ann Arbor, MI: UMI, 1997.

2

Acquiring New Materials

When records, papers, or other items are offered to the local historical society, public library, or historical property, someone must decide whether the organization should accept them. *Acquisition* is the term for both the process of obtaining new records, by donation or purchase, and the records that are so obtained.[1] What is the process for evaluating potential new additions to an institution's holdings? How is a decision made?

An organization should have a written *collection policy* to guide its collection development in a coherent manner. This is an important document that details what the organization will and will not collect. It should be sufficiently specific to answer the question of whether a particular set of records falls within the scope of the policy, yet allow some leeway for the acceptance of unexpected but suitable records. The policy might limit the dates, location, subject, or format of acceptable records. An organization may not wish to collect objects, art, or other materials. Such decisions should be recorded in the collection policy. It should also provide a method for *deaccessioning*, the removal of unsuitable material that is already in the *collection*.

If designated people have the authority to make acquisition decisions, they should be named in the collection policy by title, not the individual's name. If the process goes through a committee, the policy should describe the process as well as the composition of the committee. The same policy applies for deaccessioning. Decisions to deaccession materials from the collection should be documented. Other components of a collection policy include the mission of the archives, how collecting is done, who may use the collection, and the process for revising the policy. The policy may include or refer to separate, lengthier policies for collecting a particular subgroup of items, such as rare books or museum pieces. Refer to Additional Reading/Resources at the end of this chapter for examples of collection policies.

Appraisal

If a potential acquisition falls within the scope of the collection policy, then it should be evaluated for its informational, evidential, and intrinsic value. Archivists call this evaluation *appraisal* and distinguish this process from a monetary appraisal of the fair market value of something. Do the records have "sufficient long-term research value" to be worth the labor and expense that will be invested to preserve them and make them available to researchers?[2] Only a small percentage of records merits permanent retention in an archives.

Government, corporate, and organizational records are intentionally created to serve a purpose, such as to document a transaction. The records are created, kept, and maintained while they have value to their creator: that organization. The value may be fiscal, legal, or administrative. At some point, this value expires, and the records are no longer useful for their original purpose. Some of the records have *secondary values*. This is a different use from the one for which they were originally created. For example, tax records are created to assess and collect money to pay for government expenses. Later, genealogists can use them to document where and when people lived. Historians or economists might study them to make conclusions about wealth or financial trends. The foregoing are examples of the potential *informational value* of records—the degree of usefulness they have for providing information about people, places, or subjects. The more ways in which a set of records can be used to provide information, the higher its informational value is. Some records have very high informational value, and others may have very little. Sometimes the informational value can be increased by improving the *arrangement* or organization of the information so that it is easier to access the information. Sometimes records with high informational value will require a large expense to preserve or access the information. The cost can be more than the organization can afford. These factors need to be weighed as part of the appraisal process.

Papers created by private individuals lack the initial fiscal, legal, or administrative value of institutional records because they are created for different reasons than institutional records. Private individuals create different *types* of records that are potentially rich sources of informational value: diaries, journals, correspondence, and identified photographs. These types of records are highly desirable for gaining insight into the thoughts and opinions of their creators. They may also contain information about daily life, hobbies, or activities in a particular location or period. This would be informational value.

Some institutional records have *evidential value*, that is, information about the structure, functions, and activities of the institution that created them. Annual reports or meeting minutes typically include evidential information. Examples of personal papers that might have evidential value would include documents from service with civic or religious organizations or from a family business.

All types of records can have *intrinsic value*. This is their monetary value due to age; content; the circumstances under which they were created; someone's signature; seals, stamps, or attachments; and illustrations or uniqueness.

When deciding whether to acquire a potential acquisition, there are other factors to consider besides the research or intrinsic value of the records. The donor or the receiving institution may impose *access* restrictions on the records. Federal and state laws regulate access to personal information; Social Security numbers; medical, legal, and student records; information about minors and people who are still alive; and other types of records. Donors may request that records be closed until their death, or for a certain number of years, or they may request other conditions. If restrictions appear too stringent or close the records for too long, their value may not offset the storage space required or the lost opportunity to accept other records. Each institution will have to decide what restrictions it is willing to accept.

The organization may already have records that are similar to or related to the new acquisition. If space is an issue, will more of the same type of records add to the overall holdings, or would it be better to provide broader coverage of a subject? On the other hand, records that are related to material in the collection may increase the research value of both.

Another consideration is the physical condition of the records. Are they damaged? Is the damage easily repaired, or will it require expensive *conservation* work? Is there mold? Once contracted, mold never goes away completely; it is only dormant. Given the right temperature and humidity combination, the mold will return and can spread to previously clean items. Can the moldy items be discarded or replaced? How good are the environmental controls of the organization's storage areas? It is a greater risk to accept records that have had minor problems with mold if the temperature and humidity in the organization's storage areas are uncontrolled.

If you are offered a large quantity of paper records, how well are they organized? Will they require a lot of time to organize and make them available to researchers? Will their informational content be worth the time you will have to invest in them? Is similar information available from other sources, even if another organization owns it? Are there gaps in the records that decrease their usefulness? Maybe the correspondence files only include A through C, or maybe N through Z are missing. Do the records contain large quantities of unidentified newspaper clippings or copies of published material available elsewhere, or are they actually original, unpublished archival records? Newspaper clippings are highly acidic, transfer acid to adjacent materials, and deteriorate. Their value is in their information content; originals need not be kept. They can be photocopied onto acid-free paper, but this takes time and money and may not be the best use of limited resources. Someone else holds their copyright, restricting how they can be used. Newspaper clippings that do not include the date and name of the source newspaper are less useful than clippings for which the original source is identified. Many newspapers have already been microfilmed or digitized and are easier to search than loose clippings or even scrapbooks of clippings.

Most cultural organizations have limited resources. It is unethical to collect records if an organization has insufficient money, staff time, or storage space to properly care for them. Organizations in the same geographic area should refrain from competing for similar records. This helps to make the most of limited resources. An organization usually has other functions besides collecting records to make available for research. A successful organization must balance priorities with available resources. A collection policy that provides a clear focus, coupled with sound appraisal, will make acquisition decisions easier.

Role of the Donor

Sometimes the organization will have contact with a donor only once—when he brings the donation in. This may be the only chance to ask the donor what he knows about the donation. How did the donor get the donation: inheritance, yard sale, auction, gift, found in the attic of the old white house on Johns Hill Road, or found in the file cabinets of the such and such business? Does the donor know anything else about the previous owners of the records or objects? What does the donor know about the records or objects themselves? What is their significance? Does he know what type of information they may contain, who created them, or how old they are? Is there a person or a written source that can provide more information about the donation? What is their contact information? Even if it is speculation or secondhand information, record it. The notes can indicate the uncertainty of the information or the donor's source of information. The information can be researched later if the details are captured. Even if it is uncertain whether the donation will be accepted, record what the donor knows. This may be the only opportunity to obtain this information.

The donation information can be handwritten on paper, recorded in a word-processed document, or entered in a **Temporary Custody Receipt** (form) in PastPerfect software. The ideal situation would be to record the information during the discussion about the donation. This will minimize the loss of information and increase its accuracy. Note the source of the information (normally the donor), donor's contact information, the date, and the name of the volunteer or staff person with whom the donor spoke.

Donor Agreement or Deed of Gift

The potential new acquisition is evaluated using the collection policy and appraisal criteria discussed above. The decision is made to accept the new acquisition. Now what happens? The donor and the organization should execute a *donor agreement* or *deed of gift* legally transferring all the donor's physical and intellectual property rights in the acquisition, such as copyright, to the organization (see appendix B.1). The agreement should name the donor and the recipient with their legal address, describe the material donated in specific terms because it will be the organization's proof of ownership, describe the rights being transferred, and state the disposition of unwanted materials that are weeded out.[3] Both parties should sign and date the agreement. The receiving organization should keep the original and provide the donor with a copy. In order to create a deed of gift in PastPerfect, the donation must be at least minimally accessioned.

Note in appendix B.1 the donor may suggest possible disposition of materials the institution may choose to weed out or deaccession. An older practice of offering the donor the right of first refusal, or first choice of having these items returned, becomes problematic when the donor has passed away or moved out of contact with the institution. Language for suggested disposition allows the institution to still act rather than being stuck in limbo.

Copyright law is increasingly complex. Donors can transfer only those rights that they own. For example, donor A corresponds with relative B. The donor owns the copyright only to what he has written, not to what he has received. Although he physically owns the correspondence from relative B, he does not own the copyright. Physical ownership is not the same as copyright, whether for correspondence, photographs, art, or other copyrightable materials. Copyright will be covered in more detail later in this book, but institutions may desire to consult a lawyer regarding copyright questions particularly for significant questions or to review a sample contract.

The donor agreement may contain language restricting access to the records, provide for future additions of more material to the original donation, or address special provisions. If, for example, parts of the donation are to be copied or scanned and the originals returned to the donor, this should be documented in the agreement. A donor agreement is a contract. It is recommended that an attorney review a draft agreement for validity in the state in which the organization operates.[4]

Sometimes donors ask for an appraisal when they make a donation. All appraisals for tax purposes or monetary value must be performed by a third party. It is unethical for employees of the receiving organization to do so and may specifically be prohibited by the receiving organization's policy or their professional association's ethics statements.

After the donor agreement is executed, the next step is to create a *donor file*. This is where the organization's copy of the donor agreement should be filed. Any preliminary correspondence, notes taken about the donation, or other pertinent paperwork created prior to signing the agreement should also be put in this file. The purpose of a donor file is to assemble the records and information necessary for managing the collection, object, or items given. It might contain an appraisal, conservation records, or loan documents. Everything important to know about the donation is located in one spot, making it easier to answer questions that will occur when managing the donation.

Send the donor a thank-you note. A copy can be retained in the donor file or managed electronically. PastPerfect can extract information from the **Temporary Custody Receipt**, if one was made, and generate a thank-you letter. An alternative is to create an electronic folder titled "Thank yous" in word processing software and manage the letters there. Thank-you letters can also be filed in each respective donor's donor file.

Accessioning the New Donation

After the donor file is set up, the next important function is to *accession* the donation. Donor agreements are the written contract legally transferring rights to the new acquisition. *Accessioning* is taking physical and legal custody of the acquisition and documenting its receipt in a register, log, or database of the organization's holdings (see appendixes C.1a and C.1b).[5] When an institution transfers its own records from inactive use in an office to the archives, it doesn't need a donor agreement because the legal ownership has not changed. The institutional archives may use a *transfer form* to document the change in custody from the records to the archives. Institutional records are also accessioned to establish control over the records. A new acquisition should be segregated in a holding area for new acquisitions and accessioned as soon as possible after its arrival at the organization. Be careful not to mix new acquisitions or *accretions* with processed records.

The institution should maintain an accession log, register, or database to document all new records, collections, objects, or other items acquired. The first step in accessioning is often the assignment of an *accession number*, a unique number assigned to each new accession in order to link all the parts of the accession with each other and to the records associated with the accession, such as the donor agreement. In archives, a common numbering system is to use the four digits of the year in which the accession is received followed by enough digits to represent the number of accessions received to date that year. The example 2010-005 signifies the fifth accession received in 2010. The number may be prefaced by letters abbreviating the institution, for example NKU2010-005. If accession numbers were to be used in any type of multi-institutional database, the initial letters would help distinguish the records of one institution from another. Archives prefer to describe their materials collectively, in units, instead of item by item. Museums add a third group of digits to record each item in the accession.[6] For example, 2010-005-009 signifies the ninth item in this accession. Museums tend to record the accession number on every item in the accession. Archives do not. They do not mark anything in a permanent manner. The accession number may be marked using a number 2 pencil on the back of a photo or on the folder(s) in which the accession is stored.

A minimal accession record will include the accession number, the date received, the donor, the quantity, and a description of varying detail of the materials in the accession (approximate volume, inclusive dates, and general subject matter).[7] It may include the status of the copyright or other restrictions on access or use, the name and unique identification number of the collection or record group to which the accession will be assigned if known, information about a box list or inventory of the contents of the accession, any *preservation* issues, the possible processing priority, or other information prescribed by the receiving institution. To help track new accessions and maintain *intellectual control* over them until they are processed, it would be a good idea to record the row and shelf number where the materials are placed on the accession form. If the organization also maintains a shelf inventory, record the new accession there as well. See chapter 11, "The Collections Storage Environment," for more details on numbering storage locations. The paper or electronic accession log contains critical permanent records that may be needed in the absence of donor agreements, for insurance purposes, or in case of theft. The accession log needs to be kept permanently. If the original accession record is created electronically, maintain a paper copy as a backup. File in a binder subdivided by the year received. An additional copy can also be placed in the donor or *control file*. The last entry is used to assign the next sequential accession number for the year (see appendix C.1a and C.1b for completed sample accession forms that can be created and maintained in word processing software).

A new manuscript collection needs to be named. Its name should include the name of the person or body that created or collected the records plus a word or short phrase that describes the nature of the materials in the collection.[8] First, identify the creator. This may be an individual, a family, the Bedford Highway Department, or the First Parish Church. A person who collected documents signed by all the presidents of the United States would be treated as the creator of the collection. Although he did not create each document, he did create the collection by bringing all the documents together. This type of collection would be named for the collector, the Shonert Presidential Signature Collection. Another example is the individual who collects letters from various family members. At first glance, many people appear to have created the collection, but if a closer look reveals that all items were received by the same individual, it would be more appropriate to identify the individual, not the family, as the creator of the collection. The descriptive phrase that follows describes the nature of the material in the collection. Archival records are frequently described collectively. Common terms are *papers* (denoting personal materials), *records* (for organizational materials), or *collection* (for topical aggregations).[9] The Mary Scott Diaries would only have diaries and no other forms of material. The Bacon Family Papers would include materials in more than one format, for example, letters and photographs. The use of "records" in Campbell County School Records would indicate that these were official records created by Campbell County as a corporate body or agency.[10]

The institution's own records are assigned to record groups usually organized according to the organizational structure. Manuscript collections and record groups are normally also assigned a unique number that may be used as a shorthand way of referring to that unique body of records. Examples are RG-001 President's Records or MS-043 Chelmsford Ginger Ale Company Records. New collections may be named when accessioned or later when they are processed. If at accessioning, record the manuscript collection name or institutional record group to which the records are assigned in the accession record to indicate their expected disposition.

Once accessioned, a work copy of the accession form can be attached to the storage containers for the new collection. Space permitting, the new accession can be moved to a different holding area to await processing. If space is limited, simply attaching the accession form in a visible location on the storage containers should help distinguish between those new acquisitions that have been accessioned and those that haven't.

The people who manage cultural collections need to have intellectual control over the collection, that is, know its size, the information content or significance, and the dates of the material. The process of gaining intellectual control starts in a very preliminary way with accessioning. It is completed through arrangement and *description*, which are discussed in the next two chapters.

Deaccessioning Records

The same criteria that are used to evaluate a potential new acquisition can be used to evaluate items already in the collection that may be outside the collection policy, in poor physical condition, of negligible research value, or otherwise inappropriate for continued retention. Deaccessioning is the process of reevaluating and removing items already in the collection. "Already in the collection" means the items have previously been formally accepted or accessioned. This is in contrast to items that have been offered for consideration and may be physically at the institution but for which no decision has been made either way. The decision to deaccession records, an item, or an entire collection should be documented and put on file. Documentation of a decision to deaccession may be placed in the pertinent donor file or a dedicated deaccession file or attached to the original accession form. All these are potentially suitable places to file these documents, and copies may be placed in more than one location to cross-reference in different ways. Valuable or desirable items may be offered to a more suitable institution or sold. If sold, auctions are often the best solution since all interested parties have an equal chance to obtain the items. If they are sold, the income should be reinvested in the collections through the purchase of more suitable materials or for conservation work. Under no condition should materials be deaccessioned for the purpose of gaining income to pay for capital expenses or ongoing maintenance costs. Neither should they be sold to a member of the organization caring for the items. This may give the appearance of a conflict of interest. Be deliberate in deaccessioning decisions and document the reasons for removing the items from the collection.

Additional Reading/Resources

Boles, Frank. *Selecting and Appraising Archives and Manuscripts*. Archival Fundamentals Series II. Chicago: Society of American Archivists, 2005. This is the updated edition of Gerald Ham's book, listed separately.

Burkett, Nancy H. "Collecting Policies." American Antiquarian Society. https://www.americanantiquarian.org/collpol.htm. This is a collection policy from a historical institution.

Catholic Diocese of Fort Wayne-South Bend. "Collection Policy." Accessed July 4, 2019. http://www.diocesefwsb.org/Collection-Policy. This is an example of a collection policy for a religious organization.

Dearstyne, Bruce W. *Managing Historical Records Programs: A Guide for Historical Agencies*. Walnut Creek, CA: AltaMira Press, 2000. Refer especially to chapter 5, which discusses collection policy details and documentation strategy.

Ham, F. Gerald. *Selecting and Appraising Archives and Manuscripts*. Archival Fundamentals Series. Chicago: Society of American Archivists, 1993. Chapter 6 explains criteria for evaluating/appraising potential donations. This was revised in 2005 by Frank Boles. See separate entry.

Hunter, Gregory S. *Developing and Maintaining Practical Archives: A How-to-Do-It Manual*. 2nd ed. How-to-Do-It Manuals for Librarians, no. 122. New York: Neal-Schuman, 2003. Chapter 3 discusses methods for appraising potential new acquisitions. Chapter 4, pp. 92–99, discusses information on developing a collection policy, and pp. 105–6 discuss information to include in a deed of gift.

Kitching, Christopher, and Ian Hart. "Archive Collection Policy Statements: Checklist of Suggested Contents." New York: Crown. Accessed July 4, 2019. https://webarchive.nationalarchives.gov.uk/+/http://www.nationalarchives.gov.uk/documents/information-management/archive_collection_policy.pdf. Keeping in mind that this was written for the National Archives of Great Britain so that governing bodies and geographic locations mentioned therein are not applicable, this document presents a clear, understandable discussion of information to include in a collection policy.

McCree, Mary Lynn. "Good Sense and Good Judgment: Defining Collections and Collecting." In *A Modern Archives Reader*, 103–13, edited by Maygene F. Daniels and Timothy Walch. Washington, DC: National Archives and Records Service, US General Services Administration, 1982. This is a good commonsense article about collection policies.

Miller, Fredric M. *Arranging and Describing Archives and Manuscripts.* Archival Fundamentals Series. Chicago: Society of American Archivists, 1990. See chapter 4 for more information about accessioning.

Peterson, Trudy Huskamp. "The Gift and the Deed." In *A Modern Archives Reader*, 139–45, edited by Maygene F. Daniels and Timothy Walch. Washington, DC: National Archives and Records Service, US General Services Administration, 1982. This article discusses the elements to be addressed by a deed of gift agreement.

Phillips, Faye. "Developing Collecting Policies for Manuscript Collections." *American Archivist* 47 (Winter 1984): 30–42. Note: The JSTOR electronic database includes full-text copies of *American Archivist* articles.

Society of American Archivists. *Describing Archives: A Content Standard [DACS].* 2nd ed. Chicago: Society of American Archivists, 2013. Section 2.3 Title, pp. 17–23, provides guidance and examples for naming collections from the most recent American archival standard. A free PDF version is available at https://saa-ts-dacs.github.io/.

Yakel, Elizabeth. *Starting an Archives.* Lanham, MD: Society of American Archivists, 1994. Chapter 5 discusses collection development/policies, appraisal, and accessioning. This book includes samples of various forms and policies discussed. Page 83 includes a sample deed of gift. This book is written for the novice.

Notes

1. F. Gerald Ham, *Selecting and Appraising Archives and Manuscripts*, Archival Fundamentals Series (Chicago: Society of American Archivists, 1993), 2.

2. Ham, *Selecting and Appraising Archives*, 2; Richard Pearce-Moses, *A Glossary of Archival and Records Terminology*, Archival Fundamentals Series II (Chicago: Society of American Archivists, 2005), s.v. "appraisal."

3. Ham, *Selecting and Appraising Archives*, 82–83.

4. Ham, *Selecting and Appraising Archives*, 83–84; Elizabeth Yakel, *Starting an Archives* (Lanham, MD: Society of American Archivists, 1994), 34–35.

5. Pearce-Moses, *Glossary*, s.v. "accession."

6. Pearce-Moses, *Glossary*, s.v. "accession number."

7. Gregory S. Hunter, *Developing and Maintaining Practical Archives: A How-to-Do-It Manual*, 2nd ed., How-to-Do-It Manuals for Librarians, no. 122 (New York: Neal-Schuman, 2003), 108.

8. Society of American Archivists, *Describing Archives: A Content Standard [DACS]*, 2nd ed. (Chicago: Society of American Archivists, 2013), 17.

9. Society of American Archivists, *DACS*, 21.

10. David W. Carmicheal, *Organizing Archival Records*, 4th ed. (Lanham, MD: Rowman & Littlefield, 2019), pp. 37–39.

3

Arranging the Collection

After a new collection or donation has been appraised, accepted, and accessioned, it is ready to be *processed*, that is, physically arranged and described. The goal of arrangement and description is to make records accessible to researchers to identify the group of records most likely to answer a research question. Good arrangement and description will enable researchers to identify which collections to examine and also to locate items of interest within each collection.

People are familiar with libraries and have used them to locate books in order to answer a research question. Books are cataloged according to subject. They are organized on the shelf with other books on the same topic. Archival records differ from books in significant ways that affect how they are arranged and described. Books are discrete units of information that are intentionally created to discuss a specific subject. Archival records are normally groups of related items that derive greater significance because of their relationship to other records, all of which are created as the result of routine business transactions or simply daily living. They are rarely about a single subject. The more subjects they cover, the greater their informational and research value. Since books are published, normally there are many copies available. Archival records are typically unpublished and unique, often with as few as one copy.[1] These distinct differences require a different method of organization for archival records.

Arrangement is a combination of intellectual and physical processes that organizes records according to the two archival principles of provenance and original order in order to reveal their contents and significance.[2] The principle of *provenance* requires that records created, assembled, accumulated, and/or maintained by one records creator be kept separate from those of all other records creators to preserve their context. Provenance is the primary inviolable principle that defines archives and distinguishes them from libraries (collections of published materials). The principle of *original order* states that the order established by their creator should be maintained either physically or intellectually whenever possible to preserve existing relationships between the documents and evidence of how the records were used by their creator.[3] "Provenance and original order provide information *about* a group of records which is not *in* those records, but which is essential to understanding them."[4]

Offices often have more than one function or activity. While original order dictates that the records of activity A are kept in their original sequence, it does not determine the order of the records of activity A relative to activity B. Archivist Oliver Wendell Holmes introduced the concept of *levels of control* as the practical implementation of provenance and original order. He proposed five hierarchical levels: *repository*, record group or collection, *series*, *file*, and *item*. Best described by Holmes, records are progressively grouped "along a continuum from the largest and most general to the smallest and most specific."[5]

Let's go back and expand on some concepts that were introduced in chapter 1. Archival records in the United States originate from two major sources: institutions (government, businesses, and organizations) and private individuals. Institutions typically maintain their own records in public or institutional archives. These records document transactions. The records are organized into record groups using their governmental or corporate organizational structure as the model for their arrangement. A *record group* is a unit of "records that share the same provenance (created by the same person, office, department, or other group) and are of a convenient size for administration."[6] As long as the institution exists or is in business, it continues to create records. Such records are described as *open* because new increments of records will be added to the ones already in the archives. Government and corporate records have a further complication. Their institutions undergo frequent restructuring. New offices, agencies, or bureaus are created. Existing offices, agencies, or bureaus are given new duties or have their functions transferred to a different office, or they merge or are disbanded. The records created by these offices must reflect these organizational changes. This poses quite a challenge to the person who processes their records.

Businesses, civic organizations, and nonprofit organizations close. The records of some of these make their way to manuscript repositories or Special Collections. Government records can also make their way to manuscript repositories. These might include public copies of documents such as annual reports, personal files kept by a committee or board member, duplicate copies, or sometimes local government records are given to the local historical society. Although the records are closed in the sense that no new records will be created, they should still be arranged according to the institution's organizational structure.

Unlike institutional records, manuscript or personal papers are organized by collection. A *collection* is "a group of materials with some unifying characteristic." The unifying characteristic may be that they were all created by the same person, family group, business, or organization or that they are about the same subject. Materials about a subject can be created naturally as the result of an activity/function or created artificially without regard to the original provenance.[7] Examples of an artificial collection would include a collection of documents signed by famous people or a collection of postcards from someone's travels. Usually manuscript collections are closed because the person who created the papers in the collection is deceased and won't be creating any more papers. No new records will be added to the collection, requiring shifts in the existing arrangement. It is easier to arrange a closed collection than an open record group.

Record groups and collections are on the same hierarchical level for the purposes of arrangement. A *series* is a group of similar records organized according to a filing system "because they relate to a particular subject or function"; were created, received, or used in the same activity; have a particular form; or because of some other relationship pertaining to their creation or use. Correspondence, applications, licenses, publicity, and theatrical programs are all examples of a series. A *file* is "a group of documents related by use or topic," typically stored in a folder (or group of folders if the file is large). A file could be all the correspondence for 1981, all the correspondence with a specific person or business, or all the correspondence on a specific topic. An *item* is the smallest archival unit or lowest hierarchical level for arrangement or descriptive purposes. It is something that can be distinguished from a group and is complete in itself.[8] An item is not the same as one piece of paper. It may consist of one physical item, such as a photograph, but can consist of more in the case of a (multipage) letter or a report (of pages bound together). See appendix C.2 for a visual illustration of this archival hierarchy.

So, how do you start arranging your collections?

Research[9]

Step 1. Conduct Background Research

Select an unprocessed collection, one that has only been donated and accessioned. So far, the collection should have a donor file with a donor agreement and possibly some additional notes. It should also have an accession record with a working collection name. One of these two sources should also name the collection creator. Now it is time to research the person(s) or organization that created the materials in the collection. For an individual (or family), identify significant dates in his or her life; cities or addresses of importance; and information about work, activities, or positions he or she might have held. For an organization, look for information about its founding, the activities and/or functions of the organization, key personnel, significant dates and locations, possibly information about organizational divisions, name changes, and mergers. Look for biographical information, obituaries, and a company history. Consult resources such as biographical dictionaries or encyclopedias, published histories including city histories, newspapers of the appropriate era and location, and even the internet. Helpful resources will vary depending upon whether the records creator was an individual or an organization. This research will be helpful when writing the *administrative/biographical history* section, which is meant to provide an overview, not to be exhaustive. Knowing some basic background information about this person or organization will also help in arranging the collection and in understanding the significance of specific items in the collection.

Step 2. Prepare to Process

Bring all the parts of the collection to a clean, large, empty table where there is sufficient space to spread the records out while sorting. Bring your research notes from step 1. Get a pencil and paper to take more notes. To protect the collection, use only pencil while working with it. If archival folders and boxes are not kept nearby, bring a small quantity of folders and several boxes to your workspace to get started. Refer to appendixes A.1 and A.2 and read about guidelines for safe handling of archival materials. These guidelines apply not only to researchers but also to staff and volunteers when they handle collection material. After reviewing the guidelines, continue with step 3.

Step 3. Examine the Collection and Take Notes

During this initial examination, look through the records carefully. Depending on the quantity, it may or may not be necessary to handle every item. Avoid the temptation to read every document whether during this initial examination, later refoldering (step 6), or item-level processing (step 8). Read enough to get an overview of the collection and complete the task at hand. Do not re-arrange anything during this step. Keep it in the same order as you find it, in the same container, in the same folder, and in the same sequence it has with the other folders. Even if it looks like everything was just dumped in a box, don't move things around yet. This is respect for the original order even if there doesn't appear to be one. Examining unprocessed archival records has much in common with going on an archaeological dig. Just as an archaeologist studies all the items found at the same depth and makes deductions about them relative to each other and to items found above or below, an archivist will make deductions about records relative to their placement with other records. Once the original order is disturbed, it may be impossible to re-create. It is better to maintain the original order while studying the collection even if it is later revised or modified. An acid-free folder can be used as a marker to show that something has been removed. The marker will show where to return the folder after examination so that the original order can be maintained. Be sure to take each folder out and lay it flat on the table so that it is properly supported. Handle the records carefully and work through the collection.

Take notes as you examine the collection. This will aid decisions about the final physical arrangement and provide information for the administrative/biographical history and the *scope and content* in the collection description (see textbox 4.1 and the discussion thereof in chapter 4). At the end of this step, you should also be able to confirm the creator(s) of the collection and the collection name. As you study the collection, try to answer questions such as the following:[10]

- Who created or compiled these records? There may be additional information that differs from original suppositions.

- What types of records are there? Correspondence, diaries, receipts, reports, minutes, photographs, newspaper clippings, and ledgers are all typical types of records.

- What type of information is in the records? Is there general information about the founding of the town, education in the nineteenth century, or World War I or specific details about particular individuals, or a natural disaster?

- What are the dates covered by the records? Record the earliest date and the most recent date; these are the *span dates*. Also record major gaps in dates. If there are dates for significant events in the life of the main person or organization discussed in the records, record those for the administrative/biographical history.

- How are the records arranged? Alphabetically? Chronologically? Geographically? Numerically? By size (in the case of photographs)? Or are they in great disorder?

- In the case of personal or family papers, is there any biographical or genealogical information that might explain who is related to whom and how? Where did family members live, including addresses if known?

- In the case of business or organizational records, are there organizational charts, lists of key officers, or a company history? Why was the organization founded? What was its purpose?

- Are there any indexes or documents that explain the filing system or other complex groupings in the records?

Note the physical condition of the records. Is there anything that should be dealt with now, or can it wait? Something severe, such as active mold, should be addressed immediately to protect the other collections stored in the same room. If it can wait, make a note of the problem. Are there items that should be unframed? Are there signs of bugs, and are they dead or gone? Have the records collected dust and debris that could be gently brushed off with a natural bristle paintbrush? Are there acidic newspaper clippings? Have things been taped together that might need to be undone?

Depending on time, the size of the collection, and available supplies, simpler problems could be taken care of now and notes made for work that is more time consuming or might require a specialist. For example, rubber bands can be replaced with an acid-free folder to group records together. The folder keeps records together but is safer for them.

If there are record types other than papers or photographs, such as audiocassettes, film, or computer files, note their presence. These types of formats have special requirements that should be addressed at a later stage. By noting their location now, it will be easier to find them when it is time to work with them.

Step 4. Decide on a Processing Plan

After the initial examination of the collection is completed, a decision needs to be made about how to arrange the collection. Depending on the size of your organization, the quantity of records waiting to be processed, the amount of staff or volunteer time available to process, and other factors, this decision will vary. The collection may be very small or simple, and the decision will be to arrange at the item level, that is, to decide which folder each piece of paper will go in and the sequence of each item in all folders. The collection may be more complex or larger, or processing time may be limited. In this case, the decision may be to identify or restore the original order of the records in each series or to rearrange the file folders in a new sequence and stop. Individual folders are not opened; their contents are left alone (file-level processing). Work on the contents of folders can be done now, later, or not at all, depending on their research value, resources, and work priorities. This step may not require much time but should be intentionally considered as collections grow in size, when processing time is at a premium, or when there is a large backlog. All collections do not have to be processed to the same level (series, file, or item). All series within the same collection might not be processed to the same level. This is a judgment call that is made based on available resources, the size of the processing backlog, the research value of a collection or series, and other factors. The physical condition of collection materials will also be a factor in determining what work is needed.

Step 5. Identify the Series

Series are the main building blocks in a collection or record group. Identification of the series is critical to the arrangement of the collection. If the original order of the records is largely intact, this step will be a matter of identifying and arranging the series.

The collection has already been examined in some detail. Look again at the containers and review your notes. Are there groups of records that appeared to be organized by a logical, consistent classification system, such as alphabetically (correspondence) or chronologically (minutes or reports)? Are there groups of records whose contents appeared to be similar? The physical format of the folders or any labels may appear the same. Labels may have the same handwriting style. The information on the folders or any extra notations may look similar in format or content. Some series consist of records that have a common format, such as maps or photographs, or all are related to the same subject or activity (licenses or receipts). As each series is identified, bring all its parts together physically in a box but separate one series from another for now.

Suppose you have the records of the Chelmsford Ginger Ale Factory. You find a series of employee files organized alphabetically by last name. Box them and separate them out. There are bound ledgers for several years labeled "Expenses"; put them in a separate stack on the table or box them if they are small enough for a box. Work through the collection, identifying, separating, and boxing as many series as exist in the collection.[11]

Personal or family papers are more likely than organizational records to arrive in disorder. If there are no clearly identifiable series, the processor will have to create or reconstitute them.

The careful examination in step 3 should identify the types of records in the collection and who created them. In step 4, list the series that were identified or the series into which you propose to organize the records. For example, Mr. Banks's papers might include series for his business papers, personal/family correspondence, and political activities. Mrs. Banks's papers might include series for personal/family correspondence and her civic activities. This is an example of arrangement according to the functions of the creator (see appendix C.3). An alternate—but unsuitable—arrangement would be to arrange all of Mr. Banks's papers chronologically regardless of the type of document. If his papers are arranged strictly in chronological order, then the same method would be used for Mrs. Banks's papers even though her papers are in separate folders from his. It is best not to use more than one system within any single collection in order to avoid having more than one logical place to file an item. The collection could also have been arranged by *type* of material with series for correspondence, minutes, diaries, and photographs.[12] Mr. Banks's records still would be arranged separately from those of his wife.

A purely chronological arrangement would be unsuitable for Mr. Banks's papers because of the numerous functions of the records in this collection. The presence of these functions would be hidden if all of them were intermingled by a pure chronological arrangement. It would be quite acceptable, however, to create functional series and *then* arrange the records within each series chronologically. If any of the series were further divided, say, there was both state and national political activity, the chronological order might be applied within each subdivision in order not to mix the state records with the national ones.

The arrangement selected for a collection may depend on the quantity and type of records to be arranged. A collection of one or two boxes is less likely to be divided into as many series as a collection of ten boxes. When there are only a few legal documents, it makes more sense to combine them with a few other documents than to have two or three folders containing a few pieces of paper. However, if there are twenty to forty folders of the same material, this merits the creation of a separate series. By the end of this step, you should have one or more series of records on your worktable.

Step 6. Arrange the Records in Each Series

Start with the first series in the collection and look at it. Hopefully, it will appear to have a logical, consistent filing system. Within the series, individual file folders should be discrete units, that is, distinctly separate files. For example, a series of correspondence might be further divided into alphabetic file folders. Each folder for one letter of the alphabet is a discrete unit. If there is a logical filing system, the arrangement for this series is done unless there are random folders that are out of order or that are accidently located elsewhere in the collection that need to be returned to this series. If this is the case, restore these folders to their proper location.

If the original order is not readily apparent, the processor will have to create one. While provenance should always be respected, the question of original order is one of balance. How much change to the original order should the processor make? Original order should not be discarded lightly without good reason, but neither should a "system" incomprehensible to all except the original creator be retained. The contents of the files should be studied closely to see whether the relationship between them can be identified. Records could have been moved from their original filing system in a careless manner or moved more than once and gotten disorganized in the process. Containers may not have been labeled in a clear and thoughtful manner. If after careful consideration the original order is too obscure to be understood or has simply been lost, then a new one must be created. The new arrangement should reflect the original activity that produced the records, if possible, while balancing the needs of researchers.[13]

Many organizations and businesses have organizational charts that illustrate how they are organized, meaning which office reports to whom. Frequently, offices are grouped together into a unit that shares common functions, such as publicity, teaching, or administration. Their records may be logically arranged by using the organizational structure as illustrated on their organizational chart. In the case of personal or family papers, the records might also be organized by function or record type. If the processor imposes a new order on the records, either changing the original order or imposing one in the absence of any order at all, this should be noted in the scope and content note of the description so that researchers can better interpret the records.[14]

Once it is determined that the files in the first series are in their final arrangement, start working through the series in sequence, *refoldering* all the files, that is, moving all the materials from each old folder to an acid-free archival one. Folder labels should include the name of the collection and concisely describe the folder contents. Folder headings are important; they help researchers decide which folders to examine (see appendix C.4 for examples). Label the new folder before placing the contents inside to prevent damage to the contents while writing. Do not number folders yet; their arrangement could still shift. If the original folder is overfilled, move the contents into as many new folders as is needed. Archival folders have crease lines on the bottom to adjust their width if necessary, but the sides should not be bulging. As the new folders are created, place them in archival boxes of a uniform size, most commonly a letter- or legal-size manuscript box (five by twelve by ten inches or five by fifteen by ten inches). Work through the rest of the collection, taking one series at a time, retaining, restoring, or creating the arrangement as necessary.

If as you arrange you find something that does not make sense to you, set it aside and keep working. As you see the rest of the collection, that item or file may eventually make sense, and you will understand where to place it.

Step 7. Arrange the Series in Relation to Each Other

The arrangement of one series relative to another may be subjective and arbitrary. If the collection arrived not only with the original order within the series intact but also with a logical sequence from one series to another, that sequence should be maintained. If that is not the case, the common practice is to progress from the general to the specific and from policymaking to policy implementation. This would place the records of an executive board before the president, a director before an assistant, a central office before branch offices, and so on.[15] In the case of an individual's papers, this may be less clear. Correspondence may precede diaries or follow business papers or civic work. The research value of a particular series or the quantity of records and their completeness might help determine which series precedes another.

What if some of the items in a series are in a different format and don't fit well in the box with the rest of the series? Photographs are dealt with in chapters 5 and 6. You may find that you have oversized items, bound volumes of varying sizes, audio- or videocassettes, film, or computer files. These belong to a particular series intellectually, based on their content, but physically storing them in boxes of predominantly paper records is not good from a preservation perspective. Records will suffer less damage if the records stored together in an individual box are of similar size and format. In general, letter- and legal-size papers should be stored in acid-free folders and filed upright in a box that is neither overfilled nor so empty as to allow the contents to slump over.

Oversized items should be physically removed from their series using a *separation sheet* in place of the item that is removed. This is a form that is filed in the original location of the removed item and describes the removed item and its new location (see appendixes B.3a and B.3b). The separation sheet alerts a researcher to the existence of the removed item and preserves its context by linking it back to the records where it was originally found. Also note the additional physical location in the description. Store the oversize item in a suitably sized flat box or map drawers with other items of a similar size and type. Clearly identify the collection name and box and folder number from which the item was removed. If all the smaller-size items were put in the larger flat box in order to keep the series together, the smaller items would be shifting around, potentially causing them damage or losing their intellectual order. Also, it costs more to store materials in a larger box than is necessary and wastes shelf space.

Depending on the overall size of a bound volume, its thickness, and its weight, it could be stored several ways. If the volume is small enough and slender, it can be stored upright in a manuscript box. Place the spine on the bottom of the box with the open edge toward the top of the box. If the covers or spine are loose, University Products sells buffered, acid-free, lignin-free wrapping paper on a roll (see Additional Reading/Resources at the end of this chapter). The weight of the paper is heavier than photocopier paper but lighter than a file folder. The wrapping paper is flexible enough to wrap a damaged book. Tie it with unbleached tying "tape" (a flat "string" sold by archival vendors) to give it support. Volumes that are larger but still not too thick or heavy may fit into a flat box similar to oversize material. Boxes are sold in a wide variety of sizes. If the bound volume is extremely large or of middling size but thick and heavy, it will probably be stored flat, stacked directly on the storage shelf. Be mindful of the weight put on the volume at the bottom of the stack. Depending on the weight, a stack of three to five volumes should be safe. Turn the spine out so that labeling can be read without having to move the books and to minimize damage to page edges. Again, if covers or the spine are loose, tie or wrap and tie the volume for additional support before stacking. Write the volume title or identification on the exterior of the wrapping paper.

Audio- and videocassettes, (movie) film, and computer files all have special requirements. It is easier to monitor their physical condition if they are physically located together and can be readily found. Archival boxes are made in specific sizes to fit many of these formats. *Housing* (storing) records with special formats in boxes designed for those formats provides a proper fit for the contents so that they are not sliding about inside an ill-fitting box.

Step 8. Arrange the Records in Each File

If it was decided in step 3 to process the collection to the item level, that is the next step. If not, this step can be omitted. Work at this level varies. The processor may arrange each item within a folder alphabetically, chronologically, or according to another appropriate sequence. Or the processor may perform minor preservation tasks and leave the arrangement unchanged. Rubber bands or rusty metal fasteners might be replaced. Some materials, such as photographs, slides, or negatives, might be removed for special handling. If this is done, a separation sheet is placed in the folder where an item is removed describing what was removed and giving its new location. See appendixes B.3a and B.3b. The item that is removed must also be labeled with the collection and the location (box and folder number) from which it was removed to clearly link it back to its original location.

Step 9. Final Tasks

Finalize the arrangement. Make sure that boxes are neither so full that it is difficult to remove a folder nor so empty that materials are falling over or curling. Shift the files to another box if necessary or use box spacers to provide support for the records. Now folders can be labeled with their box and folder number (box 1, folder 1; box 1, folder 2; box 2, folder 1; box 2, folder 2; and so on) so that they can be returned to their proper order when they are used by researchers.

Label boxes on the exterior side that will face out from the shelf. Make sure all the boxes are turned in the same direction. If they do not have a pull tab on the end to help align them, check the side on which the lid of the box is hinged and turn all the boxes so that they are all hinged are on the same side. If possible, use clear label holders that use adhesive to attach to manuscript boxes. This allows the paper label insert to be revised as necessary. Archival vendors sell them. Adhesive labels of various sizes can be fed through a computer printer so they are legible and standardized in appearance. Do not write on boxes, labels, or file folders with anything other than pencil, a typewriter, or computer printer ink. Ink pens, felt-tip pens, and markers are permanent; they are not reversible. They should not be used around archival records because they can cause permanent damage to the records themselves. They should not be used on the folders and containers for archival records because they can smear or otherwise transfer to the records. A folder label can be erased and changed when it is written in pencil but not if it is written in ink. Reversible methods are preferred over those that are not. Archival supplies are expensive, and it is wasteful to throw a folder away in order to change the label.

How to Arrange a New Accretion

Adding new material to an existing collection is simpler than arranging a new collection. It is possible to receive an accretion (new material) for a collection or series that has already been processed. Locate the collection to which this accretion is being added. Determine whether there is already a series of similar material or whether a new series needs to be created. Refolder the new material. Physically add it where it belongs intellectually. This may require some shifting in a box or the addition of new boxes, depending on the quantity of new material. Check whether any folders need to be renumbered or whether box labels need adjustment. The description for the collection will need to be revised to indicate the physical changes made to the collection.

Additional Reading/Resources

Resources for Handling Collection Material

Ogden, Sherelyn. "NEDCC Preservation Leaflets, Storage and Handling, 4.1: Storage Methods and Handling Practices." Northeast Document Conservation Center. Accessed July 5, 2019. https://www.nedcc.org/assets/media/documents/Preservation%20Leaflets/4_1_Storage Handling.pdf.

University Products. "Buffered, Acid-Free, Lignin-Free Wrapping Paper." Accessed July 5, 2019. https://www.universityproducts.com/buffered-acid-free-and-lignin-free-wrapping-paper .html. This product can be used to wrap books in poor physical condition.

US Department of the Interior. National Park Service. "Museum Management Program, Conserve O Grams." National Park Service. Accessed July 5, 2019. https://www.nps.gov/museum/publi cations/conserveogram/cons_toc.html. Particularly 19/17, "Handling Archival Documents and Manuscripts 1996" and 19/18, "How to Care for Bound Archival Materials 1996."

Resources for Arrangement and Description

Carmicheal, David W. *Organizing Archival Records*. 4th ed. Lanham, MD: Rowman & Littlefield, 2019. This is a good basic book. It includes exercises in arrangement with answers and explanations and understandable explanations for a number of archival concepts.

Dearstyne, Bruce W. *Managing Historical Records Programs: A Guide for Historical Agencies*. Walnut Creek, CA: AltaMira Press, 2000. Chapter 6 discusses arrangement and description.

Greene, Mark A., and Dennis Meissner. "More Product, Less Process: Revamping Traditional Archival Processing." *American Archivist* 68 (Fall/Winter 2005): 208–63. This article introduced the concept of intentionally trying to minimally process collections instead of performing every task possible for all records. The intention is to make records available to researchers faster. Note: The JSTOR electronic database includes full-text copies of *American Archivist* articles.

Holmes, Oliver W. "Archival Arrangement—Five Different Operations at Five Different Levels." *American Archivist* 27 (January 1964): 21–41. Note: The JSTOR electronic database includes full-text copies of *American Archivist* articles.

Hunter, Gregory S. *Developing and Maintaining Practical Archives: A How-to-Do-It Manual*. 2nd ed. How-to-Do-It Manuals for Librarians, no. 122. New York: Neal-Schuman, 2003. Chapter 5, pp. 122–28, explains how to arrange a collection.

Miller, Fredric M. *Arranging and Describing Archives and Manuscripts*. Archival Fundamentals Series. Chicago: Society of American Archivists, 1990. Especially chapter 6.

Rubenstein Library Technical Services Department, Duke University. "Student Processing Manual Zine." Accessed July 10, 2019. https://library.duke.edu/rubenstein/about/technical-services-department. This processing manual is humorous and brief, but provides good guidance on processing archival records.

Society of American Archivists. *Describing Archives: A Content Standard [DACS]*. 2nd ed. Chicago: Society of American Archivists, 2013. Section 2.3, Title, pp. 17–23, provides guidance and examples for naming collections from the most recent American archival standard. A free PDF version is available at https://saa-ts-dacs.github.io/.

Sustainable Heritage Network, Center for Digital Scholarship and Curation at Washington State University. "Processing Plan Form and Levels of Processing Matrix." Accessed August 17, 2019. https://sustainableheritagenetwork.org/digital-heritage/processing-plan-form-and-levels-processing-matrix. This form helps the reader to develop a processing plan for processing a collection. It includes a grid describing work that would be done for processing tasks if performed at differing levels of effort.

Notes

1. Gregory S. Hunter, *Developing and Maintaining Practical Archives: A How-to-Do-It Manual*, 2nd ed., How-to-Do-It Manuals for Librarians, no. 122 (New York: Neal-Schuman, 2003), 7–11. This is a good basic discussion of the differences between libraries and archives.

2. Hunter, *Developing and Maintaining Practical Archives*, 113; Lewis J. Bellardo and Lynn Lady Bellardo, comps., *A Glossary for Archivists, Manuscript Curators, and Records Managers*, Archival Fundamentals Series (Chicago: Society of American Archivists, 1992), 4.

3. Society of American Archivists, *Describing Archives A Content Standard [DACS]*, 2nd ed. (Chicago: Society of American Archivists, 2013), xvi.

4. Fredric M. Miller, *Arranging and Describing Archives and Manuscripts*, Archival Fundamental Series (Chicago: Society of American Archivists, 1990), 20.

5. Lois D. Hamill, "Provenance and Original Order: The Evolution of Their Acceptance as Principles of Arrangement and Description" (master's thesis, University of Massachusetts–Boston, 1997), 29; Miller, *Arranging and Describing Archives*, 28–29.

6. Richard Pearce-Moses, *A Glossary of Archival and Records Terminology*, Archival Fundamentals Series II (Chicago: Society of American Archivists, 2005), s.v. "record group."

7. Pearce-Moses, *Glossary*, s.v. "collection."

8. Pearce-Moses, *Glossary*, s.v. "series, file, item."

9. The idea to specifically name and number the steps came from David W. Carmicheal, *Organizing Archival Records: A Practical Method of Arrangement and Description for Small Archives*, 2nd ed. (Walnut Creek, CA: AltaMira Press, 2004), chapter 3. The idea to conduct research as the first step came from Mark Savolis, telephone conversation, February 2010.

10. Carmicheal, *Organizing Archival Records*, 25.

11. Carmicheal, *Organizing Archival Records*, 31.

12. Hunter, *Developing and Maintaining Practical Archives*, 127.

13. Bruce W. Dearstyne, *Managing Historical Records Programs: A Guide for Historical Agencies* (Walnut Creek, CA: AltaMira Press, 2000), 89–90.

14. Dearstyne, *Managing Historical Records Programs*, 89–90.

15. Miller, *Arranging and Describing Archives*, 66, 74.

4

Describing the Collection

Arrangement and description are two halves of a whole. Arrangement must be done in order for description to occur. Description completes the work that begins with arrangement. A collection that has only been arranged is not fully processed and is not very useful to a researcher. Arrangement intellectually identifies groupings within a collection and physically places material in a particular sequence.[1] *Description* is the process that records the physical arrangement. The purpose of description is twofold. First, it aids the institution in gaining intellectual and physical control over its *holdings*, that is, the totality of all the collections or records it owns. This means that the institution knows which collections or records it owns; their size, completeness, and physical location; and has at least some knowledge of the information contained in them. The second purpose is to help researchers locate relevant materials.[2]

Description takes the form of a *finding aid*—a tool that provides information about the collection's content and may include contextual information about the collection. Finding aids have a variety of formats, each with its own name, depending on the information each includes and how it is organized. Their form varies from a typed document or index cards, to a print copy of a word-processed electronic file, information in an online electronic database, a web page, or more. The *inventory* is the most common type of finding aid. Not only does it describe the information content for a collection, but it also includes information about its creator and other aspects in order to better understand or interpret the records in the collection. Researchers use an inventory to find information in the set of records it describes.

Finding aids use one of two methods to guide researchers to the information they seek. The first method describes records based on the organizational structure of the person or office that created the records and their original filing system for those records. This makes sense for local businesses, units of government, or cultural or social organizations. When applied to manuscript collections created by a private individual or family, this type of finding aid would ideally describe the records the way their creator organized them for his own use. These records would simply lack references to a larger institution. An inventory is an example of a finding aid that uses this method. The second method indexes subjects, events, names, and other significant terms discussed in the records to create a paper card catalog or index, or an online electronic catalog or database. The researcher searches the index or catalog and is directed to records in collections. Although the second method allows the researcher to search by subjects or names, he should be directed back to the inventory for the pertinent collection in order to provide context to the specific subset of records identified through the subject search.[3]

Description that uses both approaches would be the most helpful. American archivists adopted a new descriptive standard called *Describing Archives: A Content Standard* (DACS) in 2005 and the second edition in 2013. Although DACS does not require the creation of search terms, called *access points*, it does support their use and standardize their formation. This means they can be included in collection inventories, improving searchability of the inventories. Ideally if an institution's inventories are delivered electronically, they are either delivered by software that enables all inventories to be searched simultaneously or formatted so that a web browser can search them all at once.

In 1960, the Xerox Corporation sold its first commercial automatic copier.[4] The introduction of photocopying caused an explosion in the quantity of records created and the number of copies produced of the same document. Prior to this time, it was not uncommon for archivists to describe every item in important collections. As the quantity of records arriving at archives and manuscript repositories dramatically increased, archivists had to refine their methods of arrangement and description. Today, archivists generally practice *collective description*, describing groups of related records together as a single unit.[5] Unless the collection has exceptional research value, most professional archivists no longer use item-level description. Most institutions do not have the resources for that kind of work.

The person who processes a collection should also write the narrative sections of the finding aid. The box and folder list can be prepared by someone else if necessary. The sections in the inventory are not necessarily written in the sequence in which they appear. The scope and content, an overview of what is in the collection and its research strengths, will be written nearly last. Processing does not have to be complete to write some sections. This can be done as arrangement progresses. Either take notes or start recording information in a draft document as it is collected during arrangement. The inventory is meant to be a factual document that conveys information about a collection or record group, what it contains, the conditions of its creation, and information about its creator. The language and writing should be neutral, not an expression of the processor's personal opinions.[6] Whether the institution has a collection from a tobacco company, the Ku Klux Klan, or another controversial group, the processor's writing should be factual. The researcher should form his opinion based on his own research. Further, the inventory should be concise, informative, and accurate; include pertinent information; and provide an overview rather than focus on one event or period to the neglect of the rest of the collection.[7] The writing should be clear, avoid technical jargon, and explain any acronyms.

The goal of a well-written inventory is to assist a researcher by narrowing his search and saving him time in identifying the most pertinent records for his research. The researcher will proceed from there to examine the details in the records for himself. The inventory is not meant to be a book describing the entire collection in great depth. The writing should be succinct. Just as the narrative should be to the point, the visual presentation of the information should be an efficient use of headings, spaces, and font types and sizes so that a researcher can quickly "grasp the essence of the collection at a glance."[8] Depending again upon the software used to deliver the inventories, the inventory author may have limited control over the visual presentation.

DACS has twenty-five fields of which eight are required, one more is highly recommended, and the remaining sixteen are optional. DACS is a content standard, which means it controls how information is formatted within a description field, but not the sequence of the fields themselves. Archivists have been experimenting with how organization and presentation of information in collection inventories might make them easier for researchers to understand and use. While inventories were created to aid collection use by researchers, when they existed only in paper they also contained information used by the organization's personnel, for example from whom did the organization obtain the records or whether there are restrictions on their use. When the author led the last inventory redesign at her archives, she intentionally located the fields thought to most rapidly aid researcher decisions about whether to examine a specific collection toward the top and some of the fields used by staff toward the bottom of the inventory. The new inventory template includes all required DACS fields and previously used optional fields the staff still valued. In some cases, the original field names were retained, but their use follows the applicable DACS rule.

Textbox 4.1 Finding Aid Template[9]

[Record Group or Collection Title]
RG-[#] or MS-[#]

ABSTRACT

This section is for the abstract.

SUMMARY INFORMATION

Creators:

Span Dates: **Bulk Dates:**

Extent:

Languages:

Repository location: Eva G. Farris Special Collections and Schlachter University Archives, W. Frank Steely Library, Northern Kentucky University, Highland Heights, Kentucky

ACCESS POINTS

Subjects:

Names:

Places:

Formats:

Functions:

Occupations:

RELATED MATERIALS

Separated materials:

Related archival materials:

Existence and location of originals:

Existence and location of copies:

Publication note:

ADMINISTRATIVE/BIOGRAPHICAL HISTORY

This section is for the administrative/biographical history.

SCOPE AND CONTENT

This section is for the scope and content.

(continued)

SYSTEM OF ARRANGEMENT

This section is for the system of arrangement.

CONTAINER LISTING

Description	Date	Box	Folder
Series I:			
Indent two spaces if folder title spills on to second line			
Subseries 1:			
Leave blank			
Series II: leave one blank space above to distinguish series			

CONDITIONS GOVERNING ACCESS AND USE

Conditions governing access:

Physical access:

Technical access:

Conditions governing reproduction and use: The copyright law of the United States (Title 17, US Code) governs the reproduction of copyrighted material. The user assumes full responsibility and any attendant liability for the fair use of materials requested in total compliance with the copyright law of the United States (Title 17, US Code) that may arise through the use of any requested materials.

Preferred citation: "Box #, Folder #, RG-#, Name of Record Group, Schlachter University Archives" OR "Box #, Folder #, MS-#, Name of Collection, Eva G. Farris Special Collections," "W. Frank Steely Library, Northern Kentucky University."

ACQUISITION AND APPRAISAL

Immediate source of acquisition:

Custodial history:

NOTES

Processing information: Processed by [Name], [Date]

Variant title information:

Instructions for using template:

- Open template NKU_finding_aid_ver4_template.docx.

- Save As with the new file name and folder location.

- Close template NKU_finding_aid_ver4_template.docx.

- Complete work using new file. Do not change the formatting of the finding aid template (and make sure you are working off a copy of it), other than to delete fields.

- When completing finding aid using this template, department staff should follow the Finding Aid Application Guide (table 4.1).

(continued)

- Brackets indicate information that will change for each record group/collection. Complete the information that is required and remove the brackets.

- If **Creators** field is unknown, enter *Unknown*.

- This template includes boilerplate language where appropriate.

- Other than the Creator field, if not using fields indicated as optional in the Finding Aid Application Guide (table 4.1), delete those fields from the finding aid.

- Enter metadata next to field name. For Abstract, Administrative/Biographical History, Scope and Content, and System of Arrangement, enter it below header.

- Use Arial 14 pt bold for section headers, Arial 12 pt bold for element names, Arial 12 pt for text body, with 1-inch margins on all sides.

- All fields will be plural where it makes sense (e.g., subjects, creators, location of copies). Rely on *Chicago Manual of Style* for formatting.

- If text is a complete sentence, use a period. If a field contains an incomplete sentence (e.g., Repository Location), do not use a period at the end.

Sections of an Inventory

The inventory template shown in textbox 4.1 is created first as a word-processed document. The header may display the name of the organization that owns the records. Depending upon how the inventory is delivered electronically to researchers, the header may be omitted, but the same information is included in the repository location field. If the inventory can be designed so that the same document is used internally and externally without having to reformat the contents, it will be more efficient. For example, the word document could be converted to a portable document file (PDF) and delivered via the web or a digital repository. In some cases, it may be necessary to copy the information field by field to a specialized software to deliver the information, but the field labels and information can be reused. Refer to table 4.1 to correlate field labels used in the inventory template with DACS element labels, element rules, and requirement status.

Title and Number

Title: required, may be called name or title. Capitalize the first letter of each noun. Name formation was previously discussed in chapter 2.

Number: required, called a *reference code* in DACS Element 2.1. The reference code is comprised of three components: a country code + a repository code + a unique local identifier for the specific materials being described.[10] Because archives collectively describe their materials, the collection or record group number qualifies as the requisite unique identifier. Whether or not an institution decides to apply DACS, manuscript collections and record groups should be assigned a unique number in addition to a name. It is a useful shorthand, an identification number, that can be used to describe a specific set of records. It makes sense to assign a collection name and number during processing when an overview of the collection is ascertained. The first collection processed is Manuscript Collection MS-001. The next one is MS-002 and so on.

Once an organization's structure is identified, depending upon its complexity, a single record group number can be assigned to the whole organization or to each component. For example, the president's office is RG-001, while the finance officer's division is RG-002. When newly transferred records are accessioned, the office that created them is identified. They are added to other records from that unit and use its assigned record group number. If a new organizational unit is created, then the next sequential number available would be assigned. In both cases, record the numbers that have been assigned and the collection name or record group to which they have been assigned. If these lists are maintained in a spreadsheet, it will be easy to sort the information into two separate lists, one in numeric order and the other alphabetical by collection or record group name. These lists will become useful reference tools for managing the records they describe.

Finding Aids >> UIU00162

Descriptive Summary

Handle: http://hdl.handle.net/10111/UIU00162
Creator: Scheetz, George
Title: George Scheetz ("Madonna" Intellectual Freedom) Collection
Date Span: 1990-1993
Number: UIU00162
Physical: *extent:* Hollinger (4)
                  link: UL6 C02 11.01, 11.02
Library :   The University of Illinois Urbana-Champaign
               Rare Books and Manuscript Library
               WorldCat Registry ID: 89813 [ISIL:OCLC-89813]

Restrictions

Open

Box and Folder Listing

Box and Folder listing in repository

Figure 4.1. An example of a very minimalistic finding aid from the University of Illinois at Urbana-Champaign. The Rare Book & Manuscript Library, University of Illinois at Urbana-Champaign.

Abstract

Abstract: this is not a DACS field. However, a very succinct overview written last and summarizing the most important qualities of the records would help researchers decide whether to examine the inventory or collection further. Use the scope and content and administrative/biographical history fields to write the abstract. In some software systems, the abstract might be displayed separately from the rest of the inventory, for example in a list of collection names. While names alone are insufficient to select a collection, an abstract would be a helpful indicator.

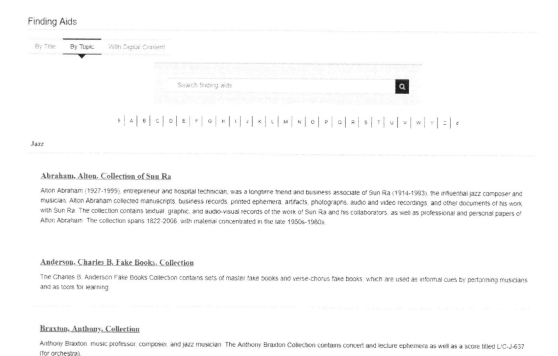

Figure 4.2. This is a good example of the use of the abstract field in a list of collections to help researchers initially identify potential collections for use. https://www.lib.uchicago.edu/scrc/finding-aids/?topic =Jazz&view=topics. Special Collections Research Center, University of Chicago Library.

Summary Information

This section provides factual information that might rapidly help a researcher decide whether the collection is from the desired time period, potentially has sufficient information, or mentions the name of a relevant person or topic.

Creators: required, record if known. This may have already been recorded in an accession record. There are professional resources for those who are trained, like the Library of Congress *Name Authority File* (LCNAF) or Resource Discovery and Access (RDA), with rules for how to create standardized personal or corporate names for records creators. If a name authority system is not used, names can be created locally by the organization, but try to use the same form of the name for an individual or organization in all your records to produce more complete search results. See the Standards: Controlled Vocabulary and Additional Reading/Resources sections later in this chapter for additional information. If there are significant creators other than the primary one who have a role in the provenance of the records, mention them in the administrative/biographical history field. Significant creators might also be included in the names field for access points.

If the records creator is not known, it might be preferable to enter "unknown" in this field than leave it blank. Depending upon the software used to display the inventory, leaving this field blank might produce undesirable display or sorting results. Since the creator is such a key piece of information for records, entering "unknown" shows the field was not accidently skipped.

Describing the Collection

Span Dates: dates are required; use span, bulk, or both. Span dates are the dates of the oldest and most recent materials in a collection, record group, series, folder, etc.[11]

Bulk Dates: dates are required; use span, bulk, or both. Bulk dates are the earliest and most recent dates for the majority of the records. Use when the majority of the materials were created between two dates within the span dates, but outliers exist more than twenty years outside the bulk dates. For example, the span dates are 1910–1970 but the bulk dates are 1950–1960. The oldest item in the collection may date to 1910, but based on the bulk dates, this would not be a good collection to use to study World War I.

Extent: required, record the quantity of analog records in linear or cubic feet; be consistent in the unit chosen. Measure digital records separately in a consistent unit size such as kilobytes, megabytes, or gigabytes.

Language: required, list the languages used by the materials being described.

Repository Location: required, provide the name of the repository, its parent organization if there is one, and geographical information so that someone from outside the local area can locate the organization. For example, Eva G. Farris Special Collections and Schlachter University Archives, W. Frank Steely Library, Northern Kentucky University, Highland Heights, Kentucky.

Access Points

Access Points or search terms: include names, places, subjects, formats [of the records] like minutes, diaries, watercolors, functions [of an office] and occupations. DACS does not treat access points as required or even optional.[12] Description in other fields is likely to include or describe this information in narrative form, but a specific, organized list in a designated field will aid researchers and software search engines, improving search results. Access points should describe the most significant information in the collection, not be an exhaustive list. Unless an individual item is exceptionally significant, do not mislead researchers into thinking there is substantive information on a topic or person by creating an access point.

Access points can be used to call attention to underrepresented populations or topics that historically have not been well documented. Consider setting a numeric range for how many access points to create as a general rule to guard against spending excessive time on these fields at the expense of others.

Archivists or librarians who create access points often take professional training on resources to use and the latest standards or rules for their formation. Some software systems include thesauri in pulldown menus to aid in this task, PastPerfect among them.

Related Materials

This section indicates the existence and location of other archival materials that are closely related to the materials being described by provenance, activity, or subject, either within the same repository, another repository, or elsewhere.[13] If an organization decides to include these fields in their inventory template and they do not apply to a specific collection or record group, they can simply be omitted.

Other Inventories: optional, this is a catch-all field for other finding aids, guides, indexes, lists, or descriptive tools, whether created by the records' creator or the archives, that provide information about the records being described.[14]

Separated Materials: optional, this is not a DACS field. Use this field to note separated book collections or other types of materials. Separated archival materials, like photographs or oversized items, are typically described where they belong intellectually. Their removal to a different location is shown physically in the box from which they are removed, but items like book collections or objects are unlikely to be interfiled with archival materials; hence this optional field.

Related Archival Materials: optional, this would include other archival collections, books, subject or clipping files or such with a "direct and significant connection to" the same records creators, activity/function, or subjects.[15] Indicate the nature of the related materials, how they are related, and their location.

Existence and Location of Originals: optional, sometimes archives have copies of material owned by another institution, a private individual, or from a resource with limited availability. Indicate who has the originals and details needed to locate them.

Existence and Location of Copies: optional; sometimes additional copies are given to archives other than where the original is given, or duplicate copies of materials are given to several archives. Materials might also have been microfilmed or digitized. If known, indicate what has been duplicated, where the copies are located, and details needed to locate the copies (e.g., collection name or URL).

Publication Note: optional, cite any publications or other works about or based on the use of the materials being described.[16]

Administrative/Biographical History

Administrative/Biographical History: highly recommended but not required; the purpose of this field is to provide the researcher with a ready reference to the people or organizations who created the records and the activities documented therein so that the rest of the inventory has greater meaning. Give key dates or events focusing primarily on the period covered by the records. This is not an in-depth biography of the creator. Life dates (birth and death dates) can be included even if the records focus on a narrower period. Although an agency history is about an organization instead of an individual, the concept is the same. Describe significant events or key dates in the history of the organization, focusing primarily on the period documented by the records. It may be appropriate to explain how a committee was created (appointed by the town manager) or the organizational structure of major divisions. If citing a source in the sketch, use footnote notation (Chicago Style) and place at the end of the field.

Scope and Content

Scope and Content: required, this is one of the most important fields in the inventory because it enables researchers to judge the collection's potential relevance to their research question.[17] The description should include the creators, dates, quantity and type of records, and major subjects.[18] Record information concerning the nature of the materials being described as well as the function(s), activity(ies), transaction(s), and/or process(es) that led to their creation.[19] Describe the types and forms of material found and their creation dates: family correspondence describing the education of women during the nineteenth century, Henry Bruce's business correspondence, and legal documents showing the purchase and sale of land. Note the presence of nontextual material: illustrations, maps, drawings, photographs, blueprints, audio or visual recordings, or computer files.

Note the geographic location(s) or places to which the records pertain. Describe the most important subjects, events, people, and organizations represented. Include any other information that helps the researcher evaluate the relevance of the materials. Mention the unexpected presence or absence of materials, and significant chronological gaps. If the collection consists of the papers of a local family during the Civil War, a letter signed by Abraham Lincoln would be unexpected and should be mentioned. Explain significant gaps in materials. For example, twenty-five boxes of unprocessed records that were damaged when a water pipe broke had to be thrown out. Boxes included constituent correspondence from 1970 to 1973 asking for assistance from the congressperson.

After providing an overview of the collection, provide more specific information at the series level only about the records in that particular series. The MS-37 Patricia A. Renick Stegowagen-volkssaurus Collection finding aid[20] illustrates collection level versus series level description in the scope and content field. DACS rules 2.3.18 to 2.3.22 can be used to form series titles. Series headings can be formatted as bold while subseries headings are italicized to distinguish between the two. MS-21, the Charles J. McLaughlin Family Collection, illustrates the use of formatting to help visually distinguish the organization of series.[21]

System of Arrangement

System of Arrangement: optional, the need to use this field will depend upon how complex the collection is, not the length of the Container Listing. Describe the "chunks" in the collection, usually series, subseries, or files; and their relationship to one another. This collection includes Series 1. Business Papers; Series 2. Personal Correspondence; and Series 3. Family Photographs. The business papers in Series 1 include an account book, day books, and ledgers that primarily document the general store he ran during the period 1829–1868. Series 2 has been subdivided into Outgoing and Incoming Correspondence, both of which are arranged alphabetically by the last name of the correspondent. Most of the photographs in Series 3 are unidentified.

Container Listing or Box and Folder List

Container Listing: Not a DACS field, but in archival practice for the last fifty years or more, inventories have included some type of list of box contents. A minimal entry would be a list of each series in sequence. A more detailed list includes the file folder headings within each series. While the physical folder heading includes additional information, the folder title, the box number in which the folder is kept, the sequential folder number for that folder (folder numbers start at 1 for each box), and possibly the dates of the material within the folder are typically what is included in a container list.

Conditions Governing Access and Use

Conditions Governing Access: required, this field states whether there are restrictions on access, meaning use, for any of the records being described. Restrictions may be imposed by legal, policy, or donor requirements. Develop several standard, succinct statements for use, such as:

Preliminary Guide to the Peter Storey papers, 1950-2006

Summary ▾

South African Methodist Church leader and anti-apartheid activist. The Peter Storey Papers contain correspondence, datebooks, articles, lectures, sermons, committee and subject files, clippings, scrapbooks, videotapes, and electronic records. The collection documents Peter Storey's leadership and active involvement in the Methodist Church of Southern Africa, the South African Council of Churches, the Central Methodist Mission in Johannesburg, the Truth and Reconciliation Commission, Gun Free South Africa, and other religious and anti-apartheid groups. Major subjects include Nelson Mandela, Winnie Mandela, urban ministry, crisis intervention, and political violence and elections in South Africa. Materials range in date from circa 1950 to 2006. Acquired as part of the Human Rights Archive.

More About This Collection

Collection Details ▾

Collection Number	RL.01260
Title	Peter Storey papers
Date	1950-2006
Creator	Storey, Peter John, 1938-
Extent	9 Linear Feet, 5000 Items
Repository	David M. Rubenstein Rare Book & Manuscript Library
Language	Material in English

Series in This Collection ▾

1. Correspondence, 1971-1997 and undated
2. Datebooks, 1963-1996
3. Subject files, circa 1970-2006 and undated
4. Clippings, 1970-2003
5. Videocassettes, circa 1995-2004 and undated
6. Electronic records, circa 2001-2003

Figure 4.3. This is a good example of a clean layout presenting key information at the beginning to help researchers determine whether to read the rest of the finding aid or use the collection for research. Note the use of DACS fields in Collection Details and that more information is available than what is shown. https://library.duke.edu/rubenstein/findingaids/storeyp/. Image used Courtesy of Duke University's David M. Rubenstein Rare Book and Manuscript Library.

- This collection is open for research access.

- This collection is open for research access with the exception of [identify the restricted section(s)], which is closed to all researchers due to [reason, for example FERPA (Family Education Rights and Privacy Act) restrictions].

Physical Access: optional, if applicable this field describes limitations on access due to physical characteristics of the materials or storage locations such as offsite storage or fragile materials that require the use of copies for preservation reasons.[22] Some materials, like audio cassettes, might require duplication and *migration* prior to researcher use.

Technical Access: optional, this field describes access limitations due to technical requirements, such as equipment or specific hardware/software required to use the materials.[23]

Conditions Governing Reproduction and Use: optional, this field identifies restrictions on reproducing materials due to copyright, other intellectual property law, or donor requirements; and on further use, such as publication, of the materials described after access is given.[24] This is another field where an institution could develop several standard entries for use depending upon what is known about the copyright status. Copyright is discussed at length elsewhere in this book and DACS element 4.4 provides additional commentary and sample statements.

Preferred Citation: optional, researchers use the citation to document their research sources. Develop a standard citation format for this field. Northern Kentucky University (NKU) uses [Box #, Folder #], MS-[#] or RG-[#], [Name of Collection or Record Group], [Eva G. Farris Special Collections (for historical records) or Schlachter University Archives (for NKU records)], W. Frank Steely Library, Northern Kentucky University. Some publications locate photograph credits along the edge of the published image or just underneath. This may require a shorter citation.

Acquisition and Appraisal

This is an example of information more useful to the institution than researchers; hence its relocation following the Container Listing.

Immediate Source of Acquisition: optional, this is the source from and date on which the repository acquired the materials in question, whether by gift, records transfer, or purchase. Some acquisition information may be considered confidential by the institution so the appropriate language for this field may require a policy decision. NKU includes the accession number(s) for all materials being described. This field may have been labeled Provenance or Creator prior to DACS.

Custodial History: optional, the institution may have additional information about who owned the materials between leaving their creator and reaching the repository. If that information is significant to the authenticity, integrity, or interpretation of the records then include it here.[25]

Notes:

This DACS field is used as a catchall for information that does not fit any of the other defined fields. It can be used on an as-needed basis or institutional policy may determine certain information is always included here.

Processing Information: optional, this is administrative information about who worked on the collection and when. NKU uses this field to document both processing and inventory creation. If a collection is reprocessed, the earlier information would be retained and added to. Format as Processed by [Name], [Date].

Finding aids are long-lived documents potentially existing as long as a collection exists and worked on by multiple people. For word-processed finding aids, and most electronic documents, the author recommends creating a standardized "signature block" on the left at the bottom of the last page (not in the footer) of the document. On line 1, record the electronic file name including the file format (DOCX, PDF), line 2 the date the document was created and name of the creator, line 3 the last revision date and the name of the person who made it. Use this information to compare print and electronic versions to quickly determine whether one is out of date. It answers questions such as "Was this inventory written before or after a new accretion was received; that is, has the inventory been updated yet? Was this inventory written or this collection processed before or after some other action such as changes in software or work processes?" The file name on a print copy can be used to locate the electronic file if necessary. Computers change the date on electronic files for actions other than revising the contents. If this information is recorded and updated manually, it will provide reliable and useful assistance from an administrative perspective. See appendix C.5 for a more complete sample inventory.

Table 4.1 Finding Aid Application Guide

Special Collections and University Archives (SC&UA) Finding Aid Element	Use	DACS Element	DACS Rule	Requirement
Header	Enter: Special Collections and University Archives, W. Frank Steely Library, Northern Kentucky University	N/A	N/A	Locally Required
Record Group or Collection Title	The first letter for each noun is capitalized in the title. Title = name of creator(s) or collector(s) + a term indicating the nature of materials being described + optional topical segment for collections documenting a very specific topical concept.	Title	DACS 2.3	DACS Required
Record Group or Collection Number	RG-[#] or MS-[#]. This number is assigned during accessioning and in some cases in processing. Special Collections numbers can be found in K:\Special Collections \L Inventories_Spec_Coll\ Processing Information\ manuscript_collection_numbers	Reference Code	DACS 2.1.3	DACS Required
Abstract	Use scope and content and administrative/biographical history information if available to construct abstract. The abstract is important for resource discovery.	N/A	N/A	Locally Required
Summary Information				
Creators	If creator is unknown, SC&UA requires that "unknown" be entered in this field. If there are significant creators other than the main one, include them in the Administrative/Biographical History if they have a role in the provenance of the collection.	Name of Creator(s)	DACS 2.6	DACS Required if known
Span Dates	Dates of creation: supply an inclusive date range comprising of the date of creation for the earliest and latest materials in the collection, separated by a hyphen.	Date	DACS 2.4	DACS Required
Bulk Dates	Dates of majority of material. Use only when a majority of the materials were created between these dates but a few outliers of more than twenty years exist outside of the span dates.	Date	DACS 2.4	Optional, use as needed

(continued)

Table 4.1 Finding Aid Application Guide (*continued*)

Special Collections and University Archives (SC&UA) Finding Aid Element	Use	DACS Element	DACS Rule	Requirement
Extent	Record physical quantities in linear feet or cubic feet. If the collection includes digital content, express digital extent (15 megabytes) separately.	Extent	DACS 2.5	DACS Required
Languages	"The materials are in (English)."	Languages & Scripts of Material	DACS 4.5	DACS Required
Repository Location	Enter: "Eva G. Farris Special Collections and Schlachter University Archives, W. Frank Steely Library, Northern Kentucky University, Highland Heights, Kentucky."	Name and Location of Repository	DACS 2.2	DACS Required
Access Points	*Goal is 5-10 terms per record group or collection.*			
Subjects	Use LCSH, AAT, other controlled vocabulary as necessary.	Subjects	DACS xxii–xxiv, 9	Locally Required
Names	Use LCNAF, local authority records. Includes names of persons, organizations, and corporate bodies.	Names	DACS xxii–xxiv, 9	Locally Required
Places	Use LCSH, TGN, local authority records.	Places	DACS xxii–xxiv, 9	Optional, use as needed
Formats	Use TGM, AAT, other controlled vocabulary as needed. Generally skip "paper" and "photograph."	Documentary Form	DACS xxii–xxiv, 9	Optional, use as needed
Functions	Use LCSH, AAT, other controlled vocabulary as necessary.	Functions	DACS xxii–xxiv, 9	Optional, use as needed
Occupations	Use LCSH, AAT, U.S. Department of Labor's *Dictionary of Occupational Titles*, other controlled vocabulary as necessary.	Occupations	DACS xxii–xxiv, 9	Optional, use as needed
Related Materials				
Other Inventories	This field can include references to indexes. It is a catch-all for other guides, finding aids, and descriptive tools. It could contain information about portions of the finding aid that are presented as spreadsheets to present detailed information about single items and to enable sorting the data in various ways.	Finding Aids	DACS 4.6	Optional, use as needed

(continued)

Table 4.1 Finding Aid Application Guide (*continued*)

Special Collections and University Archives (SC&UA) Finding Aid Element	Use	DACS Element	DACS Rule	Requirement
Separated Materials	Use this field to note the existence and separation of book collections or other separated materials.	N/A	N/A	Optional, use as needed
Related Archival Materials	Include if there are related materials in subject folders, other SC&UA collections, or collections at other institutions closely tied to the one held by SC&UA. Sample language: (1) "For related secondary material, see subject folder '___.'" (2) "For directly and significantly related collections use the collection citation. 'MS-[#] ___.'" (3) "For records at other repositories, use 'Other records directly pertaining to ___: [citation].'"	Related Archival Materials	DACS 6.3	Optional, use as needed
Existence and Location of Originals	Enter: "Originals of ____ held by [name of institution]." Include readily available information for locating collection materials.	Existence and Location of Originals	DACS 6.1	Optional, use as needed
Existence and Location of Copies	Enter: "Copies of [name of materials] are held at _____." Can include information about nature of copies (e.g., microfilm, access copies). Include readily available information for locating collection materials.	Existence and Location of Copies	DACS 6.2	Optional, use as needed
Publication Note	Cite any publications about or based on the use of the materials being described.	Publication Note	DACS 6.4	Optional, use as needed
Administrative/ Biographical History	The purpose of the note is to provide the researcher with a ready reference to the subject's activities so that information in the rest of the finding aid will have greater meaning. Emphasis should be on that portion of the subject's career or life to which the bulk of the collection relates. If citing a source in the sketch, use footnote notation (Chicago Style) and place source at end of sketch.	Administrative/ Biographical History	DACS 2.7	Locally Required

(*continued*)

Table 4.1 Finding Aid Application Guide (*continued*)

Special Collections and University Archives (SC&UA) Finding Aid Element	Use	DACS Element	DACS Rule	Requirement
Scope and Content	Can be brief or full, depending on what level the collection is being processed at or to. In most instances, describe collection at series level, noting the overall type and function of the contents as well as dates and creators. Use DACS title rules to form series titles. See DACS rules 2.3.18–2.3.22. Use the "Scope and Content" to explain significant chronological gaps in the materials. Bold series headings and italicize subseries headings.	Scope and Content	DACS 3.1	DACS Required
System of Arrangement	The need for using the "System of Arrangement" element is based on the complexity of the collection but not the length of the container list. Describe arrangement like "Collection (or Series) is arranged chronologically."	System of Arrangement	DACS 3.2	Optional, use as needed
Container Listing	Table settings for Microsoft Word: ½ point solid line, light gray (2nd one down on far left side). Color settings all at 217. All table components should be left-justified. For locations in the container list, use "O/S Box #," "Map Drawer #," "Art Rack Location #," "See staff," "Row 103."	N/A		Locally Required
Conditions Governing Access and Use				
Conditions Governing Access	Enter one of these options as applicable: (1) "This collection is open for research access." (2) "This collection is open for research access with the exception of [_____]. These have restricted access and are unavailable to any researcher." (3) "This collection is open for research access, with the exception of one folder due to FERPA restrictions."	Conditions Governing Access	DACS 4.1	DACS Required

(continued)

Chapter 4

Table 4.1 Finding Aid Application Guide (*continued*)

Special Collections and University Archives (SC&UA) Finding Aid Element	Use	DACS Element	DACS Rule	Requirement
Physical Access	This field provides information about access restrictions due to any physical characteristics or storage locations that limit access to the materials being described. Such restrictions include location, physical condition of the material that limits use, requirement to use copies instead of originals for preservation reasons. Example language: (1) "For fragile images, researchers will be asked to view digital copies of originals. Department personnel will authorize use of originals on a case-by-case basis." (2) "Some audiotapes may require duplication and migration prior to patron access."	Physical Access	DACS 4.2	Optional, use as needed
Technical Access		Technical Access	DACS 4.3	Optional, use as needed
Conditions Governing Reproduction and Use	Enter: "The copyright law of the United States (Title 17, US Code) governs the reproduction of copyrighted material. The user assumes full responsibility and any attendant liability for the fair use of materials requested in total compliance with the copyright law of the United States (Title 17, US Code) that may arise through the use of any requested materials."	N/A	DACS 4.4	Locally Required
Preferred Citation	Enter: either "Box #, Folder #, RG-#, Name of Record Group, Schlachter University Archives," OR "Box #, Folder #, MS-#, Name of Collection, Eva G. Farris Special Collections," "W. Frank Steely Library, Northern Kentucky University."	Citation	DACS 7.1.5	Locally Required

(continued)

Table 4.1 Finding Aid Application Guide (*continued*)

Special Collections and University Archives (SC&UA) Finding Aid Element	Use	DACS Element	DACS Rule	Requirement
Acquisition and Appraisal				
Immediate Source of Acquisition	Enter one of these three options to indicate method, source, date, and accession numbers: (1) "Transfer from [Name], [Date] (Accession Number)" (2) "Gift from [Name], [Date] (Accession Number)" (3) "Purchase by Steely Library, [Date] (Accession Number)"	Immediate Source of Acquisition	DACS 5.2.5	Locally Required
Custodial History		Custodial History	DACS 5.1	Optional, use as needed
Notes				
Processing Information	Enter: "Processed by [Name], [Date]." If reprocessing, add name and date below the initial processing information to capture revision history. SC&UA uses this field to indicate both processing and finding aid creation.	Description Control Element	DACS 8.1.5	Locally Required
Variant Title Information	Use if collection material has been published under a significantly different name (e.g., Mary Northington Collection instead of the NKAAHTF Records)	Variant Title Information	DACS 7.1.7	Optional, use as needed

Standards: Controlled Vocabulary

Using a template for collection inventories provides consistency in the organization of the information about a collection. This helps researchers because they can locate the same type of information regardless of which specific inventory they are reading. They must learn how to "read" the inventories at your institution only once instead of for every inventory.

In the same way that consistency in communicating information in the inventory makes research easier, consistency in access points and names ensures that a researcher can find all records with information about a particular topic, person, or location. If the word "car" is used in one finding aid and "automobile" in another, searches on "car" will overlook those finding aids that use "automobile" and vice versa. Researchers will miss potentially useful information. If John Bacon is also called J. Bacon and Squire Bacon, it may be more difficult to determine whether the records describe one, two, or three different people. Women's names are also problematic. Are Nora Jones, Eleanor Jones, and Mrs. George Jones the same woman or different women?

These are examples of the confusion that can occur if *standards*, commonly agreed-on rules, are not used to provide consistency when describing records, photographs, or other material in finding aids, catalog records, or other descriptive systems.[26] Consistency, or standards, in the creation of access points or subject terms and in the formation of names will improve the useful-ness of written description. A *controlled vocabulary* is a limited set of terms or phrases that is used as subject terms in an index, catalog record, or finding aid. Only one term represents a concept so that all material related to that concept can be retrieved using that term.[27] For example, the term "automobiles" would be used instead of "autos" or "cars." Some fields of study have devel-oped vocabulary lists, called *thesauri*, of preferred terms used to describe concepts, methods, or objects associated with that field.[28] A thesaurus is an example of a controlled vocabulary.

When *standards* are used to create a single preferred form for a name, everyone who describes records by or about that person, family, or organization uses the same form. In order to remember what the agreed-on form is for a name, people make lists of names created using the standards. These lists are called *name authority files*.[29]

Librarians developed a controlled vocabulary for subject terms called the *Library of Congress Sub-ject Headings* (LCSH). They also developed standardized rules for creating the preferred form of a name and codified them in the *Anglo-American Cataloging Rules* (AACR) first released in 1967, revised as *Anglo-American Cataloging Rules*, 2nd edition (AACR2) in 1978 and then succeeded by *Resource Description and Access* (RDA) in 2010.[30] During the last half of the twentieth century, as libraries evolved and adapted their work to perform tasks using computers, they had to agree on a consistent way to communicate information so that it could be understood by computers. Librarians developed a standard called MARC (machine-readable cataloging), which became available in 1969, for sharing computerized information about books.[31] All three of these stan-dards are used to describe published materials.

Because most archival material is unpublished, archivists normally use different descriptive standards than librarians. American archivists adopted DACS as their descriptive standard for ar-chival records. DACS describes archival materials in finding aids, as just illustrated in the section on inventories, catalog records, indexes, and elsewhere, but for the formation of access points and names, it recommends standardized vocabularies such as LCSH or rules for name formation such as those in AACR2 or RDA.

RDA says to use the form of name for a person, family, or corporate body found most commonly in resources associated with that person, family, or corporate body.[32] Associated resources means materials, records, correspondence, etc. How did the individual, family, or organization usually sign their own name or record it in organizational documents? Real names, pseudonyms, nicknames, or initials are all acceptable if that is how the person, family, or corporate body called themselves most frequently.[33] For example, if you have the papers of Eleanor Jones and she signed everything as Mrs. George Jones, the form for her name in an authority file would be Jones, George, Mrs. If, however, she always signed her name as Eleanor Jones, it would be Jones, Eleanor. Mrs. George Jones would be listed in the authority record as a variant of her name so that people consulting the name authority file would know that Eleanor Jones and Mrs. George Jones were the same per-son. If it is difficult to determine the most common form of name by using records created by the person, family, or organization in question, the next best source is the most frequently occurring form of name in reference sources *about* the person, family, or organization.[34]

Once the first person uses the standards to form the approved version of any name, other people can simply look up a particular name in a name authority file without having to know how to apply the standards used to create it. Authors and better-known people who have been written about are likely to have a name authority record on file with the Library of Congress. See Additional

Reading/Resources for a link to their website. Lesser-known local people probably will require someone at the institution to establish a standardized form for their name. If the institution agreed to maintain its own internal name authority file for the standardized formation of local names found in its holdings, but not existing in LCNAF, it would serve as an in-house tool for everyone who works on collection description.

The PastPerfect Subject authority field comes preloaded with relevant thesauri, while the People and Search Terms authority files allow the institution to create customized lists.[35] For search terms, use LCSH or other standardized thesauri when possible. For people, try to use LCNAF when possible. PastPerfect's People authority file can serve as the institution's internal name authority file. For those not using PastPerfect, a spreadsheet of alphabetically ordered names, how they are formed, and possibly variant names is a perfectly suitable alternative.

Archival records by or about the same person, family, organization, or activity often exist at multiple institutions. Researchers have difficulty locating the many places where related archival records exist. About 2009 the idea developed of linking access points, or subject terms, using linked (open) data. This technology can even link related family members. While this requires advanced technology and skills, the use of controlled vocabulary and standardized name formation is a good first step. The use of standardized names positions an organization to take the next step in sharing its inventories and publicizing its records more broadly through linked (open) data or other methods when it has the resources.

Controlled vocabulary and standards for naming enable organizations to share information about their collections with other organizations. This means that a researcher can search for the same information simultaneously at more than one institution. Although the use of standards will be more beneficial to institutions that share descriptive records (finding aids or catalog records), even those that do not will find their use beneficial or possibly even necessary. Small organizations that manage archival records may be able to make information about their collections available only on-site in their research room. Consistency in description will make it easier for researchers and the staff or volunteers who assist them to find the records that will answer their questions.

The Library of Congress has published a *union catalog* of descriptions for manuscript collections since 1959. A union catalog is one that includes descriptive records from more than one institution. The National Union Catalog of Manuscript Collections (NUCMC) originally appeared in print until 1993, when it went electronic. Organizations that own manuscript collections and are open regularly for research but lack the trained personnel or resources to create their own MARC records are eligible to have them made free of charge by NUCMC. The institution completes an online worksheet providing information about each collection and submits it to NUCMC. NUCMC creates a collection-level MARC record and submits it to a national union catalog managed by the Online Computer Library Center (OCLC) called WorldCat. Institutions who subscribe to OCLC's services will make the records available to researchers. Submitting information to NUCMC is a free and easy way to spread the word about your collections. The NUCMC home page is located at https://www.loc.gov/coll/nucmc. There is an online version of the form and two word processing versions that can be submitted by e-mail. To contact the NUCMC team, e-mail them at nucmc@loc.gov, call (202) 707-7954, or write the Library of Congress, Cooperative and Instructional Programs Division, NUCMC Program, 101 Independence Avenue SE, Stop 4231, Washington, DC 20540-4231. Because of issues in recent years with mail delivery in Washington, DC, e-mail or telephone is recommended for timely responses.[36]

Description Is More Than Just Inventories

Collection description includes more than just the inventory; for example, the labels on the file folders holding the records are also description. These labels are recorded in the container listing, so they should also be intentionally planned out. If you use the style of file folder with a one-inch tab on the back edge, this will provide room to record several important pieces of information. The edge can be visually divided into thirds. Starting at the left edge, in the first third write its manuscript or record group number (MS-003 or RG-047) or possibly add a short unique version of the collection name. This will leave space to also record the series name, such as correspondence. In the center third, record the file name/folder title. This could be the name of the correspondent, the year in which the correspondence was written, or whatever is appropriate. The span date for the material in the folder can be written in this middle third but on a second line under the folder heading. Depending on the nature of the files, in the last third write the box number in which the folder belongs and the sequential folder number for that specific folder. Folder numbers for each box start at 1. For example, Box 1, Folder 1; Box 1, Folder 2; Box 1, Folder 3 and so on until all the folders in Box 1 are numbered. Repeat with the next box—Box 2, Folder 1; Box 2, Folder 2; Box 2, Folder 3. If all the files in the box are arranged either alphabetically or chronologically, numbering the folders might be less critical; however, this information will help minimize misfiled folders. Researchers will know where to return material to within the box and the organization's personnel will spot missing folders faster.

Try to use succinct description for folder headings. Use of common standardized terms for series is helpful: correspondence, annual reports, minutes, programs, reports, press releases, deeds, legal papers, and receipts. Try to avoid labels such as miscellaneous or assorted. They are not good description. No one knows what is in those folders. Records being processed may or may not arrive in folders with labels on them. If they do, the labels should be evaluated for clarity and consistency. If they are not well written, improve or revise them. Use of acronyms and abbreviations other than commonly recognized ones should be avoided.

The front edge of the folder tab can be used to record other information if it is needed. For example, if the folder names are long, the box and folder number could be recorded on the right third of the front edge instead of the back edge. The left third of the front edge might be used for an item count for the folder contents. This would be more appropriate for photographic materials or valuable collections. Whatever is decided should be documented for future use. This ensures that everyone who processes will work in a consistent manner. A template and examples are also helpful for training new people. Examples can be as easy as photocopies of folders that illustrate a variety of heading information.

A good descriptive program for all the institution's holdings is efficient. Try to reuse information collected or recorded in one step at another stage when possible. If a deed of gift includes a list of the materials donated, the list can be attached to a paper accession record or copied and pasted into an electronic accession record. If the donation arrives with a container list, it can be the start of the container listing for the inventory. Information about the donor and donation can be taken from the deed of gift or accession record and inserted in the administrative/biographical history, scope and content, or other pertinent fields in the inventory. Paper copies of inventories available only on-site can be used to complete forms to submit to NUCMC. They can also be made available on a website as PDF versions of word-processed documents. In time, an institution might acquire the resources to purchase software, such as PastPerfect. Information from the inventories can be used to create a catalog that searches all the collections instead of just the one described by each inventory. It is even possible to make the records in the PastPerfect catalog available via the World Wide Web to researchers when the institution is closed. All this takes planning and time, but if it is organized, each step completed makes the next one possible.

It is advisable to create description in stages. If most of an institution's holdings are unprocessed, it is more important to get minimal control of all the holdings at the collection level than to focus on one or two collections. Create a minimal inventory for each collection. Once this is done, prioritize. Resources permitting, go back and arrange and describe each collection to the series level. If appropriate, collections can eventually be processed further. Not all collections merit processing to the file and even fewer at the item level. It is also preferable to have a reasonable level of control over all the holdings before proceeding with in-depth work, such as indexing a large collection.

How to Use PastPerfect for Archival Description

The description discussed so far can be created with word-processing software, file folders, and pencils. Many local historical societies, small museums, and archives use a version of PastPerfect software. This software manages objects, books, archival papers, and photographs, all of which are commonly found at organizations like these, and is more affordable than most professional software. PastPerfect was originally developed for museums. Descriptive practices for museums and libraries differ from those for archives. The first two use a one-to-one correspondence between description and what is described; one catalog record equals one physical item. This is item-level description. Archivists practice collective description. Archival description corresponds to a body of records that shares a complex, hierarchal relationship. Most archival description corresponds to an intellectual unit, not to a physical item. Only at the lowest hierarchical level does description describe one item.[37]

With the understanding that the one-to-one correspondence that is a design principle for PastPerfect does not accurately represent sound archival description, let's examine how to create description using this software. A well-written inventory will include most of the information that PastPerfect records in multiple tabs and fields. One of the benefits of using both inventories and PastPerfect would be to create an integrated catalog. Such a catalog would make it possible to search all the inventories simultaneously as well as all other formats of material cataloged in PastPerfect. Another benefit would be to make this integrated catalog available not only in the institution's research room but also after hours and to distant researchers via the internet. Remember that this is just one method of providing wider access. Written inventories combined with free cataloging by the NUCMC team is a comparable alternative. A third option would be to locate all the collection inventories on the same website and rely on web browsers to crawl the inventories, index them, and make them searchable by browsers like Google Chrome, or others. These decisions depend on available resources and the goals of those who manage the cultural collections.

Assuming that PastPerfect will supplement word-processed inventories, I will discuss those fields that would create a good minimum catalog record. Fields that repeat information from the inventory without adding a lot of value to the catalog record are skipped.

Steps to Create a Catalog Record in PastPerfect

1. Double-click on the PastPerfect icon on the Windows desktop to start the software.

2. From the **Main** screen, under the **Collections** menu, select **Archives**.

3. On the top navigation bar, select the **+ Add** button to create a new catalog record.

4. A message box will open. Enter an **Accession #** for the material to be cataloged; review how to create accession numbers in chapter 2. This can be typed in, or you can click on the folder symbol to the right of the box and select the accession number from the list. The software requires an **Object ID #**. In archival practice, the **Accession #** is the only number assigned, and it applies to all items in the accession to which it is assigned, whether that is one item or five hundred boxes of records. Archivists do not assign individual item numbers to each piece of paper in an accession. Use the same number for the **Accession #** and the **Object ID #**. Put a check mark in the box under the **Accession #** field that says **Pre-fill Object ID # with Accession #**, and the information will be entered automatically.

5. An **Object Name** is required to create a catalog record. Since this first catalog record will be a collection level to describe the whole collection, type the term "Manuscript Collection." The very first time a new object name is entered, when you select the **Add New Record** button a little later in this process, a new message box opens and asks you to either **Add this Object Name to the Lexicon** or **Select a Different Object Name from the Lexicon**. For this first time, select **Add This Object Name to the Lexicon**. When the catalog records for subsequent collections are created, you will be able to click on the **Authority File** button to the right of the **Enter Object Name** box and highlight "Manuscript Collection."

6. As you catalog more material, the software will build your own custom authority file. When you select **Authority File** instead of **Lexicon**, your custom list will open, and you can select from the terms you have previously used.

7. The **Lexicon** is preloaded with 8,500 object names from Chenhall's Nomenclature. Because this name authority file was created for museum objects, its terms may not always fit archival collections. If you do use the **Lexicon**, most manuscript materials will fall into Category 8—**Communication Artifact**. Select **Communication Artifact**. From **Subcategory**, select **Documentary Artifact**. Note that the information in the textbox below changes. Read it to see whether the material you are describing fits that definition. If it doesn't, select another **Subcategory**. Continue to the **Object Names** box, scroll through the list, and select the appropriate one. The term you highlight will appear in the **Object Name** box. When you click on **Select this Name**, you will return to the message box.

8. On the right-hand side, under **Add Options**, select **Add a Single Record** and **Fill New Record with Blank Data** to retain the information you have just entered. If you anticipate cataloging a lot of material of the same type, you may want to select **Set Current Record as Default Data Record**. Refer to the software manual for information on how to use the **Add Options** to save time by prefilling new catalog records, depending on the material you are cataloging.

9. When you have finished, select **Add New Record** (near the bottom left of the message box) to keep the record you have just created. This is a minimal catalog record that will require more information to be useful.

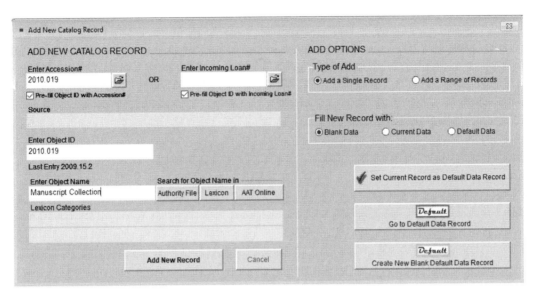

Figure 4.4. The completed message box that produces a minimal catalog record. Image used courtesy of PastPerfect Software, Inc.

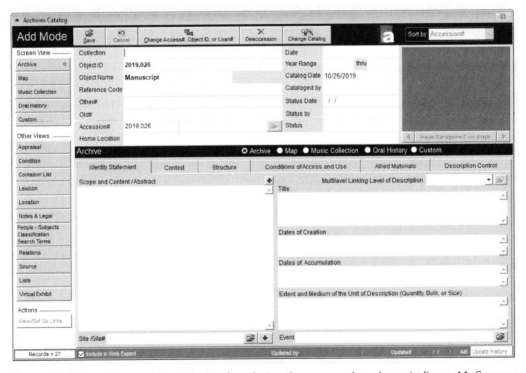

Figure 4.5. The catalog record as it looks after closing the message box shown in figure 4.1. Common catalog record fields are located above the horizontal black line labeled Archive. Image used courtesy of PastPerfect Software, Inc.

Common Cataloging Fields for All Records

10. Selecting **Add New Record** will bring you to a new screen with many fields. On the left-hand navigation, you will see three groups of screens labeled **Screen View**, **Other Views**, and **Actions**. Note that the first screen under **Screen View** is **Archive** and that it has a green dot on the right. The dot indicates that there is information in that screen, which is the same screen you are currently viewing. The five screens listed in **Screen View** represent the five choices for record types in the archives catalog. To view any of the screens on the left-hand navigation, either hold your mouse over the button or left-click on the screen you want. Note that each of the five record types has a matching radio button on the horizontal blue bar in the middle of the catalog record. Use these buttons to select the record type and set the default view for that particular catalog record.

11. The common catalog fields that appear in all four catalogs (Objects, Photos, Archives, and Library) appear in the upper half of the catalog record, as shown in figure 4.5. Much of the information to complete these fields should be in the accession record for the collection being cataloged. If this collection was already accessioned in PastPerfect, the donor's name will automatically be entered next to the accession number. To the right of the donor's name is a small file folder icon. Click on the icon to go back to the accession record. During accessioning, the name of the collection was recorded in the **Instructions** field. Look up this information. Select **Exit** on the top navigation bar to return to the catalog record and enter the collection name in the appropriate field.

12. The reference code was discussed earlier in the sections of an inventory. While the manuscript collection or record group number might be assigned at accessioning, it could also be assigned at processing when the collection name is formed. Regardless of when it is assigned, once it has been, record in the reference code field of the common cataloging fields.

13. The current storage location for the collection is entered in the **Home Location** field. This may be a temporary storage location where the collection sits waiting for or during processing, designated as new accessions holding area or processing holding area. Ideally, each storage row and shelf, flat file drawer, art rack, or other type of storage will have a sequential yet unique number that can be entered in this field. Refer to chapter 11 for specifics on how to organize the collection storage room/space. Once processing is complete, or if the collection is moved for any reason, return and update this field for the permanent collection location.

14. Dates are tricky. There are a variety of ways to format a date, depending on whether the date is definitely known or is estimated to the nearest year, decade, or century. Acceptable dates for this field include September 11, 2001; 9/11/2001; ca/circa/about/approx 1956; 1960s or 70s; and 1923?; 194_?; 18__?. Because this field will accept so many date formats, it is not a reliable search field for locating records.

Despite the potential uncertainty of dates, try to standardize how they will be written as much as possible. Use all four digits for years to avoid confusion. Aug 7 or August 7 is less ambiguous than dates such as 7/8. Is this August 7 or July 8? Decide the organization's rules for date formation, record them for reference, collect examples, and use the rules consistently.

A collection often has several dates associated with it. The **Date** field is for the date the records being described were created. Because this first record is for a whole collection and because archival records will usually be described as a group (i.e., not just a single item), the date of creation will quite possibly be a range of years. Enter the date of the oldest item and the most recent item in the collection. The **Date** field for series- or item-level catalog records may be for a shorter period than a range of years.

If an artificial collection is being cataloged, there could be two date ranges. The first, the creation dates, would be the dates the items were written, recorded, or published. The second, the acquisition dates, would be the dates during which the collector acquired the items in his collection. Family members wrote postcards from the 1900s through the 1970s. Mrs. Gilliam collected them from 1960 to 1980, when she put them into albums. The **Date** entry for the Gilliam Collection might be "Postcards written 1900–1970s; collection created 1960–-1980."

15. Because the dates entered in the **Date** field will be problematic for searching, the formation of dates in the **Year Range** field is more rigid so that it will be searchable. Enter the span dates for the years of creation as four-digit dates, 1900–1979.

16. The **Catalog Date** is the date the catalog record is created. If you are familiar with function keys on the computer keyboard, the F8 key will automatically fill in the current (today's) date. Also complete the **Cataloged By** field.

17. The **Status** field can be used to alert users to special information about the cataloged material. Examples include restricted access, copyright restrictions, missing, and damaged. If an entry is made in this field, also note who assigned the status in **Status By** and when in the **Status Date**.

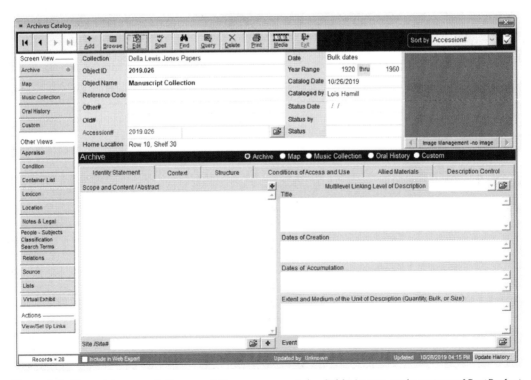

Figure 4.6. The catalog record after completing common catalog fields. Image used courtesy of PastPerfect Software, Inc.

Archives Catalog: How to Create a Collection-Level Record

On the left-hand navigation, under **Screen View**, there are five types of archival materials listed: **Archive** (this is for paper records of all types except photographs/images), **Map**, **Music**, **Oral History**, and **Custom**. Depending on which of these record types is selected, the screen(s) on the lower half of the catalog record will change to display pertinent fields. I will discuss the **Archive** screens because this will be the most frequently used format.

First, some general notes. The authors of PastPerfect have used international archival standards, so some fields or menus may use slightly different vocabulary than in this book because I am using American archival vocabulary. For example, the word *fonds* is used outside the United States to refer to either a collection or a record group, depending on who created the records.

Second, enter data only in those fields that are appropriate for the records being cataloged. If something doesn't apply, don't use it. In some cases, the information being requested is unknown to the cataloger (the person creating the catalog record), but it might be useful to enter "Unknown" in the field rather than leave it blank. For example, if the donor of a collection is unknown, enter Unknown in the field rather than leave it blank and give the impression that the field was simply skipped.

Finally, PastPerfect includes many fields, most of which are optional. The cataloger can decide how much information to enter. This may well depend on the time available to devote to extra fields, such as biographical entries for creators, photographers, or authors. Decide what is most important to do with the available staffing.

18. On the bottom half of the catalog record for **Archive**, there are six tabs: **Identity Statement**, **Context**, **Structure**, **Conditions of Access and Use**, **Allied Materials**, and **Description Control**. The first field in the **Identity** tab is for the **Scope and Content** information, which was previously discussed in the inventory template. If a word-processed inventory has already been created for this collection, copy the information right out of the inventory and paste it here. This is an example of reusing a previously created description to save time.

19. **Title**: For a collection-level record, repeat the collection name as given in the **Collection** field of the common catalog fields. Title was discussed above in the sections of an inventory.

20. The **Dates of Creation** and **Dates of Accumulation** are also listed in the common catalog fields above. Simply reenter them here.

21. **Extent and Medium**: Extent is the quantity of records being cataloged. It was also discussed in the sections of an inventory. Be consistent in the measurement unit (linear or cubic feet; kilobytes or gigabytes) used. Medium, or format in DACS, describes the *documentary forms* of the records (minutes, diaries, reports, correspondence, maps).

22. This tab also has two interesting fields at the bottom: **Site/Site#** and **Event**. The collection being cataloged may have a connection to a physical location, such as a family home or the location of a company. Records may also be about an event instead of a location. Use these fields if they are applicable. Entries in these fields will help index the records and make it easier to find detailed information. Try to be consistent in the language for these fields and make use of the authority lists that can be created for these fields. When the cursor is in

the **Event** field, a large letter **"a"** (for authority file) appears on the top navigation bar. Any time the **"a"** is visible, either right-click on the **"a"** or press the **F7** function key to call up the authority file for the appropriate field. Clicking on the folder icon next to the **Site** field will link to a site list the cataloger creates. Unfortunately, PastPerfect will allow only one site to be associated with a catalog record because of the premise that each catalog record represents one item. Pick the most important location for the records being cataloged.

23. The **Context** tab has fields for the **Name of Creator** and **Other Creators**. The **Other Creators** field does not appear to be indexed and will not be found by any type of search. If a name is entered only in the **Name of Creator** field, it can be found by only one specific search method. Go to the **Main** screen of the software, select **Research**, and select **All 4 Catalogs**; in the field labeled **Field**, select **Artist-Creator** from the pulldown menu, enter the name in the **Value** field, click on the **Add to Statement** button, and click on the **Run Query to Select Records** button. The name should turn up in the results if it is entered the same way in both fields. A further condition is that the name entered in the **Name of Creator** field must be listed in the biographical file. To do this, click on the folder icon next to the **Name of Creator** field. A message box will ask whether you would like to add the name to the Artist/Author/Creator/Photographer authority file. Click **Yes**. A new screen will appear from the biographical file. The creator's name will automatically fill in. Select **Exit**. This is sufficient to cause the name in the **Name of Creator** field to be indexed. The cataloger can return and make a more complete entry at any time.

Enter only one name in the **Creator** field, whoever either created the bulk of the collection or the most significant material. This field links to the Artist/Author/Creator/Photographer name authority list created by the cataloger. As previously discussed, decide on the formatting for these names and be consistent in their formulation and the use of the authority lists.

On the **Context** tab, I would complete only the Name of Creator field, make the minimum entry required to establish the biographical file link, and use the **Archival History** field if it is useful for your institution. Because the name fields on this tab are not well indexed, it would be more efficient to spend data entry time on the **People—Subjects Classification Search Terms** screen to be discussed below.

24. The **Archival History** field would be a good place to document information *about* the records being cataloged or their management, actions taken, or decisions made. For example, since the link to the accession record goes back to an alternate view of the temporary and accessioned records, who made the decision to accept this collection and when could be entered here, as could decisions to deaccession material. Note the immediate source of acquisition and custodial history inventory fields record some of this information. The notes field can be used to record the processing history of the collection being described as well as the finding aid. A processing plan (see chapter 3 and appendixes B.2a and B.2b) can also record some of the information PastPerfect suggests for this field. If this type of information is maintained elsewhere in paper files such as control files or processing plans, and the system is effective, skip this field.

The **Structure** tab does not seem to add useful, pertinent information. The **Conditions of Access** and **Allied Materials** tabs repeat information already recorded in the inventory (conditions governing access and use and related materials sections) and can be skipped. The **Description Control** tab is designed for use by professionally trained archivists. The

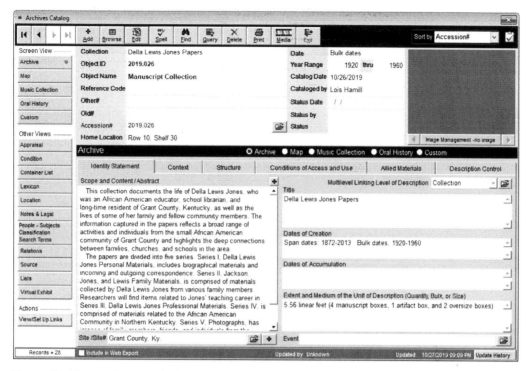

Figure 4.7. The catalog record after completion of the identity statement tab. Note the entry in the multilevel linking level of the description field. Image used courtesy of PastPerfect Software, Inc.

name of the cataloger and the date the catalog record is made are already recorded in the common fields above. The name(s) of the people processing the collection and dates are recorded in the inventory notes field. If there are details about how or why the collection is (re)arranged or described a particular way that are important enough to record, it would make the most sense to record it in the collection's processing plan, which would be kept in the collection's donor file after processing. This would keep all the processing information in a single document. If the information does not fit elsewhere in the processing plan, use the other notes field. If it was strongly desired to record this information in PastPerfect, it could just as easily go in the **Archival History** field of the **Context** tab (step 23 above) and keep all the information about managing the collection together. Readers should decide which of these several locations works best for their institution and its practices.

Completing the common catalog fields and select fields in the archive catalog that were discussed above will produce a good basic record for a whole archival collection. There are one or two more tasks to complete that will make it possible to search the collection by specific names of people, places, or types of records. On the left-hand navigation, there is a screen called **People—Subjects Classification Search Terms**. Click on the screen. There are four fields labeled **People**, **Subjects**, **Classification**, and **Search Terms**. This is the best place to create access points for the collection in PastPerfect. The access points field of the inventory, controlled vocabulary, and name authority files have already been discussed in this chapter. If access points were created for the inventory, simply copy them here as much as is possible. It is very important to consistently form the names and words used as index or search terms. If they are entered more than one way, regardless of the search term used, it is unlikely that all the pertinent records will show up in search results even though the material is described in PastPerfect.

1. Put the cursor in the **People** field. Click on **Edit** on the top navigation. This automatically moves the cursor to the **Collection** field as the first field, and the authority file symbol **"a"** appears on the top navigation bar. Put the cursor back in the **People** field.

2. PastPerfect recommends the following format for names: last name, first name, and middle name or initial. For women and people who have changed their names, use nicknames, or have titles, these can also be indicated in the **Other Names** field of their biographical record. This is comparable to the variant names field in the LCNAF. Type in a name associated with the collection being cataloged.

3. Click on **Save**. This highlights the folder icon by the **People** field. Click on the icon to bring up a list of names with biographies.

4. Click on the name that was just entered in the **People** field to open a Biographical Record for that person. New records have the person's name at the top formatted the same way as it was entered in the **People** field. The **Other Names** field is located here. A married woman's record might be Stearns, Abigail. Her **Other Names** field would include her birth name (if known): French, Abigail. Entering her husband's name in the **Spouses** field would show that she was married and to whom.

5. Click on **Edit** to enter information in any of these fields. Put the cursor in the field you choose; it should turn yellow, and then you can enter information. Complete as much as is known of the person's genealogy. Click on **Save**, then **Exit**, and then **Close**. Continue entering names in the **People** field and creating biographical records until done. Any names entered previously as the **Creator** of the records being cataloged (**Context** tab) will need to be entered again in the **People** field and have a biographical record made. Each field seems to create separate index lists.

6. After you have saved the names in the **People** field, click on **Edit**, put the cursor back in the **People** field and then open the authority file (right-click on the **"a"** or press the **F7** key). You will see that all the names have been transferred to the name authority file. The next time one of those names needs to be used again, simply click on the name to select it. When you select **Close**, the name will be transferred into the **People** field or whichever other field into which you are entering data. This is how you use the name authority file to maintain the consistency of the form used.

7. Put the cursor in the **Subject** field. Click on **Edit** on the top navigation. This automatically moves the cursor to the **Collection** field as the first field, and the authority file symbol **"a"** appears on the top navigation bar. Put the cursor back in the **Subject** field. Open the subject authority file. Think about the collection you are cataloging. What subjects does it have enough information about to be helpful to a researcher? Search the authority file for terms you think best describe the subject. You may need to try several terms before you find what you are looking for. If you are unsure about a term, highlight it and click on the folder icon next to the **Close** button. Some entries have additional information to help choose between entries. Try this with the term **Abolitionists**.

8. Highlight each choice and press the Enter key on your keyboard or double-click. When you finish, click on **Close**, and all the terms you selected will be entered in the **Subject** field. Click **Save** to save your **Subject** entries.

9. The **Search Terms** field is similar to the **People** and **Subjects** fields. The authority file for this field contains only those terms already entered in the **Search Terms** field in other catalog records from your institution. It may or may not be useful to enter terms from the **People** and **Subject** fields in the **Search Terms** field too. A **Keyword** search will locate terms entered in all three of these fields, so there would be no benefit to repeating terms. You may wish to experiment with some of the searches under **Research** on the **Main** menu to determine whether to repeat terms.

Well-written inventories prepared using word-processing software can be printed, filed alphabetically, and put in binders for use by researchers in a reading room. The same word document can be converted to a PDF file and hosted on a website for more distant researchers to use or when your institution is closed. Such a description program would provide good access to the collections. PDF files are searchable. This model would require researchers to search one collection at a time; however, if your organization's website has a comprehensive search box, it should enable searches across all inventories simultaneously. Results will not be limited to just the inventories, however. Similarly, as long as your institution does not block Google Chrome or other web browsers from your site, those search engines will potentially also include information from your inventories. This is not quite as efficient as a single web page, portal, or software database that searches your inventories exclusively, but it does provide 24/7 worldwide access to your holdings, which is valuable. If the institution is able to create MARC records itself or submits collection description to NUCMC, this raises the visibility and accessibility of the collections and will also allow simultaneous searching of all collections. If the institution has the resources to go a step further, collection management software, such as PastPerfect, allows it to create an online catalog that researchers can use in the reading room to search across collections. Inventories provide context and access through provenance, while PastPerfect provides more detailed indexing that directs a researcher to a collection and its inventory. Based on this blended approach, it is not necessary to complete every field in PastPerfect. A good minimum record with thoughtfully created search terms will complement the inventories instead of duplicating them.

Additional Reading/Resources

Getty Research Institute. "Getty Vocabularies." Accessed June 18, 2019. http://www.getty.edu/research/tools/vocabularies/index.html. This page links to three specialized but useful thesauri: the Getty Thesaurus of Geographic Names (TGN), which includes names of current and historical places such cities and nations as well as physical features like mountains and rivers that are associated with art, architecture, and material culture; the Art and Architecture Thesaurus (AAT); and the Union List of Artist Names (ULAN).

Hazell, Alastair. "The Calculator Site." ARGH Industries, Ltd. Accessed June 18, 2019. https://www.thecalculatorsite.com/misc/cubic-feet-calculator.php. This site has a handy, easy-to-use calculator to determine the cubic footage of a quantity of records.

Hunter, Gregory S. *Developing and Maintaining Practical Archives: A How-to-Do-It Manual.* 2nd ed. How-to-Do-It Manuals for Librarians, no. 122. New York: Neal-Schuman, 2003. See chapter 6, particularly pp. 131–42, for guidance on how to prepare description.

Joint Steering Committee for Development of RDA, *Resource Description and Access (RDA)*. Chicago: American Library Association, 2010. Chapter 9 addresses how to form names. An online version is available by subscription, but one thirty-day free trial online is available per institution at http://access.rdatoolkit.org/freetrial. If your organization isn't associated with a library cataloging unit, consider consulting a local library for some professional advice.

Library of Congress. "ID.LOC.GOV—Linked Data Service." Accessed June 1, 2019. https://id.loc .gov/. Go to Subjects, Thesauri, Classification>LC Subject Headings (LCSH). This site is used by library catalogers to look up standardized subject terms. The Thesaurus for Graphic Materials (TGM) is also in this category. To look up proper names of people, organizations, or even literary works, drop down to the Agents category and the LC Name Authority File (LCNAF). Try Herman Melville. The second result would be the most general entry for Melville, while others are for specific aspects of his work. Also search on Adams, Mrs. John to see how married women's names are handled. Scroll down to see the variant names compared with the preferred form.

National Union Catalog of Manuscript Collections. "National Union Catalog of Manuscript Collections." Library of Congress. Accessed June 18, 2019. https://www.loc.gov/coll/nucmc is the home page for NUCMC with guidance on how to submit collection description for cataloging.

Society of American Archivists. *Describing Archives: A Content Standard [DACS]*. 2nd ed. Chicago: Society of American Archivists, 2013. Copies may be available to borrow by interlibrary loan through the local public library for those considering the use of this standard. An online version is available at https://saa-ts-dacs.github.io/, while a downloadable PDF version is available at http://files.archivists.org/pubs/DACS2E-2013_v0315.pdf. The overview includes information about access points. Element 2.3 provides information about name formation with examples. Element 2.7 includes examples of administrative/biographical histories.

Walch, Vicki, comp. *Standards for Archival Description: A Handbook*. Chicago: Society of American Archivists, 1990. This is now available online at http://www.archivists.org/catalog/stds99/ index.html. Chapter 6 lists several specific thesauri. Chapter 7 discusses dates and geographical locations.

Wikipedia. s.v. "linked data." Accessed June 21, 2019. https://en.wikipedia.org/wiki/Linked_data. This gives a basic introduction to linked (open) data.

Witt, Betsy S., Jennifer C. Whitfield, and Adam J. Stepansky. *PastPerfect Software for Museum Collections: Version 5 User's Guide*. Exton, PA: PastPerfect Software, Inc., 2010. Chapter 3, p. 47 discusses thesauri that can be used to create access points or subject terms. Chapter 9 includes a brief cataloging tutorial for books while chapter 10 discusses the lexicon, which uses standardized terms. Chapter 6, p. 113, discusses adding a catalog record, with basic information that is true for all four types of catalogs; p. 122 explains the fixed fields; and p. 142 has more information about the **People-Subjects-Classification-Search Terms** fields.

Notes

1. Richard Pearce-Moses, *A Glossary of Archival and Records Terminology*, Archival Fundamentals Series II (Chicago: Society of American Archivists, 2005), s.v. "Describing Archives: A Content Standard."

2. Pearce-Moses, *Glossary*, s.v. "description."

3. Fredric M. Miller, *Arranging and Describing Archives*, Archival Fundamental Series (Chicago: Society of American Archivists, 1990), 79–80.

4. Wikipedia, s.v. "xerography," accessed July 1, 2010, http://en.wikipedia.org/wiki/Xerography.

5. Pearce-Moses, *Glossary*, s.v. "collective description."

6. Gregory S. Hunter, *Developing and Maintaining Practical Archives: A How-to-Do-It Manual*, 2nd ed., How-to-Do-It Manuals for Librarians, no. 122 (New York: Neal-Schuman, 2003), 152.

7. Hunter, *Developing and Maintaining Practical Archives*, 137.

8. Hunter, *Developing and Maintaining Practical Archives*, 153.

9. This template was originally created as a collaborative effort with my staff. Thanks to Anne Ryckbost and Vicki Cooper for their contributions.

10. Society of American Archivists, *Describing Archives: A Content Standard [DACS]*, 2nd ed. (Chicago: Society of American Archivists, 2013), 39–40. If the reader is using PastPerfect software, see p. 171 of the user's manual.

11. Pearce-Moses, *Glossary*, s.v. "inclusive dates (also span dates)."

12. Society of American Archivists, *DACS*, xxii–xxiv.

13. Society of American Archivists, *DACS*, 73.

14. Society of American Archivists, *DACS*, 61.

15. Society of American Archivists, *DACS*, 73.

16. Society of American Archivists, *DACS*, 75.

17. Society of American Archivists, *DACS*, 45.

18. Hunter, *Developing and Maintaining Practical Archives*, 137.

19. Seth E. Shaw, "Arrangement and Description of Electronic Records, Part 1," Society of American Archivists Digital Archives Specialist workshop, Chapel Hill, NC, June 11, 2015, course booklet, 180; Society of American Archivists, *DACS*, 45.

20. The MS-37 finding aid is located at https://inside.nku.edu/library/find/unique-collections/special -collections-archives/alphabeticallist/renick-stegowagenvolkssaurus.html.

21. The MS-21 finding aid is located at https://inside.nku.edu/library/find/unique-collections/special -collections-archives/alphabeticallist/mclaughlin-family.html.

22. Society of American Archivists, *DACS*, 53.

23. Society of American Archivists, *DACS*, 55.

24. Society of American Archivists, *DACS*, 57.

25. Society of American Archivists, *DACS*, 63.

26. Pearce-Moses, *Glossary*, s.v. "standard."

27. Pearce-Moses, *Glossary*, s.v. "controlled vocabulary."

28. Pearce-Moses, *Glossary*, s.v. "thesaurus."

29. Pearce-Moses, *Glossary*, s.v. "name authority file."

30. Salman Haider, "Anglo-American Cataloguing Rules (AACR, AACR2, AACR2R)," Librarianship Studies & Information Technology, accessed June 15, 2019, https://www.librarianshipstudies.com/2018/12/anglo -american-cataloguing-rules-aacr.html.

31. Miller, *Arranging and Describing Archives*, 110.

32. Joint Steering Committee for the Development of RDA, *Resource Description and Access (RDA)* (Chicago: American Library Association, 2010), Rule 0.4.3.4 on p. 0-5.

33. Joint Steering Committee, *RDA*, Rule 9.2.2.3 on p. 9-2.

34. Joint Steering Committee, *RDA*. Rule 9.2.2.6 on p. 9-9.

35. Betsy S. Witt, Jennifer C. Whitfield, and Adam J. Stephansky, *PastPerfect Software for Museum Collections: Version 5 User's Guide* (Exton, PA: PastPerfect Software, 2008–2012), 37–38.

36. Bruce W. Dearstyne, *Managing Historical Records Programs: A Guide for Historical Agencies* (Walnut Creek, CA: AltaMira Press, 2000), 99.

37. Pearce-Moses, *Glossary*, s.v. "archival description."

5

Photographs

Part 1—Handling, Arranging, Identifying, Rehousing, and Describing

The previous two chapters explained how to physically arrange archival records and then how to describe them once they have been arranged. The bulk of archival records consists of paper documents; however, archival collections frequently include photographs. Because of their composition and the processes used to create them, photographs have their own unique preservation requirements. This chapter discusses tasks to prepare photographs for use: how to safely handle and *rehouse* them as well as arrange, identify, and describe them. The next chapter discusses topics pertaining to their use.

Let's start with how to handle photographs, negatives, and slides. Some repositories require staff and researchers alike to wear white cotton gloves when handling these types of materials. This is to prevent the transfer of oils that naturally exist on our hands or other residue that can mark or permanently damage irreplaceable material. While wearing gloves prevents this type of damage, they also reduce a person's manual dexterity and can cause damage from clumsiness. If photographs are sleeved, the use of gloves is less critical because the sleeve serves to protect the image. There are arguments for and against the use of gloves. Each institution should consider their particular situation, set a policy, and adhere to it. There are special antistatic gloves for work with negatives or slides. Even if the general practice is against wearing gloves, one might still wear antistatic gloves for a large project involving the use of negatives.

Guidelines for Safe Handling of Photograph Collections[1]

Prepare

- Wash your hands before working with photographs. Do not apply hand cream or anything oily to your hands when working with photographs or negatives. It can transfer to the materials and mark them. A damaged negative means that all prints made from it will show the damage.

- Your work surface should be physically clean of food, adhesives, dirt, oily furniture polish or cleaning products, chemicals, or other residue that might transfer to the photographs.

- Do not eat or drink while handling these or other collection materials. Food attracts bugs that may eat your photographs.

Plan

- Make sure you have sufficient workspace to accommodate the items with which you intend to work in order to prevent damage to them.

- Make sure you have pencils, notepaper, acid-free folders, and boxes or other necessary supplies on hand.

- Use number 2 pencils when working with or near collections, not pens or markers. Ink marks are irreversible. Pencil is erasable. Number 2 pencils are soft and don't leave pressure marks, unlike harder leads or mechanical pencils.

- Always check the condition of items before moving them. If they are damaged, use care. It may be necessary to seek advice before moving them.

- Some oversize items require two people to safely move them. You may also need to prop doors open or have someone hold them. Plan ahead before starting to move them from storage.

Handle with Care

- Do not lean on or set heavy objects on top of photographs, even if they are covered or in a folder. The pressure can break older photographs mounted on cardboard stock if they are not perfectly flat or fully supported underneath.

- Do not write on paper, folders, or envelopes while they contain photographs. Pressure marks can go through to the photographs and cause damage. The pressure from bearing down in order to write can also cause older photographs mounted on cardboard stock to break if they are not perfectly flat or fully supported underneath.

- To prevent scratches, avoid touching the surface of images or dragging anything across the face of an image. Also, be careful not to drag negatives or slides across surfaces.

- Always keep photographs completely flat on a level, well-supported surface. Do not place photographs on your lap or under a stack of books, or let part of the photograph hang unsupported over an edge. Accidental application of pressure can cause breaks.

- Support items carefully when moving them. Use both hands to hold parallel sides of a photograph or place one hand underneath and hold an edge with the other to prevent bending, tearing, or breaking. Use interleaving paper that is larger than the item to be moved to transport large or damaged photographs. When necessary, ask for assistance to move oversize material.

- Do not stack photographs of widely varying sizes or weights on top of each other. Instead, stack items of a similar size together. Be mindful of the weight on the bottom photograph in a stack. Do not stack so high as to cause damage. Apply the same precautions to stacks of flat boxes of photographs.

- Store photographic sleeves and other supplies in their original packaging to help keep them clean and undamaged. It is easier to reorder the same supplies if the product information remains on the package. The packaging also clearly differentiates archival supplies from ordinary office supplies.

- Never attach paper clips to photographs, not even plastic or plastic-coated clips. Metal paper clips rust and will mark the image. All paper clips cause photographs to buckle, distorting the image. To keep items together, use an acid-free folder or an acid-free piece of paper folded in half.

Other Tips

- Never use tape, staples, rubber bands, glue or other adhesives, or sticky notes on photographs. All of these can damage the image.

- Avoid removing photographs from their photo sleeves unless absolutely necessary.

- Work slowly and move with care to avoid damaging your materials.

- Consult copies when they are available in order to protect originals.

How to Arrange Photographs

Photographic materials, whether prints, negatives, or slides, need to be arranged. Provenance and original order apply to them the same as for paper records. Photographs created, collected, and maintained by one creator need to be maintained and managed together but separate from other creators. The true creator of a photograph is the photographer, even though many times his identity is unknown. However, for arrangement purposes, the owner or collector of the photographs is often treated as the creator.

To some extent, the arrangement for photographs may depend on whether the collection consists exclusively of photographs or the photographs are physically interfiled or strongly linked intellectually to paper records. When photographs arrive interfiled with paper records as part of a collection with a discernible original order, for their own protection they will need to be physically separated out. Because the paper records may identify or explain what is illustrated by the photographs, it will be important to intellectually maintain the link between the two record types. The easiest way to do this is to replace the original photograph with a photocopy that is annotated with the new location of the now removed original, essentially creating a variant of a separation sheet. By photocopying the photo there is no mistake which photo belonged in that location. Also, it is easier to show a copy of the photo than to try to describe it with just a few words, especially if there is a series of relatively similar photos. Depending on the quantity and condition of the original photograph, it could be sleeved and left in its original location. This last option might be acceptable for a single item in good condition but should be practiced sparingly. In a collection composed of papers and photographs, frequently the photographs are designated as a separate series in the arrangement and stored in their own boxes because of their differing preservation needs.

If a collection arrives that consists entirely of photographs or the photographs are already separated from any paper records and there is no discernible order, then the processor must create one. The best way to arrange photo formats, like paper records, will depend upon factors like the quantity of photos, their context (what works for a small collection of family photos may not work for a newspaper photo morgue or photos created for a business function) and their relationship to nonphotographic records. Photographs are often separated by their format, then arranged and housed separately, meaning photos will be foldered and boxed with photos but not slides or CDs/DVDs. Negatives are also recommended for separate storage, but more on that shortly. It is perfectly acceptable to shelve boxes of photos next to slide storage boxes and CD/DVD storage boxes if that is their intellectual arrangement. Oversize photos are also separated out, arranged, and stored separately. Once the photographic materials are subdivided by format, take one format at a time and start arranging based on the image content, meaning the subject of the photo. First, review the photos, retaining their original order to get an overview of what they document, whether they are already organized in a discernable manner, whether similar or duplicate photos are scattered throughout or clustered, and whether there are any dates or identification. The results of this survey will inform the decision of a workable arrangement. The photos might be arranged by subject: people (family, friends, associates, unidentified), places (street address or geographic location), events (anniversaries or graduation), things (boats or buildings), activities (sports or classes); chronologically; or by creator or function (portraits, advertising photos, or book illustrations).[2] A collection of family photos arranged by image subject might group all the photos of Person A together, all of Person B together, etc.; or family, friends, unidentified people. Even if the identity of a specific individual or group of people is unknown, the images can be assigned to a generic category: women, students, buildings, and so on.

Professional literature recommends separating negatives from prints partly because negatives can be stored at cooler temperatures, if such environmental conditions are available. The negatives are also considered the originals while prints are copies made from the negatives. In today's digital environment, prints are often used in lieu of negatives, but that was not always an option. In the last half of the twentieth century the average person took film to the local pharmacy or grocery store to be developed. The negatives and prints were returned together in a divided envelope. A roll of film might document the events of one day or a year's worth of activities. In this example, separating the negatives and their prints can be problematic. If the prints document more than a single event, intellectually the prints are likely to be arranged into different folders. Cutting the corresponding negatives into individual pieces is not recommended. This destroys the ability to potentially date or identify as much as the whole roll of film based on identification of one or several prints. The negatives also document the sequence in which the photos were taken. This contextual information would also be lost by cutting up the negatives. One option would be to use a numbering system to link negatives and prints. The whole roll of film negatives would be rehoused in an appropriate archival film sleeve with a unique number written on the paper sleeve or printed on an adhesive foil label adhered to the paper sleeve. The label acts like a barcode. Use a number system like 000001, 000002, 000003, 000004, etc., so the same number is not repeated in a different collection or record group. The same number would have to be recorded on either the folder where the prints are stored or possibly written on individual prints depending upon the number of locations in which they would be filed. Acceptable writing implements for recording the number on a photograph itself would be either a number 2 pencil or a Pigma Micron pen with archival ink. The number would be recorded on the back, near the upper or lower edge, starting at the left to avoid running out of room. Allow the ink to dry sufficiently that it does not smear onto an adjacent photo. This numbering system requires a lot of work and tracking of the next number available for use. Unless there is a sufficient volume of negatives to track, it would be inefficient to use. An administrator should carefully consider current holdings, anticipated types of records to be collected, the skill level of staff/volunteers, and the storage environment among other factors before deciding to separate negatives and prints. If this practice is instituted, do not separate prints from negatives until all components have been properly marked.[3] Once numbered, they can be separated and arranged.

Photographs may be separated out during arrangement, as is the case when they become their own series, or during the refoldering or rehousing stage, in the case of photographs interfiled with paper records. In either case, depending on their size, quantity, and format, the photographs that are separated out are frequently put in a different box than the paper records but shelved with the rest of the collection. If any are oversize, they are shelved in the designated oversize storage area. If they are even larger, they are stored in flat files of the same type used for maps.

Photo Identification

Identification is part of the process of arranging photographs. It is easier to arrange them when they are identified. From a practical perspective, they are also more useful. Researchers request photographs of specific people, places, events, and activities. Sometimes a generic, unidentified photograph can be used in an exhibit or book, but many times it is passed over. How much time is spent on identification will vary by the significance and research value of the collection, the number of photographs, the likelihood of identifying the images, and the time available to spend on the task. One option is to arrange unidentified photographs into generic categories such as "unidentified men," "unidentified fishermen," or "unidentified buildings, probably located in Cincinnati." In this case, identification is left to the researcher who uses the collection.

Photographs transmit information using images instead of words. "Seeing a photograph is a form of literacy. . . . The greater one's experience, the more one is able to read in a photograph."[4] Visual literacy is a process of observation, critical thinking, and understanding to derive meaning from information presented in the form of an image. It is based on the premise that it is possible to "read" an image and gain meaning through the reading. While visual literacy can be applied to any graphic image from charts and graphs to art, it can be applied to photography to aid in the identification of specific photographs.

How is it possible to tease additional information from a photograph that might yield a partial or full identification? Start by studying the photograph as an object. The history of photographic processes can be a useful starting point to identify a time period for a photograph. There are a number of excellent books on the history of photography that can be consulted to aid in dating of specific photographs. James M. Reilly's *Care and Identification of 19th Century Photographic Prints* is one; several others are listed in Additional Reading/Resources at the end of this chapter. While I will not provide an exhaustive history of photographic processes, I will describe some of the more common nineteenth-century photograph types that may appear in archival collections. The photography timeline found on the Image Permanence Institute's website or chapter 2 of the Ritzenthaler book (see Additional Reading/Resources) are but two resources that illustrate the photograph types described below.

Tintype (1856–1920s, Most Popular in the 1860s)

The tintype was produced on a thin sheet of iron coated with black lacquer. Predominantly used for portraiture, images are dull gray with creamy highlights, although they might be hand colored. Each image was actually a negative, not a print, and therefore unique. Unlike mid-to-late-twentieth-century negatives, they couldn't be used to create multiple prints of the same image. The fact that tintypes were less expensive than other contemporary photographic methods contributed to their popularity. Due to their greater durability they were put in paper mats, collected in book-like albums, or left loose. Dents, scratches, and rust are the common forms of damage for tintypes.[5]

Daguerreotype (1839-1865, Most Popular in the 1840s and 1850s)

Daguerreotypes were produced on a copper plate coated with silver that underwent a chemical process and resulted in a unique, highly reflective image with sharp definition, also frequently hand colored. The image was commonly reversed laterally, especially for portraits; a wedding band would appear to be on the right hand instead of the left, and letters on signs were backward. Images were made in a variety of standard sizes from 1/16th to 1/6th, 1/4th or a full-sized glass plate (8.5 in. × 6.5 in.). They are encased in a series of layers to protect the image: copper plate, mat, glass, all held together by paper tape and inserted into a sturdy case of wood or leather. From the early 1850s a decorative preserver frame was inserted between the glass layer and the case. The distinctive layers in a daguerreotype can sometimes help date the image. Be aware that years afterward, collectors or dealers may have switched mats, preservers, or cases, which could cause inaccurate dating. Daguerreotypes are one of several types of images that were put into cases for protection. They can also be referred to as *cased photographs*, but note that not all cased photographs are daguerreotypes, only those that underwent the unique chemical process used for daguerreotypes.[6]

Ambrotype (1854-1865, Most Popular Early 1860s)

Ambrotypes were produced as the result of an emulsion layer chemically applied to a glass plate. Like daguerreotypes, ambrotype images show sharp definition, are direct positives (meaning they are nonreproducible and unique), were hand colored, and consisted of layers inserted into a case. They also came in various fractions of a full glass plate, like daguerreotypes. An ambrotype image is not reversed, unlike the daguerreotype, and lacks the silver metallic look characteristic of the daguerreotype. Ambrotypes were less expensive than daguerreotypes and replaced them for portrait photography.[7]

Albumen Print (1850-1920, Most Popular 1855-1895)

Approximately 80 percent of extant nineteenth-century photographs are albumen prints. They were the first photograph in which the image was suspended on the surface of the paper instead of embedded in the paper fibers. Albumen prints were created when a glass negative was put in contact with a sensitized paper, the albumen print, and exposed to light for a sufficient time. This was a negative-positive process, which meant that the glass negative could be put in contact with many pieces of sensitized paper to create multiple identical copies. Because albumen prints were created through extended light exposure, they are also susceptible to fading. They did, however, produce detailed images. One identifying characteristic of albumen prints is yellowing of highlights and mid-range tones caused by storage in high humidity and the natural aging of the albumen (egg white) used to sensitize the printing paper.[8]

Albumen prints were printed on very thin paper that was prone to curling and tearing. For this reason, they were usually mounted on card stock in a variety of thicknesses, colors, sizes, and designs. The card stock can be used to help date the image. In his book *Cartes de Visite*, William C. Darrah describes in detail the evolution of changes in the card stock and the information the photographer printed on the card stock. Although albumen prints were mounted on card stock, so were other nineteenth-century photographic processes not described here. Caution is advised when identifying the type of photograph to separate the technical process by which an image was created from the method of presentation—whether in a case or mounted on card stock.[9]

Stereographs (Popular from the 1850s to the 1920s)

Stereographs are a format, not a process. Two nearly identical images were created, printed, and attached to cardstock. Processes used to create stereographs included daguerreotype, ambrotype, and albumen prints, among others. When viewed through a special viewer, the image appeared to be three-dimensional, giving it a sense of depth. A popular nineteenth-century form of entertainment, stereographs illustrated natural wonders, geographic locations, and other sights. Stereography enjoyed a resurgence of popularity in the form of the View-Master reels and viewers, evolving in the latter part of the twentieth century into a children's toy.[10]

If you are able to determine the photographic process for a nineteenth-century image, note the date range for that process. Continue identification by examining the paper or mount on which the photograph is printed. Is there any writing on the front or back? This may be handwritten or recorded by a machine. The back may be stamped with the name and contact information of the photographer who took the photograph. A mounted photograph may be embossed or stamped with the photography studio's name on the front. The original paper jacket or holder for a photograph may carry the name of the studio and even a location. Knowledge of when and where a professional photographer or studio worked can narrow the date of the image, indicate the geographic location where the photo was taken, or possibly provide additional information about the subject of the image.

What information is provided about the photographer or the studio? Does it have just a name or does it include a telephone number or address? How current are they? Telephone numbering systems have changed in the number of digits used, the use of letters as part of the telephone number (FF9-1234), and the area code assigned to a particular geographic location. Some streets have been renumbered. The photograph may carry the stamp of a military branch of service, identifying it as the photographer. Is there information about when the studio was (or perhaps still is) in business? A variety of useful print and electronic resources for this type of research is listed later in the chapter.

Does the photograph have crop marks or other indications that it was published? Is it possible to tell where, perhaps in a local newspaper or a regular column in a weekly or quarterly publication? For instance, if the photograph looks like it might have been published in a newspaper, consult newspapers that published in the location appropriate for the photograph, the records, the collection, or the donor. The choice of geographic location and date depends on the information available to you in the collection itself or known about the collection or donor. A photo may look like it was published, but not in a newspaper. If you are processing the records of a business, organization, or other institution, check to see whether the business or organization produced internal publications. Use information such as the date.

When there is information recorded on the photograph that appears to identify the image, this information needs to be authenticated, evaluated, and interpreted. Just as newspaper photo captions and obituaries contain mistakes, so does information written on photographs. A person may record information about the photo many years later instead of shortly after the fact. The information may be secondhand to the person making the note, not known by them personally. Substantiate the information from other sources whenever possible.

In working with unidentified photographs in an academic setting, the author found head shots of students. Some photographs had a name written on the back, but after consulting yearbooks and alumni directories, it was clear the name didn't match the person in the photograph. What to conclude? The name was actually that of the student photographer. This information very quickly narrowed the date range for the photograph to the four years the student photographer attended that college. When numerous student head shots all had the same brick wall background (observation of a pattern), review of the weekly student newspaper revealed a regular opinion column with the same background.

The back may be completely blank or have the name of the manufacturer of the paper on which the photograph was printed. When examining a group of photographs, the simple observation that the back of one print says "Fuji" and another says "Kodak" will indicate that the two photos are not from the same roll of film, and may not have been taken on the same day. Processing information may have been printed on the back when the photograph was developed; this may or may not contain a date. Comparison of late-twentieth-century processing codes can be used to determine whether several photographs are from the same roll of film or not. The codes may even contain the number of the negative, resulting in the ability to restore the original sequence of the photographs. When working with groups of photographs that can be proven to be from the same roll, if one photograph is dated, suddenly all of them might be.

Some photographers used their own numeric or alphanumeric coding system for their images long before late-twentieth-century film processing plants. This can be seen on nineteenth-century glass plate images, but this author also saw it used on photographs from the 1960s and 1970s. If correctly deciphered, the numbers may reveal the sequence of a group of images, the year in which the photograph was taken, or whether the images were from the same event/location/client or photographer, depending on what information the photographer recorded with his coding.

When working with groups of photographs, attentiveness to patterns found on the photographs can help determine whether a specific example does or does not belong to a certain group. For example, Michael J. Novia operated as a commercial photographer in the 1960s and 1970s in central Massachusetts. Most of his prints bear his name and his own unique numbering code. However, this author found prints with numbering only and no name on them. Comparison with the numbering on a reasonable quantity of other prints clearly attributed to Novia demonstrated the unnamed ones as consistent with Novia's system, thus making it reasonable to conclude he also took those photographs.

When the specific date of a photograph is not obtainable, a month, year, or date range can be an acceptable option. May 1968 is more specific than 1968. The date range 1978–1982 is better than 1950–2000. More information is always preferable to less. New information may be discovered later, which can build on what is recorded initially and result in a more precise date or identification. If there is something special about a photo or group of photos, such as Grandma's seventy-fifth birthday or Mary and Joe's thirtieth wedding anniversary, add that information also when known.

These examples demonstrate that, before the image itself is even looked at, examination of a photograph as an artifact can provide quite a bit of useful information. Some photographs will carry more information of this nature than others.

Let us turn now to the image itself. If the photograph includes people, examine their clothing, hairstyle, and eyeglasses. Knowledge of clothing and hair styles can help date a photograph.

Joan L. Severa's book *Dressed for the Photographer: Ordinary Americans and Fashion, 1840–1900* will be helpful for dating nineteenth-century photos. For more recent photos, use your personal knowledge of clothing and hairstyles typical in your lifetime. What clothing styles have you worn or observed and when? To go back a bit further, think about your parents or grandparents. How did they dress?

Look for writing, slogans, or graphics on T-shirts; calendars in the background or on a desk; banners or posters on a wall, building marquees, business names, or street signs. Examine objects visible in the photograph. Can you identify them? Can you connect any to a particular event, date, or era? Overlapping date ranges derived from the photographic process, clothing, and objects in a photo can be compared to determine whether two or three of these factors only existed simultaneously for a narrower range than any one individually. A photo of two men with hairstyles from the 1970s or early 1980s also shows a soda can with a pull-off tab. The current soda can style with the attached tab was invented in 1982. The photo must pre-date 1982.

Do you recognize the location shown in the photograph? Is it the interior or exterior of a building? Has the building's appearance changed through a renovation or addition? Is something that used to be there gone, or is something present that was not there before a known date? Perhaps a road in the background has changed, a dirt road was paved, or a local road became an interstate. With research, it is often possible to date these types of changes.

Photographs of groups of people can provide helpful information. If Library Director A worked for an institution from 1990 to 2001 and Employee B worked from 1985 to 1997, then the photograph was taken between 1990 and 1997. Employment dates and life dates can also be used to narrow the date range of a photograph.

If the identity of several people in a photograph is known, it might be possible to extrapolate the identity of the others or make a guess about the function or activity captured by the photograph. If half the people in a group are faculty members or administrators, maybe the others are too. Maybe they are all faculty from the same department. If you recognize the president or chairperson, but everyone else is a stranger, perhaps these are donors giving money or the chairperson is accepting an award on behalf of her organization. Make educated guesses and weigh their probability based on other known information. Test them out if possible. Even if you rule a possibility out, you know more than before. No is also an answer.

When identifying photographs of people, always record the names from left to right, the same way text is read. If there is a mix of identified and unidentified people, say "Henry Jones, unidentified man, Mary Smith, two unidentified women, Toby Barnes." This helps the viewer align the names correctly with the people, reducing the risk of attaching the wrong name to a person. Consider saying "front and back rows" instead of "first and second rows." Not everyone will pick the same row as row one. Record whatever information is known. If the information is incomplete or there is some doubt, indicate that using underlining and question marks to differentiate the known from the unknown. For example, "Ma*ry*?" indicates that the processor is confident the first two letters are "Ma" but is less sure about the "ry." It could be just "y" as in "May," not "Mary."

Groups of photographs can be like logic puzzles. If it can be established that all of them date from a particular era or specific day, then what is true or false about one can be applied equally to the others. For example, examination of a group of photographs of a baseball game revealed cars parked along a roadway. While not all the cars were present in all the photographs, all the cars present in every photograph were parked in the same sequence. There were gaps where cars had left or arrived at different times, but a particular black car was always present in the same place along the fence in every photograph in which it was found. The cars in front of or behind the black car were never found in a different location relative to the black car. Thus, it was possible to conclude that the entire group of photographs was from the same game on the same day. Any similar photographs that did not match the sequence of cars were assumed to be from a different game. If it is possible to read the jersey of the opposing team in any one of these photographs, this information can be compared with a season schedule, and it may be possible to actually date the game. Especially in the case of high school or college athletics, if the graduation date of even one player in the photograph is known, this information can be used to further narrow the possible dates for the photograph. This is how small pieces of information can be combined to identify one photograph or a group. The process is similar to assembling a puzzle.

Sometimes several photos initially look the same yet are not identical. Are they duplicate copies made at the same time in the past (e.g., two prints from 1955), or is one an original from 1955 and the second a more modern copy of the original made in the 1970s? Look at the photo paper or printing marks on the back—same day, same period, or not? Can you see the edges of one photo in the image of another? Did someone take a photograph of an older photograph? Is one eight inches by ten inches and the other a wallet size or has a larger photo been cropped to appear smaller, but the image is the same size in both? Look at features such as men's ties—the same tie or not will indicate whether the photograph was taken on the same day.

When observation, analytical thinking, and research are combined, it is possible to make reasonable conclusions about the identity of a photograph. For a very readable and interesting account of the use of deductive reasoning, logic, and research to reinterpret Civil War photography, read William A. Frassanito's *Gettysburg: A Journey in Time*. Photographers' codes played a minor role in the process.

Safely Housing Photographs

Once photographic items have been identified and arranged, and are ready to be rehoused, suitable products must be selected for their storage. Many products are available for the safe storage of photographs, negatives, and slides. The choice will depend on the format of the items to be stored (photograph, negative, or slide), their physical size, usage practices, cost, the stability of the temperature and humidity of their storage environment, and even personal preferences. Whenever possible, select products that have passed the *Photographic Activity Test* (PAT). This is an international standard that "predicts possible [chemical] interactions between photographic images and the enclosures in which they are stored."[11] Enclosures, housing, or boxes that have passed the PAT are safe to use with all types of photographic materials.

In general, the products in which photographs are stored are made of either paper or plastic. Archival paper, envelopes, folders, and boxes have special qualities that distinguish them from ordinary office products. They are acid-free. Acid speeds up the deterioration process for paper and shortens its life. The papermaking process changed shortly before the start of the American Civil War. Compare paper made in the early nineteenth century with last week's newspaper. When stored under similar conditions, the newspaper will deteriorate sooner. Newspaper clippings that have been stored in a folder with other papers or slipped into a book will eventually cause a yellow stain on the adjacent papers or pages. The stain is caused by the migration of acid from the newsprint, causing damage to the adjacent materials. To counteract acid that occurs in materials stored in archival containers, these products are also available with buffering added to them. For an extensive collection of color photographs, do not use buffered materials to store them; the buffering may interact with the color photographs. If your collection is primarily black and white with a few color photographs scattered throughout, it should be safe to use buffered products.

Many paper-based archival products are also lignin-free. When left in paper products, lignin also causes deterioration.[12] Purchasing acid-free, lignin-free, buffered archival containers means not only that the containers will not harm their contents, unlike ordinary office products, but that they will actually protect and extend the life of the photographs or records stored within them.

Photographs are frequently stored in clear "plastic" sleeves so that researchers can see the image without directly touching it. If photos are sleeved, the use of gloves during handling is less critical because the sleeve serves the same purpose. There are three plastics that are safe to use with archival materials: polyethylene, polypropylene, and polyester. Other formulas for plastic contain chemicals that will damage or shorten the life of whatever is stored in them.

Archival vendors sell an inexpensive "pen" that tests for the acidity of paper, folders, boxes, or other paper-based products. As a general rule, yellow indicates acidic and purple signals acid-free; but be aware that current office paper used in computer printers and photocopiers contains brighteners that seem to give a false reading for their acid content. There is no comparable method to test plastic storage products once they have been separated from their original packaging. Purchase supplies from reputable companies that are in the business of selling archival products. Read the product description and look for the terms *polyethylene*, *polypropylene*, *polyester*, or *passed the PAT*. If in doubt, call the vendor or shop elsewhere. Be skeptical of sources that primarily sell office supplies as a source for archival products.

The following is a comparison of some basic differences between enclosures made of paper and the three types of safe plastic.[13]

Paper Enclosures

- protect from light and the buildup of gases and moisture inside the enclosure;
- are less expensive and easier to label with a pencil than plastic enclosures;
- do not allow for viewing of an image without removing it; and
- should be chosen based on whether they passed the PAT.

Plastic Enclosures

- allow for viewing of an image without removing it; and
- are heat sealed on the edges to eliminate the use of adhesives.

Polyethylene

- protects from dust, handling, pollution, and moisture;
- is a smooth, nonrigid plastic with good clarity; and
- high-density polyethylene has a slightly frosted appearance.

Polyester

- is also known by the trademark names Mylar, Melinex, and Estar;

- is hard, semirigid, and has the highest optical clarity; and

- is more chemically inert than other plastic enclosures.

Polypropylene

- is economical;

- is excellent for slide storage; and

- is very similar chemically to polyethylene.

The author prefers to use clear sleeves in a style called "fold-lock" to store photographs. Photos are placed in the sleeve, not slid, to avoid scratching the image surface. The clear sleeve allows people to quickly see the image, unlike an opaque envelope. The image is protected from direct contact, in case gloves are not worn, yet the photograph is not sealed inside the plastic so there is some air circulation. A person can reverse the photograph and see any identification on the back. Fold-lock sleeves are made of a more rigid plastic, so they also provide physical support for the photographs during viewing and storage. Depending on the stability of the temperature and humidity in the storage location for your photographs, there is some concern that plastic enclosures might collect moisture or stick to photographs.

For negatives, the author prefers to use nonbuffered paper enclosures. Paper is easy to write on for labeling and identification purposes. It protects against light, which causes fading, and does not collect moisture. Large quantities of negatives of the same size, particularly strips such as 35 mm, can be stored in small paper envelopes that are grouped in trays that in turn are stored in a large flat box with a lid. There are similar storage systems for slides that use small compartments instead of envelopes. Such systems make it easier to organize groups of negatives and slides. They are designed for standard dimensions of negatives and slides so that the contents do not slide around inside oversize boxes, and storage space is maximized.

It is recommended to store negatives separately from prints. To an archivist, negatives are considered the original, while the print is a copy made from the original. A negative can be used to create a new print if the print is damaged or destroyed. Without the negative, a print can serve as a "master" to create a new print either by taking a photograph of the print or by scanning the print and making a copy. The primary reason for storing negatives separately from prints is to protect them from damage, in the hope that if one is damaged, the other will not be and the institution can recover from any loss. However, if there aren't many negatives, it might make sense to store the negatives and prints together. If they are separated, which prints have negatives or even their existence can be forgotten.

Slides can be stored in boxed sets if there are many of them. If there are only a few, they can be slipped into a plastic sheet with pockets sized for slides, put into a file folder, and stored with photographs based on their image content. For the random slide or negative of an uncommon size, such as four by three inches or four by six inches, fold an acid-free piece of paper in half, write any identification on one side, insert the slide or negative inside the fold, and then carefully fold each side over about one-half inch to create a pocket. Just the top edge will be open. This custom envelope addresses problems of irregular sizes, or quantities of negatives or slides too small for storage as a separate format. This storage method safely protects a single negative or slide filed with photographs or even with paper records. Often there are several safe methods for storing photographs and the deciding factor may be the quantity of material to be stored.

When processing large quantities of photographs, they are arranged just like paper records. For photographs no larger than legal-size folders, group them using file folders to organize them according to the arrangement plan decided for them. Record the description on the tab of the empty file folder. Put a reasonable quantity of photographs in the folder. Do not overfill with photographs; the folders should not bulge. If necessary, utilize the fold lines on the bottom of the folder; crease the appropriate one before inserting photographs. From the side the folder will resemble the letter "U" instead of "V." Store it upright in a manuscript box. Fill boxes reasonably full. There should be room to easily remove and refile folders during use or add a few more folders if necessary. If folders are leaning over or slumping, there is too much room. Either use a half-size manuscript box instead of a full-size one (e.g., two and a half rather than five inches wide) or insert a spacer to provide support.

Photographs that are larger than a legal-size folder should be stored flat. Oversize photos come in every size imaginable. Try to select two or three different-sized boxes that will store the bulk of the oversize photographs; boxes that are seventeen by twenty-one inches and twenty-one by twenty-four inches are good candidates for consideration. Ordering and storing forty-three different sizes just complicates matters. Boxes should be one to two inches deep. A stack of more photographs than that will be heavy to move and easier to drop. The photographs at the bottom of the stack are more susceptible to damage because they are bearing most of the weight. Extremely large photographs can be stored in two-inch-deep flat file/map cases. For their protection, put them in oversize map folders first. The folders provide a place to write description and protect against damage as the drawer is opened and closed.

When organizing photographs in a folder or oversize box, consider the relative size of the photographs. Smaller photos might be placed toward the front or on the top. There can be logical reasons for placing smaller and larger photographs together. For example, if wallet-size and eight-inch-by-ten-inch prints of the exact same image are filed in the same folder with other photographs that might obscure the relationship between the small and large pair, then file them next to each other to make the relationship more obvious.

Depending on the quantity of photographs involved and the overall size of the collection, one to ten photographs can be filed together in the same folder and stored in a single manuscript box with the rest of a one-box collection. If the collection requires more than a single box, often the photographs form their own series. This means that they are boxed separately, but the boxes are shelved with the rest of the collection to which they belong. Some institutions might decide to store all photography in the same physical area. In this case, be sure to label boxes well to identify the collection to which they belong. Make sure the description clearly indicates where to find the separated box or boxes.

In general, any photographs that arrive in a frame should be unframed in order to store them more safely. The exception to this would be if unframing would cause damage to the photograph, in which case consider consulting a conservator. For example, if water got between the glass in the frame and the photograph, the photograph may stick to the glass and tear bits of the picture off if not removed carefully. Light causes photographs to fade. Sunlight causes the most damage, but fluorescent and incandescent light also cause damage. Some nineteenth-century formats are even more sensitive than mid-to-late-twentieth-century prints. The effect is cumulative and irreversible. Light damage is one of the reasons why framed photographs, and other archival material, are normally unframed. Framed photographs are also more susceptible to other damage. Appropriate archival containers are designed to protect their contents and give them the longest life possible. Unframed photographs are easier to arrange and require less storage space. It is acceptable to keep the original frame and store it separately from the photograph if it would be useful for an exhibit. If the frame itself has value as an artifact, keep it as part of the collection it came with, but store it separately from the photograph.

Be careful not to confuse nineteenth-century *cased photographs* with twentieth-century framed ones. Typically daguerreotypes and ambrotypes were cased because the images were on glass, but sometimes tintypes were cased to protect the image from scratching. The cases are shallow hinged boxes made of wood, some elaborately carved, while others are covered in leather, paper, or cloth. This class of photograph is in a case to protect it. Leave it in the case.

A suggested sequence for processing photographs is as follows: arrange them; separate from paper records if necessary and mark their original location with a separation sheet or photocopy of the item; divide by format; identify to the degree it is possible, if needed; refine the arrangement on the basis of new identification information; and sleeve smaller items or put oversize photos in a box or flat file drawer.

Description for Photographs

Description is the next step. Photographs are more challenging to describe collectively than paper records. A file folder or an entire series might be described as "Correspondence." It might be further subdivided by year or topic. In the case of very famous people, researchers might request the name of specific correspondents. It is possible to have one or several folders with photographs of the same individual, building, or event. However, photos tend to have greater use as individual items and a greater need for item-level description than documents.

As mentioned in the previous chapter, the information recorded on the file folder in which archival records are arranged is one part of description. Folders of photographs have the same types of information already mentioned for paper records but might have additional notations. An item count might be recorded on the front left corner of the folder because it is easier to misfile photos than it is paper records. If negatives are retained with their matching prints, note that "Folder includes: 1 negative, 11 prints." The negative should be sleeved in a paper enclosure that is further labeled with the collection, series, and folder name and description for the specific print it matches.

Sometimes the processor wants to cross-reference other material related to the contents of a specific file. Let's say there exist two generic categories of photos called "Students" and "Athletes" with the files arranged alphabetically in each. If there are photos of the same person in both categories, it would be possible to note on the Student file for "Jones, Henry" to "See also Athletes—Jones, Henry" and make a reverse reference on the folder in Athletes to "See also Students—Jones, Henry." In an ideal world, a researcher would be able to know about the existence of both folders from an electronic index or database, but not everyone has the resources to produce such a tool. Don't try to document every single cross-reference. There isn't sufficient time. However, if one answers a reference request and discovers a connection such as this, it might be worth the time to record it on the appropriate folders. List the "see also" reference halfway down the left-hand side of the front of the folder. This information is probably not the most significant on the folder, but it is reasonably visible, and it should be helpful. Pick another place if you like but be consistent in the formation and location of such information.

For a collection with high research value, a high dollar value, or high anticipated usage, the processor might decide to label individual photographs. This would be a further example of description. The practice of sleeving photographs would help with individual labels. In keeping with a philosophy of doing nothing to archival material that is not reversible, many people prefer not to write on the back of photographs, even to label them. Labels can be word processed and printed on acid-free paper, cut into slips, and inserted in the photo sleeve so that it can be read when the photograph is turned over. This method links the identification to the individual photo but without writing on the item itself.

Again, the manner of description should be consistent and well thought out. The collection number, as a shorthand for its name, and the series name would help return a stray photo back to the correct folder, MS-3 Stearns_S_001_1978. "MS-3" stands for Manuscript Collection number 3, Stearns is the last name of the person photographed, the initial "S" represents his first name, this is the first photo processed (or scanned) of Stearns, and it was dated to 1978. Identification of people should always be left to right. The label could even say "l to r: Henry Jones, Mary Smith, two unidentified men, Susan Scott." Indicate the date of the photo as specifically as possible whether that is a combination of a month, day, or year; a date range; or a decade; May 1974; ca. 1969; 1970s; 1976–1980. Any one of these dates is preferable to no date. If the date is in question, indicate that with "ca." (for circa or about) or underline the questionable portion and add a question mark. If the date might be 1973 or 1974, say "ca. 1973," or "1973/4?" Either would be more specific than 1970s and equally acceptable. If the location is known, add that in the form of city, state; city, country; or even street address, city, state. If there is additional explanatory information, such as the activity or event being shown, familial or other relationships between people, or something else significant that could not be deduced from the photo or known from readily available sources, record it.

Digital cameras and flatbed scanners have now been in use for about twenty-five years creating digital files. Because local historical societies and other small organizations tend to work more with older records and personal or manuscript papers as opposed to more recent or institutional records, they are less likely to have received many digital images as part of a new collection. However, these types of organizations engage in projects to borrow and scan images owned by community members or may scan some of their own photographs or paper records. Such work will produce digital files (whether images or text) that need managing.

Let us start with digital files that are not copies of original material already in your holdings. An organization might receive digital files either taken with a digital camera or scanned by someone else. A group of digital photos would be arranged the same if they existed as prints or electronically. Separate one collection from another, identify series, group the photos, subdivide further if necessary. Put the images into electronic folders labeled with the series name. See appendix C.6 for samples. Arrangement is not difficult; description is the challenge. Physical photos simply exist; electronic ones require a file name to exist. Think carefully about naming conventions for digital files. Just as good description for physical file folder headings will help a person to decide whether to examine the contents, good description in naming a digital file will produce similar results. It also reduces the number of digital files that must be opened to locate an image. This is another time when standardization will help.

Photographs are requested or arranged by categories such as a specific individual or categories of people (family members, students, doctors, World War II soldiers); places (a specific home, business, or historical or geographic location); or activities or events (graduation, an anniversary, a natural disaster, or people using a computer). The individual identification or their descriptive categories can be used to create file names in a systematic manner. Some generic tips for digital file names are to use lowercase letters only and an underscore symbol "_" to separate words. Sometimes it is advisable to use a prefix or suffix to help group or distinguish similar photos. For example, if there are thumbnail and full-size copies of the exact same image, use the prefix "t_" to signify which images are the thumbnail size. Using a prefix will force all those digital images to be grouped together, helping visually differentiate them from those that are not thumbnails. If a building is named for a person and there are quite a number of photos of each, use the prefix "b_" to separate the photos of the building from the person. For multiple photos of the same person, family, building, or location over time, use sequential numbers to distinguish one image from another. For identified people, file names might be constructed using the following format, and as illustrated in table 5.1 and appendix A.4:

File series + individual file name + sequential number + YYYY_MM_DD + image resolution.

Table 5.1 Sample File Name Formation

First Photo	Second Photo
last name_first initial_001	last name_first initial_002
perna_family_001	perna_family_002
steely_f_001	steely_f_002
steely_f_001_1980_300	steely_f_002_1974_300
chicago_001_72	chicago_002_300

If the photo is dated, that can be worked into the file name to produce file names like the above if needed. Such file naming conventions require some planning and consideration of how the files may be used. The method of forming the file names should be written down and referred to by everyone who might need them to ensure consistent use.

Digital photos taken by a camera are typically assigned a sequential number by the camera. Bear in mind that those numbers tell you the sequence in which the photos were taken, just like the numbers on a strip of negatives. This can help you determine which photos belong together, that is, which are from the same date/event/activity. If the files are renamed, that information is permanently lost. If there is no doubt about the identification of the images, renaming is not a problem. If there are some doubts about the image identification, perhaps renaming should wait. If the digital images arrive with a descriptive name (not simply a series of numbers), the names should be evaluated the same as labels on a file folder. Is the name or identification clear and helpful? If digital files would be improved by renaming them as part of the arrangement and description process, keep the above discussion in mind.

If you are arranging and describing digital files that your institution is creating by scanning photos or documents that it owns, this is different. The digital version is a copy of something else the same way a print is a copy of a negative. The digital image needs to be linked to the paper original the way a print is linked to its negative. Ideally, the paper originals have already been arranged and described before any scanning work is done. This allows you to simply re-create the original arrangement electronically. The series and file divisions are already known. The photos have already been identified or assigned to a generic descriptive category. They may even have an item-level label. The originals have folder labels assigned.

Use this information to create file names for the originals similar to what has already been discussed. Assign them to electronic folders using the collection, series, and possibly folder labels/structure already developed for the paper originals. The electronic naming and parallel use of the information from the originals helps link the digital copies back to their original source. How are the originals linked to the electronic copies? That is, how would a researcher or staff member examining the originals know there was an electronic copy? With photographs, an easy solution is to create a label on acid-free paper and put it inside a photo sleeve on the back side of the original photo. The label would provide the file name and location for the digital copy. See appendix C.7 for samples.

For documents, the best method for linking may depend on the quantity of documents digitized. If an entire folder has been digitized, perhaps a note on the front of the folder pointing to the location of the electronic folder would work. If an entire series or collection has been digitized, it might be more appropriate to mention this information in the scope and content field of the inventory rather than trying to label every document or folder.

When digital images are produced through scanning from an original, sometimes it is helpful to know the scanning resolution of the finished image. While software like Photoshop can read the resolution, others like Microsoft Office can't. If the resolution will be important, for example, low-resolution images will be displayed on the internet, but higher-resolution scans will be used to reproduce images for exhibits or publication and need to be separated, the scanning resolution can form part of the file name as a suffix. The file name turcotte_r_001_1973_600 would identify the first photo scanned of Triple Crown jockey Ron Turcotte, date it to 1973, and indicate its resolution as 600 dpi. Again, file names like this require planning and the method of their formation should be recorded for consistent use.

File names can't provide a complete description for digital images. How can you attach a label to something electronic? Use your computer's file management software to open the electronic file folder of images; select the View tab and the small or medium icons option to display them on the computer screen as thumbnails, then print the screen out. Microsoft Office will do this. Optionally, Microsoft has a snipping tool that can be used for a screen capture that can be pasted into a word document. A color printer might be nice for color images, but black and white will still do the job. The file name should print below each image. Create a spreadsheet listing the file names and record the image description the same as if you were working from a print. See table 5.2 as an example.

The printed copy of the thumbnails and the spreadsheet with the image identification can even be put into a file folder and physically placed in the collection as a surrogate for the digital originals

Table 5.2 Image Description Sheet for Images Only Existing Digitally

Image #	Image Description	Date	Location
PC250160148.jpg	Steve Cauthen	May 1978	Churchill Downs, KY
PC250160149.jpg	Steve Cauthen with Affirmed	May 1978	Churchill Downs, KY
PC250160150.jpg	Steve Cauthen with Affirmed and trainer Laz Barrera	May 1978	Churchill Downs, KY

if they only exist electronically, or the institution does not own the physical original. Include the electronic location of the digital files either with the thumbnail printout or with the image identification. Using a spreadsheet makes the image identification more portable. For example, this spreadsheet as shown would be suitable to use for a batch upload into an institutional repository, a more advanced method for delivering digital files via the internet.

Using PastPerfect to Describe Photographs

Now let's look at using PastPerfect to describe photographs. The process for creating a new catalog record in the **Archives** catalog was discussed in chapter 4. It is nearly the same for photographs. Review it if necessary. Instead of selecting the **Archives** catalog, select the **Photos** catalog. The other difference will be the vocabulary used for the **Object Name** field. If you have nineteenth-century photographs, you might want to look at some books on the history of photography and try to identify the photographic process that created the particular image(s) being cataloged. They usually include sample photographs of the types discussed. There is a difference between the process used to create a photo and its format. See textbox 5.1 for a short sample list. Be consistent in the terms you use for the **Object Name** field for photographs.

Once you have completed the initial catalog record message box, you will see a screen fairly similar to the **Archives** catalog. The top navigation and the common catalog fields are identical. The left-hand navigation is missing those fields that do not pertain to photographs. The primary difference is the fields on the bottom, which are tailored to the unique qualities of photographs. Data entry for the common fields has already been discussed in chapter 4. If you place the cursor in a particular field, click with the mouse and then press the **F1** function key on the keyboard, the software displays information about that specific field to guide data entry. Otherwise, from the main PastPerfect page, select **Reports**, on the top left navigation select **Photos**, then double-click on **Photos Field Descriptions** in the center box to bring up a message box. Here you can select **Print** to get a copy of all the photo field descriptions.

The photo catalog does not have multilevel links to link an item-level description of an individual photo to a folder of similar photos or the collection to which it belongs, unlike the **Archives** catalog. Currently, in order to see what other items are part of the same collection or accession, you have to click on the folder icon to the right of the **Accession #**, **Donor Name** fields at the bottom of the common catalog fields. This links to the accession record that would describe other items in the collection. However, this would not clearly tell you the collection arrangement or whether there were other similar photos foldered together.

Textbox 5.1 Sample Nineteenth-Century Photographic Processes and Formats

Photographic Processes	Formats
Albumen prints	Cabinet cards
Ambrotype	Cartes-de-visite
Daguerreotypes	Stereograph
Tintype	

In the **Description** field, describe what you are cataloging: one photo, a folder of photos of various buildings from the 1893 World's Columbian Exposition in Chicago, or a series of photos of the Kennedy family. Be clear about the quantity/level of records you are describing. Dates will already be indicated above. Possibly describe the photo process or format, the subjects depicted in the photo(s), or other pertinent information. Because photographs are not normally named, the processor will have to create the **Title**. "Ideally, titles are concise labels that help researchers . . . distinguish among many images in a catalog." Unique titles are not required, but descriptive ones are the most useful.[14] Name the person, place, or activity shown, or use a generic phrase like "Unidentified young woman." Complete fields like **Photographer**, **Studio**, and **Place** (geographic location of the studio) as completely and accurately as possible. They will be helpful for searching the **Photos** catalog. Click on the folder icons for the **Photographer** and **Studio** fields and add whatever information you can to the message boxes that open. A database of information about photographers and/or studios can be very useful in helping to date or identify photos with incomplete information. Don't forget to use the authority files for both these fields to maintain consistency in names. If you are describing nineteenth-century photos, try to complete the **Processing Method** field.

Information linking prints and negatives should already be recorded on the negative sleeves, possibly the prints themselves, and/or the folders housing these items. Complete the **Provenance** and **Copyright** fields if they are not clearly described in the written (word-processed) collection inventory. Both of these can be important pieces of information for managing the use of photos. If you are describing more than one photo, however, and there are differences in either the **Provenance** or the **Copyright** for the photos being described, it would probably be easier to deal with this information somewhere else and leave these blank.

If you are describing photos that are only electronic, enter the electronic file location in the **Home Location** field. If the images exist both physically and electronically, list both locations. Use the **Description** field to clarify that there are electronic copies of the physical originals and enter "Digital Photograph" for the **Processing Method**. Also indicate in the **Orig[inal]/Copy** field whether you are describing originals or copies.

One of the nice features about the **Photos** catalog is the option to attach digital copies of photos to the catalog record. This would be a useful way to allow researchers to examine a photograph without handling it, at least initially, which helps preserve them longer. It is also useful for distant researchers to determine whether a certain photo really does interest them. The software makes it possible to display these photos for viewing without having to design a website. It even has the capability of taking photos that you select and creating a virtual web exhibit for you without requiring that you have web design skills. Note that both the Multimedia and Virtual Exhibit modules are separate added options for an extra fee beyond the basic software.

The most important screen to complete other than the basic photo view is the **People—Subjects Classification Search Terms** screen. This is how you will create the indexing for your photos, just as it does for your archival records. All four of these fields have authority lists attached to them. Use them as much as possible. Even if you add terms that reflect your holdings, you can be sure that you are always using the same terms or form for names after the first entry. This helps researchers find all the material on a particular topic instead of only some. Notice that all four of the fields here have a small "A–Z" icon at the upper right of the field box. If you click on the icon, it will alphabetize everything in that field. However, it is not reversible if you later decide that another sequence is preferable. You would have to delete all the entries and reenter them.

In the **People** field, obviously list the names of all identified people in a photo, but also include unidentified people or generic terms such as unidentified man, unidentified young woman, unidentified African American. These are descriptive enough that someone searching for a particular person could call up people of the same gender, age, ethnicity, or other quality and potentially identify him or her. For the **Subjects** field, try to include the most obvious or important subjects illustrated by the photo(s). If appropriate, index what the photos are "about" as well as what they are photos "of." A photo "of" a cat may also illustrate the cat being a "pet." The photo would be "about" the cat as a pet. Include proper nouns and generic equivalents, for example, "Laurel Street School" and "elementary school." Include terms for the photographic process and format of the photos. They can be general or specific: photographs, digital photographs, albumen print, or stereograph. A helpful question to ask when assigning subject terms is, "If I needed photos of X, Y, Z topic, would I want to see this photo or is X, Y, Z just a minor feature and hard to see?"[15]

The **Classification** field is designed to parallel the actual physical organization of photos in boxes and folders. However, the organizing principle for the authority file is by subject, which is not how archival records, including photographs, are arranged. Archival material is arranged first by provenance: the collection of which it is a part. At the folder level, it may be arranged topically, but the authority file does not reflect this arrangement. Skip this field and move on to the **Search Terms** field.

The **Search Terms** field is similar to the **People** and **Subjects** fields but will be tailored specifically to your institution's collections because the authority file for this field is built from the entries that the processor enters here. Names of individuals, families, the collection of which this photo/these photos form a part, locations represented in the photo, the photographer and/or studio that took the photo, and words describing what the photo is "about" are all possible entries. It may or may not be worthwhile to also enter all the terms from the **People** and **Subjects** fields again here. Some of the software searches may take terms only from a specific field rather than from all fields associated with a catalog record. Be careful about the terms selected for this field. Where possible, draw them either from the authority files that come with the software or the custom authority files that will be built as the processor enters terms describing archival records. This will result in the consistent formation of names or the use of terms to describe something. This means that researchers will find all the material on a topic or person because the same words are used to describe all the pertinent materials.

Additional Reading/Resources

Resources for Photo Identification[16]

Photographic Processes

Baldwin, Gordon, and Martin C. Jürgens. *Looking at Photographs: A Guide to Technical Terms*. Rev. ed. Los Angeles: J. Paul Getty Museum, 2009. This book defines and illustrates the vocabulary of photography from its earliest processes through today's digital photography. It is both a glossary and a history of the medium.

Crawford, William. *The Keepers of Light: A History and Working Guide to Early Photographic Processes*. Dobbs Ferry, NY: Morgan & Morgan, 1979. This is an excellent book for more detailed information about early photographic processes.

Darrah, William C. *Cartes de Visite in Nineteenth Century Photography*. Gettysburg, PA: W. C. Darrah, 1981. This book includes photographs illustrating the wide range of subjects appearing in cartes de visite.

Eastman Museum. "Eastman Museum, Collections, Photography, Photographic Processes Video Series." Accessed July 13, 2019. https://www.eastman.org/photographic-processes-video-series. This page links to videos that illustrate and describe the photographic process used to create some of the most common nineteenth-century photo formats as well as several twentieth-century formats. They are well done and discuss the history and impact of photography.

Image Permanence Institute. Photographic Process Identification Webinars. Rochester Institute of Technology. Accessed July 13, 2019. https://www.imagepermanenceinstitute.org/process-id-webinars. This site has a series of webinars that discuss the materials and processes of nineteenth- through twenty-first-century photographic prints; teach how to identify a photographic process and use the Graphics Atlas; and care for, handle, display, and store photographs.

Leyshon, William E. "Photographs from the 19th Century: A Process Identification Guide." Accessed July 13, 2019. https://oldhtmlarchive.sharlothallmuseum.org/photographs/19th/book/index.html. This website presents a book on how to identify nineteenth-century photographic processes.

Reilly, James M. *Care and Identification of 19th-Century Photographic Prints.* Rochester, NY: Eastman Kodak Co., 1986. This book explains nineteenth-century photographic processes, provides illustrated examples of each process, and discusses appropriate care. The book includes an illustrated pullout reference chart.

Vitale, Tim. "Brief History of Imaging Technology." Accessed July 13, 2019. http://videopreservation.conservation-us.org/library/BHoIT.pdf. This is an informative brief history.

Photographers

Photography dictionaries and directories can assist with photographers' names and dates. There are also published directories for various geographic locations or other categories of photographers.

City directories and telephone books can help locate and date photographers and research businesses shown in a photograph.

Kelbaugh, Ross J. *Directory of Civil War Photographers.* Baltimore, MD: Historic Graphics, 1990.

Other Helpful Resources

Daguerreian Society. Accessed September 27, 2019. https://www.daguerreiansociety.org/. Despite its name, this organization studies nineteenth-century photography and its processes. An annotated bibliography is located under Resources.

Frassanito, William A. *Gettysburg: A Journey in Time.* Gettysburg, PA: Thomas Publications, 1975. This book is a very readable and interesting account of the use of deductive reasoning, logic, and research to reinterpret Civil War photography. Frassanito played a pivotal role in the interpretation of historical photography. The book is well illustrated and includes some of the iconic photos of this battle. Photographers' codes (p. 19) played a minor role in the process.

Image Permanence Institute (IPI). IPI is a resource for scientific information about the preservation of archival records, particularly photographs and film. They are part of the College of Art and Design, Rochester Institute of Technology/IPI, 70 Lomb Memorial Drive, Rochester, NY 14623-5604. Their web address is https://www.imagepermanenceinstitute.org. At the time of this writing, they are selling copies of James M. Reilly's *Care and Identification of 19th-Century Photographic Prints*. Select Resources, then Publications from the homepage menu. Other useful resources, such as A-D strips, are under Store.

NEDCC Staff. "Preservation Leaflets, 5.5 Storage Enclosures for Photographic Materials." Northeast Document Conservation Center. Accessed July 13, 2019. https://www.nedcc.org/assets/media/documents/Preservation%20Leaflets/5_5_photostorage_2018.pdf. This leaflet discusses an assortment of enclosures and the advantages and disadvantages of each.

Preservation Directorate, Library of Congress. "Care, Handling, and Storage of Photographs." Accessed July 9, 2019, http://www.loc.gov/preserv/care/photolea.html. This has additional advice on the care and handling of photograph formats.

Ritzenthaler, Mary Lynn, Diane Vogt-O'Connor, Helena Zinkham, Brett Carnell, and Kit Peterson. *Photographs Archival Care and Management*. Chicago: Society of American Archivists, 2006. Chapter 3 discusses how to "read" photographs and has practice exercises. Appendix I lists sources for equipment and supplies for the care and storage of photographic materials. Appendix IV lists resources for help with various aspects of managing and caring for photographs, including research and identification. Appendix V presents sources for training, including tutorials and online study guides. There is a short glossary followed by a seventeen-page bibliography with references to many more resources. This is a very thorough reference tool.

Severa, Joan L. *Dressed for the Photographer: Ordinary Americans and Fashion, 1840–1900*. Kent, OH: Kent State University Press, 1995. This book will assist in dating nineteenth-century photographs based on the clothing, hairstyles, jewelry, and other fashion items worn by the people in an image. Information is broken down by decade and includes illustrations.

US Department of the Interior. National Park Service. "Museum Management Program, Conserve-O-Grams." Accessed July 13, 2019. https://www.nps.gov/museum/publications/conserveogram/cons_toc.html. See particularly the following:

14/2, "Storage Enclosures for Photographic Prints and Negatives 1993,"

14/3, "Chronology of Photographic Processes 1993,"

14/4, "Caring for Photographs: General Guidelines 1997,"

14/5, "Caring for Photographs: Special Formats 1997," and

14/6, "Caring for Color Photographs 1998."

Vitale, Timothy, and Paul Messier. "Albumen Photographs: History, Science and Preservation, a Gallery of Albumen Prints." John Burke, Walter Henry, Paul Messier, Timothy Vitale, and Stanford University Libraries and Academic Information Resources. Accessed July 13, 2019. http://albumen.conservation-us.org/gallery/loc.html. This website provides information about the albumen photographic format.

Notes

1. Prints & Photographs Division, Library of Congress, "Safe Handling Tips for Pictorial Collections," accessed July 13, 2019, https://www.loc.gov/rr/print/tp/SafeHandlingTip.pdf.

2. Mary Lynn Ritzenthaler, Diane Vogt-O'Connor, Helena Zinkham, Brett Carnell, and Kit Peterson, *Photographs: Archival Care and Management* (Chicago: Society of American Archivists, 2006), 158.

3. Ritzenthaler et al., *Photographs*, 149.

4. William C. Darrah, *Cartes de Visite in Nineteenth Century Photography* (Gettysburg, PA: W. C. Darrah, 1981), 1.

5. Image Permanence Institute [IPI], *The Archival Advisor, Photography Timeline*, accessed July 19, 2011, https://www.archivaladvisor.org/index.shtml; Eastman Museum, "Glossary," accessed July 19, 2011; Ritzenthaler et al., *Photographs*, 36.

6. Eastman Museum, "Glossary"; Ritzenthaler et al., *Photographs*, 29–30; IPI, *Archival Advisor.*

7. Ritzenthaler et al., *Photographs*, 34–35; Eastman Museum, "Glossary."

8. IPI, *Archival Advisor*; Eastman Museum, "Glossary"; Ritzenthaler et al., *Photographs*, 38–39.

9. Darrah, *Cartes de Visite*, 171–79; Ritzenthaler et al., *Photographs*, 40.

10. Eastman Museum, "Glossary"; Ritzenthaler et al., *Photographs*, 41, 43.

11. IPI, "Photo Activity Test," accessed July 19, 2011, http://www.imagepermanenceinstitute.org/shtml_sub/srv_pat.asp.

12. Richard Pearce-Moses, *A Glossary of Archival and Records Terminology*, Archival Fundamentals Series II (Chicago: Society of American Archivists, 2005), s.v. "lignin."

13. Angela Blauvelt, "How to . . . Properly Store Your Negatives?" *Archival Methods Newsletter* no. 3 (December 10, 2009), accessed March 10, 2020, https://www.archivalmethods.com/newsletters/issue3.

14. Ritzenthaler et al., *Photographs*, 172.

15. Ritzenthaler et al., *Photographs*, 175–76.

16. Ritzenthaler et al., *Photographs*, 70–71.

6

Photographs

Part 2—Management and Use

The previous chapter dealt with the work that needs to be done to prepare photographs for use by researchers. This chapter focuses on managing the use of photographs once processing is completed. It assumes that a researcher has already located the photographs he wants and is now asking to use them.

Private individuals create photographs using their personal camera to take photos of friends, family, pets, or vacations. Generally, the photos are used to share with others, whether they were carried to war to remember loved ones or posted on social media for the world to see. The person who snaps the photo is the photographer and the owner of the intellectual rights to that photo. No money has changed hands, and no release forms were signed by the people in the photos giving their consent to be photographed. This individual may later donate his photos to a historical institution. If they are interesting enough, they are accepted. Hopefully, the donor signs a donor agreement and gives his intellectual rights to the photos to the institution. This is the simplest example and perhaps most desirable.

Someone gets married and hires a photographer to take wedding photos. They go to a studio and have a portrait taken, or a photographer comes to your child's school and takes photos there. Your prize bull wins at the 4H fair, or you are photographed at your high school graduation and the photo is published in the local newspaper. These are all examples of work for hire. Someone hires a photographer and pays them money to take the wedding photos, the school photos, or the studio portrait. In more formal cases, the person hiring the photographer signs a written contract outlining conditions of the transaction. The photographer creates the photos; he owns the rights to his photos. He sells only copies of the photos he takes, not the intellectual rights to them; those he keeps as his own. If the person who hired the photographer wants additional copies of the photos, normally he must go back to the photographer who took the photos and pay to buy more copies.

In the case of the photo that is published in the newspaper, the photographer has been hired by the newspaper publisher. The contract between the photographer and the publisher can vary. If the photographer is an employee of the newspaper, then most likely the publisher owns the rights to the photograph and can publish and sell copies of the photo. In the case of a freelance photographer who is not the publisher's employee, the publisher may have purchased the right to onetime only or limited use of the photo with the photographer again retaining the intellectual rights. So, in this example, the intellectual rights may belong to either the publisher or the photographer and would require research to determine which it is.

An individual who hired a photographer and bought photos from the photographer could donate the photos he bought to a historical institution and may even sign a donor agreement, but he is unable to donate the intellectual rights to the photos because he does not own those rights. He only bought the photos. Ownership of a physical print or even possession of a negative or digital file does not equal ownership of the intellectual rights. Ownership of the photos—the objects— allows a person to show them to others or display them in the sense of hanging them on the wall or putting them into a physical display case. It does not allow for publication or distribution of the photos, even if the person gains no money from the transaction. Publication, distribution, and other activities are rights reserved to the person who owns the intellectual rights, not the object.

Intellectual rights are rights to intangible property—the ideas, creativity, skill, and knowledge of an individual, group of people, or business that uses those qualities to create something. The US Constitution and US law give the creator the rights to or the ownership of his creation for a time so that he may profit by his labor. Intellectual rights are divided into industrial rights, such as patents and trademarks, and copyright and related rights, including reproduction, distribution, adaptation, exhibition, performance, and moral rights.[1] Copyright is a property right. This means that it can be bought, sold, given, inherited, donated, or otherwise transferred from the original owner to someone else. It should also be pointed out that not everything is copyrightable. Copyright requires some element of creativity. A person can't copyright a slavish reproduction of something—such as a photo of a painting. There is no creativity in a copy, especially of a two-dimensional object. With a three-dimensional object such as a sculpture, the photographer can add lighting and be creative, which is copyrightable.

Copyright law is complex and getting increasingly so as new legislation is passed that builds on prior legislation. The Copyright Act of 1976 serves as the basis for modern US copyright law. In 1998 two copyright acts were passed. The Copyright Term Extension Act of 1998, also called the Sonny Bono Act, added twenty years to the Copyright Act of 1976. The 1998 act meant that works created in 1923 whose copyright was about to expire received another twenty years of copyright protection. Effective on January 1, 2019, the 1923 works moved into the public domain. Disney's Steamboat Willie version of Mickey Mouse was one of the most visible beneficiaries of the twenty-year extension. In 2024 he will move into the public domain.[2] In 2020 works from 1924 will become public domain and so on.

Whereas the Sonny Bono Act extended the length of time copyrighted work was protected, the Digital Millennium Copyright Act (DMCA), also passed in 1998, focuses on efforts to circumvent copyright protection of digital creative works. It controls how a person can play or use digital film and music even if he has purchased a copy. The most recent legislation is the Music Modernization Act (MMA) passed in 2018, which affects commercial sound recordings and *orphan works*. Prior to this legislation, pre-1972 commercial sound recordings were not copyright protected. The MMA includes them and provides for their gradual transition into the public domain. Although orphan works are not specifically addressed in the MMA, it includes provisions for nonprofit streaming of out-of-print pre-1972 sound recordings whose rights holder can't be located *if* there are no commercially available recordings. Fair use now also applies to sound recordings.[3]

A good resource is the Copyright Term chart found at Cornell University's website, which Louis Smoller illustrates clearly in a visual graphic (see Additional Reading/Resources). A brief review of the chart quickly shows how complex this question is. It is important to note that copyright law applies differently to unpublished material than to published material. Although archives and, to varying degrees, historical organizations hold primarily unpublished material, they usually also have published newspapers, books, and publications.

The following discussion focuses on copyright as applied to archival records, including photographs. The author is not a lawyer and is not giving legal advice. She has had sufficient training and experience to apply it to archival material and to know when to get legal counsel. If in doubt, speak with a lawyer who is experienced in copyright or intellectual property rights.

Documenting the status of the copyright of any material donated to a historical institution is one of the reasons for obtaining a donor agreement. More will be said on this subject later in this book. Working with copyright is frequently described as risk analysis. Identify what is known about a photograph or even other records or formats. Consider the use that the institution itself or a researcher is requesting. Weigh the risks and make a decision. Some institutions will be conservative in the risks they are willing to take; others will be more aggressive.

Start with what is known about a specific photograph. Consult the donor file to see what it may say about the copyright status. If there is no clear answer on who the owner is, proceed with an analysis. How old is the photo? Was it ever published? Making a print of an image from a negative is not necessarily publication, but appearing in a newspaper, magazine, or book is. Refer to the Cornell Copyright Term chart. If the photo was published prior to 1923, it is in the public domain, meaning that there are no copyright concerns. If the photo was published in 1923 or later, consult the chart again and attempt to categorize it by date and copyright information. You may or may not know the definite date of the photo or whether the copyright notice appeared or was renewed. Make your best guess.

If you are inclined to believe, on the basis of factors such as the subject of the photo, past history of ownership, how long it has been at your institution, and past research use, that it was not published, do you know who took the photo and when the photographer died? It is very common that both the photographer and his date of death are unknown for archival materials. This is a frequent problem. If you know both the photographer's name and date of death, add seventy years, and the photo goes into public domain after that date. Unfortunately, if you know only one of these key pieces of information, the wait extends to 120 years after the date the photo was taken. If the date of creation is unknown and there is a desire to use the photo, some research may be required. Refer to the previous chapter for techniques for identifying and dating photographs.

Even if very little is known about the photo in question, some obvious information based on the photo itself as a physical object may suggest more or less risk. If the photo lacks a professional photographer's stamp or mark, the chance is greater that it was taken by a private individual; therefore, there is less risk. Weigh the age of the photo; older is less risk. What is the subject matter? Famous people or public figures—people who have very visible jobs, such as a well-known politician, athlete, or entertainer—are not treated the same as private citizens. If I buy a ticket to a Toby Keith concert and take a photo of him onstage with my personal camera, as long as photography was not prohibited as a condition of concert attendance, I can take the photo, display it, and should even be able to sell it. He is a public figure in a public place. If I have a professional photographer's photo of a well-known figure, especially if the subject is still living, that is higher risk. Chances are good that the photographer had the person's permission to take the photo or that the person hired the photographer to take the photo for him as a work for hire. One of the two of them is likely to complain about unauthorized use of such a photo.

How does either the institution or the researcher wish to use the photo? If the researcher requests a copy of a photo for a personal use—to hang on his wall because he likes photos of riverboats or famous people from his hometown—that is low risk. It is not going to be very visible to a copyright holder (if there is one). The request may be for a copy of a photo to give to the individual in the photo. It could be from an athletic or theatrical performance from their younger days given by a coworker on the occasion of a milestone birthday or retirement. Perhaps it is for an event honoring that person, an award ceremony, or a memorial ceremony after that person's death. These are onetime uses. The copy is not intended for print or electronic publication. These are still low-risk uses.

The researcher would like to publish the photo in a magazine, scholarly journal, or book. The more well known the publication or the greater the circulation—something regional or national versus the local newsletter—the greater the visibility and the greater the risk. Some publication is done for the purpose of sharing knowledge: about local history, a personal hobby, or a faculty member writing a scholarly article. Some publication is for the purpose of earning money; the request is for a commercial project. Copyright protection is for the purpose of giving the rights holder the chance to earn money. If someone else infringes on the copyright in order to make money for himself, he is taking that earning opportunity away from the rights holder. That is definitely high risk.

Copyright law does permit some uses that do not require the copyright holder's permission. This exception is called "fair use." Copies of a photograph can be made for private study, scholarship, or research; for news reporting; or for satire, parody, commentary, or criticism of the original. Section C at the end of chapter 9 of the Stanford University Libraries website on Copyright and Fair Use (see Additional Reading/Resources at the end of this chapter) gives examples of uses that have and have not qualified as fair use, including ones involving images. Four factors are used to evaluate fair use. Remember the acronym PANE:

P— *purpose* and character of the use: Uses that add new value or content or change its function or character are considered "transformative." Transformative uses are judged more favorably, as are nonprofit uses versus commercial ones.

A—*amount* and substantiality of the portion taken: Using all of a work or its most significant section is not recommended. This factor is more easily applied to text than images.

N—*nature* of the copyrighted work: Has it been published before? Fine art photography is given greater copyright protection than grade school or passport photos.

E— *effect* of the use on the potential market: Is there a market at all for the item? Would the proposed use affect future demand?[4]

Students and teachers may be permitted uses in an educational situation that might not otherwise be allowed. Although not specifically written as part of the Copyright Act, publishers and the academic community agreed to educational fair use guidelines to provide some guidance: "Educational institutions include K–12 schools, colleges and universities. Libraries, museums, hospitals and other nonprofit institutions also are considered educational institutions under most educational fair use guidelines when they engage in nonprofit instructional, research, or scholarly activities for educational purposes." Educational uses must be noncommercial for the purpose of teaching or researching or presenting research findings at peer conferences, workshops, or seminars. The guidelines focus primarily on published text, music, and moving images (film or television), not unpublished photographs or material, so it is difficult to say how this would apply to images.[5]

The Technology, Education, and Copyright Harmonization Act, known as the TEACH Act, which was passed in 2002, applies to photographs used in teaching either in formal distance learning or face-to-face courses with a live instructor. When they are used in distance learning, the images must be protected so that only registered students have access. Students are not allowed to copy or distribute the protected images.[6]

So, documentation for the photos that the institution or researcher would like to use does not exist or does not name the copyright holder. Someone does a risk analysis. The University of Minnesota has a fair use analysis tool, and Columbia University has a fair use checklist. Refer to Additional Reading/Resources at the end of this chapter for web addresses. Print and keep the checklist or otherwise record your risk assessment in order to document efforts to respect copyright. The combination of what is (un)known about the photos is combined with the requested usage. Several factors together may all be low risk, all high risk, or somewhere in the middle. The institution will have to decide whether it is comfortable with the risk level and is willing to reproduce the photos and allow their usage.

If someone wants to use a photograph that appears to be copyrighted, it is advisable to try to identify and locate the copyright owner to ask permission to use the photo. The person who does the research should record how and where he searched to find the copyright holder and the results. These steps show due diligence and would be favorably noted should there later be a problem. The US Copyright Office "Circular 22" explains how to investigate the copyright status of a work (see Additional Reading/Resources at the end of this chapter). The Copyright Office will even conduct a search for you and give you a report of their findings for a fee. "Circular 22" has those details.[7]

Sometimes people who aren't sure what to do or perhaps are unwilling to go through the process of a risk analysis and search for the copyright holder think that an easy solution is to simply include the photographer's name with the photo. According to the Stanford University Libraries Copyright and Fair Use website, it isn't. Acknowledging the potential copyright holder by citing the photographer's name may be considered in a determination of fair use but is not protection against a claim of copyright infringement. When in doubt, they also recommend trying to get permission from the copyright holder.[8]

When an institution clearly knows it owns the rights to a photo, it can agree to let it be used. When the institution knows it does not own the copyright but is unsure who does or whether the photo has gone into the public domain, the typical response is to require the patron to assume responsibility for gaining permission from the copyright holder. Depending on their risk tolerance, the institution won't replicate the photo until the researcher can document permission, or it will replicate the photo with the understanding that the matter is the patron's responsibility. Normally, the institution has a copying or photo usage contract whereby the researcher agrees in writing that he will assume all responsibility for clearing copyright and that the institution will not be held liable (see appendix B.4). While this language may not guarantee that the copyright holder, if one comes forward, won't try to also hold the institution responsible, the institution has the responsibility to respect copyright. In those instances when the institution knows that it does not own the copyright, if it knows who does or has information about the potential owner, such as the photographer's name stamped on the back, it can share that information with the researcher. It would also be wise to have a qualified lawyer review a copying or photo usage contract prior to putting it into use. If the institution wants to use photographs internally for, say, the marketing or public relations department or for an educational project of its own, another option is to be prepared to pay for the use of the photos after the fact if the copyright holder comes forward.

So far, the discussion has focused on print usage of photographs. What about images on the internet? Those are free, aren't they? Can't people just use them or put other photos up there? No. The fact that a photo is not locked behind a password-protected site that requires a fee to gain access does not mean it is not copyrighted. Some people also falsely assume that because they have the technical skill to copy a photo, it is not copyrighted. Photographs or images are also subject to copyright and fair use. They should also be credited or cited when used in scholarly or published works, the same as text would be. The fact that they are a visual image instead of words doesn't somehow change the rules.

If the owner of a physical copy of a photograph has the right to display the photo, does that mean he can scan it and put it on the internet for people farther away to see? Organizations sometimes digitize a group of photos and create what they may call a virtual exhibit or web exhibit. Isn't that about the same as a real exhibit in a physical case somewhere? No, it isn't. Although such a display may be described as an exhibit, it has generally been treated as a form of publication, a right reserved to the copyright holder. If the institution itself would like to display photos it owns, either it must also own the copyright to the photos or it should conduct a risk analysis and try to obtain permission from the copyright holder. In addition to these steps, some websites will also include language to the effect that although they have attempted to be diligent, they welcome any copyright owner who was missed to contact them and identify themselves. OCLC's document "Well Intentioned Practice for Putting Digitized Collections of Unpublished Materials Online" includes possible disclaimer language (see Additional Reading/Resources at the end of this chapter). If someone does come forward or complain about unauthorized use, the most frequent response is to simply remove the disputed photo. Again, it may be possible to negotiate an agreement after the fact and pay a fee in order to use a desirable photo.

Suppose that after some research the institution determines either that it docs in fact own the copyright to a photo or that it is able to locate the copyright owner. What happens next? This depends on how the institution would like to use the photos. If it merely wishes to display them on the internet to let researchers know they exist and where, possibly to add to the body of knowledge for educational purposes, it asks permission to do so. The photos may be of the institution itself, its buildings, its people, or activities held on its property; that is, they may be of limited use to someone else. The institution may want the ability to reuse the photos in its own publications or on its website or even charge outside researchers a fee for them to use one of these photos. It may not be possible to predict details of the future times the institution would like to use the photos.

In the case of a nonprofit or educational institution, the institution should consider asking for unlimited future usage, including the right to charge a fee to outside researchers on the condition that the institution will always require a credit given to the copyright holder. If the initial inquiry is verbal, always follow up with a request for the copyright holder to sign a written agreement. Have a lawyer review the written agreement before sending it to ensure that it is a legal contract.

The author has negotiated such agreements several times. In the first case, several local photographers had taken photos of buildings, students, and events at a local college. The photographers owned their own business, were elderly, and had either already closed their business or were close to closing. They agreed to allow unlimited use by the institution, only of photos related to the institution, on the condition of use of a credit line that was agreed on. They requested no fee as a condition of the agreement. Had the author not pursued this agreement when she did, the photographers might have died without an agreement being made. Then the matter would not have been as easy.

The second example involved photographs of a different college taken by the local newspaper, which was bought out by a much larger and more visible newspaper. The former closed, and the latter is still in business. The author made a similar request as before. The newspaper agreed to unlimited reuse of the photos that related to the institution with the appropriate credit line. They permitted a reasonable charge to outside researchers for the recoup of staff time. A larger fee for a commercial project would probably require contacting them again. The newspaper also required that any fees be waived for them or their affiliates should they ever request reuse of a photo that they had originally taken. The agreement was put in writing, reviewed by lawyers for both parties, and reached with little difficulty. All it took was asking and some time.

If the institution already owns the rights to photographs in its physical possession, it may display the photos however and wherever it chooses; it may publish them or charge others a fee to use the photos in a like manner. Archives and cultural collections are expensive to care for. Even if there are no paid staff members at the institution, there are many other potential expenses. The ability to charge a fee for the use of photographs is a wonderful opportunity. The institution may not get rich unless it owns some extraordinary photos of great significance, but it is still worth the trouble to establish some policies, fees, and forms to bring in a small, steady income. Institutions need to recognize that they may have materials that have value, that it is reasonable to charge for their use, and that the income could add up over time. People also tend to take better care of things that cost money or that are perceived to have value.

So, a researcher has identified one or more photographs she or he would like to use. The copyright status of the images has been reviewed and the institution is willing to authorize their reproduction. Does the institution have the ability to reproduce the requested images? Chapter 7 provides step-by-step guidance on how to scan photographs, documents, postcards, maps, etc.

If the institution itself is unable to digitize photos for its patrons, then another option is to locate a photo shop that can scan the photo for you. Here you run the risk that the people at the photo shop don't know how to safely handle archival photos and may damage them. Another risk is theft, especially if the photos are at all desirable. Perhaps there is another cultural organization in your area that would be willing to digitize photographs for you at some expense. Cooperative or consortial agreements are often developed to share resources like equipment or technical skills. There are commercial vendors who will happily digitize materials, but they aren't normally used for small quantities of photos. If your institution is able to develop a system by which it can get digital copies with a minimal risk to its photographs within a reasonable amount of time, then the next step would be to establish fees and develop a photo contract.

Anyone who spends even a little bit of time researching fees charged for the reproduction of photographs will find a variety in how the fees are calculated. Fees may be flat or nominal, may vary depending upon the number of copies to be published, may vary depending upon the status of the patron (student, nonprofit, or commercial), may be set by city ordinances or law in the case of governmental units, or may be what the market will bear. They may vary by the institution's status (government, educational, nonprofit, or commercial) as well as geographic region. Ask other cultural organizations in your community, region, or of a similar nature to share their fee schedule and contract if they use one. Check with professional organizations you, other volunteers or staff, or your institution may be affiliated with, including any listservs where a query could be posted. Also do a search on the internet. Again, a good place to start is other institutions from your area that are similar in nature to your institution.

The fee may be called a use fee, a copying fee, or a research fee. Some people have argued that a use fee implies ownership of the copyright; the fee would be charged for using the image and the term should not be applied to photographs for which the institution does not own the rights. Calling it a reproduction or copying fee may be more neutral. A research fee would charge for the staff time involved in locating, copying, and mailing or transmitting the copy or copies. It might be expected that a copying fee would only cover the cost of making copies.

Consideration should be given to what the costs will be to make the digital copies. If the work is being sent out, that expense should be passed along to the patron. Other potential expenses include CDs or DVDs to put the images on and packaging and postage to mail the same. Some patrons are in a big rush and want copies right away. Perhaps an overnight delivery fee or rush fee is appropriate. The institution should at least break even and ideally would actually make some amount of profit to cover the value of the staff time to scan photos or deliver and pick them up if the work is sent out. Each institution will have to evaluate what the market will bear, what its expenses are, possibly even what its mission is or what its governing body will permit, or other factors in setting a fee schedule. Fees can be increased over time. It is also possible to charge less per photo when someone requests more photos. For example, if the fee is $100 per photo for commercial use and five or ten photos are requested, the institution may decide to charge $75 or $50 per additional photo over the initial five.

Recognize that your materials have research value of varying degrees. Frequent handling will cause wear and tear and may shorten their life. Also, there are always people who will take advantage and be unreasonable. If one institution is willing to give away for free that for which another charges, no matter how reasonable the cost, chances are that everyone will go to the former. This may also result in indiscriminate requests for more material than the researcher really needs or so many requests that nothing else gets done. Does the institution want to become the local stock photo shop or just support a reasonable amount of research and scholarship? The answer to this question depends upon the institution's mission, values, priorities, and resources. The answer to this question will also guide the institution in establishing and applying a fee structure. See appendix C.8 for a sample fee structure.

Once a method has been established for reproducing the institution's photographs and a fee structure has been agreed upon, the last component is a written photo contract. This is an agreement between the institution and anyone from outside who would like to use the institution's photographs. It is particularly important to use a contract for any commercial request. This includes the traditional printed books or journals but can include still images used in a film or television program, photographs that are on a for-profit website, note cards, calendars, posters, or whatever else can be imagined.

A contract may or may not be used for requests for personal use or by nonprofits. This may depend on how desirable the requested image is and how concerned the institution is about others infringing on the institution's ability to earn money from the sale of its images. The institution can always change its policy about when the use of the photo contract is required if something doesn't seem to be working after a trial period. At its most basic, the photo contract should state that the institution gives permission to the researcher to use the photo, specify the authorized use, and any conditions for that use. For example:

- The researcher has purchased the right to use the photo(s) as agreed, but not the right to reproduce the photo(s) or allow others to do so.

- Written permission is required to publish, exhibit, or otherwise use the photo(s) excepting personal uses. (The photo contract is the method for obtaining the required written permission.)

- Permission is given to use the photo(s) once in the manner and format agreed to. If the initial request is to publish the photo(s) in a book and later a new edition is to be published, another request is required. If the publisher decides later to develop a website to accompany the published (text)book, separate permission is required for the website.

- The agreement is nonexclusive so that the institution may use the same photo(s) itself and also give permission to other researchers.

- The contract is with the person, company, or institution named in the contract. That party may not transfer their permission to anyone else by any method.

- The institution should request an appropriate credit line for the use of its photo(s) and provide the exact wording of the credit line.

- It is not uncommon to ask for one complimentary copy of any commercial product made that uses the photo(s), regardless of the media format. First, this allows the institution to confirm appropriate credit was given. Second, this allows them to display scholarship or other work that it has supported.

- As was mentioned earlier, the contract should state that copyright compliance is the responsibility of the researcher, not the institution.

Once these three main components have been put in place, the institution is ready to accept requests to reproduce its photographs. Researchers need to be informed of all pertinent details before they place an order. This helps to minimize problems after the reproduction work is completed. It is important to be clear on how the researcher intends to use the images, what he needs copied, and when. If the institution does not feel comfortable copying a specific photo for copyright reasons, or is unable to meet the requested deadline, tell the researcher. However, if both parties are agreed, a signed contract and payment should be received before any reproduction is done. If the researcher changes his mind, the institution could be out money if it contracts out for the reproduction work. The best result is a happy researcher, the knowledge that the institution has contributed to a worthwhile project, and increased visibility for its collections.

Additional Reading/Resources

Clement, Gail P. "The Copyright Self-Help Movement: Initiatives in the Library Community." *College & Research Libraries News* 72 (July/August 2011): 404–7, 415. This article discusses OCLC's document, "Well Intentioned Practice for Putting Digitized Collections of Unpublished Materials Online" mentioned in the text and below.

Cohen, Daniel J., and Roy Rosenzweig. "Digital History a Guide to Gathering, Preserving, and Presenting the Past on the Web," page labeled Owning the Past. Accessed August 3, 2019. http://chnm.gmu.edu/digitalhistory/copyright/1.php. This page presents a brief history of copyright. Depending upon the reader's need, other sections may be useful.

Columbia University Libraries/Information Services Copyright Advisory Office. "Fair Use Checklist." Accessed July 4, 2019. http://copyright.columbia.edu/copyright/fair-use/fair-use-checklist/. This site has a fair use checklist. Keeping a print copy of your analysis would document reasonable and good faith efforts to apply fair use.

Copyright Information Center. "Homepage." Cornell University. Accessed July 4, 2019. https://copyright.cornell.edu. This website has information on fair use, how to research whether something is in the public domain, tutorials, and other resources on copyright. Particularly take note of the Copyright Term chart found at https://copyright.cornell.edu/publicdomain.

Jenkins, Amanda. "Copyright Breakdown: The Music Modernization Act." National Audio-Visual Conservation Center Blog. Accessed August 3, 2019. https://blogs.loc.gov/now-see-hear/2019/02/copyright-breakdown-the-music-modernization-act/. This explains the difference between a sound recording and a musical work, and includes the graduated timeline for sound recordings transitioning into the public domain.

Kansas State University Intellectual Property Information Center. "Copyright Basics Online Tutorial." Accessed July 4, 2019. www.k-state.edu/academicpersonnel/intprop/webtutor/sld001.htm. This short tutorial gives a nice general overview of copyright and fair use.

Nolo. "Copyright and Fair Use Overview/Resources." Stanford University Libraries and Academic Information Resources. Accessed July 4, 2019. http://fairuse.stanford.edu/Copyright_and_Fair_Use_Overview/index.html. This website has extensive information about copyright. Chapter 7, Academic and Educational Permissions, particularly section B, discusses fair use, specifically in academic or educational applications. http://fairuse.stanford.edu/Copyright_and_Fair Use_Overview/chapter7/index.html. Chapter 9 discusses fair use and the four factors that should be evaluated. http://fairuse.stanford.edu/Copyright_and_Fair_Use_Overview/chapter9/.

OCLC. "Well Intentioned Practice for Putting Digitized Collections of Unpublished Materials Online." Accessed July 4, 2019. https://www.oclc.org/research/activities/rights/practice.pdf. This document, created through the work of OCLC (a nonprofit, membership library service) proposes a method for addressing copyright issues in the event an organization chooses to digitize an archival collection. For more information follow this link: https://www.oclc.org/research/events/2010-03-11.htm.

Ritzenthaler, Mary Lynn, Diane Vogt-O'Connor, Helena Zinkham, Brett Carnell, and Kit Peterson. *Photographs Archival Care and Management.* Chicago: Society of American Archivists, 2006. Chapter 10 discusses legal issues for photographs including copyright and fair use and includes samples of a variety of related forms. Chapter 11 discusses policy issues for establishing a program to reproduce photographs.

Rowe, Jeremy. "Copyrights and Other Rights in Photographic Images." Accessed August 1, 2019. http://vintagephoto.com/reference/copyrightarticle1.htm. This article discusses copyright and other intellectual rights specifically for photographic images.

Schlipp, John. *Intellectual Property and Information Rights for Librarians*. Santa Barbara: ABC-CLIO, 2019. This book teaches intellectual property literacy, enabling the reader to easily understand a range of issues, explaining the rights of both creators and consumers, providing fair use examples and real life examples of how to apply intellectual property law, including copyright, in libraries, archives, and museums. It includes information about the Music Modernization Act. This is a good comprehensive resource.

Smoller, Louis. "Using Orphan Works (Copyright Holder Can't Be Located)." *Artrepreneur Art Law Journal* (November 14, 2018). Accessed August 3, 2019. https://alj.artrepreneur.com/using-orphan-work/. This has a nice visual flowchart of the Cornell copyright chart.

UCLA Online Institute for Cyberspace Law and Policy. "The Digital Millennium Copyright Act." Accessed July 4, 2019. http://gseis.ucla.edu/iclp/dmca1.htm. This is a shorter summary of the Digital Millennium Act.

University of Minnesota Libraries. "Copyright Services: Thinking Through Fair Use." Regents of the University of Minnesota. Accessed July 4, 2019. https://www.lib.umn.edu/copyright/fairthoughts. The site has a Fair Use Analysis Tool, which may provide some assistance. Although it focuses on published material for teaching or scholarly research, there are examples for unpublished material.

US Copyright Office. "Circular 21: Reproduction of Copyrighted Works by Educators and Librarians." Accessed July 4, 2019. https://www.copyright.gov/circs/circ21.pdf. This discussion, particularly on pp. 5–11, focuses primarily on text, not images, but there is no specific exclusion of images from the discussion.

———. "Circular 22: How to Investigate the Copyright Status of a Work." Accessed July 4, 2019. https://www.copyright.gov/circs/circ22.pdf. This provides guidance on how to conduct a copyright search.

———. "Copyright." Accessed July 4, 2019. https://www.copyright.gov/. This page has information about copyright and includes a link for teachers and students to teach/learn about it.

———. "The Digital Millennium Copyright Act of 1998: US Copyright Office Summary." Accessed July 4, 2019. https://www.copyright.gov/legislation/dmca.pdf. This is the summary of the Digital Millennium Copyright Act prepared by the US Copyright Office of the DMCA.

Notes

1. Richard Pearce-Moses, *A Glossary of Archival and Records Terminology*, Archival Fundamentals Series II (Chicago: Society of American Archivists, 2005), s.v. "intellectual property," "copyright."

2. Timothy B. Lee, "Mickey Mouse Will Be Public Domain Soon—Here's What That Means," *Ars Technica*, copyright by Conde Nast, January 1, 2019, accessed August 3, 2019, https://arstechnica.com/tech-policy/2019/01/a-whole-years-worth-of-works-just-fell-into-the-public-domain/.

3. John Schlipp, *Intellectual Property and Information Rights for Librarians* (Santa Barbara: ABC-CLIO, 2019), 48; Stephen Carlisle, "The Music Modernization Act: What's In It, Why Is It In There, and Is It a Good Thing?" accessed August 3, 2019, http://copyright.nova.edu/music-modernization-act/. See Schlipp, p. 295, for a brief discussion of steps for use of orphan work sound recordings. See also the US Copyright Office for detailed guidance on how to search for the copyright holder, accessed August 3, 2019, https://www.copyright.gov/rulemaking/pre1972-soundrecordings-noncommercial/. My thanks to my colleague John Schlipp for an informative update on recent changes in copyright law.

4. Mary Lynn Ritzenthaler, Diane Vogt-O'Connor, Helena Zinkham, Brett Carnell, and Kit Peterson, *Photographs: Archival Care and Management* (Chicago: Society of American Archivists, 2006), 312–13; Nolo, Stanford University Libraries Copyright and Fair Use website, Chapter 9, section A, "What Is Fair Use?," Board of Trustees, Leland Stanford Junior University, accessed July 4, 2019, http://fairuse.stanford.edu/Copyright_and_Fair_Use_Overview/chapter9/9-a.html; Chapter 9, section C, "Summaries of Fair Use Cases," accessed July 4, 2019, http://fairuse.stanford.edu/Copyright_and_Fair_Use_Overview/chapter9/9-c.html; Chapter 9, section B, "Measuring Fair Use: the Four Factors." accessed July 4, 2019, http://fairuse.stanford.edu/Copyright_and_Fair_Use_Overview/chapter9/9-b.html. The use of the acronym PANE as a mnemonic aid came from my colleague John Schlipp, who has dealt extensively with copyright as applied to published materials. I thank him for some interesting discussions on a tortuous subject.

5. Nolo, "Stanford University Libraries Copyright and Fair Use website, Chapter 7, section B, "Educational Uses of Non-coursepack Materials," Board of Trustees, Leland Stanford Junior University, accessed July 4, 2019, http://fairuse.stanford.edu/Copyright_and_Fair_Use_Overview/chapter7/7-b.html.

6. Ritzenthaler et al., *Photographs*, 314–15.

7. Ritzenthaler et al., *Photographs*, 332n18.

8. Nolo, "Stanford University Libraries Copyright and Fair Use website, "Chapter 9, section B, Measuring Fair Use: the Four Factors," Board of Trustees, Leland Stanford Junior University, accessed July 4, 2019, http://fairuse.stanford.edu/Copyright_and_Fair_Use_Overview/chapter9/9-b.html.

7

Managing Digitization Projects

The last chapter addressed the management question of whether a requested use for a photograph does or doesn't infringe on the rights of the copyright holder. This chapter will address the actual process of digitizing archival materials: photographs, text documents, postcards, maps and other nonphotographic images, and relevant management questions to consider. The need to digitize an item may originate with a reference request for a photograph or it may be part of an intentional decision by the institution to increase access to its collections. This author has managed both a scan-on-demand program for photographs used by outside researchers and my own institution, and planned digitization of specific bodies of records to improve access. The former may appear to be just a few photographs for a onetime use, but in more than ten years we have scanned thousands of images, resulting in a sizable body that requires active management as images are repeatedly reused.

Digitization

Fifteen years ago, researchers asked for a print copy of a photo that they wished to publish. Today they request digital copies of photographs unless they only want to display them for personal purposes. The creation, storage, and preservation of digital (electronic) files require thinking, planning, and intentionality. It is easy to slap a photograph on a scanner bed and push a button, about as difficult as photocopying. The uninformed assume that is all there is to the process. They would be wrong. It is the tip of the iceberg. What guarantee is there that the quality of the image will meet the proposed usage? Will someone else be able to locate the digital file in a week? Will it still exist in a year or will the same image need to be scanned repeatedly because of poor choices for technical specifications, poor naming conventions, a disorganized electronic file structure, or the lack of a plan to preserve the digital image? Most aspects of the digitization process for photographs or archival records have been studied in great depth by specialists, and literature on the subject is plentiful and at times quite complex. This chapter will provide a basic introduction and refer to helpful resources where possible.

Let's start with a basic workflow for scanning a few photographs, images, or documents on demand for a reference request, publication, or possibly an exhibit. Determine the final use of the scanned image. Is it to publish in a print book or journal? Is it for an exhibit by your institution? Will it be used for a blog post or website? Different uses require different scanning resolutions and possibly the addition of a watermark. The most frequently requested resolution for a print resource is a 300 dots per inch (dpi) JPG. Images that are enlarged, say an 8" x 10" photograph enlarged for a 16" x 20" poster, will require a much higher resolution. Slides and most negatives also require scanning at a higher resolution because the original is much smaller than the final size at which it is used. Because the priority for images delivered via the web is fast loading, their resolution typically ranges from 72 to 150 dpi. Another concern is unauthorized use of copyrighted images. Low resolution web images won't provide good quality print images. In the case of documents, the ability to search them for specific words is often a goal. Knowing the final purpose and functionality of items to be scanned will influence decisions to be made during planning and workflow design. The process of working backward from the end to the beginning is called reverse engineering.

Equipment

Let's start with equipment. The equipment available to create scans and its associated software will impose limitations on your final product. According to Kit A. Peterson, digital conversion specialist at the Library of Congress, there are three methods of digital capture that are safe for historical photographs: a flatbed scanner, a digital camera, and a film scanner. Peterson recommends selecting a digital capture method appropriate for the format of the originals and capable of capturing digital images that meet your digitization specifications. Additionally, your organization must be able to afford the equipment selected. A film scanner digitizes strips of film negatives (such as 35 mm or 126 or 110 cartridge film) or slides. It doesn't handle photographic prints or documents. A digital camera is good for photographic prints, a variety of documents including oversize materials, and even three-dimensional objects. A flatbed scanner accepts photographic prints and documents. Some are designed to also handle negatives and slides.[1] Peterson, writing in *Photographs: Archival Care and Management*, compares the advantages and disadvantages of each method in a chart on page 395.

Flatbed scanners are not all the same. Those with an auto-feeder are not intended for archival photographs or documents. A general use flatbed scanner is designed to handle reflective materials, meaning documents or photographic prints. The lighting that creates the scan is located below the item being reproduced, like it is in a photocopier. A scanner designed for documents won't produce as good a quality scan of photographs as a photo scanner will. A photo scanner that accommodates negatives and slides, that is, transparent materials, uses lighting from above the item being scanned, in the lid. It should also be capable of scanning at the much higher resolutions required for negatives and slides. Epson is a manufacturer that makes good-quality flatbed scanners designed for photographs, negatives, and slides. Having first used a scanner that must have been designed for modern office papers, and then switched to an Epson photo scanner, the latter produces much better results even if the original is a published photo in a print source like a magazine, newspaper, or yearbook. For these types of sources, the photo scanner should be set to descreen the resulting image. The final product is much better starting from a negative or a photographic print than a published picture, but a photo scanner that can descreen will produce visibly better results than an office document scanner. The photo scanner is quite capable of digitizing paper documents too. In fact, when digitizing aged paper that may have yellowed or have contrast problems, the photo scanner produces more satisfying results than a general document scanner. It picks up the shading differences that make the scans look more authentic when compared with the source document. This is useful if copies of original documents are used for exhibits; what is displayed still conveys the look of being aged while protecting the original.

On a modest budget, it is possible to purchase a single flatbed photo scanner that will handle negatives, slides, and photographic prints up to about eight inches by ten inches as well as documents of a similar size. If the majority of materials your organization would like to digitize do not fit this description, you will need to consider alternate methods of digital capture. Options include a scanner with a larger flatbed, software and technical skills to stitch together piecemeal scans of a single larger photo or document, or a digital camera. This decision may require research, advice from more experienced people, and discussion to determine the best fit for your organization based upon its resources and needs.

Assuming the photo scanner does work for the majority of your collection, what next? Originals, whether slide, negative, print, or document, need to be placed on the scanner bed without damaging them. If the original is bowed, the top of the scanner must be held open far enough to avoid putting pressure on the original and cracking or breaking it. If the original is contained in a bound volume, say a yearbook, the side not being scanned needs to be supported to protect the binding and other pages. A sufficiently thick book or even a box lid can be placed next to the scanner bed to provide the necessary additional support.

Technical Specifications

The next question is what technical settings should be used. The answer is it depends. There is no single all-purpose setting. Settings vary for black-and-white text, black-and-white images, and color images. They also vary for a digital *preservation copy*, an access copy, and a web thumbnail. A digital preservation copy is created at the highest-quality specifications possible within the scope of a digitization project. It is used to create the master copy, which in turn is used to create all derivative files: access copies, web thumbnails, print or digital reproductions. A digital *access copy* is intended to replace the original in the sense that the access will answer most reference requests, limiting the need to see and handle the original. What physical properties of the original need to be captured by the preservation copy? What technical specifications will meet those needs? For example, does the preservation copy need to capture the entire photograph or negative from edge to edge? Are images mounted in an album? Does the whole page need to be captured in addition to all individual images? Is there significant information on the back that needs to be digitized?[2]

A policy to digitize all images from edge to edge including mountings and casings will create a surrogate that appears the same to a researcher as viewing the original in person. The researcher will be able to distinguish nineteenth-century photographs from twentieth-century, a postcard from a photograph. This additional information may be important to his research question and he will be able to get it from the digital surrogate. Digitizing the whole album page in addition to individual images, if possible, is a similar example of providing as much information digitally as the original provides. It gives contextual information for each of the individual images.

The technical specifications for digitizing a photograph depend upon selecting a spatial resolution (dpi); color (color or grayscale); color system (RGB—red, green, blue or CYMK—cyan, yellow, magenta, black); *bit depth* (1, 8, 16, 24); dynamic range (the difference between the lightest and darkest areas of the original photo), and the tonal values (the numeric values assigned to black and white to help the scanner define the full range of tones to use). These decisions will determine how large the file size is for a particular image. There are no standards to answer these questions, only recommendations, and no one set of specifications will fit all situations.

Generally, the higher the scanning resolution, the more clearly the details are captured and the larger the file size (i.e., digital storage space requirements). The level and quality of detail must be balanced with the resulting file size. This should include evaluation and planning to reach an informed decision. Dots per inch alone is not a sufficient measure of the quality of a scan; the resolution must be relative to the size of the original. If a four-inch by five-inch photo is scanned at 300 dpi but printed at eight inches by ten inches, the resolution of the print will be less than the original 300 dpi. The size of the original (height x width) multiplied by the scanning resolution equals its resolution in pixels, so (four-inch by five-inch) x 300 dpi = 1200 x 1500 pixels. When the pixel size is divided by the desired print size, eight inches by ten inches, the resulting resolution for the print is only 150 dpi. This example illustrates that the final use of the digital image is important in determining the original scanning resolution. The size of the original is also a factor. Appendix A.5 compares originals of varying sizes with the resolution required to produce preservation or master copies and access copies. It is highly recommended when planning a digitization project to determine what users should be able to do with the final digital files and work backward to determine the technical specifications. Ask "What level of resolution captures enough information from the original object to be considered high resolution in the anticipated uses?" not "How high should the resolution be?"[3]

To calculate the file size of an 8-bit grayscale scan, multiply (the pixel height x pixel width), divide by 1,000,000 = __ approximate MB (megabytes); for a 24-bit RGB color scan, multiply (the pixel height x pixel width x 3), divide by 1,000,000 = __ approximate MB. The RGB color system has three channels (red, green, blue), each composed of 8 bits. This comparison illustrates that an RGB color scan creates three times the file size as a grayscale of the same original. It may be an easy decision to scan a color photo in color, but what about a sepia-colored albumen print? Would a grayscale copy be an acceptable substitute for color in order to keep the file size manageable? There will be trade-offs as decisions are made about scanning specifications. It may be preferable to have a higher resolution or *bit depth* grayscale scan that produces greater detail than a color scan of a sepia-toned photograph, or even text on aged paper that is low in resolution or makes it difficult to read the text. Bit depth is another choice that can capture more or less color information and affect the resultant file size. Peterson says that a commonly accepted minimum standard for bit depth is 8 bit for grayscale and 24 bit for color for a preservation copy. The most accepted file format for preservation copies is the uncompressed TIFF file.[4]

Once a high-quality digital preservation copy is created, it is used to create a duplicate master copy, which is in turn used to create derivative files such as access copies used for study or reproduction purposes and a thumbnail for quick viewing to select images for further study or on the web. Access copies are 640 to 1240 pixels long (approximately 300 dpi) and use the JPG format. Thumbnails tend to be 150 to 300 pixels long and also use the JPG format. It is acceptable to compress derivative files.[5] If there are copyright concerns, any derivative can also be watermarked. In order to keep the watermark in proportion to the image size, it would be added after the access copy is made, but before it is reduced in size to make a thumbnail or web version.

File Management

Managing multiple digital versions of the same original source photo or document and linking them to the original will require good file naming conventions and file management practices. The file name can provide information about both the digitized image or document and the original, as well as aid in file retrieval and management. If collections (MS) or record groups (RG)—institutional records—are given both a name and a unique collection number when they are processed, the collection number can be used as a shorthand identification for digital file names. For example, if the Charles H. Elston Legal Collection is MS-3, and the collection has been processed so that records have been assigned to a series, possible file names could be Manuscript Collection[fill in number]_series[fill in number]_folder[fill in number]_item[fill in number] as illustrated in tables 7.1 and 7.2.

Table 7.1 File Naming Sample 1

ms3_s2_f3_017**p**.tif	p denotes preservation copy
ms3_s2_f3_017**m**.jpg	m denotes master copy
ms3_s2_f3_017**a**.jpg	a denotes access copy
ms3_s2_f3_017**t**.jpg	t denotes thumbnail copy

Table 7.2 File Naming Sample 2

ms3_s2_f3_017_600.tif	TIFF designates both a preservation and a master copy; they are duplicates but stored in different folder locations.
ms3_s2_f3_017_300.jpg	JPG with no added tags designates an access copy.
ms3_s2_f3_017_72.jpg	JPG + 72 dpi resolution indicates a thumbnail or web copy.
ms3_s2_f3_017_72_w.jpg	JPG + w + 72 dpi resolution indicates a watermarked web copy.

If a collection has not been processed it really is not ready to digitize, but a system designating the source box and folder number has also been used. See table 7.3. This work sequence is not recommended and likely will require more work when the collection is processed to maintain the link between each scan and the original source because the originals will probably be reordered and grouped differently during processing than they were at the time of scanning. This might require labeling each item with its digital file name or possibly renaming scanned files.

Scans of photographs that are part of a large institutional record group comprised solely of photos might have names like those in table 7.4. Refer to appendix A.4 for an explanation of how the file names in table 7.4 were constructed. Note the use of the resolution in dpi in the file names in tables 7.2 and 7.4. While the file format, JPG versus TIFF, certainly distinguishes master copies from access copies, the dpi also suggests one or the other. Also, if standardized scanning resolutions are used based on the size of the original and whether the copy is a master or for access, the resolution can be compared with that written table and the dpi will indicate the size of the original. See appendix A.5 for a sample table. Note that while software like Photoshop will read the file size, Microsoft Office Photo Manager and other simple viewers cannot. A standard practice of inserting the resolution in the file name is very useful for a number of reasons. Written guidance for file naming will standardize file names, increasing consistency in colocating similar photos or related documents.

Table 7.3 File Naming Sample 3

ms3_b1_f3_017.tif	b = box + specific box number
	f = folder + the sequential folder number in that specific box
	017 = the 17th item in folder 3

Table 7.4 Sample File Names Decoded

classroom_003_2001_04_adj_600.tif	photo #3 taken April 2001 of unknown classroom
staff_casson_g_001_1970s_adj_600.tif	staff employee G Casson, identified only to decade
m_basketball_smith_s_001_1986_600.tif	m = men's athletics, player S Smith, photo #1
campus_life_registration_002_adj_900.tif	adj = signifies photo has been adjusted somehow
greek_delta_zeta_001_1970s_600.tif	greek life photo #1 of delta zeta sorority from 1970s

These sample naming systems link the digital copy back to the paper original. The file name actually has a meaning that can be decoded as opposed to file names like 0000109, 0000110, 0000111, which require an index to link each scan to the source collection and item location. Descriptive file names make it possible to locate a particular file without having to open every scan to visually search for a desired item. Each item has a unique name. It is easy to determine which preservation, master, access, and thumbnail copies belong together.[6]

Another necessary component of file management that supports good file naming is a clear and orderly file structure. It is very desirable that records and files be organized such that there is a single location to search for a specific item. Multiple locations where similar or related files are kept leads to inefficient searches and potentially overlooked information, redundant copies of the same files resulting in wasted storage space, or different versions in multiple locations causing confusion. It is also strongly recommended that electronic file structures parallel arrangement structures used for analog records. Record groups, collections, series, and file names need to be the same regardless of the format used to record the information (i.e., paper documents, audio or video formats, or electronic files whether stored on CDs, DVDs, hard drives, or server space). As much as possible, consistent arrangement needs to extend even to the software used to provide public access to digital surrogates of analog originals. A researcher will inevitably view a photo or document online and ask to see the original or request similar material from another period that has not yet been digitized. Or a researcher will browse analog material and request a digital copy. Staff needs to know how to determine whether it has already been digitized, and where to locate the requisite copy. They need to be able to locate all copies or versions of the same item and all related records regardless of time period, format, or even unit name changes in the case of organizational records. A logical and consistent digital file structure will support these goals.

At some point digital file management requires the copying or moving of files. Frequently these actions change the date of original files unnecessarily. No one would change the date on correspondence just because it was moved to a new folder. The date helps provide context for the information in the document whether analog or digital. TeraCopy is a software for quickly copying files that reports errors, permits the pause and restart of file transfers, and does not change creation dates.[7] Highlight a file to copy, use your preferred method to indicate the need to copy, and a message box pops up asking which of several options to use for the copying. Select TeraCopy and that is all that is necessary after the software is loaded onto the computer being used for this work. The TeraCopy software can also be loaded on an external hard drive or flash drive to move files between computers.

Just as distinct manuscript collections and record groups are created and managed as separate bodies of records, so the starting point for a parallel and consistent electronic file directory structure is to create a separate folder for each collection or record group that has electronic files. The number of subfolders created within any individual collection or record group will depend upon the quantity of electronic files and their relationship to each other, the same as when a collection is physically arranged. The electronic file directory should mirror the analog file structure as represented in the finding aid description. Only those sections of the physical arrangement that have corresponding digital files should exist in the electronic file directory. If only one series or folder has been digitized, only one electronic folder is needed.

An intentional program of scanning photos on demand or digitizing records to make them available for access from off site will result in the creation of multiple copies of the same image or document. At the least there will be a preservation copy, a master copy, and one access copy, although there could well be more access copies (thumbnails, web, or watermarked copies). Organizing and linking all digital copies to each other and the analog original, if one exists, requires planning. The same institutional practices used to arrange analog records into series and individual folders should be applied to electronic files. (Sub)folders will separate series and files. A simplistic arrangement would locate all formats (preservation, master, and access copies) in the same folder, as shown in figure 7.1.

Figure 7.1 illustrates the file structure for electronic files as named in table 7.1. Figure 7.1 assumes there are electronic files in series 1 that are not shown in the figure. Table 7.2 presents a file naming system that relies on the use of standardized file resolution indicators and file formats to distinguish preservation copies from access and thumbnail copies. File location distinguishes preservation copies from master copies. Figure 7.2 illustrates the electronic file structure for files named as shown in table 7.2. The TIFFs in figure 7.2 are master copies based on their colocation with the access or derivative copies.

Figure 7.3 illustrates just part of the electronic file structure for digital copies made from a large, complex, institutional photograph collection. The electronic folder headings shown parallel series and subseries from the print collection. The file structure also shows preservation copies (TIFFs) colocated with access copies (JPGs).

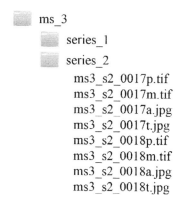

Figure 7.1. Electronic file structure for table 7.1.

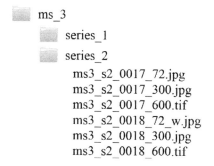

Figure 7.2. Electronic file structure for table 7.2.

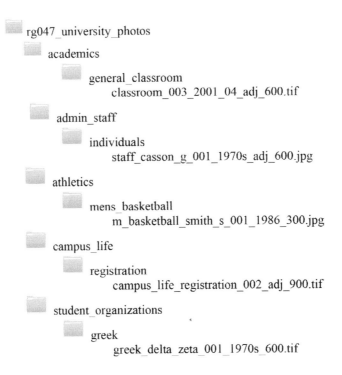

rg047_university_photos
    academics
        general_classroom
            classroom_003_2001_04_adj_600.tif
    admin_staff
        individuals
            staff_casson_g_001_1970s_adj_600.jpg
    athletics
        mens_basketball
            m_basketball_smith_s_001_1986_300.jpg
    campus_life
        registration
            campus_life_registration_002_adj_900.tif
    student_organizations
        greek
            greek_delta_zeta_001_1970s_600.tif

Figure 7.3. Electronic file structure for table 7.4.

While this certainly can be done, it isn't desirable. The purpose of creating separate access copies is so the preservation copies can be set aside and left untouched avoiding accidental deletion or change to dates or other metadata. If access copies are lost, master copies are used to create new ones. Since the preservation copies are intended to protect against loss, it doesn't make sense to store them in the same directory or on the same server as the access copies. Figure 7.4 illustrates the same complex photograph collection, but the preservation copies are filed in a separate directory, or preferably a separate server.

Notice too in figure 7.3 that some file names repeat the name of the subfolder in which the digital photo is located and sometimes even the name of the folder another level up. The file named m_basketball_smith_s_001_1986_300.jpg abbreviates the folder label men's basketball but omits athletics. The file campus_life_registration_002_adj_900.tif includes its own folder name and the one above. Depending upon how well the file directory is organized when a specific image file is named, some of the folder name redundancy inserted in the file name can be omitted. Separate storage locations and the file structure can also eliminate the need for prefixes or suffixes separating preservation, master, and access copies, including watermarked and thumbnail copies.

A Word about File Storage

How and where files are stored will be affected by the technical skill level of personnel at an organization and its resources. Preservation files should be stored on Location 1 while master and access copies are stored in Location 2. This means physically or electronically they are in two distinct locations, not two different file folders on the same hard drive, external hard drive, or cloud storage. Location 2 access copies would be used for daily work. If the access copies

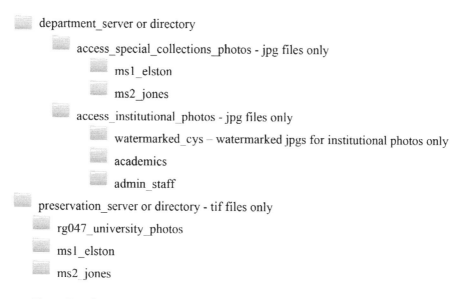

    department_server or directory

        access_special_collections_photos - jpg files only

            ms1_elston

            ms2_jones

        access_institutional_photos - jpg files only

            watermarked_cys – watermarked jpgs for institutional photos only

            academics

            admin_staff

  preservation_server or directory - tif files only

    rg047_university_photos

    ms1_elston

    ms2_jones

Figure 7.4. Separate electronic file structures for access and preservation copies.

were damaged and needed to be replaced or higher resolutions copies were needed, the Location 2 master copies would be used to replace them or create higher-resolution derivative files. The Location 1 preservation files would be monitored for file deterioration and file obsolescence requiring migration to a new format. Otherwise, they would be opened only to make new master copies to replace lost or damaged Location 2 files.

Depending upon the amount of storage space required for Location 2 files, they could fit on a laptop or desktop computer. If the storage requirement is larger, an external hard drive would be an inexpensive option. If there are many image files or audio or video files that would require considerable storage, several external hard drives could be used. Drive A could be audio files, Drive B video, Drive C master copies of photos, while only access copies of photos or text type files were stored on the computer's hard drive. Location 1 preservation files could have their own dedicated external hard drive. Many permutations are possible. There does need to be some organization to whatever system is developed. The structure might need documentation depending upon how many people create and access files.

When files are on computers, external hard drives, or other storage devices under the organization's control, it can be easier to protect them, control access to restricted or confidential files, and control access to copyrighted material whose rights are not owned by the organization, as well as copyrighted material owned by the organization. At the same time, the organization also bears the responsibility for actively managing those same files: protecting them against viruses, unauthorized access or usage, accidental deletion or damage, monitoring file formats to ensure they can still be opened and used, and more. If personnel have strong technical skills, they might develop their own server for increased live storage space that could even be networked to provide several employees simultaneous access to the same file locations so documents can be easily shared with minimal duplication. If funding is available but technical skill is limited, an organization might choose to use free or paid file hosting services, cloud storage, or a vendor for some services. Dropbox, OneDrive, iCloud, Google Drive, and Amazon Drive provide free storage.

File hosting services or cloud storage providers are responsible for keeping your data accessible, managing the hardware and software storing your files, and providing access thereto. They may also provide you with backup copies of your files. They should also provide security for your files.[8] When considering a service to store your data, evaluate how experienced they are, how long they have been in business, how likely they are to remain in business. Consider how easy it is to use their software to access your files, how secure the data will be, whether you can get your data back if the provider closes, what provision they make to protect the data in case of natural disasters.

Selecting Records for a Digitization Project

When scanning photos or documents on demand, the researcher making the request selects the materials to be scanned based on their research requirements. Archival staff need to consider the physical condition of the requested materials. Will the physical manipulation required to place the items on the scanning bed damage them? Are they in a bound volume or oversized scrapbook or warped so they cannot be laid flat? Putting excessive pressure on such items to get a clear or complete image can damage bindings or cause warped items to crack or break. Oversized scrapbooks need additional support for the part that hangs over. Items may fall out of their original location, etc. Institutions have the right to refuse reproduction of records that will be damaged by the process. Alternate methods like photographing the requested photo or information may be possible pending the institution's capabilities. Sometimes just a simple snapshot on a cellphone or tablet will suffice.

Another consideration besides physical condition is whether the institution has the right to reproduce the records in question. Copyright was discussed extensively in the last chapter. If an organization does not own the copyright to the requested records, and determines the probability is too high that the copyright holder will complain, again it can refuse a reproduction request or better yet, recommend the researcher obtain permission directly from the copyright holder. If the researcher obtains such permission and provides a copy to the organization, they should feel comfortable reproducing the records.

How does an organization select records for an intentional digitization program? Several common reasons for an intentional program are to increase access to the records, to provide access to damaged, fragile, or high-value records while minimizing handling of the originals, or to migrate records from an obsolete format to a more accessible format. As a rule, digitization is best done after records have been processed, arranged, and described; because the final arrangement of the records has been determined, the relationship of one series of records to another is known. The processing stage is when the records will receive the most intensive scrutiny by staff. Damaged materials, high-value items, unique or interesting items, and more are potentially identified during processing. If the processor is also familiar with topics or records that are frequently requested by researchers, he can also flag those in his processing notes.

Digitization is labor- and time-intensive work. Not all records in an archives are of equal research value. An experienced manager should consider the potential research value of specific records based on archival appraisal, the organization's strategic plan or upcoming new initiatives, patterns of usage based on past reference demands, potential funding from grants or donors, in addition to other factors already mentioned. It is acceptable to scan a single series of a collection or record group.

Workflow

Once the organization either receives a research request or decides to digitize a specific body of records, it needs to identify equipment, assign personnel, and develop a workflow for the task. Appendix B.12 is a workflow used to scan photographs using an Epson Perfection V 700 photo scanner capable of also scanning negatives and slides. The SilverFast software version illustrated is one between 6.6 and 8.8, although the process is similar for older versions in use since about 2010 when we purchased the Epson scanner. While the specific method used to perform a task, like setting the scan resolution, may vary based on the scanning software used, the tasks to perform and their sequence are representative. Alternate software and older versions can be substituted for Adobe Photoshop. What is recommended is a software that performs basic photo manipulation (contrast adjustment, resizing, image rotation, cropping, watermarking) tasks.

When working with photographs, the process is to create a high-grade preservation copy first. If possible, a duplicate copy of the preservation copy should be made and labeled as a master copy. Then software like Adobe Photoshop is used to resize the master copy to make an access copy. If watermarking is desired, create the watermark before the photo is reduced in size. The size of the watermark will be legible and in better proportion to the image than if the sequence is reversed. As each version is created, be sure to Save As the new version to avoid overwriting the original, revise the file name as appropriate, and file each copy (preservation, master, access, or watermarked thumbnail) in its designated digital file location.

The workflow for scanning multipage text documents is different from photographs because the individual pages need to be linked together to re-create the whole document. Appendix B.13 documents the workflow used to digitize a large body of meeting minutes using the same Epson scanner and SilverFast software as described above and in appendix B.12. They are part of an intentional digitization project to add documents to an institutional repository. The institutional repository delivers access copies via the World Wide Web in a publicly accessible repository. Since the purpose of the access copies is delivering information via the web, the governing criteria for the file's functionality is fast loading time. A resolution of 300 dpi provides legible text while balancing file size to provide respectable loading times and acceptable file storage requirements. Since this is a public repository, restricted or confidential materials are not put in the repository.

In the workflow described in appendix B.13, all the pages in an individual document are scanned as PDF files. The meeting date for minutes or agendas, newsletters, or a constitution and the individual page number are incorporated into the file name of each individual page scan. After all pages for a document are scanned, basic quality control work is done to ensure no pages are omitted or repeated, pages are correctly oriented, not cut off, and of sufficient contrast to be legible. At this point, Adobe Acrobat Pro or a similar software is used to combine the individual files into a single PDF document. A new combined file is created bearing a file name similar to the individual pages but omitting the page number. The individual page files and the combined file are saved into the same folder and all are retained until after the final quality control check later. Once the combined file is created, Adobe Acrobat is used again to perform optical character recognition (OCR) on the combined file. This file is Saved As again to allow prior steps to be repeated if necessary without having to rescan pages. The new file includes the tag _ocr in the file name to distinguish the final product from the files created in the two earlier stages. A second more skilled person performs the quality control check. As files pass the quality control check, all files from the first two stages are deleted. Running the OCR compresses the file size, which improves its download time. Another benefit is that adaptive software for people with vision problems is more likely to successfully read OCRed text. Depending upon how the files are delivered, the OCR may also aid word searches of the documents or automated indexing of the document contents by web browsers or other software. A 300-dpi text document is of sufficient quality and the PDF file format sufficiently portable that this file can also be used as both a preservation copy and master copy. For this purpose and bearing in mind that preservation and master copies should be retained in case something happens to the access copy, a duplicate copy of the combined, OCRed PDF file should be placed in the same location as other digital preservation and master copies.

Creating written documentation of the specific process for your equipment tailored to the institution's file management practices will help train new staff and develop consistency in the work produced. If the institution engages in one-day community scanning projects or uses interns or others who do not normally perform scanning, clear written directions like appendix B.13 will improve the outcome of their work. Documentation for scanning tasks can be printed out and kept in a binder next to the scanner for ready reference.

Delivery of Digitized Records

The beginning of this chapter mentioned the impact of the final functionality of the records to be scanned on technical decisions for the scanning workflow. The final functionality will also be affected by the method used to deliver the scanned files. The simplest delivery method is files conveyed directly to an individual researcher or an organizational office for their use as needed. Digitization to create resources for a public that may never contact the organization is very different. Delivery options include web pages, an institutional repository using software like DSpace[9] or Digital Commons, or a web page portal accessing digital records in PastPerfect.

My institution has changed its website four times in the last thirteen years, requiring hundreds of web pages for my department alone to be migrated to new formatting. The migrations required a tremendous amount of work to re-create the same resources instead of creating new ones. For organizations that don't change their site as frequently or have a small site, web pages may be a good option. Delivery via basic web pages requires technical skill to use web page design software while advanced presentation of scans may employ computer languages to design searchable, custom databases. Additionally, each image requires a minimal description of what is being displayed, the collection of which it is a part, the holding institution, possibly rights and citation information, otherwise known as metadata. Depending upon the organization and the technical knowledge of project personnel, archival or library descriptive standards such as Describing Archives: A Content Standard (DACS) (a *data content standard*) or Dublin Core (a data structure standard) might be used. Decisions about what standards and data fields will be used and other details should be recorded, both to execute the project and for future reference in case the project needs to be migrated. There is also a growing need, in some cases a legal requirement, to make web pages handicap accessible. Scanned text that has been run through OCR software, or the addition of a descriptive label to images are examples of adjustments that improve accessibility. Also retain backup copies of all scanned files as well as description in file formats that can be edited for use in case the project is migrated in the future. This preparation will save time in the future and increase the ability to successfully migrate such work over the long term. If every document or photo must be rescanned and the metadata re-created, it is less likely the project will be migrated.

When resources allow, an institutional repository provides greater stability for digitization projects than a website, meaning the same information does not have to be re-created as frequently. The software used to manage the repository will determine at least some of the descriptive standards, acceptable file formats, and presentation. Some organizations hire a vendor to host their repository because they lack the technical skill to manage servers, software upgrades, and system backup. This option means they have less ability to customize aspects of functionality and presentation. My institution uses a hosted version of DSpace software. DSpace uses Dublin Core fields. A librarian uses MARC to describe the published works she adds to the repository while the Archives uses DACS and batch uploads archival documents and images. Figure 7.5 shows one scanned postcard and its associated DC metadata as delivered via a web page. Figure 7.6 shows the same postcard and metadata as presented via our institutional repository.

Man O'War, the Wonder Horse

Postcard Information

- **Description:** Postcard of a picture of Man O'War, the Wonder Horse, bred in Old Kentucky
- **Subject:** Gilliam Family
- **Subject:** Horses--Kentucky--Lexington
- **Date:**
- **Format:** jpeg
- **Source:** Digital copy of postcard: Man O'War, the Wonder Horse
- **Language:** English
- **Rights:** This postcard is in the public domain, so this image may be freely used. Please cite as follows: Gilliam Collection, Eva G. Farris Special Collections, W. Frank Steely Library, Northern Kentucky University.
- **Publisher:** Genuine Curteich
- **Resource Identifier:** gilliam_ky_lexington_11
- **Provenance:** Donated by Dr. Katherine Kurk in 1991 to the Eva G. Farris Special Collections, W. Frank Steely Library, Northern Kentucky University.
- **Type:** Image, postcard
- **Relation:**
  Is part of - Gilliam Collection
  Is part of - Kentucky Postcards Series
  Is part of - Lexington File

Figure 7.5. Scanned archival images delivered by a basic web page.

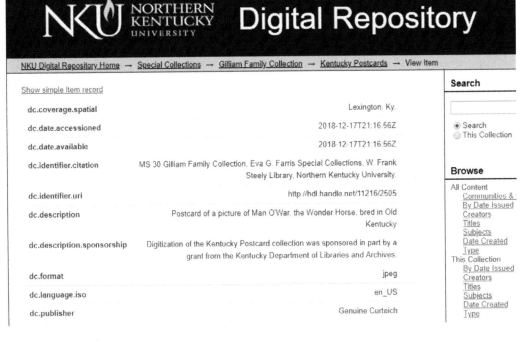

NKU Digital Repository Home → Special Collections → Gilliam Family Collection → Kentucky Postcards → View Item

Show simple item record

dc.coverage.spatial	Lexington, Ky.
dc.date.accessioned	2018-12-17T21:16:56Z
dc.date.available	2018-12-17T21:16:56Z
dc.identifier.citation	MS 30 Gilliam Family Collection, Eva G. Farris Special Collections, W. Frank Steely Library, Northern Kentucky University.
dc.identifier.uri	http://hdl.handle.net/11216/2505
dc.description	Postcard of a picture of Man O'War, the Wonder Horse, bred in Old Kentucky
dc.description.sponsorship	Digitization of the Kentucky Postcard collection was sponsored in part by a grant from the Kentucky Department of Libraries and Archives.
dc.format	jpeg
dc.language.iso	en_US
dc.publisher	Genuine Curteich

Search

◉ Search
○ This Collection

Browse

All Content
Communities &
By Date Issued
Creators
Titles
Subjects
Date Created
Type
This Collection
By Date Issued
Creators
Titles
Subjects
Date Created
Type

Files in this item

Name: gilliam_ky_lexing ...
Size: 74.98Kb
Format: JPEG image

View/Open

Name: gilliam_ky_lexing ...
Size: 57.93Kb
Format: JPEG image

View/Open

Figure 7.6. Scanned archival images delivered in DSpace Institutional Repository.

Community Scanning Days

Identify Needs

Many local historical organizations and public libraries like to hold community scanning days. These are often written up in the local news and bring the organization beneficial publicity; however, managing such a project presents logistical problems as well as copyright problems. Whoever proposes holding such an event should clearly articulate the purpose for the event and what is being sought. What does the organization or library hope to gain? What is its collection policy? What does it collect and what doesn't it collect in terms of time periods, formats, topics, geographic locations? Are there gaps in the collections compared with the collection policy? If yes, will the scanning event focus on them or also consider material for areas that are already reasonably well documented in the collections? Can planners develop a prioritized list of topics, images, or information it will seek? Does the organization only seek to acquire information, or does it hope to stimulate offers of new collection donations, financial support, or something more? Do these other objectives fit the organization's strategic plan or other governing documents? Will someone be on hand to make immediate decisions regarding the organization's interest in a proposed donation of materials, accept a financial donation, or otherwise field questions? If not, consider focusing solely on acquiring new images, documents, or information for the collections.

Address Copyright Questions

Assuming a prioritized list of topical and geographic collection gaps can be identified for specific time periods and formats, and this can be clearly communicated to a prospective audience of people likely to own the targeted information, copyright and documentation of the information are the next problems. A community scanning event asks people who physically own photographs, maps, visual records, or documents to bring them to a designated location for them to be scanned on the spot, after which the original is taken back home. The community member bringing materials to the event may or may not own the copyright to the materials or may not know. The organization will need to know whether it should or shouldn't scan the items brought to the event. Someone knowledgeable about copyright should either be at the event to prescreen materials or be prepared to review all scans and documents after the fact and decide whether any of the materials are a high risk for copyright infringement. Consider having several stations prior to reaching the scanning station(s), one of which would include some minimal copyright assessment. Although the copyright information presented in chapter 6 focuses on photographs, it is equally applicable to other type of materials likely to appear at a scanning event. This would include unpublished original documents like family correspondence, diaries, or journals; paper certificates, diplomas, licenses, or awards; original poetry, stories, or written narratives; unpublished maps or original drawings.

The organization will only have a digital copy. It needs to obtain consent to preserve and back up the digital copy; create access copies; digitally deliver access copies to the public, hopefully through the World Wide Web, possibly through proprietary software; and allow researchers to use, cite, and publish the scanned records. Because the institution will only own a copy of the original, it makes more sense to license its use from the copyright holder than execute a deed of gift.

What if the community member doesn't own the rights to the materials or doesn't know who does? The on-site designated copyright specialist should speak with the community member to see whether a reasonable determination can be made. For example, with photos, ask the person how they got the photos. Did she or a family member take the photos? Were they bought from the public-school photographer or other professional photographer? Examine the photos for clues. These are the same types of questions a person asks when conducting a copyright risk analysis as discussed in chapter 6. This information should be recorded at the time of the conversation, possibly using one of the risk analysis forms already referenced in the copyright section. Consider asking the community member to sign and date the document recording the information collected to affirm it was recorded accurately. If she doesn't, the institutional representative conducting the interview should sign and date the document, which should be put on file for as long as the scanned copy is retained. If it is concluded that the community member probably owns the copyright, execute a license agreement with them. If it seems unlikely they own the copyright, try to obtain contact information for whoever does in the case they are someone the community member knows (a relative, neighbor, etc.). If the copyright holder is unknown, the organization may decide to scan the item anyway if it is highly desirable for their collection and conduct further research later. It is always possible to discard or sequester items of questionable copyright. But again, document the information gathered at the time from the community member, and sign and date the notes.

Forms and Documentation

Besides documenting pertinent copyright information for the records to be scanned, the organization will want to collect information from community members about themselves and the materials they bring for scanning. This may be the only time the institution interacts with the community member, or he might be readily available by telephone to answer follow-up questions. Better to plan for the former while hoping for the latter.

Create a separate form to collect the donor's contact information and whatever information is known about the records brought for scanning. What are they? What is their date or best estimate? Who created them? If known, collect biographical information about the creator. If the creator is unknown, record that. Where geographically were they created and for what purpose? How did the community member acquire the records? Did he create them, buy them, receive them, or inherit them? Did they come out of someone else's attic? Whose attic and where (complete address). Also gather any other information that might provide context for the records and how to interpret them. Ideally this information would be recorded electronically for legibility and manipulability, enabling text to be copied and pasted into an accession record or other reuse. This information gathering can be another station in the workflow process on scanning day.

Conditions or Limitations

A scanning event will have a set capacity for the number of potential scans that can be created based upon the number of scanners and scanner operators available, the time the equipment requires to create a scan based on resolution settings, and the number of hours set for the event. Event planners should decide beforehand what scanning resolutions will be used (create a printed chart), set up a file structure in the (temporary) directory where the images will be scanned, and settle on file naming conventions (write those out also) and other details so time is maximized in scanning. Using this information, an experienced scanner operator should be able to make a rough estimate of the number of scans possible in the time available.

Use the estimate of total possible scans to potentially set a cap on the maximum number of items per person to scan. It won't be possible to accommodate a person who brings in twenty-five or fifty pieces. The event should provide an opportunity to start relationships with people new to your organization, a bit like a first date. Based on what they bring in and describe, the organization might like to follow up with them individually, spending more time on their materials. At a certain point in the event, if the time required to scan the materials that have been prescreened equals the amount of time left for the scanning event, it might be necessary to shut the door and not allow additional people to get in line. Depending upon the number of people, how long they have been waiting, and other factors, it might require some tact to explain that the event has reached capacity. Have a plan for how to handle such a happy circumstance. Do you want to take the contact information for local people who could return another day? Do you want to chat with them to determine how well their materials fit your collection policy? If their materials sound on target, how much do they have? Is this material you would prefer to acquire versus scan? Can you set a date for them to bring their materials back for scanning or would a house call to assess the materials be possible?

Another option might be to offer online registration for the event. This would ideally make it possible to limit the number of people in advance by asking how many items they plan to bring. If an individual cap is set, build that into the registration form. Close registration once the maximum number of scans is reached. The registration can capture contact information in advance as well as contextual and biographical information. This method requires the community member to interpret your form questions, which could result in incomplete information. An in-person interview allows the organizational representative to respond to the initial information and redirect it if it seems off target or ask follow-up questions. In the case of a limited number of people to carry out all the tasks on scanning day, this option might be a compromise. Set the registration up such that the forms are completed online and submitted at the time of registration to avoid paperwork being left at home. Be prepared with blank forms though, just in case.

Another question is whether the institution will offer copies of the scanned items back to the community member. Sometimes people are happy to share their history and find others who also value it and that is enough for them. Some people want digital copies of family records but are unable to make them themselves. Perhaps a public thank-you as a supporter will suffice. Think about your purpose for the day, collection building, relationship development, potential expenses, and the logistics of delivering something in return, then decide.

Workflow

Preliminary screening of materials brought for scanning to confirm they are what the organization seeks topically and otherwise; a copyright assessment; completion of a licensing agreement; and collection of contact information, contextual information for the records, and biographical information of the records' creator have all been identified as tasks to perform prior to scanning. Depending upon space and personnel, each of these could be separate stations the community member progresses through before reaching the scanning station(s), or a single person could complete all the tasks in sequence. Balance the length of time required to complete these steps with people's willingness to wait. Is it possible to make waiting more comfortable with chairs to sit? Might light refreshments ease waiting and be a nice thank-you to those who share their materials?

Alternate to One Scanning Day

Instead of trying to accommodate a large number of people with records to scan in a single day, one northern Kentucky public library publicizes their desire to scan local records to distribute via the internet for researchers to use. Residents bring materials to the library and leave them for two weeks for library employees to review and scan as their schedule permits. The library signs a digitization agreement with the owner of the material, documenting their consent to distribution of digital copies of the materials to the public via the internet. See appendixes B.11.a and B.11.b.

Other Information

Newspaper articles might be offered for scanning. Those are published. Any actively published newspaper is likely to object to unauthorized digitization of their publication. Many newspapers, whether currently published or closed, have already been digitized and are offered commercially in microform or in a subscription electronic database. Clippings that fail to record the name and date of the original source can't be cited by researchers. When undated, they are not helpful in determining an accurate sequence of events. An article written a week after an event versus fifty years later presents dissimilar historical contexts. The socially accepted norms will have changed in that time but minus a date this can't be easily determined. Random news clippings have low research value and present copyright problems. The author would recommend against scanning them.

Additional Reading/Resources

General

American Association for State and Local History. *StEPs: Standards and Excellence Program for History Organizations Workbook*. Nashville, TN: American Association for State and Local History, 2009. See Stewardship of Collections, standard 2, pp. 183–85.

Code Sector. "TeraCopy for Windows." Accessed August 17, 2019. http://www.codesector.com/teracopy. This is a Windows tool for quickly copying files that reports errors, permits pause and resume of a file transfer, and doesn't change file creation dates, which helps maintain authenticity of files.[10]

Drake, Nate. "Best Cloud Storage of 2019 Online: Free, Paid and Business Options." *TechRadar Pro IT Insights for Business*. Accessed October 21, 2019. https://www.techradar.com/news/the-best-cloud-storage. This article compares five cloud hosting options, presenting pros, cons, and prices.

Jain, Neeru. "Best Free Cloud Storage Solutions." Accessed October 17, 2019. https://www.whizlabs.com/blog/best-free-cloud-storage/. © Copyright 2019. Whizlabs Software Pvt. Ltd. This article presents free cloud options.

Vlajin, Branko. "Best Cloud Storage for Personal Use in 2019." Accessed October 2019. https://www.cloudwards.net/best-cloud-storage-for-personal-use/. © 2007–2019 Cloudwards.net. This article discusses the pros and cons of some cloud storage services, both free and paid.

Equipment Selection

Peterson, Kit A. "What to Look for in a Scanner: Tip Sheet for Digitizing Pictorial Materials in Cultural Institutions." Prints & Photographs Division, Library of Congress. Accessed August 17, 2019. https://www.loc.gov/rr/print/tp/LookForAScanner.pdf. This is a somewhat less technical explanation of factors to consider when selecting a scanner for digitization.

Sanders, Steve. "Steve's Digicams." Accessed August 17, 2019. http://www.steves-digicams.com/. This website reviews digital cameras, photo scanners, and printers. The Knowledge Center includes recommended reading, a technical dictionary, and how-to articles. There are also help forums. Bear in mind this site is about photography, so many aspects will not apply to care and preservation of older, archival photographs, but it can be very helpful for those topics that are pertinent.

Williams, Don. "Guides to Quality in Visual Resource Imaging, Chapter 2: Selecting a Scanner." Council on Library and Information Resources. Accessed August 17, 2019. https://www.oclc.org/research/publications/library/visguides/visguide2.htm. This is somewhat technical advice on selecting a scanner.

Digitization

Cornell University Library Research Department. "Moving Theory into Practice: Digital Imaging Tutorial." Accessed August 17, 2019. http://preservationtutorial.library.cornell.edu/conversion/

conversion-01.html. This is a good basic online tutorial explaining how to digitize archival documents and photographs. It explains vocabulary, factors in selecting material for digitization, factors to consider when digitizing, and workflow; discusses scanners and how to manage files of images or documents; asks how the digitized material will be presented or used, which impacts other decisions; and addresses how to preserve digital files. The tutorial is broken into small, manageable chunks and includes examples to test understanding and additional resources.

J. Paul Getty Trust. "Introduction to Imaging, rev. ed." Accessed August 17, 2019. http://www.getty.edu/research/publications/electronic_publications/introimages/intro.html. This site explains terms and concepts associated with digitization and discusses standards and metadata. Then it proceeds to workflow: project planning, equipment, delivery of scanned material, and more. Includes a glossary and resources.

Library of Congress. "Preservation Guidelines for Digitizing Library Materials." Accessed September 19, 2019. http://www.loc.gov/preservation/care/scan.html#skip_menu. This site discusses how to care for materials during digitization to prevent damaging them.

Lyrasis. "Digital Toolbox." Accessed August 31, 2019. https://www.lyrasis.org/services/Pages/Digital-Toolbox.aspx. Participants in the Colorado Digitization Program created many of the resources available here.

Peterson, Kit A. "Digital Master Images Sample Technical Specifications for Photograph Collections." Prints and Photographs Division, Library of Congress. Accessed August 17, 2019. https://www.loc.gov/rr/print/tp/DgtlMastersSamplSpecsSelctdRcmndFinal7_2004.pdf. This chart lists recommendations from various institutions for spatial resolution and tonal values for different-size originals.

———. "Introduction to Basic Measures of a Digital Image for Pictorial Collections." Prints and Photographs Division, Library of Congress. Accessed August 17, 2019. https://www.loc.gov/rr/print/tp/IntroDgtlImage.pdf. This article defines vocabulary for digital images and explains image resolution in a manner that aids decisions about choosing the image resolution when digitizing photographs, and some other basics. This may seem technical, but many resources are even more so.

Ritzenthaler, Mary Lynn, Diane Vogt-O'Connor, Helena Zinkham, Brett Carnell, and Kit Peterson. *Photographs Archival Care and Management.* Chicago: Society of American Archivists, 2006. Chapter 12, "Digitizing Photographs," addresses planning a conversion project, digitization guidelines, and managing digital images.

Sustainable Heritage Network, Center for Digital Scholarship and Curation at Washington State University. Accessed August 17, 2019. https://sustainableheritagenetwork.org/digital-heritage/digitizing-scrapbooks-tutorial. This site includes PowerPoint presentations or video tutorials on how to digitize photographs, negatives, and scrapbooks; how to develop a digitization workflow with a sample workflow, and how to batch convert preservation TIFFs to access JPGs. It includes many additional resources.

US Department of Interior. National Park Service. Museum Management Program. "Conserve O Grams." National Park Service. Accessed September 19, 2019. https://www.nps.gov/museum/publications/conserveogram/cons_toc.html. See particularly:

19/21, "Planning Digital Projects for Preservation and Access" and

19/22, "Managing Digital Projects for Preservation and Access" for guidance on planning and managing digitization projects.

Notes

1. Kit A. Peterson, "What to Look for in a Scanner," Washington, DC: Library of Congress, accessed August 17, 2019, https://www.loc.gov/rr/print/tp/LookForAScanner.pdf. See also Mary Lynn Ritzenthaler, Diane Vogt-O'Connor, Helena Zinkham, Brett Carnell, and Kit Peterson, *Photographs: Archival Care and Management* (Chicago: Society of American Archivists, 2006); the chart on p. 395 compares and contrasts the advantages of each of these three methods of digital capture.

2. Ritzenthaler et al., *Photographs*, 388–89.

3. Ritzenthaler et al., *Photographs*, 390–91; Kit A. Peterson, "Introduction to Basic Measures of a Digital Image for Pictorial Collections," Washington, DC: Library of Congress, accessed August 17, 2019, https://www.loc.gov/rr/print/tp/IntroDgtlImage.pdf, particularly the table labeled "There's More to High Resolution Than DPI."

4. Kit A. Peterson, "Digital Master Images—Sample Technical Specifications for Photograph Collections," Prints and Photographs Division, Library of Congress. https://www.loc.gov/rr/print/tp/DgtlMastersSampl SpecsSelctdRcmndFinal7_2004.pdf.

5. Ritzenthaler et al., *Photographs*, 392.

6. Ritzenthaler et al., *Photographs*, 388.

7. Code Sector, "TeraCopy for Windows," accessed June 28, 2019, http://www.codesector.com/teracopy.

8. Wikipedia, s.v., "file hosting service," "cloud storage," accessed October 21, 2019, https://en.wikipedia .org/wiki/File_hosting_service, https://en.wikipedia.org/wiki/Cloud_storage.

9. On January 23, 2019, it was announced that DuraSpace and Lyrasis plan to merge: https://duraspace .org/amplifying-impact-lyrasis-and-duraspace-announce-intent-to-merge-2/. Management of DSpace software will move to a new division of Lyrasis.

10. Code Sector, "TeraCopy for Windows."

8

Reference and Researchers

The previous chapters of this book have discussed obtaining and preparing archival records for their eventual use by external researchers or by the institution itself for exhibits or possible digitization. Once a new collection of interest has been processed, the institution might announce its availability for use in the institution's print or electronic newsletters or on its website or blog. It may also post notices in professional association newsletters. Not every new acquisition will merit the effort to publicize it. For those that do, it is worth the effort because it provides positive publicity for the institution and may attract new donations.

What happens when a researcher asks to use archival records? What is the reference process like? What are the staff member's responsibilities? When researchers arrive for the first time to conduct research in an archives, they are often unfamiliar with how the archives functions, how collections are arranged and described, how to conduct archival research, and how to safely handle archival records.

Bruce W. Dearstyne, former program director at the New York State Archives, says that new archival researchers "are often not well prepared to use historical records." They fail to conduct preparatory research in secondary sources before visiting the archives. Since people are more familiar with how libraries operate and since so many archives are located in libraries, new or casual researchers often "assume that historical records are in reality library materials" and therefore are organized the same way as library materials. They expect quick, easy, direct access to exactly the information they need. They assume that the historical records custodian will act as their research assistant and that the institution must be open for the convenience of the researcher. These same researchers are surprised by security requirements and restrictions on how materials may be used or handled.[1]

Knowing that inexperienced researchers are initially not well prepared to conduct archival research, how does the staff interact with a researcher to obtain the most productive outcome? The staff and the researcher must have a two-way exchange of information in order for the reference process to move forward successfully. The primary purpose for this exchange is for the staff member to determine the researcher's information needs and meet them to the best of his ability. How well he is able to accomplish this depends in part on the researcher's preparation and time constraints, the amount of time the staff member can devote to an individual researcher, the records available to answer the reference question, and the state of their finding aids, among other factors.[2]

A logical first step in the reference process is to provide at least a brief orientation to the institution: the subjects, formats, or focus of its collections; rules, guidelines, or policies for the use, handling, and citation of materials; and services available to the researcher, including rules and policies for photocopying, requests for photo reproduction, and any applicable fees. The format for an orientation may be a film, written documents, or a verbal explanation (see appendixes A.1 and A.2 for sample guidelines for researcher conduct in the reading room).

During registration, the research patron should be asked for identification in order to verify his identity and to provide written consent to follow important policies or guidelines. In addition to the formal registration process that often is valid for a period of time, researchers should register every day they conduct research. This is useful not only for statistical purposes but also as a security measure. In case of theft, the institution would have proof in the individual's own handwriting that he was in the reading room on a given day.[3] More will be said about the registration process in chapter 9, "Security."

The reference interview, sometimes called an entrance interview, is a dialogue between the reference staff and the patron. It requires good communication skills from both participants in order to be successful. The staff member gathers information from the patron; tries to determine what the patron is really seeking; provides information, advice, or instruction as needed; and requests feedback to determine whether the patron's information needs have been met. This process may be repeated several times as the question is refined or narrowed.

In order to determine what the researcher's topic or question is, the staff member should ask a lot of questions. He should ask the patron to describe his research question in detail, about completed preliminary research, and how much time he has available to research. As he conducts the interview, the staff member is considering which collections may provide the requested information. Specific information such as names, dates, and locations may eliminate a collection under consideration.

The biggest problem the staff member faces is that many patrons' research questions are poorly formed.[4] Many times, the true question is not the one initially posed. The researcher does not ask for the information he really needs. He may not want to divulge his real question. Sometimes he thinks he knows what he wants and arrives requesting a specific item that he believes will answer his question. This may be based on his review of information the institution makes available to the public through a catalog or website, the instructions of a teacher, or another source. Sometimes he is correct, but sometimes his assumption is inaccurate or incomplete. If the researcher does not ask clearly for what he wants, he may fail to receive the full benefit of the staff member's knowledge and miss important information. Some researchers don't even know what information they really want. Researcher inexperience or misassumptions as described by Dearstyne above—their lack of understanding about how archival records are organized or how archives function—contribute to difficulty in clearly explaining the researcher's information needs.

Many researchers may be uncomfortable asking for research help or may be unaware of the services available to them. Sometimes their command of English contributes to their reluctance to ask questions. The staff person should try to put researchers at ease about asking questions or for assistance.

As the staff person moves between refining the research question and identifying which archival records could potentially answer the question, he may ask further questions about how the information will be used. Is the research for something to be published, used personally, or submitted as part of a homework assignment? The staff member must mediate between what he knows is or is not permitted—by copyright, fair use, donor restrictions, other laws, or even institutional policies—and the researcher's request. He asks questions to help him sort through potential restrictions, identifying which may apply. Some answers may eliminate material from consideration. Sometimes the restrictions come in to play later, once specific records have been identified as useful. Another question is whether a specific format is required for the information the researcher needs. Is a photocopy acceptable, or is a publication-quality electronic file required? The format type, its quality, and the time available to obtain it may further eliminate records from consideration.

Depending on institutional resources, the number of people available to answer research questions, and other demands on their time, a staff person will have a limited amount of time to spend with an individual researcher. He balances his time with the researcher's information needs, research skills, and the records most likely to yield an adequate answer in his recommendation of which records to consult. At this point, he recommends potential collections, materials, or resources to the researcher and offers advice on how to proceed with his research. If there are any inventories or other finding aids for those particular materials, he should explain where they are located and how to use them. He may even refer the researcher to resources he knows about that are located at other institutions. If there are likely to be any fees involved for the proposed line of research, these should be explained up front. Sometimes another researcher is pursuing a related line of research that would be of interest to the current researcher. Researchers have a right to privacy about their research topics and the resources they have used. Some researchers are willing to share this information with other researchers, but they should give the institution permission before a staff member shares this information with a second researcher.[5]

After the reference interview, the researcher proceeds to the research area or reading room where he will work. For security reasons, before he reaches the reading room, he should leave his personal belongings in a secure locker, taking only notepaper and pencils (or a laptop) and research notes into the research room. If lockers are not possible, provide a secure place as far away as possible from the research tables to store coats, wet umbrellas, and other personal possessions. A coat rack and umbrella stand would be a start. If the location can be monitored by staff, book bags and everything except women's purses can still be left at a distance from the research tables. The purpose is twofold: security and preservation minimize the risk of theft and avoid clutter or moisture that could damage the records.

Once the researcher has reached the reading room, he is likely to review finding aids or other forms of description to decide which records he would like to use. He will call for or request records. In professionally managed archives, the records are stored in an area accessible only to staff members. This is a *closed stack* system. The procedure for records retrieval varies by institution. Some institutions require researchers to submit a written request for specific material, and in others the researcher simply asks verbally. For the security of your collections, a written record is preferable. It is also advisable to limit researchers to one container of records at a time. Not only is this preferred for security purposes, but it also reduces the likelihood of misfiling records. A staff member retrieves the desired material and provides additional instruction about the use of the particular material or related finding aids if needed. This is an opportune time to provide further instruction about how to safely handle archival records, explain less well-known formats, or provide additional information about the organization of the records that were requested. The staff member should check back with the researcher after he has worked a while to determine whether he has further questions, the records are actually pertinent to the research, or he needs other assistance. If his research appears to be going well, this should be a quick inquiry that only minimally interrupts progress. If the records do not seem to yield the information being sought, perhaps further discussion to clarify, confirm, or refine the research question would be useful, or perhaps it is time to try another group of records. Experience and the researcher's response will guide you.

When the researcher completes his work, he should have contact with a staff person again prior to his departure. In institutions with a high priority on security, boxes may be examined to ensure that no records are missing or misfiled. Some institutions reserve the right to examine the researcher's papers, materials, or laptop. The staff person should at least briefly inquire how useful the collections were, how helpful the finding aids and staff members were, and whether there were any problems with the finding aids or the records. This information may help the staff identify weaknesses and make improvements. Sometimes the researcher is more knowledgeable than the staff person about the subject content of the records. He may be able to provide additional information or point out errors in the finding aid or mislabeled or misidentified items. Establishing a good rapport with knowledgeable researchers is mutually beneficial.[6]

Duplication of Materials

In addition to wanting to examine records, researchers are likely to request duplication of the information they locate in order to reuse it for their own purposes. They may request copies of material instead of taking notes. They may request copies of photographs to use in a publication or other commercial project. The original material they request to be copied will be either published or unpublished. Copyright, fair use, educational use, and the TEACH Act were all discussed at some length in chapter 6 relative to photographs. Resources for further research were listed at the end of that chapter. The same laws that apply to photographs also apply to text. Someone will have to evaluate the nature of the original material to be copied, the researcher's intended use, and the previously mentioned laws along with other factors to determine whether a request to photocopy or duplicate material can be fulfilled.

If an institution is so small that it does not have a photocopier or scanner, this discussion is moot; researchers will be required to take their own notes. A cautionary warning is merited. Dishonest researchers may resort to theft of originals if legitimate copies are not easily obtainable. If the institution does have a photocopier, it will have to decide who will photocopy material—the staff or the researchers themselves. While it may be faster to allow researchers to conduct self-service photocopying, it is more common that staff perform photocopying for several reasons. First, all institutions reserve the right to refuse to duplicate (photocopy or scan) any archival material that might be damaged by the process. The condition of the source material may be so fragile or unwieldy that it would be damaged. Second, staff members are more likely to handle the originals with care during duplication, less likely to misfile material after duplication, and less likely to accidently give the original to the researcher. Finally, staff members are more likely to be better informed about copyright and therefore not infringe on copyright when duplicating published or unpublished materials.

In either case, it is highly recommended to post a copy of the Copyright Warning Notice near the photocopy machine to reduce the institution's risk and raise the patron's awareness about his responsibility for copyright infringement (see appendix A.3). Some institutions require written requests for photocopies. Their form includes the Copyright Warning Notice just mentioned. The researcher acknowledges his responsibility for copyright compliance when he signs the photocopy request form.[7]

Researchers will also request copies of photographs. Chapter 6 included extensive information about setting up a method for the reproduction of photographs, potential problems and solutions, issues regarding copyright, and the development of a fee structure and photo contract.

Any fees that the institution is likely to charge a researcher should be brought to the researcher's attention before he incurs an expense. The most common fees might be mentioned right away during the reference interview. The other logical time would be once the research question has been clearly defined and potential records have been identified. Reproduction fees vary by format. Knowing that a researcher will work with photographs, oral histories, or manuscript records should indicate the fees most likely to apply to his line of research. The institution should formally develop a fee structure and make it available to researchers via the internet or in print.

Institutions often require researchers who conduct research for publication or other commercial purposes to submit a written request describing the specific material they would like to use and the final product in which they would like to incorporate the institution's records. Contracts describing the conditions for publication or commercial use of photographs were also discussed in chapter 6. While it is common practice to charge fees for the publication of images, it is not common when quoting text from unpublished manuscripts. However, written requests are still made for the institution's permission to quote from its documents or records. The requests document who used what material, when, and how.

In the case of records that are fragile or are in poor physical condition, that are anticipated to receive heavy usage, or have high intrinsic value (making them desirable to thieves), institutions should consider the use of *surrogate copies*. The originals would be removed from their respective collections, locked up, and replaced with surrogates that researchers would use for most requests. If a request absolutely required the examination of the original, it would be done in a more controlled setting than usual. Depending on the condition of the originals, the surrogates might be created by photocopying, scanning, or digital photography. The surrogates could be made available in the reading room or even over the internet, also increasing access.

Care of Records During Research

Once processing is completed, new collections of records are ready to be used. Archival records are preserved in order to make them available for use. However, depending on the physical condition of the records and how they are handled by staff and researchers, usage and exhibition can cause damage and shorten their life span. People who manage and care for archival, historical, or cultural collections must balance the needs of people who use the collections and the needs of the collections to be used in a safe manner that causes the least damage. The same safe handling practices already described for archival records during processing or for photographs apply during their use by patrons (see appendixes A.1 and A.2 for guidance on safe handling practices for archival records and photographs). These apply equally to staff members and researchers. If anything, staff members should model safe practices for researchers.

When staff members retrieve books for researchers, if they place a *pull card* (see appendix B.5) on the shelf where the book was removed, this will aid in reshelving the book in its correct location. It also calls attention to the fact that something was removed and needs to be returned. This can be useful in reducing misshelving by new people as well as quicker identification of potentially lost or misplaced books. A pull card can be as simple as an acid-free file folder that is placed on the shelf. It would be useful to annotate the date on which the book is removed from the shelf, the call number, and the initials of the person removing the book. All this information will be helpful if a book does go astray or should be stolen. When the book is returned to the shelf, the pull card is annotated again with the date and initials of the person who reshelves it. The pull card is returned to a convenient location near where books are shelved. Acid-free pull cards are also available from archival vendors. They have preprinted lines for recording the information already mentioned.

Pull cards are also useful when folders are removed from a manuscript box, whether by a staff member or a research patron. The sequence for filing folders will be very clear in some boxes because the folders are numbered or there is an alphabetic or chronological sequence for the folder titles. When the folder headings do not follow an obvious sequence, pull cards are useful for ensuring that the folder arrangement is maintained. Use only acid-free folders as pull cards in the manuscript boxes. Whereas they are meant to mark the removal of a folder for only a very short time, annotations shouldn't be necessary.

A book pillow and book snakes are other accessories that may aid in the safe handling of books, scrapbooks, or other bound items in poor or fragile condition. A book pillow is just what it sounds like: a pillow made of archivally safe materials on which a bound item is placed to provide support for the spine and covers. The pillow should be larger than the bound item. Book snakes are long, skinny tubes of unbleached fabric containing weights. When placed at the edge of a page, the weight will hold the page open. The weights reduce the amount of time a person's hand comes in contact with the page itself, minimizing potential for the transfer of harmful substances to the archival item or rare book. Unless there are issues getting a bound item to open most of the way, a book snake could be placed on both pages of a book to make it stay open for examination.

Sometimes pieces of foam in combinations of flat rectangles and triangular wedges are used in lieu of a book pillow to provide support for fragile items. Purchase them from an archival vendor to ensure that they won't chemically interact with the archival items or rare books. Another option is to place a book of similar thickness under the open cover to support the binding.

Security for Records

Archival records may be removed from their collection for longer periods of time if they are used for exhibits, sent out for conservation or digitization, or loaned to other institutions. If an item is removed from the collection for more than several hours and leaves the archives, its removal should be marked. A good technique would be to photocopy the item that is removed and note the date, the reason the item was removed, and where it went. For example, a document is removed for an internal exhibit that will last two months. Two photocopies of the document are made and annotated "Jan 15, 2011, equestrian exhibit, L. Hamill." The first copy marks the place in the manuscript box where the original belongs. If the original is not returned or is misfiled, whenever that box is used, the photocopied placeholder will flag that the original is missing and that someone should check on it. It also informs researchers of the existence of the original even if it is not currently in its storage box. The second photocopy is annotated with the identity of the manuscript box from which the original was removed. In the case of an exhibit, a master file is created for each exhibit, and the second photocopy is put in the exhibit folder. When the exhibit is taken down, there will be no doubt about where the material should be returned. This eliminates reliance on staff memory and accommodates changes in personnel.

A centralized withdrawal log that records the departure and return of anything that leaves the archives can help keep track of records, objects, or equipment. People are busy with numerous responsibilities; staff, volunteers, or others may not work full-time; and personnel can change. The withdrawal log provides a single point of control for anything that leaves and serves as a reminder that there is material that is still out. It makes it easier to ensure that whatever leaves also returns. The second photocopy mentioned above can be attached to a withdrawal form to be very clear about what was removed from the collection. For example, five photographs are removed to be taken to a reliable vendor to make duplicate copies for a reference request. Attaching a photocopy of each photo to a single withdrawal form documents precisely which photos left for duplication. The withdrawal forms should be kept permanently. They are useful for answering other questions besides whether an item was returned, especially in the case of photographs that are reproduced for researchers (see appendix B.6).

How to Locate Records for a Reference Request

Various methods can be used to locate records in response to a reference question. To some extent, the search process will depend on specific institutional practices. In general, the archival records at each institution will be unique. This means that a staff person who answers research questions needs to know the institution's collection policy, the specific collections it owns, the kind of material in each collection, and the type of information that is typically found therein. This knowledge takes time to acquire and is valuable. It is called *institutional knowledge*.

The staff person should ask, "Who would have created records with the kind of information or about the topic that the researcher is seeking?" If collections have been processed, the staff person will be able to use the collection inventory or other finding aids to help locate relevant material to answer the research question. If collections are unprocessed or poorly processed, whatever finding aids exist will not be very helpful for locating suitable material. If finding aids are poor or nonexistent, the tendency is to search the boxes directly, resulting in excessive handling and an increased risk for damage or loss. Or suitable materials are simply overlooked because of ignorance of their existence. Doing a proper job of arranging and describing a collection is an investment that pays off whenever the collection is used. It makes it easier to find information more reliably and efficiently and reduces unnecessary handling and potential damage.

Depending on institutional resources and practices, the staff person tries to locate the box of records that will answer the research question. It is the researcher's task to examine the records and determine what is pertinent or useful to him. If the question originates from an important internal office or person, the staff person may continue the research himself until he answers the question or determines the absence of sufficient information to answer the question. At this point, he would inform the office or person of the results.

Searching for Records in PastPerfect

Chapters 4 and 5 explained how to create description, or catalog records in PastPerfect. During searches for pertinent records, the information that was previously entered into the software will be used to locate records. This would be a good way to test the catalog records and determine whether changes should be made to the descriptive process. Refer to chapter 14 of the PastPerfect Version 5 user's guide for details on how to search by **Keyword**, **People**, **Search Terms**, or **Lexicon** in one, several, or all catalogs simultaneously.

The Value of Research Use

Funding for archives, museums, and other cultural heritage organizations is often limited. Demonstrating the value of your archives will prove useful when arguing for resources, applying for grants, speaking with donors and supporters, and promoting the organization through social media, print publicity, or other opportunities. Knowing who your researchers are and which materials they are using is useful for management decisions. Should a potential donation on a particular topic be accepted? Are there items in more heavily used collections that would benefit from preservation work? Are more heavily used collections or subsets thereof candidates for digitization to reduce wear and make them more widely available?

Assessment of research activity will help answer questions like these. A joint archival-library task force developed a standard for assessing public service/reference interactions that was adopted by the respective professional associations in late 2017 and early 2018. The *Standardized Statistical Measures and Metrics for Public Services in Archival Repositories and Special Collections Libraries* defines eight domains or different areas of public service and provides specific definitions for each data to collect, specific examples, and rationale for how the data could be used. Each domain defines baseline data to collect and then offers optional advanced data the institution might choose to collect. This tiered approach enables an organization to select what is within its ability to document and allows for a range of technology to gather and record the data. Start with a minimum set of manageable statistics for a trial period of one year. Think about which statistics are likely to answer basic management questions. Also consider what information, if any, might be required for annual reports or other types of reports the organization might be required to complete. At the end of the year, assess what did or didn't work and determine whether adjustments are needed. If the process is working, additional helpful statistics can be added over time. Paper and pencil forms, electronic spreadsheets, or other software can be used to record statistics.

Sometimes during the course of assisting a researcher or answering a reference question it is possible to determine how the information will be used, that is, the final product. Is it helping a student complete a school assignment or an employee to create a slide show for the president's gala to thank donors? Will the researcher publish an article or book? Is the request for an image to include in a film or external exhibit? These are a few examples of how the archives is supporting student success, donor work, faculty publication or humanities research, or products that raise the visibility of the organization. Many requests will be routine, but where the final use is known and more notable, documenting it will be beneficial. The requests might be reported as specific examples of support provided in the annual report. Very visible uses might be reported to donors, especially when a credit line is given for the institution's contribution. The institution might publicize its contribution to an exhibit or published work in social media or other publicity. Some grant applications specifically ask for measurements of and examples of support for humanities research. If the organization can collect examples before they are needed, they will have examples to cite, thus strengthening their application.

Additional Reading/Resources

American Association for State and Local History. *StEPs: Standards and Excellence Program for History Organizations Workbook.* Nashville, TN: American Association for State and Local History, 2009. Section 2: Audience discusses collecting visitor information, access to archival resources, and programming, all of which would benefit by collection of standardized data about usage.

Dearstyne, Bruce W. *Managing Historical Records Programs: A Guide for Historical Agencies.* Walnut Creek, CA: AltaMira Press, 2000. Chapter 7 discusses the role of a person providing reference assistance and typical steps in the process. Appendix 9 has a nice checklist of questions an institution can ask about what it does, its policies, and so on to make records available to researchers.

Hunter, Gregory S. *Developing and Maintaining Practical Archives: A How-to-Do-It Manual.* 2nd ed. How-to-Do-It Manuals for Librarians, no. 122. New York: Neal-Schuman, 2003. See chapter 9, particularly pp. 219–23, for a discussion of the entrance interview, reading room activities, and the exit interview.

Pugh, Mary Jo. *Providing Reference Services for Archives and Manuscripts.* Archival Fundamentals Series II. Chicago: Society of American Archivists, 2005.

Ritzenthaler, Mary Lynn. "Preservation of Archival Records: Holdings Maintenance at the National Archives." Technical Information Paper No. 6, 1990. National Archives and Records Administration. Accessed August 13, 2019. https://www.archives.gov/files/preservation/holdings-maintenance/table-of-contents.pdf. This is a free online resource with good basic preservation information, including some illustrations and lists of supplies where appropriate.

———. *Preserving Archives and Manuscripts.* 2nd ed. Archival Fundamentals Series II. Chicago: Society of American Archivists, 2010.

SAA-ACRL/RBMS Joint Task Force on the Development of Standardized Statistical Measures for Public Services in Archival Repositories and Special Collections Libraries. "Standardized Statistical Measures and Metrics for Public Services in Archival Repositories and Special Collections Libraries." Accessed August 10, 2019. https://www2.archivists.org/sites/all/files/Standardized%20Statistical%20Measures%20and%20Metrics%20for%20Public%20Services%20in%20Archival%20Repositories%20and%20Special%20Collections%20Libraries_011718_0.pdf.

Society of Georgia Archivists. Accessed September 26, 2019. https://soga.wildapricot.org/resource/forms. This website provides a variety of examples of forms to use with researchers as well as others like deed of gift and loan documents.

US Department of the Interior. National Park Service. Museum Management Program. "Conserve O Grams." National Park Service. Accessed August 13, 2019. www.nps.gov/museum/publications/conserveogram/cons_toc.html. See particularly:

19/3, "Use and Handling of Rare Books,"

19/17, "Handling Archival Documents and Manuscripts," and

19/18, "How to Care for Bound Archival Materials."

Witt, Betsy S., Jennifer C. Whitfield, and Adam J. Stepansky. *PastPerfect Software for Museum Collections: Version 5 User's Guide.* Exton, PA: PastPerfect Software, Inc., 2010. Chapter 14 explains how to conduct searches and use results to manage the collection.

Resources for Locating Archival Records

Library of Congress. "Browse Finding Aids by Collection Title." Accessed August 13, 2019. http://findingaids.loc.gov/browse/collections/a. The A-Z index list of collections held by the Library of Congress.

_____. NUCMC. The National Union Catalog for Manuscript Collections. Accessed August 13, 2019. https://www.loc.gov/coll/nucmc/index.html. Originally people processed archival or manuscript collections and submitted information about the collection to NUCMC, which published information in their next print volume. This is now available electronically. This is a way to search nationally for processed collections on particular topics, people, etc.

Notes

1. Bruce W. Dearstyne, *Managing Historical Records Programs: A Guide for Historical Agencies* (Walnut Creek, CA: AltaMira Press, 2000), 103.

2. Telephone conversation, December 31, 2010, with archivist Mark Savolis; Dearstyne, *Managing Historical Records Programs*, 107.

3. Gregory S. Hunter, *Developing and Maintaining Practical Archives: A How-to-Do-It Manual*, 2nd ed., How-to-Do-It Manuals for Librarians, no. 122 (New York: Neal-Schuman, 2003), 221–22.

4. Telephone conversation, Savolis.

5. Dearstyne, *Managing Historical Records Programs*, 107–8; Hunter, *Developing and Maintaining Practical Archives*, 220–21.

6. Hunter, *Developing and Maintaining Practical Archives*, 223; telephone conversation, Savolis.

7. Hunter, *Developing and Maintaining Practical Archives*, 228–29.

9

Security

Now that your archival records are ready for use by researchers and in other ways, it is important to discuss how to keep them safe. Unfortunately, many small to midsize organizations, especially those that are managed predominantly by volunteers, are not well prepared to protect their collections from theft. They fail to recognize the historical or cultural significance or the financial value of what they own. They are largely unaware of professional practices to safeguard their collections. Unfortunately, there are many unscrupulous people who have taken advantage of ignorance or laxness on the part of these organizations and stolen materials that can never be replaced. All too often, even professionally run organizations have been the target of clever and persistent thieves. It is embarrassing to admit that material has been stolen, but publicity about a theft may alert potential buyers, aid in recovery or prosecution, and serve as a warning to other institutions.

A well-publicized thief named E. Forbes Smiley III stole antique maps from the Boston Public Library, Harvard University, and other libraries primarily in New England. Smiley was caught in 2005, convicted in 2006, and started serving a three-and-a-half-year jail term in 2007. Additionally, he was ordered to pay $2.3 million in restitution.[1]

In September 2008, James Lyman Brubaker was convicted for stealing and transporting hundreds of books, maps, lithographs, and more from libraries in the western United States. Fortuitously, a librarian realized within about a week of its occurrence that maps had been cut out of some bound volumes. Realizing that they were probably going to be sold, he monitored e-Bay and identified two maps that matched descriptions of maps owned by his employer, Western Washington University. Arrangements were made to have someone else purchase the maps, which were analyzed and proven to belong to the university. The ability to prove ownership and theft of the maps led to a search warrant being issued for Brubaker's home, where an incredible quantity of stolen historical material was found. Brubaker was sentenced to thirty months in jail and restitution of $23,000.[2]

In recent years, representatives of the National Archives have attended professional conferences and shows at which private collectors buy and sell materials, such as Civil War documents and photographs, to publicize the fact that stolen records from the National Archives or the presidential libraries may occasionally turn up for purchase.

In 2006, a sharp-eyed Civil War buff who had conducted research at the National Archives twenty-five years earlier realized that documents from the National Archives were being sold on e-Bay. Denning McTague stole 164 documents during a two-month internship at the National Archives Regional Branch in Philadelphia. McTague was convicted in 2007 and sentenced to fifteen months of jail time.[3]

These are but a few highly publicized examples of thieves who stole significant historical items from professionally managed institutions. According to a 2008 Society of American Archivists Security workshop, theft of historical cultural material is among the top four most lucrative crimes. In 1987, the Rare Books and Manuscript Section, a division of the American Library Association, started maintaining a list of publicly reported thefts of cultural heritage materials (see Additional Reading/Resources at the end of this chapter for the website). Specific examples of materials most susceptible to theft include autographed documents; presidential records; material about lighthouses and railroads; black history, especially related to slavery; Native American items; stamps; ephemera; sports and war records; photographs; and vintage blank paper that can be used by forgers.[4]

Thieves may be personnel who work or volunteer in the archives or from other departments, researchers, or outside people, such as contractors or repair people. A study revealed that 15 percent of people are honest, 40 percent are relatively honest, while 45 percent are very dishonest and, given the opportunity, would steal.[5] These statistics suggest it would be unwise to test people's honesty by tempting them.

What Can an Institution Do to Protect Its Collections?

Good Practices[6]

- Conduct a security survey to assess needs.

- Assess the security of the building exterior and interior in which the institution and its collections are housed.

  o Are there ground-level access points?

  o Are there shrubs or other hiding places around the outside of the building that can be removed?

  o How secure are the locks on the doors? Are there panes of glass close enough to door or window locks to break them and unlock the door or window from the inside?

  o Are entrances and exits lit well enough to see people coming or going when the institution is closed?

- Install appropriate security systems and take other preventive measures.

- Establish good work practices and provide equitable supervision of staff and volunteers. This is as much to protect personnel from false accusations as it is to protect collections from insider theft.

  o Disgruntled employees have been known to steal from or damage collection items.

  o Employees may steal from financial need or to add to their personal collections.

  o Consider background checks for staff when consistent with institutional policies.

- Establish policies for patron behavior.

    o The most valuable items in the collection should be locked up, and researchers should use *access copies*—photocopies, microfilm, or digital copies of the originals.

    o Establish a policy of no access to unprocessed collections and apply it equally to all researchers.

- Establish policies for visitors, contractors, and those who are neither department personnel nor researchers.

    o Be clear about who has access to storage areas. Always escort people with a need for temporary access, such as repair people, and remain with them for the duration of their work.

    o Do not publicize the storage location of highly valuable items to people outside of department staff.

    o Do not give tours of the storage room and *closed stacks*.

    o Do not give keys to collection storage rooms to custodians or security police.

Security and Researchers

The physical layout of each institution will vary. Some may require a researcher to pass through at least one anteroom before reaching the research room, while others won't. Although the exact sequence of some of the following and whether they occur in the research room or prior to arrival there is not critical, it is important that the following take place before a researcher is given access to records.

Researcher Orientation and Registration

A staff member should greet researchers on their arrival to confirm that the researcher is in the right place and desires to conduct research. Researchers should not be allowed to take any unnecessary personal materials, such as coats, bags, backpacks, notebooks, or books, into the research room. Even sheaves of loose research notes can be used to hide stolen documents. Ideally, lockers or some type of secure space is provided for researchers to store their personal possessions, including women's purses. It is acceptable to require a researcher to leave photo identification on deposit when issued a locker key. If lockers are not possible, consider an alternate system to locate personal possessions away from the research tables. If this area is under regular observation, it should be safe to leave bags and backpacks, but if you can't guarantee the security of an alternative system, you may need to allow women to keep their purses.

Orientation and registration are next. As part of this process, address conduct in the research room. Clearly explain what materials and behavior or activities are or are not allowed, such as only pencils or laptops being allowed for writing and no use of cell phones, scanners, or digital cameras. If laptops are allowed in the research room, exclude their cases. It is reasonable to require researchers to sign a document that delineates (un)acceptable behavior in the reading room or how collections must be handled. A researcher's signature documents his consent to abide by the stipulated practices. An institution can refuse access to a researcher who fails to follow the institution's policies and guidelines.[7]

All researchers should register to document their identity and often their research topic as well (see appendix B.7 for a sample researcher registration form). Registration forms are typically valid for a limited duration, say, one year. This form includes information such as the researcher's name, permanent address, and other contact information; the number on the identification presented and what type it is (e.g., Kentucky driver's license); and a written signature. The researcher should present at least one photo identification card to establish his identity. Confirm that the researcher looks like his photo. Compare the information on the identification card with the completed registration form to check their consistency.

After completing registration forms, researchers should sign in on a daily research register, a formality they should complete every time they visit. The register proves the specific days that a particular researcher was at the institution. It also documents who else was in the research room on the same day in case missing documents were misfiled and not stolen.

The third component that documents researcher activity is *call slips*. Call slips should indicate the researcher who requested the material (printed legibly); the information requested by collection name or number, depending on how it is identified; the researcher's signature; and the date he received the records. A staff person initials and dates the call slip when the researcher returns the records after use. The institution needs to be able to link a specific researcher to use of a particular item. Call slips are one such link. Since many losses remain undiscovered until months or years after the fact, all these research documentation records need to be retained permanently. Research registration and call slips are filed by the researcher's last name, while the daily register is kept chronologically. In order to prosecute for theft, it is necessary to prove a person had access to the stolen items. Consistent and reliable use of these three forms, assuming that writing is legible, should provide the required proof.[8]

Depending on how busy and large an institution is, multipart call slips can be used. The first copy goes on the storage shelf from which the box of records or other item is retrieved. The second copy goes to the person or station responsible for monitoring the reading room to indicate the records currently present in the room. The third copy remains with the material itself. When the researcher returns the material, his copy of the call slip is matched with the one at the reading room station. The box can be checked to confirm that all material has been properly refiled in order. When the box is returned to the shelf, the call slip is matched with the one on the shelf to ensure that the records are returned to the correct location. The top copy is retained and filed by the researcher's last name.[9]

Some institutions use request forms for photocopying or photoduplication. These forms document not only the researcher's activity but also the institution's ownership of specific materials as of a particular date.

Managing the Research Room[10]

After storage of personal belongings, registration, and orientation, the researcher arrives at the research room or table. Once a research interview is concluded, records will be brought to the researcher.

- Ideally, the research room and access points are monitored by surveillance cameras whose recordings are retained permanently.

- In addition to security cameras, a staff person should supervise the room at all times when a researcher is present. Ideally, one person would monitor while a second retrieves records.

- The research room supervisor should move about the space regularly to observe researchers and determine whether any require additional assistance or a new box of records.

- An institution has the right to limit access to its most valuable records but should try to provide legible reproductions in their place. Photocopies qualify as acceptable reproductions.

- If a researcher absolutely must have access to originals of higher monetary value or at greater risk of theft, he can be required to use them under even more secure conditions. For example, he might work at the same table as a staff person or directly in front of the research room monitor's station, depending on the room layout.

- Limit the quantity of records a researcher uses at one time. One box is a common limit.

- It is recommended to check each box before delivering it to a researcher to review the box contents and ensure that everything is there and in order. The box is again inspected when the researcher finishes with it and returns it. If file folders are sequentially numbered in the box or can be matched against a finding aid, it will be easier to determine whether one is missing or misfiled.

- Do not allow researchers to hide behind stacks of boxes or books, archival carts, or anything else that blocks the room supervisor's view of researchers.

- Do not allow one researcher access to records requested by a different researcher in case they are working together for dishonest purposes.

- Discourage anyone who is not actively conducting research from loitering in the research room.

- Don't make photocopying overly difficult or expensive. It may encourage theft.

When researchers have finished, they should not be able to leave the room without checking back with a staff person. At a minimum, examine the material they were using when it is returned to ensure that the original file folder order has been restored and nothing looks suspicious. The call slip copy with the records can be matched with the research desk copy. An exit interview can inquire whether the researcher intends to return or whether there were problems that the institution can work to improve.

Security and Internal Processes

Collection material can be at risk not just from researchers but also from staff, volunteers, interns, and others who work for the institution. Even if a theft is committed by a researcher, the institution's employees may still undergo intense scrutiny until they are eliminated from consideration. Good work procedures protect the institution's personnel from false accusations as much as they protect the collections themselves.

Security during Processing[11]

- Provide security for collections while they are processed, not just when they are in the research room, on exhibit, or in storage.

- Be attentive to what is left out unattended, whether it is overnight or for an extended period during the day. People other than the staff responsible for collection materials can wander by—custodians, contractors, and so on. Minimize the opportunity for them to take items.

- An individual staff person should not be left alone for long periods of time working with collections. It would be better to have two or more people work where each can observe the other.

- Staff should have offices where they can work late or alone that are separated from partially processed materials or collection storage rooms.

- All personnel should store their personal belongings away from the location where processing is done or collections are stored.

- During processing identify, duplicate, and sequester the most valuable items. Some categories of high-risk archival materials were mentioned earlier in this chapter. Nineteenth-century books with photographs, engravings, maps, or other types of illustrations are also prime candidates for theft. The value of just the illustrations, if cut out, may exceed the value of the intact book.

  o Do not label boxes with words such as "valuable." Don't make it easy for thieves to identify highly desirable items.

  o Consider photographing some of these items and keeping one copy in the donor file for the collection and a second copy (locked up) off-site.

  o Consider having items worth $1,000 or more professionally appraised and photographed/photocopied. Make a list of these items and keep the list secure.

- A good finding aid enhances security because it highlights the presence of items of high value in the collection, helping to document the institution's ownership of said items. The finding aid would not say "the photo of astronaut Neil Armstrong is very valuable." It would say "photographs of the Cincinnati Airport include a group photo of Neil Armstrong with the board of managers."

- Consider a policy prohibiting researchers access to unprocessed material. If the material has not yet been thoroughly examined by staff, unless it arrived with detailed documentation, there will be no way to know if something goes missing during research use.

Security during Exhibits/Loans

Whether an institution removes materials that it owns from storage to use for an in-house exhibit or to lend to another institution for exhibit, or borrows materials from someone else for an exhibit, security should be considered. The location of all exhibit materials, whether the institution's or someone else's, needs to be tracked and accounted for throughout an exhibit. Just as a pull card or call slip is put on the storage shelf to show that a book or manuscript box has been temporarily removed for a researcher, one photocopy of each item removed from a box to use in an exhibit should be left in place of the original. Use of a photocopy avoids mistaking which item should be returned to which box. It also flags that something is missing from the box; if it is not returned, someone can check on it. The photocopy could serve as a use copy if a researcher calls for the material while the original is on exhibit. Should anything happen while the original is out of the box, there is a copy to establish what the original looked like. Annotate the place marker in the box with the reason the original was removed (exhibit, loan, etc.), when (date), and by whom.

A second copy of each photocopy is put in the exhibit file. A separate folder is created for each exhibit. The second copy is annotated with the identity of the manuscript box from which the original was removed. When the exhibit is taken down, each item is matched with its duplicate in the exhibit file to determine the proper location to which it should return. When the staff person reaches the correct box, he will see the placeholder marking the exact folder location. The original is returned to its box, and the placeholder is removed and disposed of. The duplicate set in the exhibit file is retained to document the exhibit. In the case of objects or art, especially if it is borrowed, substitute a photograph for a photocopy.

Reference requests and exhibits are not the only reason that collection materials leave permanent storage. Records, objects, or materials may leave for conservation, framing, or other purposes. Regardless of the reason, their departure should be documented and tracked. A centralized withdrawal log should be used to track what leaves the department or institution, when, who removed it, where it went, and why. When the material returns, note the return date and who received it (see appendix B.6 for a sample form). A binder with paper forms provides a low-tech solution. It is important to track the location of everything and regularly check the withdrawal log to ensure that everything is returned in a timely fashion.

Documentation that Enhances Security

An institution needs to be able to identify the materials it owns in case of theft.[12] It can create documentation from the time a new collection arrives to help protect it, starting with the deed of gift transferring legal ownership. Establish a *donor file* or *control file*, depending on the method of acquisition, in which to collect the deed of gift or other important documents about the collection. A new collection may arrive with an appraisal for monetary value or a photograph of the donation. Its donation may have been publicized. If it was bought, purchase documents should go in the control file to establish its value and *provenance* (from whom it was obtained).

As soon as possible after arrival, an accession record should be made. Restrict access to accession records so that they can't be used as a browsing list to identify potential material to steal. Some institutions have locator files or *shelf lists* that detail the specific shelf location for their holdings. New collections are likely to be entered here too. Restrict access to these lists for the same reason.

If an item is discovered missing, complete a missing item record. The form includes a description of what is missing, who discovered its absence, when and which places were checked, who double-checked locations, the last time it was seen, and to whom this information was reported. If used, retain these forms permanently in a master file. File a duplicate copy where the missing item belongs just in case it was misfiled and returns at a future date.

Good description in various finding aids has already been mentioned. During processing, especially of more valuable materials, photographs can be taken to document what items look like, their condition, markings, and so on. If the collection is lent out, put a copy of the loan form in the donor or collection file to document its departure and return. If an appraisal is obtained after arrival, put that in the collection or donor file. A variety of documents can establish continued ownership, changes in value or condition, or other pertinent information. Call slips will track usage by specific researchers on specific dates. If theft or damage should occur, all this documentation should provide the information required to respond to the situation. Without sufficient documentation, even if the thief is caught, the institution might not be able to prove ownership or prosecute.

Additional Reading/Resources

Antiquarian Booksellers' Association of America. "Stolen and Missing Books." Accessed August 23, 2019. http://hq.abaa.org/books/antiquarian/databases/stolen_search.html. Use this site to report stolen or missing books to commercial dealers.

Association of College and Research Libraries. "ACRL/RBMS Guidelines Regarding Security and Theft in Special Collections." Accessed August 23, 2019. http://www.ala.org/acrl/standards/security_theft. These guidelines focus on rare books, so some of the discussion is less applicable to archival records, such as recommendations to mark material. Discussion about the facility, staff, and researchers are all pertinent. Part II describes how to respond to a theft with detailed specific actions. It also illustrates the importance of good processing, description, and procedures with researchers. Appendix III, section IV, contains a comprehensive list of where to report thefts, depending on the format/type of material.

_____. "Guidelines on the Selection and Transfer of Materials from General Collections to Special Collections." Accessed August 23, 2019. http://www.ala.org/acrl/standards/selctransfer. Section 3.0, "Transfer Criteria," discusses criteria that may be helpful in identifying more valuable books in an institution's holdings. This could be helpful in identifying volumes that should be sequestered and given higher security and documentation.

Brown, Karen E., and Beth Lindblom Patkus. "Emergency Management 3.11: Collections Security: Planning and Prevention for Cultural Heritage Institutions." Accessed August 23, 2019. https://www.nedcc.org/assets/media/documents/Preservation%20Leaflets/3_11_CollSecurity_2020.pdf. This is an excellent presentation of security basics that will help even the smallest volunteer-run organization. It covers a wide range of security basics and lists additional resources.

Campbell, Tony. "E. Forbes Smiley III Map Thefts: Reports and News Stories." Accessed August 23, 2019. http://www.maphistory.info/smileynews.html. A compilation of articles describing the thefts committed by E. Forbes Smiley, how he was caught, and his prosecution.

Crowe, Jonathan. "Breaking News: Smiley Sentenced to 3½ Years." The Map Room, a Weblog about Maps. Accessed August 23, 2019. http://archives.maproomblog.com/2006/09/breaking_news_smiley_sentenced_to_3_years.php. More reports about the Smiley thefts.

Denver Public Library. "Recovered James Lyman Brubaker Photographs: Are They Part of Your Institution?" Accessed August 23, 2019. https://www.flickr.com/photos/dplwesternhistory/sets/72157623286262023. Details about the thefts by James Lyman Brubaker, including photographs of stolen material whose owner has not yet been identified.

Rare Books and Manuscripts Section. "RBMS Security Committee." Accessed August 23, 2019. http://rbms.info/committees/security/. This site has links to an audit tool (checklist) for security practices; resources for best practices, guidelines, and reporting thefts; a list of publicly reported thefts of cultural heritage materials; and to state laws on stolen/damaged library materials.

Society of American Archivists. "ALA/SAA Joint Statement on Access to Research Materials in Archives and Special Collections Libraries." Accessed August 23, 2019. https://www2.archivists.org/statements/alasaa-joint-statement-on-access-to-research-materials-in-archives-and-special-collection. See especially section 4 on policies.

Trinkaus-Randall, Gregor. *Protecting Your Collections: A Manual of Archival Security*. Chicago: Society of American Archivists, 1995. This book presents the basics for protecting archival records.

Twomey, Steve. "To Catch a Thief." *Smithsonian*, April 2008. An article about Denning McTague's theft of Civil War documents from the National Archives Regional Branch in Philadelphia.

US Department of the Interior. National Park Service. Museum Management Program. "Conserve O Grams." National Park Service. Accessed August 23, 2019. https://www.nps.gov/museum/publications/conserveogram/cons_toc.html. See particularly 19/2: "Care and Security of Rare Books."

Notes

1. Tony Campbell, "E. Forbes Smiley III Map Thefts: Reports and News Stories," accessed August 23, 2019, http://www.maphistory.info/smileynews.html.

2. Denver Public Library, "Recovered James Lyman Brubaker Photographs: Are They Part of Your Institution?" accessed August 23, 2019, https://www.flickr.com/photos/dplwesternhistory/sets/72157623286262023.

3. Steve Twomey, "To Catch a Thief," *Smithsonian*, April 2008, 89, 90, 94, 96, 99.

4. Mimi Bowling and Richard Strassberg, "Security in Archives and Manuscript Repositories," Society of American Archivists workshop, Louisville, KY, June 26–27, 2008.

5. Bowling and Strassberg, "Security" workshop.

6. Gregor Trinkaus-Randall, *Protecting Your Collections: A Manual of Archival Security* (Chicago: Society of American Archivists, 1995), 6; Karen E. Brown and Beth Lindblom Patkus, "Emergency Management 3.11: Collections Security: Planning and Prevention for Libraries and Archives," accessed August 23, 2019, https://www.nedcc.org/free-resources/preservation-leaflets/overview; Association of College and Research Libraries, "ACRL/RBMS Guidelines Regarding Security and Theft in Special Collections," accessed August 23, 2019, http://www.ala.org/acrl/standards/security_theft; Society of American Archivists, "ALA/SAA Joint Statement on Access to Research Materials in Archives and Special Collections Libraries, Section 4 Policies," accessed August 23, 2019, https://www2.archivists.org/statements/alasaa-joint-statement-on-access-to-research-materials-in-archives-and-special-collection.

7. Society of American Archivists, "ALA/SAA Joint Statement on Access to Research Materials."

8. Bowling and Strassberg, "Security" workshop.

9. Telephone conversation with Tom Knox, staff member at the American Antiquarian Society, Worcester, Massachusetts, October 24, 2007.

10. Association of College and Research Libraries, "ACRL/RBMS Guidelines," Section 6, Researchers; Society of American Archivists, "ALA/SAA Joint Statement"; Brown and Patkus, "Emergency Management 3.11."

11. Association of College and Research Libraries, "ACRL/RBMS Guidelines," Section 5, Staff; Brown and Patkus, "Emergency Management 3.11"; Trinkaus-Randall, *Protecting Your Collections*, 3, 5, 7, 10.

12. Association of College and Research Libraries, "ACRL/RBMS Guidelines," Section 8, The Collections.

10

Exhibits

Exhibits are one of the ways in which collections can be used after they have been arranged and described. Usually, archival exhibits highlight material from the institution's collections. They encourage people to study and learn about the past, preserve and donate historical items, or learn about archival/historical work. Well-done exhibits can pique interest and be enjoyable while educating visitors. They honor individuals or classes of people (e.g., veterans), commemorate tragedy or accomplishments, or explain a process, event, or movement. They celebrate anniversaries or are simply entertaining.

Exhibits provide opportunities to develop goodwill and new relationships, for example, with institutions or individuals involved in lending or borrowing materials. They announce newly received collections, not only in hopes of attracting new visitors, researchers, or potential donors but also to recognize and thank the donor of the new collection. The subject of an exhibit can be linked to topics taught or assignments given in formal classes or other educational programs. If the staff monitors educational initiatives in their community or a particular academic department with which their collections fit well, they may be able to identify opportunities for exhibits that support the educational program. For example, when all incoming freshmen were required to read a book by an illustrator/author about whom the archives had a modest collection, I offered to create an exhibit about the artist. This had the potential to introduce hundreds of freshmen and their professors to the archives. It was the first time the archives had worked with the Office of First Year Programs, which managed the Freshman Book Connection. It was also an opportunity for the archives to develop a stronger relationship with the artist in hopes of someday acquiring original art or records documenting his creative process. Another benefit was the increase in visitors, publicity, and visibility that can be used to argue with resource allocators for additional resources.

Archives are one example of an organization that creates exhibits, museums being another well-known example. Archives and museums both vary in size and collecting focus. Archives collect heavily in the area of paper records (text, photographs, drawings, maps) or recorded words (audio, video, or digital documents). First, because institutional archives preserve records created by their organization, archives tend to collect similar record formats when acquiring manuscript collections. Second, the types of questions these formats support often differ from what museums collect. While archives do have objects, art, and other three-dimensional items, they are not usually the primary collecting focus. Objects require a lot of space to store and specialized expertise at times beyond the norm for archivists.

The nature of the archival materials influences selection, display methods, and the stories or information their exhibits can communicate. For example, only a limited number of text documents can be used and not too densely. Photographs, T-shirts with colors and graphics, and other visually appealing materials help break up documents. Archival exhibits can be interpretive if the collections provide sufficient material with which to work. Often, they are more illustrative or factual. According to Beverly Serrell, noted museum exhibit professional, interpretive exhibits "tell stories, contrast points of view, present challenging issues, or strive to change people's attitudes." Interpretive exhibits have learning objectives. Their labels tell stories, explain, guide, question, inform, or provoke the visitor to interact with the exhibit; they do not instruct. The exhibit creator should communicate knowledge to the visitor, who adds his or her personal life experience to depart with a new understanding of the topic.[1]

Archival exhibits tend to be temporary if originals are displayed. Archivists try to preserve their collections so that the material is available for researchers as long as possible, meaning hundreds of years, not a decade or two. This goal requires constant watchfulness to protect collection material from risks that can cause deterioration or damage. Exhibits are a use that poses risks. Care must be taken, and, in some cases, modifications made to protect materials during use in an exhibit. More will be said later on this topic. Archives display original documents, photographs, and other paper-based materials, but they also create replicas to protect originals.

Exhibit Planning and Development

Choosing a Topic

Do you start with a topic and then look for examples that illustrate it, or do you start with the materials and figure out what story they tell? Exhibit ideas originate in different ways. Archives that are part of a larger organization are intermittently requested to create an exhibit on a specific topic or for the anniversary of a particular historical event. Examples include African American History Month, Veterans' Day, graduation/commencement, a war or battle, the death of a significant person, or the founding of a community, organization, or business. It can highlight a recently donated or processed collection or one that is rich in materials that lend themselves to an exhibit. It may relate to an educational program or public lecture. In this case, the exhibit theme comes first, and staff determines whether the collections can support the proposed theme.

The Kentucky Derby is an important annual event in Kentucky. Our institution collects local history materials. Although the Derby is held in another part of the state, one of our collections has many publications focusing on horse breeding and racing. Some are illustrated. Another collection includes postcards of scenes from around the state, several of which include the Churchill Downs racetrack and Derby-winning horses. A third collection includes several women's hats in older styles. One of the Derby Day traditions includes women wearing stylish hats. A sheet music collection included one or two related pieces with illustrations. Additionally, several items were borrowed. While no collection was specifically devoted to the topic, a thoughtful review of the collections found a few pieces here and an item there sufficient to create an exhibit. It was not serious and scholarly, but visitors enjoyed it, nonetheless. Over the long term, exhibits should provide variety, so it is quite acceptable to include an exhibit like this.

Author Gail Farr believes starting with the materials is more likely to result in an original exhibit. Successful exhibits also tend to draw on the collection's strengths, areas in which the institution collects, although loans can address gaps. Suppose your institution collects materials related to military history. This is a broad topic. Think about which aspect(s) of this topic collections illustrate particularly well. Is it a particular battle, military uniforms, or the history of a local unit? Large institutions with rich resources will have more material to select from and will be able to illustrate a topic in greater breadth. It is unnecessary for an exhibit to address all aspects well, but it should address at least one. A small institution can still create a successful exhibit by bringing together groups of visually appealing materials that illustrate a story of interest to the exhibit's target audience.[2]

As staff members work with collections, whether processing a new collection, conducting research in existing collections to answer reference questions, or for other reasons, they may notice potentially interesting exhibit items. They can make note of the items, list the collection and box and folder location of representative examples, and describe them a bit and what they illustrate. This information is collected in an exhibits idea file. When the time comes to create the next exhibit, these ideas can be reviewed and evaluated.

Material Selection

Whether the idea for an exhibit originates with a specific collection or otherwise, there is a back-and-forth refinement between the initial idea and the materials themselves. The most likely collections are reviewed. If there aren't adequate materials, the exhibit idea isn't possible, or it is modified. The search is broadened to additional collections. A collection may have strong research value, but the records may be insufficiently appealing visually. The exhibit topic needs to be presented visually; visitors will not spend time reading lengthy documents. At some point, it will be clear that there is sufficient material to create an exhibit. As material is reviewed for relevance, it should be possible to group items by the aspect of the topic they illustrate. Again, how well the collections support specific aspects of a topic should determine whether to include or exclude those items and aspects.

Allow sufficient time to review collections and select exhibit materials. This stage may be the most time consuming, requiring weeks to months, depending on the size of the holdings and the time spent reviewing. Background research will be required. At the beginning, it will provide information about the people, event, or topic under consideration, including dates, names, and locations that can be used to focus review of the collections. As potential items are located, additional research may be necessary to date the item, determine its creator, identify people in photographs, or otherwise confirm details. This research may determine whether the item fits the exhibit scope—how well it illustrates a point compared to other items—or can be used later to write exhibit labels. Take notes of your research to save time backtracking for information you remember reading. Research may suggest items to look for or aspects of the topic to illustrate. To save wear and tear on the collections, make photocopies of items being considered. Note the location of the original—the collection name and box and folder number or name. The photocopies can be organized by the aspect of the topic they illustrate or used to mock up exhibit layouts. Photocopies of the items that make the final cut can be used again for the exhibit documentation described later in this chapter.

Preservation Implications for Exhibits

The ability of records or objects to illustrate the exhibit concept is just one factor in selection decisions. The physical condition of the items themselves and the likelihood that they might be damaged while on display is another factor. If an item is in poor condition, it may be eliminated from consideration if a similar item in better condition is available. If a copy can be made without harming the original, this might be a suitable solution in the case a similar item doesn't exist. An exhibit can be an opportune time to perform basic preservation tasks such as mending, cleaning, or flattening, or even sending an item to a professional conservator for more complex treatment.

Site Evaluation

Not only are exhibit items evaluated, but so too is the exhibit site. Items in perfectly good condition can be damaged if improperly exhibited. An ideal site is centrally located, attractive and comfortable for visitors, and secure, well maintained, and conservationally safe for exhibit materials. If the site isn't secure or there are other factors that might damage originals, the use of copies only is an option that would still make use of the particular items without risk to their safety. Evaluate the current condition of the site, correct serious problems, and then monitor the site regularly during the exhibit to prevent problems.[3]

Lighting

Excessive levels of light pose the greatest threat to exhibit materials. Paper, ink, fabric, and original photographs fade or yellow while their fibers weaken, hastening breakage. Light damage is irreversible, permanent, and cumulative. The susceptibility of paper to light damage varies according to the quantity of chemical impurities it contains. Paper with high rag content is the most stable, while paper with low rag content and newsprint are the least stable. Deacidified paper is still vulnerable to light damage.[4]

The amount of damage caused is directly proportional to the intensity of the light and its duration. A weak light over a prolonged period will produce the same amount of damage as a strong light for a short period of time. There are three basic types of lighting—sunlight, fluorescent, and incandescent. The first two have high levels of ultraviolet (UV) light and are the most harmful. Incandescent light doesn't produce much UV light, but it does produce heat that is a different risk. Effective January 1, 2014 in the United States, the traditional technology used to manufacture popular forty- and sixty-watt incandescent bulbs was banned. They are now required to be more energy efficient. While halogen incandescent bulbs meet this requirement, they produce a lot of heat and in the past have caused fires. Some countries have begun banning them.[5]

Compact fluorescents and light-emitting diode (LED) lights also meet the new energy requirements. LED lights do not produce UV light, so they don't require the use of UV filters. They also don't produce heat so are a safe light to use for exhibits. Traditional fluorescent light tubes are now available with LED technology. Old fluorescent light fixtures can be converted to safer LED technology while retaining the traditional tube appearance. Light levels are measured in lux or foot-candles by using a light meter. Conservators recommend between five and ten foot-candles of light for exhibit materials and three foot-candles for especially light-sensitive materials.[6]

Evaluate the exhibit cases or walls where the exhibit will be displayed. What type of lighting is used in this space? What are the problems, and how can they be corrected? Can cases be shifted to avoid direct sunlight? Can shades be used to block the sunlight or UV filtering be applied to windows and fluorescent lights? How long does the exhibit have to be up? Other possibilities include rotating materials, such as displaying one example of an item and rotating it out after a period and substituting a different example of the same type of item. Make a copy of the original and put the replica on display. If the original is in too fragile a condition to duplicate and using the original will damage it, then it should not be used in the exhibit. Rearrange materials to reduce excessive exposure of a single portion—for example, turn opened books to a different page or rotate closed books to show the back or spine. Use timing devices on case lights to turn them off at intervals or turn them on only when a visitor is present. Shorten the exhibit hours or turn the lights off when there are no visitors.[7]

Humidity and Temperature

Humidity and temperature are two other environmental conditions that can potentially harm archival records. If possible, the room environment should be controlled through the heating and air-conditioning system. Exhibit cases are not going to protect materials if the room environment is poor. Since paper absorbs water, its fibers expand and contract as the air moistens or dries out. Excesses can cause mold growth or brittleness and breakage. Purchase inexpensive humidity and temperature monitors and place them in exhibit cases. Silica gel or room dehumidifiers can be used to help mitigate humidity. The next chapter goes into more detail about the effects of light, humidity, and temperature.

Security

Another factor for consideration in exhibit design and item selection is the security of the overall exhibit space and for individual items. If cases do not have pick-resistant locks or their construction makes them easy to pry open at the seams, strongly consider the use of replicas, or items that are extras. Institutions may have an excessive number of copies of an item that are fairly similar but unidentified, in poor condition, or otherwise not qualified for inclusion in the collection. These less desirable copies may be used for a teaching collection or exhibits or may be deaccessioned. Don't risk the theft of originals. More than one institution has displayed something of historical or monetary value, trusting in the goodness of people, and eventually lost it. As mentioned before, 45 percent of people are very dishonest, while 40 percent are relatively honest. Don't tempt them.

Hopefully, the building as a whole has good security that will protect the specific room(s) in which exhibits are located. Whenever possible, exhibits should be monitored by someone, even if they are working at a desk nearby but can see the exhibit area.

Exhibit Loans

An institution may not have just what it needs to illustrate a specific aspect of an exhibit theme. Choices include modifying the theme, presenting a smaller exhibit, or borrowing material from another institution or a private source. Bear in mind your institution's ability to protect and safely handle whatever it might borrow. It would not be worth the risk if it cannot take proper care of what it borrows and something on loan is damaged or stolen.

Whether your institution borrows or lends collection material, appropriate paperwork should document the terms of the loan, including the length of the loan, the condition of the borrowed items, and whether the items are insured and by whom (normally the borrower; see appendixes B.9 and B.10 for a sample loan form and art condition report). If possible, photograph borrowed items, first, to visually link every borrowed item to its loan form. Photographs can be printed out on bond paper and attached to loan documents. This minimizes returning the wrong item to the wrong lender. Make two sets of loan documents: one for the borrower and one for the lender.

Second, photographs are a good way to document the condition of borrowed items on arrival as part of the condition report. If insurance is involved, copies of the loan documents, identifying photos, and possibly the condition reports would be useful for the insurance provider.

The Registrars Committee of the American Alliance of Museums (AAM) has authored the General Facility Report, which documents information about an institution's building: its construction; exhibit spaces; shipping and receiving areas; heating, ventilating, and air-conditioning system; lighting; fire protection; security; and insurance. A museum that has been asked to lend something to another museum for an exhibit can request a copy of the potential borrower's General Facility Report to help decide whether to lend the requested item(s).

Not all organizations will have attained the level of AAM certification and have a recent general facility report. Lending and borrowing organizations do need to consider the intrinsic and monetary value of the item(s) requested and the borrower's ability to insure; provide security for; and safely handle, care for, and display the borrowed item(s). Organizations that are unable to fulfill these responsibilities should refrain from borrowing exhibit materials until they can.

Exhibit Documentation

When work starts on a new exhibit, create an exhibit folder. Label it with the (working) exhibit title and exhibit dates once they are known. Place loan forms, photographs, and condition reports in the folder. Include a record of all the material used in the exhibit. This may be as simple as a photocopy of each document or photograph used or a sufficiently descriptive list that clearly identifies each item used in the exhibit. Also include a complete set of the final labels used. A word document with the actual wording used will be sufficient to document the exhibit; the labels don't need to be originals from the exhibit. However, it might be useful to include a representative sample of the actual labels to illustrate their design. Background research, sources of factual information for labels, and the like should also go in the file, especially if from unusual or difficult-to-obtain sources. Include a record of expenses and possibly sources (vendors) for materials used in the exhibit creation (not the items on display). If there are handouts, publicity, or print material related to the exhibit, put a copy in the file. Since most of this information must be created or gathered anyway to prepare and install the exhibit, it makes good practice to collect the exhibit documentation when it is being created and then retain it for future reference. The file contents can serve as a model for the next exhibit, answering questions of how things were done last time or how much it cost.

Sometimes the people who create the exhibit are not the ones who take it down and put everything away. At the end of the exhibit, the exhibit folder contents should answer the question, "Where did this item come from originally?" meaning in which specific box or container was it stored? This is one reason to photocopy everything in the exhibit. The photocopy can perform a double duty, first to document the exhibit and second to point to the location from which each item came. As photographs, documents, objects, or books are selected for inclusion, it is a good practice to leave a placeholder or pull card in their permanent storage location. Photocopy 1 serves as the pull card. For photographs and documents, place the photocopy in the folder where the original was stored. The photocopy should be annotated "Removed for __ exhibit (fill in the exhibit title), on __ (date), by __ (name of person or possibly job title)." For an object, try describing the item removed on paper, perhaps referencing its accession number or other unique description. Or take a photo of the objects, copy and paste the images into a word document, print the document, and add to the exhibit folder. See the process explanation below. When the original is returned, the photocopy is removed and destroyed. The pull cards allow staff and researchers to still become aware of information pertinent to their research, even if they are redirected to an exhibit case to see it. It also ensures the ability to determine that the absence of something that should be in a particular box is legitimate as opposed to having been stolen or misplaced. Finally, it ensures that exhibit materials are returned to their proper location instead of being misfiled and declared lost. Photocopy 2 goes in the exhibit file. This copy is annotated with the collection name and box and folder number from which the original was removed for the exhibit. This documentation connects the item back to its proper box. Links in both directions minimize the chance that exhibit items will go astray. Photocopy 1 or 2 may have been created originally in the selection stage when deciding which of many potential items to display. Once the decision is made and originals pulled, the selection copy can be reused.

In the case that photographs are used in an exhibit, an alternate method of documentation would be to place a digital copy of each photo used into a digital exhibit folder. View the folder contents using Windows File Explorer. Set the display method for the folder contents to medium or large icons. Use a snipping tool to copy the images as a group and paste into a new word processing document; then print the single sheet for the exhibit folder. This method also provides the photo file name, which is searchable when needed again at any future time.

Universal Design

Universal design is the concept of designing products, buildings, and environments to be usable to the greatest extent possible by everyone, regardless of age, ability, or other factors.[8] This concept grew out of the broader accessibility movement. Its application to museum exhibits goes beyond accessibility to ensure that all museum experiences are not only accessible for all ages and abilities but also enriching and satisfying.[9] It has implications for exhibit traffic flow, display methods, and labels, among other aspects.

Display Methods

The design of exhibit cases affects the methods that can be used to display materials. Vertical cases may be built in (the front of the case is even with the surrounding wall) or attached to the wall. These cases may have fixed or movable shelves or inserts of various configurations on which to display items. Some cases have a track at the top, making it possible to hang items inside the case. If there is no track system and it isn't possible to attach matted photos or documents to the case interior due to potential damage to the case, perhaps a decorative fabric could be attached to a quarter-round piece of doweling that is then screwed into the back wall at the top. Archival mats would then be attached to the fabric. Flat/horizontal cases can be attached to the wall or floor or have legs and be freestanding. Some have sloped inserts on which to display items. A single slope displays items visible from only one side of the case; a double slope displays items on two sides. If the sides of a case are not transparent, they will restrict one's ability to view its contents and impact the positioning of materials inside the case. Metal or glass exhibit cases are preferable to wooden cases because raw wood releases gases that are harmful to archival records. Wood that is sealed in some manner is slightly better than untreated wood, but also evaluate whether the product sealing the wood will interact with archival material and cause damage.

A wide variety of objects exist to physically assist with the display of exhibit items. They range from clear acrylic wedges to display books or flat items at an angle to pedestals and shelves of varying sizes on which to place small objects, plastic-coated wire book or plate stands or rare book pillows and snakes for more delicate items. Consult archival vendors' catalogs or websites or study exhibits at larger museums to get ideas for displaying objects (see Additional Reading/Resources at the end of this chapter for a sample). The Farr book discusses exhibit display techniques in great detail. Universal design recommends smaller objects be placed in the front with larger objects in the back.[10]

As long as archivally safe materials and techniques are used, the exhibit curator is limited only by his collections, his exhibit cases, and his imagination. With the right equipment, it is possible to play videos, CDs, or other film or voice recordings that illustrate an aspect of the exhibit. Photographs can be scanned and enlarged. Pertinent text from original manuscripts or correspondence can be scanned, word processed, or photocopied onto slightly yellowed paper to create a facsimile safe for situations unfavorable for originals. Regardless of the cause for risk to archival originals, whether poor condition, insecure display areas, or unsafe display methods, the use of replicas is an acceptable option.

Documents and photographs are typically matted with acid-free foam core and mats. A piece of acid-free matting is cut with a window so that it looks like a picture frame. This piece (the front) is attached to a solid piece of acid-free foam core (the back) with a piece of artist's tape that forms a hinge between the two. The mat is opened to lay a photo or document flat on the foam core. Photo corners or See-Thru Mounting Strips by Lineco are attached directly to the foam core. The archival document or photograph is merely held in place by parallel strips above and below or supported by the corners. No adhesive should ever touch the archival item. The mat frame is closed over the archival item. The mat also helps to hold the item against the foam core, keeping it flat and from falling out. Once protected by a mat, archival documents can safely be attached to a wall or propped up. Any adhesive or putty is attached to the back of the foam core instead of the documents. If mats are cut in a standard size, they can be reused repeatedly. For example, eight and a half by eleven inches is a standard late-twentieth-century paper size, while eight by ten inches is a standard photograph size. It is possible to cut the window of a mat to accommodate both of these sizes, making it more versatile than a custom-cut mat. The opening should be cut slightly smaller than the item being matted. This allows the mat to hold the item in, giving it support. The mat can be repeatedly reused for exhibits as long as it is kept clean and the front and edges remain undamaged. Select a neutral mat color that will go well with documents and black-and-white and color photographs or that harmonizes with the colors of your cases, walls, or display areas.

Continue to be mindful of security for exhibit materials while they are in transit between the safety of the storage area and locked exhibit cases. During early stages of placement in cases, the cases are usually unlocked because pieces are being added and rearranged. Don't neglect to lock them or to lock access to the room the cases are in if everyone leaves the exhibit area simultaneously to retrieve more materials or have lunch. Cases can always be unlocked to pick up work again another day. Staff should be especially attentive with items on loan—from the moment they are received until the moment they are handed back to the lender, not just while in the exhibit case.

Good documentation also adds a layer of security. As mentioned already, documenting the removal of materials from their permanent storage location using photocopies/pull cards not only aids in putting an exhibit away but also adds security for the items. The pull cards call attention to the fact that something is missing or has been removed. The photocopies retained in the exhibit file document items in the institution's possession at the time of the exhibit, a fact that may be necessary in the case of theft or disaster in the future. This was the case with Denning McTague, mentioned in chapter 9. Loan forms document the temporary location of items that are lent or borrowed and confirm their owner, value, and insurance coverage. Condition reports document the condition of lent items on their arrival prior to exhibit. If there is existing damage or unique identifying features, the report should capture the information. This protects both the lender and the borrower in case of further damage or theft; insurance provides additional protection.

Exhibit design starts with a theme or collection. Material selection is guided by how well an item illustrates the theme, preservation concerns for potential damage caused by exhibition, and security requirements for the safety of the items while on display. Once material has met these requirements and been selected, it is prepared for the location where it will be displayed. Now work begins on the labels.

Exhibit Labels

It is important that all exhibit labels are easily readable by all visitors. This includes tall and short people, people with good and poor eyesight, and people who may have additional vision disabilities. Poor label design and content can be frustrating and detract from the enjoyment of an exhibit. Canadian museum advisor Kathleen Watkin suggests the use of large font, small paragraphs, alternative formats like audio or Braille when possible, and tactile experiences as methods that expand visitor experiences beyond reliance just on text labels.[11]

To comply with the Americans with Disabilities Act, use sans serif fonts such as Arial, Calibri, or Helvetica, for all text. It is easier to read text that mixes upper- and lowercase than all uppercase. Left-justified text is easier to read than text that is centered. Do not use underlining on labels. Use bold only for titles of text. Italics can be used for foreign words, book titles, or acknowledgments for exhibit supporters. Standardize the letter and line spacing for text. Margins around text on labels should be equal on the top and left sides, while the margins on the bottom and right sides are equal to each other but greater than the other two sides. Also balance the use of white space; consider double spacing between text paragraphs. Avoid the use of red or green for either font colors or background colors so that people with color blindness can read the labels. Many people without color blindness will still have difficulty reading red, green, or yellow text on a black or very dark background. Avoid these color combinations. For greater reading ease by the most people, it is recommended to place labels at fifty-four inches from the top edge of the label to the floor. This distance works whether labels are vertical on a wall or slanted inside a case. An item label that is laid flat near an object can be read at thirty inches off the floor.[12]

Depending on the size of an exhibit, it will have several types of labels, each with a different function. Exhibit labels have a hierarchy. The largest, most noticeable label is the exhibit title. Accordingly, the text on these labels has the largest font size, anywhere from thirty to sixty points, and the fewest words per label. Its function is to clearly identify the name of the exhibit. Hopefully, it arouses interest or curiosity and helps visitors decide whether they would like to see the exhibit. The next most important labels describe the specific objects, documents, or photographs on display. They should lead the reader to mentally move back and forth between the text and the item being described, stating more than just the obvious about the item.[13] Effective text for these labels starts with interesting phrases, uses active verbs in the present tense, has vocabulary for a broad reading level, and discusses the items on display. They tell the viewer the significance of the items and provide context for them. Items that are of higher value or greater probable interest or that best illustrate the exhibit theme should get longer labels. Labels should be succinct. People will not read long, complex labels. A recommended word length is fifty to seventy-five words maximum. A point size of eighteen is suitable for item labels.[14]

Larger exhibits may include a third type of label, a text panel, that is longer and more narrative. One example is a main label near the exhibit title to orient the visitor to the exhibit. It explains why the exhibit theme is important and why the items have been assembled to create the exhibit. A text panel could be used to provide information that would apply to everything in a case. This might negate the need for individual item labels or make them shorter. Another purpose would be to provide information useful for understanding the exhibit that isn't illustrated by the exhibit items themselves. This would be a way to address a gap in the ability of the collections to illustrate a point. These are optional, depending on the complexity of the exhibit. If titles are used on these panels, they may be bolded.[15] Finally, an acknowledgments label/panel may be appropriate to recognize organizations or individuals that lent items, financial support or grant funding, or other types of aid for the exhibit.

Point size is used to help distinguish labels with different functions, but color can also be used. One method would be to change the font or background color every time the point size changes, resulting in the same color for the same function and different colors for differing functions. In another application, a three-room exhibit that presents a different idea in each room might use three different colors. All labels in room 1 use color A, labels in room 2 use color B, and so on. This may be difficult to manage once difficult-to-distinguish colors are eliminated.[16]

Whatever is decided for the use of point size, color, bold, italics, or other qualities, be consistent. Write out the label schema so that labels can be checked against it for consistency. Check labels for spelling, grammar, and accuracy of information. Avoid acronyms and technical language that is not explained. Once the final text is ready, it can be physically formatted, printed, and mounted in the exhibit.

Exhibit Publicity

At this point, your exhibit is ready, but the work may not be done. Publicity announcing the exhibit will inform potential visitors of its readiness. Depending on the size and nature of the institution, publicity efforts may have preceded completion of the exhibit installation. Where and how much publicity is created for an exhibit may depend on the significance of the exhibit, staff time available for publicity, the duration of the exhibit, and deadlines for publicity submissions.

One reason for creating archival exhibits is to publicize the institution's collections and their availability for research use. The institution wants to attract visitors, researchers, and even potential donors of new collections or money. Sometimes lectures or other events are held in conjunction with an exhibit to broaden the exhibit's appeal, focus on a subset of the exhibit audience, or recognize a donor or other supporter.

Alternative Exhibits

This chapter has focused on traditional physical exhibits displayed in floor cases or wall panels within the institution's facility. There are other possibilities. A very minimalist exhibit could consist of an eight-inch-by-ten-inch digital photo frame that cycles through a slideshow of digitized photographs from the collections. The photos can be from a single collection, limited to one topic, or a general assortment representative of holdings. The images should be changed several times a year if possible. If the institution internally reproduces its own images in answer to reference requests, seriously consider repurposing those image scans for an easy exhibit. An institution may create exhibits from its collections that are physically displayed elsewhere. The historical society may collaborate with the local public library or the town hall to place a display there. Strongly consider the use of replicas for this type of exhibit. An organization may display a traveling exhibit created elsewhere from another organization's collections.

Recent technology has made it possible to create what are now called virtual exhibits. These use digital images of collection items such as photographs, documents, objects, books, or art and display them on the internet. They are different from digital collections because the items displayed have been selected the same as they would be for a physical exhibit. They have an intellectual theme and text labels describing them. A digital collection resembles a single archival collection of papers that have simply been digitized to make them accessible outside the research room. Visitors worldwide can visit a virtual exhibit twenty-four hours a day. Simple exhibits consist of web pages displaying a number of scans with descriptive text.

Note that while these virtual presentations are called exhibits, they are legally treated as the equivalent of publication. This means that copyright is a factor and must be carefully considered. Take art as an example. Physical ownership of a piece of art, like photographs, does not include the right to publish it. Permission to display copies of copyright-protected artwork in a web exhibit requires the artist's permission to publish a copy of the image. In addition, the 1990 Visual Artists Rights Act (VARA) protects the right of attribution and the right of integrity of artists who create "paintings, sculptures, drawings, prints, and still photographs produced for exhibition" when made either as a single copy or a signed and numbered, limited edition of 200 or less.[17] "The right of attribution ensures that artists are correctly identified with the works of art they create and that they are not identified with works created by others. The right of integrity allows artists to protect their works against modifications and destructions that are prejudicial to the artists' honor or reputation."[18] These rights reserved to artists are also called moral rights.

The basic PastPerfect software that has been discussed in earlier chapters has an optional module called Multimedia. This module can link digital photographs of anything described in a catalog record to that record. For example, a digital photograph or scan of a document, photograph, or object can be attached to the item record. When the record is retrieved in a search, the image also appears on-screen. This option can be very useful for security, inventory, and insurance purposes and is worth considering. The module can also attach audio, video, PDF files, and more to the catalog record.

Another optional module called Virtual Exhibit builds further on those catalog records that include images or other types of media. This software can be used to group selected catalog records and create a virtual exhibit. When created using Virtual Exhibit, pages appear more like illustrated catalog records than exhibit pages because descriptive information, such as the collection name, number, and search terms, appear. Normally, an exhibit wouldn't include this type of information. The "Here's the Story" field appears to be where text for the item label is located. To see samples of what the software can do, go to the PastPerfect website, select Online Collections, then Virtual Exhibit and follow links from there to Featured Online Exhibits. This appears to be a relatively easy way to further repurpose work that has already been done with a minimum of technical skills.

Omeka is a free, open-source, web publishing platform originally developed by George Mason University specifically for media-rich online exhibits and sharing digital collections. It is available as a stand-alone product or hosted for those who prefer not to worry about the technical management aspect. Omeka Classic is for individual projects, sites, or institutions. It uses Dublin Core description, has an online users guide, help forums, presentation themes, and more. Omeka S manages multiple sites and can publish *linked open data* to connect your digital collections with other collections worldwide. It can also connect to your Dspace or Fedora institutional repository.

Additional Reading/Resources

Aber, Hal. "Guidelines for Universal Design of Exhibits." Accessed April 22, 2020. https://airand space.si.edu/rfp/exhibitions/files/j1-exhibition-guidelines/4/SI%20Guidelines%20for%20 Universal%20Design%20of%20Exhibits.pdf. This document discusses museum exhibit design with the goal of making it universally accessible to visitors of diverse age, gender, social and educational backgrounds, and physical and intellectual abilities.[19]

American Alliance of Museums. Registrars Committee. "General Facility Report." Accessed August 23, 2019. https://www.polishmission.com/wp-content/uploads/2013/05/aam-general -facility-report.pdf. Originally the American Association of Museums when this report was written, in 2014 the organization was renamed the American Alliance of Museums. The questions asked indicate important factors to consider for the safety of collections material on exhibit. Note the degree of detail requested.

Association of College and Research Libraries. "ACRL/RBMS Guidelines for Interlibrary and Exhibition Loan of Special Collections Materials." Accessed August 30, 2019. http://www.ala .org/acrl/standards/specialcollections. These guidelines provide "decision-making criteria to support the interinstitutional loan of special collections materials, . . . specify the respective responsibilities of borrowing and lending institutions, and . . . recommend procedures to ensure the security and preservation of loaned materials."[20] This document combines two previously separate documents on lending materials for researchers and for exhibits. The sections for exhibits discuss the role of both the lending and borrowing institutions, provide sample loan agreements and condition reports, and discuss the AAM General Facility Report.

Childs-Helton, Sally. "'You Want the Civil War Letters Exhibited Where?' Archives, Exhibits and Preservation Concerns." *MAC Newsletter* 39 (July 2011): 29–30. This is a well-written article naming specific materials to use or avoid for exhibit case construction and props to display items or use in creating exhibits.

Corporation for Digital Scholarship. Roy Rosenzweig Center for History and New Media, George Mason University. Accessed August 23, 2019. https://omeka.org/. The site includes the history of Omeka's development, details about both Omeka Classic and Omeka S, a user's guide, help forums, and more.

Esworthy, Cynthia. "A Guide to the Visual Artists Rights Act." Accessed September 7, 2019. http://www.law.harvard.edu/faculty/martin/art_law/esworthy.htm. This provides an explanation of the VARA act with examples of what is or isn't permitted.

Farr, Gail. *Archives and Manuscripts: Exhibits.* Basic Manual Series. Chicago: Society of American Archivists, 1980. This is a good basic book on exhibiting archival materials. Chapter 4 is particularly helpful, with illustrations of exhibit cases and props for displaying various types of materials. Photographs illustrate display techniques used in actual exhibits. The author discusses how to lay out an exhibit and explains a variety of display techniques.

Glaser, Mary Todd. "Preservation Leaflets, The Environment, 2.5: Protecting Paper and Book Collections During Exhibition." Northeast Document Conservation Center. Accessed August 30, 2019. https://www.nedcc.org/free-resources/preservation-leaflets/2.-the-environment/2.5-protecting-paper-and-book-collections-during-exhibition. This leaflet discusses the impact of light and materials to use or avoid in exhibit cases. Childs-Helton's article is partially based on this source.

HGTV. "Light Bulbs: Know the Different Types." Accessed August 30, 2019. https://www.hgtv.com/design/decorating/design-101/light-bulbs-know-the-different-types. This is a basic primer on light bulb types.

Library of Congress. "Preservation—Collections Care—Limiting Light Damage from Display/Exhibition." Accessed August 30, 2019. https://www.loc.gov/preservation/care/light.html. This article on the effect of lighting discusses exhibit lighting and lists the light sensitivity of various formats.

Lineco, Inc. "Conservation Products." Lineco, Division of University Products, Inc. https://www.lineco.com/. Select the conservation catalog for illustrations of use and sources for See-Thru Mounting Strips, self-adhesive photo corners, and easel backs, among other useful supplies.

Ordoñez, Margaret T. *Your Vintage Keepsake: A CSA Guide to Costume Storage and Display.* Lubbock: Costume Society of America: distributed by Texas Tech University Press, 2001. This inexpensive guide explains how to exhibit textile items.

PastPerfect Software, Inc. "Virtual Exhibit for PastPerfect 5.0." https://museumsoftware.com/online.html. This page has links to featured online exhibits developed using PastPerfect's optional Virtual Exhibit module.

Schlipp, John. *Intellectual Property and Information Rights for Librarians.* Santa Barbara: ABC-CLIO, 2019. Chapter 6 includes information on the 1990 Visual Artists Rights Act, including which categories of art are or are not protected. Chapter 10 also touches on the Visual Artists Rights Act and the Music Modernization Act mentioned earlier relative to copyright.

Serrell, Beverly. *Exhibit Labels.* Walnut Creek, CA: AltaMira Press, 1996. This is a good resource for guidance on how to write labels well.

Smithsonian Institution. "Smithsonian Guidelines for Accessible Exhibition Design." Accessed August 26, 2019. https://www.sifacilities.si.edu/ae_center/pdf/Accessible-Exhibition-Design.pdf. Section B III discusses label text and design techniques to make them more accessible.

US Department of the Interior. National Park Service. Museum Management Program. "Conserve O Grams." National Park Service. Accessed August 30, 2019. https://www.nps.gov/museum/publications/conserveogram/cons_toc.html. See particularly the following:

Packing and Shipping Museum Objects:

17/1, "Checklist for Planning the Shipment of Museum Objects 1993,"

17/2, "Packing Museum Objects for Shipment 1993,"

17/3, "Crating Museum Objects for Shipment 1993,"

17/4, "Retrofitting a Moving Van to Transport Museum Collections 1995,"

17/5, "How to Make a Paper Board Crate 2008," and

17/6, "Packing a Framed Two-Dimensional Object 2009."

Museum Exhibits:

18/2, "Safe Plastics and Fabrics for Exhibit and Storage 2004."

University Products: The Archival Company. "Exhibit and Display." Accessed August 30, 2019. https://www.universityproducts.com/exhibit-display. This section includes products with illustrations for ideas to display books, documents/photos, and objects. Acrylic display risers in a variety of heights and dimensions make it easier or more interesting to see small objects. Includes products to absorb humidity (such as art-sorb), self-stick easel backs (to attach to the backs of mats so that they stand up on shelves), gallery label putty (to attach labels near documents/objects). The Temperature & Humidity Monitoring Equipment section at https://www.universityproducts.com/exhibit-display/environmental-monitoring-and-security/temperature-and-humidity-monitoring includes several types of gauges to monitor temperature and humidity inside display cases, humidity indicator cards, and products that absorb excess moisture to aid in humidity control. Peruse catalogs from other archival suppliers to get an idea of the range of available products and how they might be used.

Watkin, Kathleen. "What is 'Universal Design?'" Museum Association of Saskatchewan (blog), December 18, 2017. https://saskmuseums.org/blog/entry/what-is-universal-design. This article explains universal design and provides examples of its application to museum exhibits.

Wikipedia. s.v. "universal design." Accessed April 22, 2020. https://en.wikipedia.org/wiki/Universal_design. This entry details the history of universal design and gives many examples but doesn't focus on exhibit application.

Notes

1. Beverly Serrell, *Exhibit Labels* (Walnut Creek, CA: AltaMira Press, 1996), 9–11.

2. Gail Farr, *Archives and Manuscripts: Exhibits*, Basic Manual Series (Chicago: Society of American Archivists, 1980), 10.

3. Farr, *Exhibits*, 19–20.

4. Farr, *Exhibits*, 20.

5. Sean Hollister, "The Incandescent Light Bulb Isn't Dead," *The Verge*, accessed August 30, 2019, https://www.theverge.com/2014/1/1/5263826/the-incandescent-light-bulb-isnt-dead; Wikipedia, s.v., "halogen lamp," accessed August 30, 2019, https://en.wikipedia.org/wiki/Halogen_lamp.

6. Farr, *Exhibits*, 20; Library of Congress, "Preservation—Collections Care," accessed August 30, 2019, https://www.loc.gov/preservation/care/light.html.

7. Farr, *Exhibits*, 20–21.

8. Kathleen Watkin, "What is 'Universal Design?'" Museum Association of Saskatchewan (blog), December 18, 2017, https://saskmuseums.org/blog/entry/what-is-universal-design; Wikipedia, s.v., "universal design," accessed April 22, 2020, https://en.wikipedia.org/wiki/Universal_design.

9. Wikipedia, s.v., "universal design," accessed April 22, 2020, https://en.wikipedia.org/wiki/Universal_design; Watkin, "What is 'Universal Design?'"

10. Watkin, "What is 'Universal Design?'"

11. Watkin, "What is 'Universal Design?'"

12. E-mail correspondence with Dr. Judy Voelker, who teaches museum methods at Northern Kentucky University, March 2011, and personal conversation, July 29, 2011; telephone conversation with Mark Rohling, senior exhibit designer for the Taft Museum of Art, Cincinnati, August 1, 2019.

13. Voelker correspondence; Serrell, *Exhibit Labels*, 22–25.

14. Serrell, *Exhibit Labels*, 26–27; Voelker correspondence.

15. Voelker correspondence; Farr, *Exhibits*, 45.

16. Voelker correspondence.

17. John Schlipp, *Intellectual Property and Information Rights for Librarians* (Santa Barbara: ABC-CLIO, 2019), 169.

18. US Copyright Office, "Circular 40: Copyright Registration for Works of the Visual Arts," accessed September 4, 2019, http://www.tabberone.com/Trademarks/defs/legal/CopyrightOffice/circ40_VisualArts.pdf.

19. Hal Aber, Smithsonian Institution, "Guidelines for Universal Design of Exhibits," accessed April 22, 2020, https://airandspace.si.edu/rfp/exhibitions/files/j1-exhibition-guidelines/4/SI%20Guidelines%20for%20Universal%20Design%20of%20Exhibits.pdf.

20. Association of College and Research Libraries, "ACRL/RBMS Guidelines for Interlibrary and Exhibition Loan of Special Collections Materials," accessed August 30, 2019, http://www.ala.org/acrl/standards/specialcollections.

11

The Collections Storage Environment

Archival collections include a wide range of materials from paper records to photographs, audio and visual recordings, digital files, books, objects, and even clothing or art. These records are physically made from a very wide range of materials: paper, glass, polyester film, vinyl, assorted metals, wood, leather, vellum, parchment, fabric, or paint, to name the more common ones. Over time, all these materials will age and break down, but a controlled environment, appropriate storage methods, and careful handling practices can extend the life of these materials.

Temperature, humidity, light, biological agents, organic materials, housekeeping practices, and disasters can all work to extend or shorten the life of archival collections. Staff members need to intentionally manage these factors in order to preserve their collections. Neglect, even if benign, will allow materials to deteriorate faster than necessary.

It is expected that collection material will spend the majority of its life in permanent storage, hopefully in a safe environment. The time it spends in the research room or on display should be short by comparison. Records with a high intrinsic value or in delicate condition may be replaced by a reproduction and nearly never leave their safe haven. Since the ability to control the conditions of the storage environment is a crucial factor in preserving collections, it is highly desirable for the storage location to be an enclosed room. While small institutions may not have a great deal of physical space or resources, if they do not yet have a self-contained storage room, it should be a high priority. Otherwise, their collections will deteriorate more rapidly, and they will lose their reason for existing.

Security

Once a dedicated storage room has been obtained, it should be made secure. Only authorized personnel, whether paid or not, should have access to the storage room. It should be clear to everyone who works in, volunteers for, or visits the institution who may and may not enter the storage room. All workers, cleaning staff, and maintenance personnel should be escorted by authorized personnel if they need to enter the storage room. This is not only for the security but also for the well-being of the collections and the protection of the people being escorted. Workers and cleaning staff are usually unaware of the harm they can potentially cause to collections while they perform their duties. Those who manage the collections should be more knowledgeable and advise on modifications that will be safer for the collections while accomplishing the task at hand. For example, it might be necessary to cover collections with plastic sheeting for a repair involving water or to make substitutions for potentially harmful cleaning products.

Sometimes people give tours of the storage room to people not normally given access. Because of the security risk, this should be discouraged unless there is a very compelling reason. Sometimes for educational purposes, staff will give behind-the-scenes tours to colleagues. Be mindful of what information is shared. It should be possible to discuss pertinent points without revealing where more valuable items are stored or security features.

Access to keys to the storage room should also be carefully restricted. Cleaning and maintenance people should not have keys, nor should interns or other temporary personnel. Security personnel employed by the institution may need to have access in case of an emergency or disaster. Policies or guidelines should address to whom or how access will be given in those cases. Will local police or fire personnel call a designated person from the historical society, library, museum, or institution to notify them? A backup key may need to be left with another manager or department in case the primary key holders are unavailable or their keys are lost.

Depending on the layout, location, and design of the storage room, doors or windows may need locks, alarms, or hinges that cannot be removed from the outside, protective grillwork, security cameras, or appropriate lighting after dark. All these precautions provide additional layers of security for collections. They should be evaluated in light of the value of the holdings, potential risk, and available resources. Basic steps can be taken while prioritizing more expensive ones.

Temperature and Relative Humidity

Temperature and relative humidity can have a significant impact on how long archival records last. There is no single ideal setting that is equally beneficial for the wide range of materials mentioned earlier. For example, color photography benefits from lower temperatures more than black and white and would last considerably longer at about freezing. However, such cold temperatures are not suitable for materials that are regularly brought to a research room kept at 70°F because problems with condensation could lead to mold. Higher temperatures cause paper and other materials to dry out, become brittle, and crack. They can also accelerate various chemical reactions, causing damage. Chemical processes are used to create photographs and blueprints. Chemical reactions can include interaction between more acidic materials and acid-free materials or chemical buffering in archival boxes.

Relative humidity is the measure of how much moisture is in the air. As the temperature increases, the relative humidity decreases because warm air can hold more moisture than cold air can. Records need a certain amount of moisture to remain flexible. Relative humidity affects whether materials dry out. High humidity can cause *foxing*, small brown disfiguring spots on paper, but worse yet is the potential for mold growth. Once papers, photographs, or books get moldy, they are forever contaminated. The mold can be physically removed with care, but spores remain. All they need is a return of sufficiently hot, humid air, and the mold will break out again. Mold can also jump from contaminated records or books to clean ones and spread; therefore it is important to deal with it as soon as possible. At a minimum, segregate moldy records until they can be dealt with.

In the past, accepted archival practice recommended temperature settings no higher than 70°F with a variation of not more than plus or minus 2°F and a 50 percent relative humidity that fluctuated not more than plus or minus 2 percent. More recent research from the Image Permanence Institute (IPI) at the Rochester Institute of Technology in New York suggests that it is safe to be more flexible about temperature and relative humidity settings. This approach reduces energy consumption and results in a more sustainable storage environment because the temperature and relative humidity targets are more achievable and more affordable, increasing the percentage of time the institution's heating, ventilating, and air-conditioning (HVAC) system is capable of meeting those goals. Jeremy Linden, formerly an IPI Preservation Specialist and now principal of Linden Preservation Services, recommends first controlling the relative humidity at an acceptable level and then lowering the temperature as much as possible while still maintaining the relative humidity, an acceptable range for relative humidity being from 30 to 55 percent. Metal corrodes when relative humidity reaches 55 percent, and mold grows at 65 percent and above. Below 30 to 35 percent, the air is too dry for vellum and other materials. The temperature depends on what the HVAC system can maintain while keeping the relative humidity within the acceptable range for the greatest number of heating or cooling days.[1]

Depending on where in the United States your institution is located, your HVAC system may heat or cool for the greater part of the year. The type of system that services your storage area will also be a factor. Purchase temperature and humidity gauges to monitor the conditions in the storage room. Inexpensive models will display the maximum and minimum temperature and relative humidity since the last time the gauge was reset. More expensive models record the temperature and humidity readings, providing data for analysis. The Preservation Environment Monitor, or PEM2 Datalogger, allows data to be downloaded onto a flash drive or USB drive. When the data are downloaded from the flash drive to a computer, they can be charted separately—just temperature, just relative humidity, or together. They can also be compared with the local temperature and relative humidity (outside the building) for the same time period. Small rechargeable models are available to monitor exhibit cases, or humidity indicator cards will provide a onetime reading in an exhibit case.[2]

Once collected, data can be analyzed to determine how much of the time the current system at the current settings is able to provide an acceptable storage environment. Data can also be studied to determine when there are problems and what their causes might be. Then it is time to consult with the personnel who manage the HVAC system to determine how it can be optimized to provide improved results. According to Linden, the goal is to achieve the best possible preservation of the collections with the least possible consumption of energy while being sustainable over time (see the IPI webinars listed in Additional Readings/Resources at the end of this chapter for pertinent information).[3]

If the relative humidity is too high or low and the building's heating and cooling system cannot be adjusted enough to deal with the problem, portable or room-size dehumidifiers, humidifiers, or air conditioners may help. Depending on the size of the space, models for commercial use may be required. They need to run continuously to be beneficial; otherwise, they will cause an artificial fluctuation by being on some days and off others. The electrical system needs to be sufficient to run the equipment without causing an electrical overload or fire. Dehumidifiers must safely drain the water without causing a flood. An automatic drain would be preferable. If the amount of water in the air is enough to cause the dehumidifier to overflow if left unattended, it will probably not be safe to run overnight or over the weekend. It will not help to cause a water problem while trying to regulate the humidity. If people are in the building five or six days a week so that the dehumidifier can work steadily, a model with an automatic shutoff when full may work. Settings could be tested to see how much water the system would draw out during the day to know whether it could be left running overnight. A model without an automatic drain would need regular monitoring. All equipment would need regular cleaning to avoid mold growth. Portable fans might be necessary to improve air circulation and minimize the chance of mold.[4]

Light

Archival materials need to be protected from UV and visible light. UV light, primarily from the sun and fluorescent bulbs, is particularly damaging to paper items. The damage from UV light can be reduced using filters over windows and fluorescent lightbulbs or special glass in framed items. The intensity and amount of light exposure should be reduced as much as possible. Storing all archival collections in closed boxes provides protection from harmful light. Manuscripts, newsprint, original blueprints, cyanotype photographs, watercolors, and non-print media are particularly sensitive to light. Excessive exposure causes fading and yellowing. Drapes or filtered shades will help with exterior windows. Materials should not be displayed where direct sunlight will fall on them. Lighting in exhibit cases should also be monitored. If excessive lighting is a concern, consider using a good-quality reproduction rather than an original manuscript item.[5]

UV filters take various forms including rolls of flexible film for windows or exhibit cases and sleeves or tubes sized for fluorescent tubes. The filters absorb varying amounts of UV light, providing varying amounts of protection. Purchasing filters with known specifications will be safer. "Filters range from colorless to those tinted with varying amounts of yellow through amber; generally, the more yellow the filter, the more visible light it is capable of absorbing." Acrylic filtering sheets last about ten years. Fluorescent lights vary in the amount of UV light they emit. If the bulbs emit more than 2 to 3 percent of UV light, sleeve them with UV filtering sleeves. Be careful that maintenance personnel do not accidently discard the filters when the fluorescent lightbulbs are replaced. If possible, check filtered light sources with a UV light monitor to check their effectiveness. It may be possible to borrow a monitor from a local art museum.[6]

LED technology has advanced in recent years. What looks like a traditional fluorescent tube can actually use LED technology, eliminating the risk of UV light and the need for filters. Additionally, LED lights save on energy consumption, saving money. Fluorescent light fixtures must be rewired to accept the LED bulbs, but a four-tube fixture takes thirty minutes or less to rewire.

Housekeeping

Good housekeeping practices can have a considerable impact on the preservation of collection material. A clean, orderly environment encourages staff and visitors to keep it tidy and discourages bugs and rodents from moving in. Eating, drinking, and smoking should be prohibited in the archives storage room as well as processing areas and the research room. Any kitchens, lunchrooms, or other food service areas should also be sufficiently distant from these rooms so as not to attract bugs to them. Food and drink encourage bugs of all types and can cause damage to collections if they come in contact. Food residue can remain on tables and other surfaces and be transferred to documents that are laid on top of sticky, oily, or unclean surfaces. If there are problems with bugs, they should be dealt with promptly. Do not use chemicals that will harm the collections to treat bug problems. Do not allow the chemicals to come in direct contact with archival materials or their storage containers. Plants and organic material should also be avoided in the same locations both for the ability to attract bugs and also to prevent possible water spills.

The storage room should be kept free of clutter and debris. It should not be used to store broken-down equipment, leftover building maintenance materials, inappropriate collection material, and the like. The archival storage room is neither a general storage room nor a place for equipment, supplies, and other items about which people are unable to make appropriate decisions.

All materials should be stored in closed archival boxes on shelving appropriately sized for archival boxes. Boxes that are intended to be stored upright should be shelved upright. Skinny oversized boxes should be stored flat and not stacked too high, or the weight on the bottom box will cause it to be crushed. Box lids should be closed properly. Boxes should not be tipped, overfilled, crushed, or otherwise shelved or stored inappropriately. No material should be sitting directly on the floor. The height of the lowest shelf should be at least three inches above the floor to provide protection from water damage. New materials should be transferred out of acidic or open boxes into acid-free archival boxes as soon as possible.

The storage room should be cleaned regularly. This includes dusting, vacuuming, or damp mopping the floor, depending on the surface as needed, but at least every week or two. Shelves, boxes, and bound volumes should be dusted on a regular cycle. If they are physically in good condition, a clean, soft untreated cloth (like the electrostatically charged "Dust Bunny") or a clean, natural-bristle brush for books and bound volumes works well. If treated dust cloths are used, they should not come into contact with archival records or surfaces on which the records may be placed for use. The chemicals used to treat the cloths could transfer to the records and damage them. A vacuum cleaner may be appropriate for flooring, shelves, or box exteriors. The suction level should be low when used on boxes, books, and collections. If necessary, place screening or cheesecloth over the nozzle to prevent fragments of labels, books, or paper from being sucked in.[7]

Fire and Water Protection

Archives, libraries, museums, and historic properties should have fire protection systems, such as smoke detectors and sprinkler systems, throughout the building, including collection storage rooms. Care should be taken to prevent fires from smoking, overtaxed electrical systems, electrical outlets with too many cords plugged in, and inappropriate use or storage of cleaning supplies or flammable materials. Extension cords and heaters should be used with care.

Enclosing all collection material in closed archival boxes, good housekeeping practices, and the use of appropriate shelving that keeps collections at least three inches off the floor will also reduce risks from fire and water damage. Boxes provide an extra layer of protection around their contents that can help against smoke or water damage. Shelving units provide a measure of protection against water coming from fire sprinklers or pooling up on the floor. This is why everything should be at least three inches off the floor and shelving should have a top or canopy if possible. If any emergency exit paths go through the storage area, they should be kept clear.

Organizing Your Collections Storage Space

Established archives usually have already organized their collections storage area, but they might undergo renovations to add space or install compact shelving, may revise work processes, or simply wish to further organize this space. New archives will also benefit from the following discussion. Archival collections tend to be paper based and therefore heavy. Metal shelving is preferred, adding more weight. Compact shelving doubles the storage capacity of a space by reducing aisle space to a single aisle, roughly doubling the weight. The life of archival records is increased and improved by avoiding hot, dry locations, humid, damp locations, or locations with water leaks or overhead water pipes. Sunlight causes damage and unsecured spaces risk loss or damage. Identifying a collections storage location that avoids as many of these hazards as possible will be easier in a nonresidential building than in a residential building, which is likely to have fewer good options. In either case, if compact shelving will be used, it might be wise to have an engineer determine whether the selected flooring will be able to safely bear the potential weight. There may be additional situations in which it would be wise to determine the load-bearing ability of a particular location.

Once a physical space has been selected, shelving would be the next consideration. Archival shelving should be made of steel because it doesn't burn and is chemically inert, unlike wood. The steel should be coated with baked-on enamel or a powder-coated finish. It should be open to allow air to circulate and have a canopy over the top shelf to protect against water or other materials falling from above. The shelving should not have plywood or chipboard shelves or panels since they contain high levels of formaldehyde, which "can cause metals to corrode, pigments to fade, and paper to weaken and become acidic." Wooden shelves, storage units, bookcases, exhibit cases, or unsealed flooring material should all be avoided for the same reason.[8] While a rectangular space will allow for the maximum amount of shelving, reality will dictate potential shelving configurations.

Once the available shelf space and configuration is fixed, some consideration should be given to the format of the materials held, in what percentage, and their physical size, and to workflow. The NKU Archives is comprised of the University Archives, which holds the university's permanent records, and Special Collections, consisting of regional and local history records. The university legally owns its records, so they are transferred to the archives while Special Collections materials are gifts requiring a deed of gift to give NKU legal ownership. The university's records are *open records* organized by record groups based on NKU's organizational structure. Special Collections are *closed records* organized into manuscript collections based upon the records creator. Due to the significant differences in ownership, organization, and their open or closed status, the processed University Archives and Special Collections records are housed on separate sides of the room. Each side has shelving for the standard manuscript boxes and separate dedicated shelving in their area for oversized bound volumes or boxes. Another part of the room has flat files or map cases for very large items like blueprints, maps, or large, unframed photos.

Each row of shelving has been given a unique number regardless of what is stored there so there is no potential duplication of the row number. The row numbers are located on a sign on the end of each row. Each shelf has been assigned a number, starting with the top shelf of the leftmost column when facing the shelving. Numbering goes down the first column, then starts at the top of column two and goes to the bottom, starts at the top of column three, etc. Number all shelves high or low on which collections can be stored. The shelf numbers were word processed, printed on skinny, adhesive labels, and uniformly adhered on the left end of each shelf edge. They say "Shelf __ [insert next sequential number]." Shelf numbers repeat by row, that is, Row 1 has shelves 1–49, Row 2 has shelves 1–49, and so on. The row and shelf numbers are always recorded together in all documentation (finding aids, shelf inventories, accession records), creating a unique address for the records on that shelf. All flat file drawers are numbered consecutively starting with 1 and continuing until there are no more drawers. Since they don't have very many drawers per cabinet, cabinet numbers are omitted. File cabinets and art racks are also numbered consecutively, vertical file 1, 2, 3, and art rack 1, 2, 3. Some version of one of these numbering systems can be used for microfilm cabinets, bookshelves, or whatever furniture is used to store collection materials.

Once an organizational structure has been given to the physical storage system, the next step is to determine what is stored where. If collections have already been shelved, numbering can be done after the fact. Manuscript collections typically have a collection number, for example

MS-19 and a collection name. Either could be used to organize the collections on the shelf, being organized numerically or alphabetically. The risk with the alphabetic system is that the institution will save space for each letter, eventually run out of space for more popular letters, and then require collections be shifted to create space where it is needed. The more efficient method would be to organize the collections by collection number, thus eliminating the need to save any space between collections. All the standard-sized manuscript boxes (those that aren't oversized) in MS-1 are shelved together generally in numeric order: MS-1 Box 1, 2, 3. If there is more than one flat box, stack them on top of each other in a column to maximize the shelf space, even if this puts them out of box number order for that collection. Refer to directions below on how to safely stack flat boxes or books. If a particular box doesn't fit on the remaining shelf space, go on to the next box in that collection that will. The important thing is to shelve as much of the collection together as will fit on that shelf size whether regular or oversize. It is okay to wrap from one shelf to another or from the bottom of column two to the top of column three or from row 1 to row 2. It is more important to keep all the boxes from the same collection adjacent to each other following the numeric sequence of the shelves than it is to have the boxes within the collection shelved in numeric sequence. Labeling every box on the outside with the manuscript number and collection name helps identify which boxes belong together. If there are oversized boxes, put them on the oversize box shelves in numeric order of the manuscript collection number and then box order within the manuscript collection. If the institution prefers to use an alphabetic sequence, follow the same process but leave some space between letters of the alphabet to insert new collections. If an institution has organized its collections by another system, and decides it wants to reorganize how the collections are shelved, it is quite acceptable to take all the containers off the shelf and start over.

Row numbers for the University Archives have been integrated with the numbering system for the entire collections storage room. Although the university records are on a different style shelving than Special Collections, the shelf numbering process was identical. The record groups in the University Archives are open because as long as the university exists, new records will be created and added to existing record groups. Due to their open nature and the shelving differences, the top and bottom shelves were initially left empty to create room for growth and where possible some space was also left between record groups. Those boxes are labeled with their record group number and name. Each box of university records has a unique, sequential number within the entirety of university records unlike the manuscript boxes, whose sequential box numbers are limited to their collection and then start over with the next collection. All boxes for a record group are shelved adjacent to each other just like the manuscript collections. Boxes shelved in these two areas are considered ready for research use.

When new collections and record transfers are received, in order to distinguish them from processed records they are shelved in a designated New Accessions holding area. Like the numbering system for the University Archives storage area, these rows and shelves were numbered as part of the overall system. Only unprocessed records are located in this area to distinguish them as records that need work. Also, some archives don't allow access to unprocessed collections for security reasons. Records are shelved on the next consecutive shelf that is available, leaving no spaces. Boxes are at least minimally labeled to indicate which records came in together. One of the first tasks is often accessioning. As was mentioned in chapter 4, it is suggested that the row and shelf number of the new materials be included in the accession record. This means the accession record can be used to locate records when someone is ready to perform the next task for those records. It also helps document what was received as part of that specific acquisition, maintaining intellectual control over the records. Ideally once records are accessioned, they would be moved along to a second holding area for records ready to process; however, many archives lack the luxury of sufficient space to do so. Accessioned records could be flagged with color-coded sticky notes or have a work copy of their accession record attached to the exterior to identify records that are ready to process.

How to Put Materials on the Shelf

Letter-size archival manuscript boxes are a standard twelve inches deep, while legal boxes are fifteen inches. Flat oversize boxes may be fifteen to thirty inches long or more in either direction. A good size for archival shelving is sixteen inches deep per row by forty-two inches wide, meaning shelving that is accessed from two different back-to-back rows actually needs to be thirty-two inches deep in total. This shelf size accommodates a variety of the most common box types: up to eight manuscript boxes, three record cartons, or an assortment of oversize boxes. Manuscript boxes and record cartons are the most commonly used archival boxes. Grouping same-size boxes together on the shelf makes the most efficient use of the shelf dimensions. Try not to fill each shelf completely full so that there is room to add additional records before having to shift boxes to make more room.

Oversize boxes should be stored in a separate designated area on shelving that is deeper than the main shelving. These boxes are usually flat and not more than two or three inches thick. Flat oversize boxes of similar dimensions should be stacked on each other. Do not stack the boxes too high to avoid crushing the bottom box, perhaps three to five boxes, depending on their thickness and weight. Do not stack larger boxes on top of smaller boxes or excessively thick or heavy ones on smaller, thinner ones. The bottom box must be able to bear the weight on it as well as provide support for the box sizes on top of it. If necessary, start a new stack.

Bound volumes, including relatively recent books and rare books, should be shelved similar to boxes. Ordinary books in good condition are shelved upright. Books that are taller or wider but not exceptionally thick or heavy should be shelved upright together in an oversize book section. Books that are oversize and thick or heavy will probably need to be laid flat on their side, much like the oversize boxes are stacked. Big, heavy volumes go toward the bottom of a stack. All books should have support under them; no upside-down pyramids.

Some books will require special storage treatment. If their covers are a bit loose, use unbleached, flat, cotton tape and tie them up like a package. Although this product is called tape because it is flat, there is no adhesive. It is more like flat ribbon or string. If the knot is on the top or open edge of the volume, it can be shelved without the knots bumping into the adjacent book. Unrepaired books in even poorer condition can be wrapped in acid-free paper before being tied with tape. The paper will provide additional support for all parts of the volume. Rare books can optionally be similarly wrapped and tied even if they are in good condition. Because of their rarity, only careful repairs by trained conservators can be done without causing the book to lose its value. The paper wrapping provides protection like archival boxes do for paper records. Custom book boxes can also be constructed but are more expensive.

Sometimes smaller bound volumes that are part of a manuscript collection are stored in archival boxes because they fit and to keep the volumes shelved with the rest of the collection. If a book is stored other than upright or flat, it should be laid on its spine with the open edges of the pages up to the ceiling. This puts the least amount of stress on the book binding. This would be particularly applicable for rare books.

An institution may maintain a noncirculating book collection in its closed-stack archival records storage to supplement research on the topics documented by its archival collections. Whether managing a nonrare collection of older books or even a collection of rare books, some types of bookends are less likely to cause damage than others. Bookends that are thicker and wider are safer for protecting the life of books. They reduce the possibility of the bookend winding up between the pages of a book and causing it physical damage.

Additional Reading/Resources

American Institute for Conservation and Foundation for Advancement in Conservation. Accessed August 31, 2019. https://www.culturalheritage.org. From the home page go to Resources. From there, Learning goes to educational resources for the general public on a variety of material types. Also under Resources, the Collections Care link leads to a preventative care wiki, information on storage solutions, and Connecting to Collections, which provides access to upcoming and past webinars on diverse topics. The archives page lists the webinars and allows topical searches of the webinars.

Archival Methods. "Archival Methods Newsletter, Issue #7." Accessed August 31, 2019. http://us1.campaign-archive2.com/?u=00f293b32ca7d4f4aecb588c9&id=72f7397 a59&e=d73eb315c7. This newsletter provides a very basic overview of factors that can cause your collection to deteriorate. Archival Methods is a vendor of commercial archival products, particularly for photography.

Glaser, Mary Todd. "Preservation Leaflets, The Environment, 2.5: Protecting Paper and Book Collections During Exhibition." Northeast Document Conservation Center. Accessed August 30, 2019. https://www.nedcc.org/free-resources/preservation-leaflets/2.-the-environment /2.5-protecting-paper-and-book-collections-during-exhibition. The discussion of the effect of light in this leaflet is why archival materials need to be stored properly. Light fixtures in storage areas should be filtered also. Although this information is still valid, due to its 1999 date, it doesn't discuss LED lighting, which has made many advances since then.

Image Permanence Institute. "Dew Point Calculator." Rochester Institute of Technology, College of Imaging Arts and Sciences. Image Permanence Institute. Accessed August 31, 2019. http:// www.dpcalc.org. The homepage for the Dew Point Calculator shows a set of sliders on the left. If they are set to the temperature and humidity of your storage room, the chart on the right will indicate the risk to various material types when stored under those conditions. Mechanical damage is listed as one of the potential types of damage. It refers to the stress on paper fibers caused by continual shifts in temperature and relative humidity. These shifts cause the paper fibers to expand and contract. This constant movement is stressful and causes damage. A series of videos located at https://www.imagepermanenceinstitute.org/resources/videos explains heating, ventilation, and air conditioning (HVAC) systems; environmental monitoring; preservation metrics; the three preservation metrics of metal corrosion, mechanical damage, and mold risk; and sustainable management of collection management, which represents a change from previous professional recommendations of maintaining specific temperature and humidity settings. Additional videos or PDFs on sustainability are located at https://ipisustainability .org/webinars.html.

———. "Standards and Sustainability." Rochester Institute of Technology, College of Imaging Arts and Sciences. https://www.imagepermanenceinstitute.org/resources/newsletter-archive /v19/preservation-practices-webinars. This article discusses the shift away from rigid temperature and humidity goals to a more flexible and sustainable practice. IPI's Sustainable

Preservation Practices Webinar Series gives examples of sustainable temperature and humidity goals that don't harm collections yet saves energy: https://ipisustainability.org/.

Library of Congress. "Preservation, Collections Care." Accessed August 31, 2019. https://www.loc.gov/preservation/care/. This webpage has links to good information about the effect of lighting and how to care for photographs and books, besides many other topics related to collections care. This page: http://www.loc.gov/preservation/care/C2CC.html links to videos including one on pest management.

Lyrasis. "Publications and Resources.". Accessed August 31, 2019. https://www.lyrasis.org/services/Pages/Publications-and-Resources.aspx. Lyrasis has free online leaflets that deal with a variety of topics, such as disaster planning, how to dry wet books and records, and how to handle mold.

National Archives. Preservation: "New Techniques for Fire Detection and Suppression." US National Archives and Records Administration. Accessed October 12, 2019. https://www.archives.gov/preservation/emergency-prep/fire-detection-suppression.html. These links may be rather technical, but halon fire suppression systems have been the Cadillac system for several decades. They are included here only to note that alternatives are being identified that are safer for people and the environment.

Northeast Document Conservation Center. "Preservation Leaflets." Accessed August 31, 2019. https://www.nedcc.org/free-resources/preservation-leaflets/overview. These technical leaflets discuss a variety of topics related to improving the storage environment and caring for collection material.

Ritzenthaler, Mary Lynn. *Preserving Archives and Manuscripts*. Archival Fundamentals Series. Chicago: Society of American Archivists, 1993. Chapter 5 has a good discussion of how to create an archival storage environment that will protect and extend the life of the materials stored within. Chapter 7 discusses desirable qualities for shelving and products that will harm collections.

US Department of the Interior. National Park Service. Museum Management Program. "Conserve O Grams." National Park Service. Accessed August 31, 2019. https://www.nps.gov/museum/publications/conserveogram/cons_toc.html. This is a useful collection of brief technical leaflets on general topics such as choosing a vacuum cleaner or UV filtering film, using silica gel, and mold prevention, and more specific ones on the care, handling, storage, and security of manuscripts and books and many other topics. See Note 13/2, "How to Flatten Folded or Rolled Paper Documents," and Note 19/24, "How to Preserve Acidic Wood Pulp Paper."

_____. "Museum Management Program, NPS Museum Handbook." National Park Service. Accessed August 31, 2019. https://www.nps.gov/history/museum/publications/handbook.html. Some of the Conserve O Grams may refer the reader to the National Park Service's "Museum Handbook," which is located here. The Museum Handbook Part 1, chapter 9 (newly revised) focuses on fire protection: https://www.nps.gov/museum/publications/MHI/Chap9.pdf.

Wilsted, Thomas P. *Planning New and Remodeled Archival Facilities*. Chicago: Society of American Archivists, 2007. Chapter 11 discusses bugs, fire safety, housekeeping, and disaster preparedness. Chapter 9 discusses appropriate shelving specifications.

Notes

1. Jeremy Linden, "Environmental Data Analysis-Tips and Tricks," webinar in Sustainable Preservation Practices series presented by Image Permanence Institute, Rochester Institute of Technology, Rochester, New York, March 23, 2011.

2. Go to the Image Permanence website at https://www.imagepermanenceinstitute.org/environmental/pem2-datalogger for further information. Examples of some of these products can be found at the University Products website at https://www.universityproducts.com under Equipment and Tools, Temperature and Humidity Monitoring Equipment (digital mini-hygrometer, humidity indicator cards, and jumbo display thermo-hygrometer for exhibit cases). Go to Gaylord Archival, another archival vendor, at https://www.gaylord.com and select Environmental Control for additional examples.

3. Jeremy Linden, "Sustainable Preservation Practices," webinar in Sustainable Preservation Practices series presented by Image Permanence Institute, Rochester Institute of Technology, Rochester, New York, May 25, 2011.

4. Mary Lynn Ritzenthaler, *Preserving Archives and Manuscripts*, Archival Fundamentals Series (Chicago: Society of American Archivists, 1993), 55–56.

5. Library of Congress, "Care, Handling, and Storage of Works on Paper," accessed August 31, 2019, https://www.loc.gov/preservation/care/paper.html.

6. Ritzenthaler, *Preserving Archives*, 61.

7. Ritzenthaler, *Preserving Archives*, 63.

8. Thomas P. Wilsted, *Planning New and Remodeled Archival Facilities* (Chicago: Society of American Archivists, 2007), 116–17; Ritzenthaler, *Preserving Archives*, 78.

12

Other Types of Material

In chapter 1 a record was defined as any type of recorded information regardless of physical form or characteristics that is created, received, or maintained by a person, institution, or organization. A record is considered archival based on its information content, meaning, and usefulness, not its age or appearance.[1] So far, this book has focused on paper records: manuscripts, photographs, and to a small extent, books or bound volumes. Archives, historical societies, and other cultural heritage organizations typically own other formats besides paper because people have not limited themselves to recording useful information on paper. Many if not all of the following formats will have specialists who focus solely on that single format. This chapter strives to provide a basic overview. More in-depth discussion will require further research by the reader.

Audio Records

Common audio recording formats may include $33\frac{1}{3}$- or 45-rpm phonograph records, audiocassettes, reel-to-reel tapes, and CDs that have recorded music or speech (lectures, presentations, or oral history interviews). Less common formats may include cylinders or 78-rpm phonograph records. All these recording formats require the appropriate machine to play them; they are *machine dependent*. They may first require identification of their format and then the location of equipment to play them. Both tasks may prove difficult, especially for noncurrent formats.

Archival records that require a machine to access the information recorded in them have special problems. Over time, it becomes difficult to find equipment that can play, read, or decode the information. If the recording is not migrated to a more current format before the last machine is gone, the information will be lost. Formats that are no longer readily available will require professional technical help to identify an appropriate new format and create a *preservation copy*. A preservation copy is replicated to create a *master copy* from which an *access copy* is made for researcher use. The preservation copy is then stored in a secure and environmentally stable environment. It is only used to create more master copies; otherwise, it is not played. Some machine-dependent records are in such fragile physical condition that they can be played only one more time before they disintegrate. Any record suspected to be in such perilous condition should not be played until it can be played for the purpose of rerecording it as a preservation copy. Researchers should not be allowed to use or handle originals or preservation copies.[2]

Machine-dependent records are often information dense, meaning that a little damage can destroy a lot of information. Dust, scratches, and fingerprints should be minimized through appropriate handling and storage, and regular equipment maintenance and cleaning. Audio cylinders, an early recording format, were made from a variety of materials, such as wax, cardboard, and plaster of paris. Cylinders tend to become brittle and crack with age. To handle cylinders appropriately, insert several fingers inside the top of the cylinder and use the other hand to provide a flat surface of support for the bottom of the cylinder. The top and bottom edges may be touched, but the grooves on the exterior should never be touched.[3]

Phonograph records vary in size and recording speed (33 1/3, 45, and 78 rpm). They have been made of materials such as shellac, acetate, and vinyl.[4] Their grooved playing surfaces also should not be touched. They should be handled by placing the palms of both hands perpendicular to the edge of the record. When records are put into or removed from their sleeves, the cover should be bowed so that the sides do not scratch the surface of the record. Place the index or middle finger in the center of the record and steady the edge with the thumb to insert or remove the record. Records should be stored upright/vertically, not laid flat on their side.

Magnetic Media

Both audio and video recordings have been made on magnetic tapes (audiocassette, reel-to-reel, and video). All magnetic media have a similar structure: a *base layer* that provides structural support and a *binder layer* that holds the magnetic particles whose configuration is translated as information. From about 1935 to the mid-1960s, cellulose acetate was the most common base layer. It is prone to brittleness and breaks cleanly when it deteriorates. It was replaced with polyester, which is much more stable, degrading at a slower rate than the binder layer. Higher grades of polyester tape were tensilized, increasing their strength but also resulting in tape that is permanently stretched out of shape. DuPont Mylar® is the most widely used polyester for magnetic tapes.[5]

The binder layer is thinner and more fragile than the base layer. Its composition varies, and its formula is a closely guarded trade secret. Problems with the binder are what usually cause magnetic media to fail. Excessive moisture in the air can cause layers of tape to stick to each other or cause the binder to separate from its base layer. Acidic pollutant gases accelerate the breakdown of magnetic tape. This layer can also be scratched by bits of dust on machine heads and guide rollers.[6]

From 1956 to 1980, the standard width for video tape was two inches. This was replaced with one-inch-wide tape. Both widths were open reel-to-reel tapes. U-matic tape, used largely by professionals, including television broadcasting, was an early cassette style with the tape on the inside of the cassette. Released in 1971, U-matic tape is three-quarters of an inch wide. Betamax, released in 1975, and VHS, released in 1977, were half-inch home videocassette tapes. In both U-matic and Betamax cassettes, the tape moved in a U shape, meaning that each sprocket went in the opposite direction, compared with VHS, in which the sprockets move in the same direction during playback.[7] U-matic still has limited use today, but Betamax is obsolete, having lost the format war to VHS.

How to Protect Magnetic Media[8]

Care for magnetic media falls into three main categories:

1. Keep them free of foreign matter deposits (solid or gaseous).

    *   House media in archival paper, boxes, or inert plastic (polyester, polyethylene, or polycarbonate). The housing must be static free.

- Do not leave them exposed to the air any longer than necessary. Return to their housing and close storage containers immediately after use.

- Handle only by the housing or plastic cases that hold them. Wear lint-free cotton gloves if it is necessary to touch the tape itself (in case of tangles or breaks).

- Keep storage rooms and surfaces where they are handled scrupulously clean. Allow no food, drinks, smoking, or sticky aerosol sprays that could gum up either the playing equipment or the playing surface. Do not store paper inside boxes next to reel-to-reel tape.

- Use filters for air-conditioning equipment and change them regularly.

- Clean playing equipment regularly per the manufacturer's instructions. When duplicating important tapes, play only on recently cleaned equipment. When duplicating deteriorating tapes, clean equipment after each tape plays in order to remove debris that might damage the next tape or playing heads.

- Remove the first one and a half winds of tape from a new reel so that the adhesive on the end does not contaminate the tape or equipment.

2. Do not apply pressure that will misshape the media.

- All cassettes, reels, or disks should be stored vertically, not flat or on a slant.

- Do not pack them tightly enough to cause pressure sideways but do provide support for them.

- Do not interfile different sizes of media together. Separating sizes from each other will more fully provide support along the sides of each type.

- Do not put heavy items on top of magnetic media.

- Keep away from heat, which causes plastic to soften and warp, and light, especially UV light, which can accelerate degradation.

- Be careful not to drop magnetic media, as the jarring can damage the magnetic particles and cause information loss.

- Magnetism can destroy data. Keep at least three inches away from all magnetic fields (twelve-volt transformers, electric motors, and antitheft detectors in libraries). Don't store media on top of or next to players. Metal shelving is okay.

- Do not use fast-forward or fast-reverse speeds, which can cause damage by creating uneven tension.

- Store tapes without rewinding after playing. This will result in more even tension on the tape. The tape can be rewound the next time it is used. Protruding edges of tape are a visual indicator that the tape is unevenly wound.

3. Store in a safe, stable environment.

- Strive to keep a stable temperature and humidity. Drastic fluctuations within a twenty-four-hour period can cause more damage than steady levels at the high end of an acceptable range.

- Maintain a relative humidity of 30 to 55 percent with as cool a temperature as the heating system can sustain.[9]

- If media are not stored and used in the same environmental conditions and there is more than a fifteen-degree difference between the two environments, allow the media four hours in its sealed container for every 15°F of difference to acclimate to the usage environment.[10]

4. Other considerations.

- It is desirable to play user copies whenever possible while keeping preservation or master copies in safe, stable storage (which may be off-site).

- DVDs and CDs that are not backed up with live server space should be checked for data deterioration every three to five years, especially for important data.

- Some sources recommend recopying magnetic and digital media every five years, before it goes bad.

- If the software required to play the DVDs or CDs is becoming obsolete, update the data to a newer version that can be read by current software or migrate to another format if necessary.

Projected Film

This section refers to projected or moving film as opposed to magnetic-based videotape discussed in the previous section. Movie film was made of cellulose nitrate or nitrate from approximately 1895 to 1951.[11] Nitrate was a transparent, light, flexible, easy-to-handle material used as a support for both black-and-white and color motion picture film and also black-and-white still photographic negatives. Nitrate film and negatives are dangerous and highly flammable. Once ignited, they can burn underwater and are almost impossible to extinguish. Burning nitrate produces lethal gases.[12]

Nitrate breaks down at an unpredictable rate over time unless stored at very low temperatures. It may appear yellowed, tan colored, stained, bleached, sticky, brittle, blistered, or powdery or may smell sweet or pungent. Not only does nitrate film self-destruct, but while it is breaking down, it also damages paper, film, many organic materials, and metals that may be stored nearby.[13] The National Park Service has several Conserv O Grams that provide detailed information on how to identify cellulose nitrate film and manage it. Its "Museum Handbook" provides additional helpful information (see Additional Reading/Resources at the end of this chapter for specific citations). Nitrate film needs to be handled and stored carefully. The primary method of preserving nitrate is to duplicate the original material onto safety film (either acetate or polyester) before it deteriorates enough to damage the images on the film.[14]

The cellulose ester family of film bases refers to cellulose diacetate (around 1901–1931), cellulose acetate (around 1931–1948), or cellulose triacetate (1948 to the present) film; all of these have also been called safety film because they will put themselves out when there is no source of flame.[15] Like nitrate, cellulose ester films are transparent and flexible; they are flammable but ignite at a much higher temperature than nitrate (above 800°F). When stored at a maximum of 70°F, they have an average life expectancy of one hundred years.[16]

Classic signs of deterioration in cellulose ester film are the development of channels created by raised blisters in the emulsion layer and tunnels in the base layer and emission of a vinegary odor, known as vinegar syndrome, because the film has been treated with acetic acid (vinegar).[17] Film that starts to give off the vinegar odor should be isolated from "clean film" because the presence of the acetic by-products will hasten the decomposition of nearby film. Storing film in sealed or closed containers also hastens deterioration by trapping the gases with the film. Like nitrate film, cellulose ester film is also prone to brittleness and breaks cleanly when it deteriorates. Recommended treatment is again preservation reformatting and cold storage for original film that has not deteriorated and has permanent historical value.

Polyester is a durable, clear plastic. It is chemically neutral, so it doesn't give off dangerous gases. It is not particularly flammable, and it has a five-hundred-year life expectancy.[18] Polyester has been the material of choice for film bases since 1960.[19]

Film has been manufactured in many different gauges, or sizes, including 8 mm, 16 mm, and 35 mm, to name a few. The size is determined by measuring the width of the film. The most common gauge of nitrate film was 35 mm; 70 mm was also used but not nearly as much. Nitrate was never manufactured as 8- or 16-mm film.[20] Super and standard are formats of 8-mm film and were typically used for family home movies, whereas 16-mm film was used in the classroom for educational purposes and 35-mm film in movie theaters.[21]

Northeast Historic Film provides the following dates as clues for film identification:[22]

1923: first 16-mm camera for amateur use

Early 1930s: 8-mm film available

1931: 16-mm sound film

1933: Technicolor film

1935: 16-mm color film, Technicolor, available

Early 1950s: 35-mm safety film in wide use

1965: Super 8 mm film available

Start by examining each film. Using gloves or very clean hands, handle the film by the edges only. Use figure 12.1 to identify the film size; 8, 16, and 35 mm are the most common sizes. Check to see whether there are sprocket holes on one or both edges. Unroll a little and determine whether the film is at the beginning or the end. Is it possible to read a title? Was any information recorded on the film canister? Is the image a positive, like a photo, or a negative (the parts that are normally light and dark are reversed)? Is the film black and white or color? Is it possible to determine whether the film has sound? Magnetic sound frequently appears as a brown stripe on one side, while optical sound is a black, wavy pattern.[23] The film size and dates may help determine whether it is made of nitrate, acetate, or polyester. Determining the film composition and size may help date the film. Some combination of information or using the tests described in the National Park Service's "Museum Handbook" (part1, appendix M) will help determine the material from which the film is made.

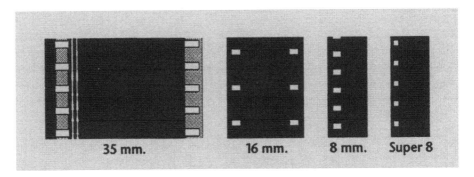

Figure 12.1. Film gauges.

Determining the material from which the film is made will guide how to handle it. Examination of the film and records about it should help determine its subject, condition, and other qualities. If the film is in reasonably good condition, it might be helpful to watch it to confirm whether it should be kept and to gather more information about the contents, possible dates, or even copyright ownership. Depending on the condition of the film, its research value, and the obsolescence of the equipment required to play the film, it may be necessary to reformat the film. If the film is deteriorating or the necessary playing equipment is not available, it may be time to consult a more knowledgeable expert. This consultant may be able to help identify the film type, evaluate its condition, or assist in reformatting the film. Professional film or conservation associations may be able to assist in locating a knowledgeable person or company to work on film in your region.

One way to evaluate the condition of your film would be to use A-D test strips, which are available from the Image Permanence Institute and archival vendors. These strips are placed inside individual film cans and left for the specified time to detect the amount of acidic vapor being given off. Then they are read by comparing them to the provided color strip to evaluate their condition. If your film is in good condition, consider whether it is affordable to replace closed or metal cans with vented plastic ones to reduce the buildup of gases. Store film in clean cans that are laid flat. Stacking cans is perfectly acceptable.

Digital or Electronic Records

Whole books have been written on electronic records, their management, and their preservation, so I will address only some basic concerns here. Electronic records are yet another group of machine-dependent records, which are even more dependent than phonograph albums or videotapes, because they also require software to assist in reading or accessing them. Start by surveying what electronic records exist, their storage medium, quantity, age, file format, and what software or hardware is required to read the files.

The first task is to determine whether you have both the necessary hardware and software to open the files, depending on their storage medium: disk or diskette, zip disk, portable flash drive, external hard drive, CD/DVD, or a computer. If the file can be opened, the next task is to evaluate or appraise the information, the same as if it were printed on paper. Does the electronic file contain textual information, a database, electronic images, or something else? Does the information fit your institution's collection policy? Is it part of a larger collection or record group that has been accepted? If yes, how does this electronic file fit with the rest of the collection? Is the information a draft versus a final copy or a duplicate of other records in the collection? Or is it a policy, minutes of a decision-making body, or information that should otherwise be kept? What is its research value?

If the file can't be opened, is there any information about what might be in the file based on labels on the storage device, material that accompanied it, or knowledge about who created or donated the file? Does it seem important enough to invest time or money getting help to open the file to evaluate it?

If the file can't be opened, it will be discarded. If the file is opened but the contents have minimal research value, are duplicated by other records, or fall outside the collection scope, it should probably be discarded. If the file is an image file but of poor quality or your institution either does not own the rights to the image or can't get the rights, it is also a candidate for weeding.

If the file can be opened and the institution wants the contents, the next question is what would be the best format for retaining the electronic record. Should it be kept as is, *refreshed* by copying onto the same or another storage device without altering the file (e.g., DVD to DVD or DVD to hard drive), or *migrated* to live server space (if available), cloud storage, or another newer storage method? Many businesses have moved to cloud storage, choosing to use a vendor that provides hardware, manages hardware and software updates, and provides technical skills and security so they don't have to. It is a model that partially or fully outsources its information technology (IT) unit.

The above options address the hardware required to access and open files; however, software is also a concern. Migration might mean converting files to a newer software version like updating document files from the DOC format (Microsoft 97–2003) to DOCX (Microsoft Office 2007 or more recent). New software versions can typically open files from the prior version, but they are only backward compatible for a limited number of versions. If the software manufacturer goes out of business or stops supporting a particular software, file conversion may become difficult or impossible. Both the hardware or storage technology and the file format made readable by software need to be kept reasonably current to enable continued access to the information for files kept in digital formats.

Printing some files out on paper may be a reasonable option. This is not a panacea for managing digital files. Maintaining ongoing access to digital files requires regular, intentional effort and time. Files of lower value might not need or be worth the expense of maintaining them electronically.

Bear in mind how fragile electronic records are. Hard drives crash, new hardware and software comes on the market in less than three years, it is easy to accidently delete files, and files on all storage media (flash drive, hard drive, disks, and CDs/DVDs) can be corrupted. Computers are wonderful for providing fast access to electronic information at all hours from around the world. Do not confuse access with preservation. Because electronic records are both hardware and software dependent and their technology changes so frequently, they are the most expensive to maintain and manage. They require a lot of attention and expense. Depending on the function of your institution and its resources, carefully weigh what must be maintained electronically. Consider whether the purpose of the electronic version is for access or because it was born digital and has permanent historic value. Server space that is actively managed, routinely backed up, and regularly undergoes software updates would be the preferred location for permanent and important electronic files. Records that were originally created in analog format can be preserved in their original format or reformatted as necessary to another format using an electronic version for access. Then, if the electronic file is lost, the original source still exists to work from again. Depending on the format and condition of the original, preservation or access copies might be kept as microfilm, printed out on acid-free paper, or saved to CD/DVD or an external hard drive. Invest in the records that are most heavily used, have the highest research value, or are best suited to the electronic medium.

Arrangement and Description

If electronic records are maintained on a server, they still need to be arranged and described. A collection may be a mix of paper and electronic formats, include additional formats, or consist solely of electronic files. Start working as if the collection were entirely paper based. Work through the records the first time, identifying the series or intellectual units of information (correspondence, business records, and meeting minutes and their creator). Separate by creator and then arrange based on the content for each creator. Eventually, as you start to box up records, you will come to formats that don't belong in the manuscript box with the paper records. Whether oversize paper records, photographs, or electronic records, they will be stored as is appropriate for that format. Whether describing them in a word-processed paper-finding aid or electronically on a web page or in a collection-management software, records are described where they fit intellectually, just as when they were physically arranged. Then, when you describe where the records are physically located, note Oversize Box 10, Photo Box 23, CD/DVD Box 2, or Kdrive\Special_Collections\elston\correspondence, as applicable. See also appendix C.6. The electronic arrangement of the file folders should structurally resemble a tree, as shown in figure 12.2.

Special Collections

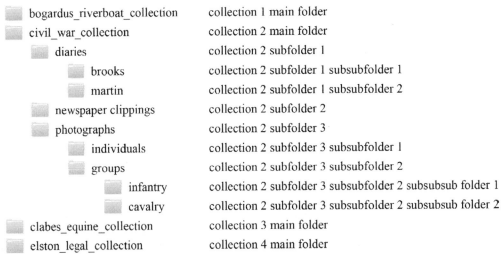

bogardus_riverboat_collection	collection 1 main folder
civil_war_collection	collection 2 main folder
diaries	collection 2 subfolder 1
brooks	collection 2 subfolder 1 subsubfolder 1
martin	collection 2 subfolder 1 subsubfolder 2
newspaper clippings	collection 2 subfolder 2
photographs	collection 2 subfolder 3
individuals	collection 2 subfolder 3 subsubfolder 1
groups	collection 2 subfolder 3 subsubfolder 2
infantry	collection 2 subfolder 3 subsubfolder 2 subsubsub folder 1
cavalry	collection 2 subfolder 3 subsubfolder 2 subsubsub folder 2
clabes_equine_collection	collection 3 main folder
elston_legal_collection	collection 4 main folder

Figure 12.2. Sample file structure for electronic records.

If copies of electronic files are kept on CD or DVD, these should be housed separately from other record formats so that they can be actively managed. Complete a separation sheet and insert it in the place from which CDs or DVDs are removed to provide context for their contents. There are archival boxes designed specifically to hold CDs or DVDs, which can be individually stored in inert, nonabrasive, antistatic, mold and tear resistant Tyvek sleeves. Foil-back labels or fine-tipped Pigma Micron pens can be used to label the Tyvek sleeves. These supplies are readily available from a number of reputable archival vendors (see appendix D.1 for a partial list).

In labeling CDs or DVDs, the following information would be helpful to note.

- A unique identification number for the disc, an accession number, or a collection number

- The collection name, series, and file, if known, to which the CD or DVD belongs intellectually

- The physical storage media (CD or DVD; CDs often have a silver or gold cast, while DVDs often have a blue or purple cast)

- How the electronic file was recorded: audio, data (includes JPG and TIFF), photo CD (Kodak only), video, hybrid (two or more of the previous)

- The name of the software required to open the files

- Copyright ownership, especially for photographs

- For photos, description, such as black and white or color, file format (JPG and TIFF), quantity of images, date taken, and event

See appendix C.9 for a sample description for sleeved CDs/DVDs.

Care and Handling

- Store discs upright, whether in plastic cases or in archival sleeves and boxes.

- Do not write on a CD or DVD with markers or other writing implements. Do not attach adhesive labels to CDs or DVDs. The layer on which information is recorded or burned is near the surface. Inks, dyes, and adhesives can bleed through to the data layer and increase the risk of data failure.

- If you absolutely must write on a CD or DVD, the safest location is the clear space/edge at the center hole.

- Handle by the edges or insert a finger in the center hole.

- Avoid scratching or accumulating dust on the surface, both of which could cause damage.

- Return discs to their sleeves or cases immediately after use to protect them from damage.

- Do not expose discs to extreme heat or humidity; avoid sunlight or storage in hot cars.

- Clean discs with a clean cotton cloth and CD/DVD cleaning detergent or isopropyl alcohol, wiping in a straight line from the center of the disc to the outer edge. Do *not* clean by wiping in a circular direction around the disc.

The life expectancy of CDs and DVDs depends on many factors but is limited. The disc type, manufacturing quality, handling, and storage conditions are major factors. Degradation of the material used for the data layer is the primary cause of disc failure.[24] Because of the importance of the composition of the data-carrying layer, gold CDs and DVDs are recommended for long-term/archival storage. A 2005 study conducted by the Library of Congress and the National Institute of Standards and Technology tested seven CD recordable products and fifteen DVD recordable and rewritable discs on the market in 2005. The life expectancy of the CD products ranged from thirty to more than forty-five years. Seven of the DVDs also tested for more than forty-five years, four fell in the thirty- to forty-five-year range, and two tested less than fifteen years. As of 2005, CDs appeared more stable than DVDs, but the technology was also more developed and stable. It is unknown whether that has changed as DVD technology has matured. All CDs in the study used pthalocycaine as the recording layer. A different material might produce a different life expectancy. Also, all test CDs and DVDs were stored in 25°C at 50 percent relative humidity. Higher temperatures and humidity or temperature and humidity conditions that fluctuate would most likely produce different results.[25]

Books

One of the differences between archives and libraries is that archives try to preserve their materials so that they will last a very long time. An archives can't simply go out and buy a replacement copy of fifty-year-old correspondence or hundred-year-old photographs if the original is destroyed. Libraries, on the other hand, are providing access to information. Normally, there are thousands of copies of the books they own, and they can be readily replaced. The difference between preserving the original and providing access to the content extends to books. Archivists and conservators will not perform preservation or conservation work that cannot be reversed. They do not necessarily use materials or techniques for books that would be acceptable to a librarian. Unacceptable examples include the use of tape and adhesives, which would cause permanent damage, or rebinding, which would, in the case of a rare book, destroy its monetary value as an artifact.

An institution may have several classes of books. Public libraries have books that circulate. The institution may own rare books, which will be handled very differently from books that circulate. An institution may also have books that don't circulate but are not rare either. In an archives, this class of books would support secondary research in the same topics in which it collects archival records. It may be appropriate either to have separate collection policies for the classes of books held by the institution or to mention them in separate sections of the institution's collection policy. A policy decision should be made regarding how the nonrare, noncirculating class of books will be treated: like replaceable library books, or like irreplaceable archival materials or rare books. This will guide how they are used and managed. The following holds if they are classified as irreplaceable archival materials. They should:

- Receive appropriate special handling when used or displayed, depending on their physical condition:

    o   Be handled with clean hands or possibly cotton gloves.

    o   Be placed on a book pillow or foam supports.

    o   May be held open with book snakes.

- Not circulate.

- Not have cataloging labels, book pockets, or other items attached to the book, or pages stamped or embossed with the institution's name or undergo other irreversible actions.

- Be cataloged by recording on rare book strips placed *between* pages, not hooked over a single page, which could lead to tears.

- Be stored under controlled environmental conditions if possible.

- Be repaired with reversible conservation treatments.

- Be supported with wider, larger bookends to minimize accidental damage.

- Be placed standing up when they fit shelving. Those books stored in manuscript boxes as part of a collection should be stored with the spine down touching the box bottom. Oversize books should stand if shelf height and/or depth accommodates or laid flat on their side as discussed in the last chapter.

Books classified as rare will receive the following treatment in addition to the conditions mentioned above. They should:

- Be subject to stricter requirements when considered for exhibition and during display *if* they are selected.

- Be handled with clean cotton gloves.

- Be placed on a book pillow or foam supports.

- Be stored under controlled environmental conditions if possible.

- Be wrapped in acid-free paper and tied with tying tape or put into archival boxes or some type of custom box, in the case of fragile volumes or books in poor condition.

Further guidance in handling and storage of noncirculating books was provided in chapter 11.

Art

Archives do not typically collect art because it does not convey information of the same kind as archival records and documents and does not usually meet the information needs of people conducting archival research. Art is more appropriate for a museum. However, art can arrive as part of a larger collection consisting primarily of other formats; for example, the papers of an artist might include representative examples. Like archival material, it should be appraised, accessioned, described, and stored under controlled environmental conditions. Some art media, such as charcoal sketches, are sensitive to prolonged light exposure, while others are not. Water, fire, bugs, humidity, food, cigarette smoke, chemicals or airborne pollutants, mold, and more can potentially cause damage, depending on the art format or medium. A lot of art is framed, adding to its size and making it more difficult to store. While framed items arriving at an archives would normally be unframed for the protection of the records they contain, framed art is an exception to this practice. Additionally, the frame for an artwork may be valuable independent of the art itself. Three-dimensional artworks can require even more storage space because of their size or shape.

Art can be easier to appraise for monetary value than manuscripts or corporate records. You may be able to conduct some basic research about the life of artists who have created pieces in your collection or the sale price of other pieces they created to obtain a general idea of the value of the art your organization owns. Depending on the age of the piece and the status of the artist, it might be wise to obtain a professional appraisal from a qualified art appraiser for insurance purposes or decisions about security.

Start your research by looking for biographical information about artists whose pieces are held by your institution. Depending on the library resources available to you, there are book series that have biographical information about contemporary or deceased artists. Information about American artists will be easier to locate than information about Asian or African artists. If your local public library does not own these resources, ask whether it can get the information for you from another library. A nearby college or university may let you examine its books even if you can't borrow them. Some art museums have an art library and allow the public to use it for research purposes. Look for basic information, such as when and where the artist was born and died and his or her name as an artist. This will help focus the search to the appropriate period and geographic location (see the specific resources listed in Additional Reading/Resources at the end of this chapter). If the artists you are researching are not found in sources such as these, perhaps they are only known locally. In this case, review local historical resources to determine dates if possible, then consider searching local newspapers or publications and records of local art organizations.

If the artist has some standing, even locally or regionally, the next question may be information regarding exhibits or sales of his or her art, including whether museums own pieces by this artist. This may be more difficult to research, depending on the artist's reputation. The Getty Research Institute of the Getty Museum has an "Appraisal Research Guide" (also listed in Additional Reading/Resources) that lists a number of helpful resources and describes the type of information each provides. Some resources require a paid subscription for access. Again, check with the local public or academic libraries to see whether any of them have a subscription or can help you locate someone who does. The local art museum is another institution that might have a subscription. Further, they are likely to maintain a collection of auction and exhibit catalogs either for their region or for artists of pieces that the museum owns. The general public may be able to conduct art research using the museum's resources. Ask.

Art can be created from a wide range of materials, some of which are different in nature from archival papers, photography, or audiovisual materials. They can be more or less sensitive to the same sources of damage as archival records. Determine the primary materials from which your art is made, then refer to the American Institute for Conservation of Historic and Artistic Works or the National Park Service's "Museum Handbook" (appendix L) for information about the care of paintings. The Northeast Document Conservation Center Preservation Leaflets and the Library of Congress Preservation website focus primarily on paper works and thus will apply to some art forms. A few of the National Park Service Conserv O Grams apply to art.

Art is a common item to use in exhibits. Chapter 10 discussed some basics of exhibit work, including preservation and security concerns. It also touched on loan documents and condition reports for art that is lent or borrowed; see appendixes B.9 and B.10. Art may require a professional appraiser to value it or a conservator to clean or repair it. Locating and working with outside specialists is addressed in the next chapter.

Objects

Objects are the final format this chapter addresses. Many archival collections include some very interesting "stuff" besides the expected documents or photographs recording the life of an individual or family, civic or community organization, business, or government. Clothing, household objects, buttons, weapons, ceremonial garb or objects, awards and trophies, and items owned by famous people and everyday people are just a few examples of what your organization might own.

In a well-staffed museum, separate specialists would manage and preserve objects based on their physical composition, format, country of origin, or other qualities. In archives, local historical societies, and other cultural institutions, objects are likely to be cared for by a generalist until such time as a specialist may be required. Intellectually, objects, like other formats, are managed the same way as paper records, meaning that they are still appraised, accessioned, arranged, and described based on their information content and creator. The processes discussed in earlier chapters still apply. Differences in format are most evident in how their information is accessed, as has been demonstrated by machine-dependent formats, and how they are stored and handled. Physically, objects are unlike paper documents and unlike machine-dependent formats.

Objects can be made of any material within the realm of physical possibility. Because of the differences in their physical and chemical composition, they will react differently to temperature, humidity, and chemicals. While the ideal might be to have a variety of storage environments suitable for accommodating these physical differences, the reality is that most institutions will have a single storage environment (meaning that the temperature and humidity settings are the same throughout) shared by all materials. This means that objects won't be organized with all the metal objects in aisle 1, glass in aisle 2, and so on.

Decisions about how to store objects are guided by factors such as size, shape, weight, the material from which an item is made, and whether it is breakable. Light and heavy items should be in separate containers to prevent the heavy item from shifting and potentially damaging the light item. Small objects, such as metal buttons, could be stored with small, heavy items, such as bullets, or light items, such as jewelry, insignia, awards, or pins but would not be stored with heavy items of a much larger size. Many small items can be stored together in a larger box with dividers. Acid-free tissue paper can be used to create a nest inside the division to keep the items from shifting around. Gaylord makes small, clear artifact boxes of polyethylene (a safe plastic) that permit box contents to be viewed without having to open them. Many small boxes could be laid flat inside a larger box. Artifact boxes that hold more than one item are available in a variety of configurations and materials from Gaylord and other archival vendors (see Additional Reading/Resources at the end of this chapter for examples of a few options).

Another option is to simply use acid-free tissue paper to carefully wrap artifacts of a similar size, weight, or nature and store them in a box that is sufficiently close fitting that it holds the objects without crushing them or allowing substantial shifting. This method also works for breakable items. Boxes containing breakable, fragile, or heavy items should be labeled with the appropriate word on the exterior to warn people when they retrieve the box.

Textile items, such as clothing, banners, flags, hats, and uniforms, should be stored separately from nontextiles. The quantity per container will depend on the size of the box, the size of the textile, and possibly provenance. If the institution owns only two garments, they can be put in the same box or two separate ones. The decision to separate them because they belong to separate collections would be as valid as the decision to put them in the same box because there are only two items. If the garments came from separate collections but shared a box, they would need to be clearly labeled. In the case of textiles, try to store them with the least number of folds possible. Use acid-free tissue paper to pad folds and prevent hard, sharp creases. Unbuffered acid-free tissue paper is best if the fabric composition is silk, wool, or unknown. Buffered acid-free tissue paper can be used with certain types of fabric, such as cotton or linen. It may be easiest to use unbuffered tissue paper exclusively because there will be no way to visually distinguish between the two types, and then the wrong type won't accidentally be used with the wrong fabric. Some items, such as banners, may be rolled to eliminate folds. Although triangular flag boxes are sold, they are not as safe as other size boxes that do not require as many sharp folds.

Silver objects can be safely stored in bags made of anti-tarnish silver cloth. Premade bags or custom-size ones sewn from specially treated silver cloth are equally acceptable.

Plaques, architectural models, and various three-dimensional objects may present storage problems because of their size, shape, or weight. For some plaques, the object itself has little value; it is the information on the plaque that has value. Options include photocopying or photographing the inscription or disassembling the plaque and removing the section with the text. Storing architectural models while keeping them dust free and intact can be challenging. Thoroughly photographing the model is one option. Sometimes it is possible to carefully partially disassemble the model for storage. It might be wise to photograph it first to aid in reassembly when required. Photographing large objects in addition to careful note taking may be the most suitable option for items that are beyond the institution's ability to store and protect.

Be careful to document what is stored in each box and the collection to which it belongs so that it doesn't accidentally become separated from its collection. It may be helpful to photograph each item and save it electronically in a folder named for the collection to which it belongs. The photos can also be printed out, annotated with box numbers and shelf location, and put in the donor or control file for the collection. PastPerfect software has an optional module that will display photos of objects. The photos can be linked to the catalog record for that item.

Objects may be easier to appraise for monetary value than paper records. Pottery, dishware, weapons, silver, items associated with (in)famous people, or other objects for which there is some type of collectable market will be easier to appraise. Individual items of high intrinsic or monetary value or of great interest because of their association with well-known people or events may be worth describing at the item level.

Objects can be challenging to care for and store because of their diverse composition, size, or other qualities, but they are often some of the most interesting pieces in an exhibit, making it worth the effort to learn how to care for them. Specialized training is available for nonspecialists from historical organizations, museum associations, preservation specialists, and professional associations.

Chapter 12

Additional Reading/Resources

Audio

Association for Recorded Sound Collections (ARSC). Accessed September 7, 2019. http://www
.arsc-audio.org. ARSC is a nonprofit organization dedicated to the preservation and study of
sound recordings, in all genres of music and speech, in all formats, and from all periods. It
publishes a journal, holds conferences, has a moderated listserv, and lists ARSC members
who provide audio preservation migration or restoration, equipment sources, and resources
for training about recorded sound, including discussion lists, training, and organizations.

Bolnick, Doreen, and Bruce Johnson. "Audiocassette Repair." *Library Journal*, November 15, 1989,
43–46. This is a good how-to article for audiocassette repair.

Casey, Mike, and Bruce Gordon. *Sound Directions: Best Practices for Audio Preservation*. Accessed
September 7, 2019. http://www.dlib.indiana.edu/projects/sounddirections/papersPresent/
sd_bp_07.pdf. Each chapter in this work includes an overview of the key concepts for people
who manage collections followed by a more technical discussion for the use of technical staff.
The project discusses the best sound practices for converting older formats to digital.

McWilliams, Jerry. *The Preservation and Restoration of Sound Recordings*. Nashville, TN: American
Association for State and Local History, 1979. This volume has a history of the first hundred
years of recorded sound, but recommendations for storage conditions (temperature and relative humidity) and preservation recommendations have been superseded.

Sturgill, Josh. "The History and Evolution of Sound Recording and its Impact on Culture and Education." Accessed September 7, 2019. https://joshsturgill.wordpress.com/2012/05/06/the
-history-and-evolution-of-sound-recording-and-its-impact-on-culture-and-education/. This
website presents a history of technologies used to create recorded sound.

Magnetic Media

Guerrero, Miriely. *Removable Media and the Use of Digital Forensics*. Accessed August 17, 2019. https://
deepblue.lib.umich.edu/bitstream/handle/2027.42/96441/Guerrero_IMLS_Removable
MediaReport_20120702.pdf. The first half of this research report describes magnetic and
optical media, their qualities, how they worked, differences between them, and factors that
damage or help preserve them in clear language with illustrations.

Film

Association of Moving Image Archivists (AMIA). Accessed September 7, 2019. https://www
.amianet.org. This organization includes professionals as well as individuals who want to protect
their personal collections. In the past, AMIA has offered a one-day basic film course available
to beginners. Other educational resources include an eight-part Introduction to Digital Formats
and Storage webinar series that addresses audio, video and digital film formats, storage and
workflows: http://www.amiaonline.org/?page_id=193; two webinars on Best Practices for Personal Audiovisual Collections: http://www.amiaonline.org/?page_id=104; and two webinars
on Best Practices for Small Audiovisual Archives: http://www.amiaonline.org/?page_id=112.

Bennett, Karen L., and Jessica S. Johnson. "Identification of Film-Base Photographic Materials."
Conserve O Gram Number 14/9. National Park Service. Accessed September 7, 2019. https://
www.nps.gov/museum/publications/conserveogram/14-09.pdf. This Conserve O Gram explains in detail how to identify nitrate, acetate, and polyester film.

Image Permanence Institute (IPI). "A-D Strips." Rochester Institute of Technology. Accessed September 7, 2019. https://www.imagepermanenceinstitute.org/store/media-preservation/ad-strips. A-D strips test for acid and measure the level of deterioration of cellulose acetate film. This web page explains what the strips do. They can be purchased from IPI or reputable archival vendors.

Knapp, Tony, and Diane Vogt-O'Connor. "Caring for Cellulose Nitrate Film." Conserve O Gram Number 14/8, 2004. National Park Service. Accessed September 7, 2019. https://www.nps.gov/museum/publications/conserveogram/14-08.pdf. This Conserve O Gram gives excellent guidelines on how to handle, store, and manage nitrate film.

National Film Preservation Foundation (NFPF). Accessed September 7, 2019. https://www.filmpreservation.org/. The NFPF offers grants for basic film preservation and free copies of *The Film Preservation Guide: The Basics for Archives, Libraries and Museums* as a download or in paper. The site also has a short primer on film decay and how to slow it by James Reilly, now retired, of the Image Permanence Institute; good storage practices and several other preservation topics.

Northeast Historic Film. Accessed September 7, 2019. https://oldfilm.org/. This is a nonprofit film archives in Bucksport, Maine, dedicated to preserving film with an emphasis on home movies.

Suits, Linda Norbut. "Hazardous Materials in Your Collection." Conserve O Gram Number 2/10, 1998. National Park Service. Accessed September 7, 2019. https://www.nps.gov/museum/publications/conserveogram/02-10.pdf. On page 2, there is a brief description of the hazards of nitrate film to people.

University of Illinois at Urbana-Champaign. "Preservation Self-Assessment Program (PSAP)." Accessed September 14, 2019. https://psap.library.illinois.edu/. This is the opening page for the PSAP. Originally developed as the Audiovisual Self-Assessment Program (AvSAP), in 2015, this open-source self-assessment program, designed for organizations with minimal or no preservation training or conservation staff, was expanded to include photographs and images, paper records, and object formats. Follow the More link on the opening page for specifics or skip to the extensive collection ID Guide at https://psap.library.illinois.edu/collection-id-guide. All that is needed is a web browser. The website includes a manual and glossary.

US Department of the Interior. National Park Service. "NPS Museum Handbook, Part 1, Appendix M: Management of Cellulose Nitrate and Cellulose Ester Film." National Park Service. Accessed September 14, 2019. https://www.nps.gov/museum/publications/MHI/mushbkl.html. This source provides guidance on identifying, evaluating, and managing both nitrate and acetate film. Pages M:12–M:14 describe the tests mentioned above.

Digital or Electronic Records

AV Preserve. Accessed September 19, 2019. https://www.avpreserve.com. Under Products, look at Exactly, Fixity, and other products for digital files.

Byers, Fred R. *Care and Handling of CDs and DVDs—A Guide for Librarians and Archivists*. Washington, DC: Council on Library and Information Resources and Gaithersburg, MD: National Institute of Standards and Technology, 2003. Accessed September 14, 2019, https://clir.wordpress.clir.org/wp-content/uploads/sites/6/pub121.pdf. This publication discusses the composition, structure, longevity, cleaning, labeling, care, and storage of CDs and DVDs.

Slattery, Oliver T., and Jian Zheng. *Final Report: NIST/Library of Congress (LOC) Optical Disc Longevity Study*. Washington, DC: Library of Congress and Gaithersburg, MD: National Institute of Standards and Technology, 2007. Accessed September 14, 2019. http://www.loc.gov/preservation/resources/rt/NIST_LC_OpticalDiscLongevity.pdf. This report describes research on the longevity of optical discs, specifically the impact of temperature and humidity on the life span of CD-R and DVD-R RW formats.

Books

Rare Books and Manuscripts Section Publications Committee. "Your Old Books." Accessed September 14, 2019. http://rbms.info/yob/. RBMS is the professional association for managing rare books. The "Resources" and "Publications" links may be helpful.

US Department of the Interior. National Park Service. "Museum Management Program, Conserve O Grams." Accessed September 14, 2019. https://www.nps.gov/museum/publications/conserveogram/cons_toc.html. See particularly the following:

19/1: "What Makes a Book Rare?" and

19/3: "Use and Handling of Rare Books"

Art

For biographical information about artists, try the following books:

Akiyama, Terukazu, Hugh Brigstocke, and Jane Turner, eds. *The Dictionary of Art*. London: Grove, Macmillan, 1996. This was previously called the *Macmillan Dictionary of Art*.

American Federation of Arts. *Who's Who in American Art*. New Providence, NJ: Marquis Who's Who, 1937–2016.

Falk, Peter H., Audrey M. Lewis, Georgia Kuchen, and Veronika Roessler. *Who Was Who in American Art*. Madison, CT: Sound View Press, 1999. Use this for more obscure artists in the United States.

Naylor, Colin, and Genesis P-Orridge. *Contemporary Artists*. New York: St. Martin's Press, 1977. This is weak on African and Latin American artists.

Turner, Jane, ed. *Grove Dictionary of Art*. New York: St. Martin's Press, 2000 (in print) or Macy, Laura Williams, and E. Bénézit. *Oxford Art Online*. Basingstoke, England: MacMillan, 2002 (electronic resource). Accessed September 14, 2019. https://www.oxfordartonline.com/. Either format includes biographies and a smattering of other information about art.

Walsh, George, Michael Held, and Colin Naylor. *Contemporary Photographers*. New York: St. Martin's Press, 1982.

Getty Research Institute, J. Paul Getty Trust, has a number of resources that are useful for art research:

Appraisals Research Guide. Accessed September 14, 2019. http://www.getty.edu/research/tools/guides_bibliographies/guide_appraisal.html. This guide provides information on how to research the background and value of a range of art formats as well as how to locate an art appraiser.

Art and Architecture Thesaurus® Online (AAT). Accessed September 14, 2019. http://www
.getty.edu/research/tools/vocabularies/aat/index.html. AAT is a standardized vocabulary for
terms relating to art or architecture. They may be used for creating catalog records or other
description.

The Getty Thesaurus of Geographic Names® Online. Accessed September 14, 2019. http://www
.getty.edu/research/tools/vocabularies/tgn/index.html. This thesaurus provides the correct
form of many geographic names related to artists or their art. These terms are also acceptable
for cataloging or descriptive purposes.

Research Guides and Bibliographies. Accessed September 14, 2019. http://www.getty.edu/
research/tools/guides_bibliographies. There are additional guides for researching artists'
biographies and their signatures.

Union List of Artist Names® Online (ULAN). Accessed September 14, 2019. http://www.getty
.edu/research/tools/vocabularies/ulan/index.html. ULAN helps identify the most commonly
used name for an artist or architect and may provide biographical information. ULAN is stron-
gest for American and European artists, weaker on Asian artists.

For the care or conservation of art:

American Institute for Conservation of Historic and Artistic Works. "Caring for Your Treasures."
Accessed September 19, 2019. https://www.culturalheritage.org/about-conservation/caring
-for-your-treasures. An assortment of guides based on material type is located here as well as
help locating a conservator.

National Park Service. "Appendix L Curatorial Care of Easel Paintings." Accessed September 19,
2019. https://www.nps.gov/museum/publications/MHI/MHI.pdf. See also "NPS Museum
Handbook, Part 1: Museum Collections, Chapter 7: Museum Collection Storage." https://www
.nps.gov/museum/publications/MHI/MHI.pdf. This chapter discusses storing paintings and
other formats. See figure 7.15 on p. 7:46.

Northeast Document Conservation Center. "NEDCC Preservation Leaflets." Accessed September
22, 2019. https://www.nedcc.org/free-resources/preservation-leaflets/overview.

Objects

Gaylord Archival. "Boxes, Specimen, Archival, Coroplast, 3mm." Accessed September 19, 2019.
https://www.gaylord.com/adblock.asp?abid=15179&search_by=desc&search_for=artifact
%20boxes&mpc=WW. This is an example of a divided artifact box made of Coroplast (polypropylene, another archivally safe plastic).

———. "Modular Box System, Artifact, Clear & Deep Lid, Archival, Buffered, Metal Edged, Corrugated
E-Flute, Blue, Gaylord®." Accessed September 19, 2019. https://www.gaylord.com/Preservation/
Artifact-%26-Collectibles-Preservation/Boxes%2C-Trays-%26-Dividers/Storage-Boxes/Gay
lord-Archival%26%23174%3B-Blue-E-flute-Clear-Lid-Modular-Box-System/p/CLMOD-SYS
TEM. An example of a modular box containing assorted sizes of smaller artifact boxes within.
The box is made of archival material but has a clear lid for easy viewing of the contents.

Ordoñez, Margaret T. Your Vintage Keepsake: A CSA Guide to Costume Storage and Display. Lubbock: Costume Society of America: distributed by Texas Tech University Press, 2001. This
inexpensive guide explains how to store and exhibit textile items.

Preservation Resources for Multiple Formats

Library of Congress. "Preservation, Collections Care." Accessed September 19, 2019. https://www.loc.gov/preservation/care. This web page has links to basic information and simple steps for good care, handling, and storage of a variety of material formats.

US Department of the Interior. National Park Service. "Museum Management Program, Conserve O Grams." Accessed September 19, 2019. https://www.nps.gov/museum/publications/conserveogram/cons_toc.html. See particularly the following:

16/1: "Causes, Detection, and Prevention of Mold and Mildew on Textiles 1993,"

16/2: "Dry Cleaning Museum Textiles 2000,"

16/3: "A Simple Storage Mat for Textile Fragments 2001,"

19/8: "Preservation of Magnetic Media 1993,"

19/9: "Caring for Blueprints and Cyanotypes 1995,"

19/19: "Care of Archival Compact Disks 1996," and

19/20: "Care of Archival Digital and Magnetic Media 1996."

Notes

1. Richard Pearce-Moses, *A Glossary of Archival and Records Terminology*, Archival Fundamentals Series II (Chicago: Society of American Archivists, 2005), s.v. "record."

2. Mary Lynn Ritzenthaler, *Preserving Archives and Manuscripts*, Archival Fundamentals Series (Chicago: Society of American Archivists, 1993), 72–73.

3. Ritzenthaler, *Preserving Archives*, 73.

4. Ritzenthaler, *Preserving Archives*, 73.

5. Dan Riss, "Preservation of Magnetic Media," Conserv O Gram Number 19/8, National Park Service, accessed September 9, 2019, https://www.nps.gov/museum/publications/conserveogram/19-08.pdf.

6. Riss, "Preservation of Magnetic Media," 2.

7. Alan Lewis, "Archives Basic Film Workshop," Association of Moving Image Archivists, Boston, November 19, 2002; Wikipedia, "U-Matic," http://en.wikipedia.org/wiki/U-matic.

8. Riss, "Preservation of Magnetic Media," 2–4; Ritzenthaler, *Preserving Archives*, 74–75.

9. Jeremy Linden, "Environmental Data Analysis—Tips and Tricks," webinar in Sustainable Preservation Practices series presented by Image Permanence Institute, Rochester Institute of Technology, Rochester, New York, March 23, 2011.

10. Diane Vogt-O'Connor, "Care of Archival Digital and Magnetic Media," Conserv O Gram Number 19/20, National Park Service, accessed September 9, 2019, https://www.nps.gov/museum/publications/conserveogram/19-20.pdf.

11. Lewis, "Archives Basic Film Workshop."

12. Tony Knapp and Diane Vogt-O'Connor, "Caring for Cellulose Nitrate Film," Conserv O Gram Number 14/8, National Park Service, accessed September 9, 2019, https://www.nps.gov/museum/publications/conserveogram/14-08.pdf.

13. Knapp and Vogt-O'Connor, "Caring for Cellulose Nitrate Film," 1; Linda Norbut Suits, "Hazardous Materials in Your Collection," Conserv O Gram Number 2/10, National Park Service, accessed September 9, 2019, https://www.nps.gov/museum/publications/conserveogram/02-10.pdf.

14. Knapp and Vogt-O'Connor, "Caring for Cellulose Nitrate Film," 1.

15. Lewis, "Archives Basic Film Workshop"; National Park Service, "Museum Management Program, NPS Museum Handbook, Part 1: Museum Collections, Appendix M, Management of Cellulose Nitrate and Cellulose Ester Film," M:8, accessed September 9, 2019, https://www.nps.gov/museum/publications/MHI/AppendM.pdf.

16. NPS Museum Handbook, Part 1: Museum Collections, Appendix M, M:8.

17. NPS Museum Handbook, Part 1: Museum Collections, Appendix M, M:9; Lewis, "Archives Basic Film Workshop."

18. NPS Museum Handbook, Part 1: Museum Collections, Appendix M, M:9.

19. Lewis, "Archives Basic Film Workshop."

20. NPS Museum Handbook, Part 1: Museum Collections, Appendix M, M:12.

21. Lewis, "Archives Basic Film Workshop."

22. Northeast Historic Film, *How Do I Identify Film?* (Bucksport, ME: Northeast Historic Film, 1994).

23. Northeast Historic Film, *How Do I Identify Film?*

24. Fred R. Byers, *Care and Handling of CDs and DVDs—A Guide for Librarians and Archivists* (Washington, DC: Council on Library and Information Resources and Gaithersburg, MD: National Institute of Standards and Technology, 2003), 12. Accessed September 9, 2019, https://clir.wordpress.clir.org/wp-content/uploads/sites/6/pub121.pdf.

25. Oliver T. Slattery and Jian Zheng, *Final Report: NIST/Library of Congress (LOC) Optical Disc Longevity Study* (Washington, DC: Library of Congress and Gaithersburg, MD: National Institute of Standards and Technology, 2007). Accessed September 9, 2019. http://www.loc.gov/preservation/resources/rt/NIST_LC_OpticalDiscLongevity.pdf.

13

Outside Specialists

At some point while managing collections, the need may arise for the services of an outside specialist, such as an appraiser, a conservator, or others. The question "What is the monetary value of this collection, or item?" arises in a number of situations. A donor may desire a value for a potential donation to claim a tax deduction. To obtain insurance for the collections as a whole, a value is required. Items that are loaned out to other institutions need to be valued for insurance coverage while they are away from their home institution. Items that still have value may be deaccessioned from the collection. They can be sold privately, through an auction, or on e-Bay. How much should they be sold for? Or perhaps the institution wishes to purchase something to add to the collection. What is a reasonable price to pay for it? These are all examples of when the monetary value of one or more items would be helpful in decision making.

Rough Estimate of Value

In some cases, a rough estimate may suffice, and some research can establish a price range. In other cases, a more definite value based on expert knowledge and experience is required. How can you obtain this type of information? For a rough estimate, current market transactions can be an indicator. Any price may be asked, but if buyers think it is grossly inflated, the item won't sell. Then again, novice buyers may overpay for something that a more experienced person would know is overpriced.

Start with some background research on the item in question. Does the institution have any information about what the item is, its age, where it might have been created, or who previously owned it? Is it art, a book, a photograph, an object, or something created on paper? For art, what is the medium? Does it look amateur or professional? Is it signed or dated? Are there any labels or marks on the piece? Does it appear American, European, Asian, or African in style? Have you ever seen anything similar? Look on the internet at museum or art sites to see if you can locate something similar. Perhaps there is a name to the specific style or type of art. This would help narrow the search. There are books, magazines, auction catalogs, and websites devoted to various schools of art or artists and encyclopedias of art and book series of biographical sketches for current and deceased artists. Sometimes art gallery managers may be able to help identify art or artists. Art faculty at the local college, university, or art school may be of some assistance. Even if they can't identify a piece, perhaps they can refer you to someone who can. As research progresses, hopefully more specific information is uncovered about this particular piece of art, how (un)common it is, and who else might have something similar.

Once sufficient particulars are determined, look for information about the sale or value of pieces like yours. Art libraries often collect auction catalogs to establish values and a chain of ownership. Museum staff need this type of information. Auction houses may maintain information about past auctions and the sales price of specific items. They may also be willing to examine your art and give you some information for no charge. Sometimes there are local *Antiques Roadshow* types of events at which representatives from an area auction house will be present to examine items for a nominal cost. There may be information on the internet about the sale of art like yours. If the category of art to which your piece belongs is uncommon, has not been written about much, or is by a little-known artist, or a professional evaluation is required, then a professional appraiser is wanted.

Books, excepting rare books, are probably the easiest to research because they usually include enough identification to research them and more than one copy exists. The title page or first few pages of most books include the formal title, author, publisher, date, and location of publication. This is sufficient information for research. Like art, there are encyclopedias and biographies of current and deceased authors. A useful resource for determining the number of cataloged copies of a particular book and their locations is an electronic database to which many libraries subscribe, for a fee, called WorldCat. This database includes only those copies of a book that have been cataloged and whose catalog record has been submitted to the database (for which there is a fee). Not every library subscribes to WorldCat, but if a library in your area does, you can get a sense of how (un)common a particular book is.

The Antiquarian Booksellers Association of America maintains databases of member book dealers, antique and rare books for sale, and missing and stolen books. Abe Books, Rare Book Hub, Powell's, or Bookfinder, among others, carry older and used or rare books (see Additional Reading/Resources at the end of this chapter for their websites). If any of these sources is offering a copy of a book you are trying to appraise, you will be able to see the asking price. There may be multiple copies, each with a different price. Read closely to compare the edition(s) being advertised and their physical condition. Use the one that most closely matches your copy. Online book sellers like Amazon or Barnes & Noble are sources for the asking price of recent books. Bear in mind that an asking price is only a rough guideline. There are other factors that can affect the value of a specific copy. If a more reliable valuation is required, an appraiser can help.

In the case of photography, some of the same resources for art research may include photographers and photography. There are also specialty resources, particularly for nineteenth-century images. Refer to some of the photography resources mentioned in chapter 5, particularly James M. Reilly's book, to identify the type of photographs being researched. This will make further research easier by focusing on one or two types of images whereas some resources are devoted to a single type of image, photographer, or subject. Baldwin's book will help with technical vocabulary for photography.

It may be possible to locate similar items for sale from antique dealers to obtain a rough estimate for objects in the collection. The Public Broadcasting Service's television show *Antiques Roadshow* has a website with resources for collectables as well as art. Under the "Appraisals Archive," it is possible to pick a category and see if anything similar has ever been appraised on an episode.

Professional Appraisers

If a rough estimate of the value of an item is insufficient, a professional appraisal will be required. How do you locate an appraiser? How do you know if they are qualified to appraise the item that needs appraising? Appraisers specialize in their area of expertise. Appraisers who value art, books, objects/collectibles, or manuscript collections fall into the broad category of personal property appraisers as opposed to real estate or business appraisers. Jewelry appraisal is also a separate specialty. According to the American Society of Appraisers (ASA), personal property appraisers are not regulated by state or federal government. They can be accredited by professional organizations, but not all appraisers are accredited. The ASA's website provides information on how to select an appraiser, questions to ask to determine their credentials and expertise, dos and don'ts for an appraiser, and what to expect.[1] No one who appraises an item should have a personal or financial interest in that item. This means the appraiser's fee is independent of the value of the item being appraised. It also means that an organization may not pay for an appraisal for an item about to be donated to them. Both examples illustrate a conflict of interest. The appraiser might be tempted to inflate the value of the item to receive a higher commission. The organization might be tempted to pressure the appraiser to overvalue an item for the benefit of the donor, something that in turn could benefit the organization.

Personal property appraisers have their own professional association, the Appraisers Association of America (AAA). Their website has a detailed outline of the information that should or may appear in an appraisal, the areas in which members specialize, the association's code of ethics for members, and a database for locating appraisers. Both the ASA and the AAA maintain standards for their members, including continuing education and certification. The Internal Revenue Service accepts appraisals for tax purposes from three US-based appraisal organizations, of which these are two. The AAA has produced an informative brochure about collecting art, *Expert's Guide to Collecting*, which briefly discusses how appraisals can be used and the role of conservators relative to art and other collectables. The brochure can be read online at their website.[2]

The International Society of Appraisers specializes in personal property appraisals. Their website includes help in locating an appraiser and a brochure on how to select a qualified appraiser. The Art Dealers Association of America appraises only art. Their appraisers also follow education and certification standards and are recognized by the Internal Revenue Service to provide appraisals for tax purposes. Curators or administrators at local or regional art museums may also be familiar with area appraisers and be able to make a recommendation. Professional appraisals or even informal research to further identify and estimate the value of collection material should be added to the donor or control file used to manage the item or materials that have been researched or appraised.

Conservators

A specialist who can aid in caring for historical or cultural collections is a conservator. Paper, photographs, or film negatives are rolled up too tightly to flatten without causing damage. A photo has gotten wet, and part of the image is stuck to glass from a photograph frame. A paper item is falling apart, has pieces missing, or is dirty. A painting has tears in the image, or the frame is missing pieces. Period clothing or historical flags need cleaning or repair. These are typical examples of damage that is beyond the normal expertise of a staff member. The right conservator can help with all these problems. Conservators specialize even more than appraisers and require a lengthy program of study and practice before they are qualified to work.

According to conservator Jan Paris, "Conservation treatment is the application of techniques and materials to chemically stabilize and physically strengthen items in the collection. The aim of treatment for materials with *artifactual value* is to assure the item's longevity and continued availability for use, while altering its physical characteristics as little as possible. Conservation also includes making decisions about which items need treatment and determining appropriate treatments."[3]

A professional conservator is highly trained in theoretical and practical knowledge of

- the history, science, and aesthetics of the materials and techniques used to produce the items in our collections;

- the causes of deterioration or damage to these items;

- the range of methods and materials that can be used in conservation treatment; and

- the implications of any proposed treatment.[4]

Although there is no license or certificate to identify who is qualified to provide the appropriate conservation treatment, "the days of apprentice training are ending and most professional conservators these days have been to graduate school." Most conservators in the United States are members of the American Institute for Conservation of Historic and Artistic Works (AIC), their national professional association. Many are "professional associates"; a smaller number are "fellows." "Becoming a professional associate or a fellow is a peer review process and requires a certain number of years in the field after completion of training as well as submission of letters of recommendation and examples of examination and treatment reports." Professional associates and fellows must agree to abide by the AIC Code of Ethics. Conservators in private practice who want to be listed in AIC's referral system on their website must be a professional associate or fellow. Before hiring a conservator, ask him or her questions about his or her training, the length and extent of practical experience, and references.[5]

Several of the Additional Reading/Resources at the end of this chapter can be used to locate prospective conservators. As with professional appraisers, the staff at a local or regional museum may also be able to suggest the names of conservators they have used. Once several names have been obtained, further research will be required to select one. Read some of the technical leaflets for the particular type of material or item that needs conservation treatment as well as some of the information about working with a conservator. Develop a list of questions to ask the potential conservators. Some candidates may be eliminated because your item type is outside their specialty, their lab facility may not be able to physically accommodate an item of the size you need conserved, or their price is higher than you can afford.

Don't hesitate to ask the conservator to explain technical vocabulary or processes or other questions that will allow you to assess the treatment he or she has proposed or to compare it with other proposals. Ask what will be done, in what sequence, and how. Will different specialists work on different parts? For example, a conservator who works on paintings may not work on the wood frame. Make sure you understand the proposed treatment and its anticipated outcome. You need to be able to evaluate the proposal and choose the work to be done and by whom. Depending on the item and its condition, you may be able to request estimates for different levels of work—good, better, or best treatment plans that would provide choices depending on the available resources. For example, the minimum work for an oil painting might be to clean the surface of the painting while it remains in its frame. A better treatment plan might be to remove the painting from the frame, clean the surface of the painting to the edge of the canvas, and replace the nails attaching the canvas to the frame. The optimal treatment might be to also clean the frame, repair any loss of the frame itself (where chunks may have broken off or the frame was gouged), touch up dinged paint, and cover the back with acid-free materials when the painting is returned to the frame.

It is part of conservation protocol to document what an item looked like before work started and after the treatment is completed. There may also be interim photos at various stages of work. Ask whether you will receive copies of the images. They might be an interesting side note for a piece that was conserved and is later exhibited. They would certainly be desirable to have for the donor or control file along with any other documents about the conservation work.

Gunsmiths

Some collections include historical weapons and their parts, attachments, or ammunition. Weapons are made primarily of metal or a combination of metal and wood. Accessories may be made of other materials. If you are unable to locate a conservator or appraiser who works with weapons, an experienced gunsmith might also have the necessary expertise to clean, repair, appraise, or identify historical weapons from your collection. An auction house or antique dealer might be able to recommend someone. Private individuals collect historical weapons from all the wars in which Americans have fought. Dealers buy and sell them at trade shows held throughout the country. There are also groups of people who reenact the American Revolution and the American Civil War. They strive to authentically re-create the uniforms, weapons, and accoutrements of their period. People involved in these activities may also be a source for the name of a qualified gunsmith.

Shipping Companies

Items that are sent for conservation or lent to another institution or even incoming donations may require the services of a commercial shipping company for transportation. Some companies specialize in transporting art and museum pieces. If you are shipping to a conservator or another institution, ask them for names of companies they would or would not recommend. Check with other institutions in your area, ask colleagues, or use professional listservs or the internet to identify potential candidates.

Contact several companies, explain what you would like to ship, and request a quote. Ask how long the company has been in business and how experienced they are with moving the type of object you need moved. Discuss who will wrap, crate, or prepare the item for shipment. Depending on the size, weight, and fragility of your item, it may be best to have the shipping company prepare the item. If it is something simpler, such as an oversize painting, you may be able to wrap it yourself. There will be an additional charge if the shipping company wraps your item. Depending on your insurance situation and the value of the item, it may make a difference who wraps it. The shipper will not provide the same coverage in case of damage if he does not wrap the item. He will not assume responsibility for someone else's wrapping job. If this is your first time shipping art, furniture, or a historical item, consider asking the conservator or receiving institution what is an appropriate method of wrapping.

If there are special requirements for handling your item, ask whether the shipper can accommodate your request. Ask about security for your item. Will the truck go directly from your location to its destination, or will it make additional stops? How is the pickup scheduled? Does the shipper have a regular circuit, or does he go directly between two points? Will your item arrive on time if there is a specific schedule?

These types of materials are preferably kept in climate-controlled environments. This should apply equally during shipping. Paintings and other items should be shipped in climate-controlled trucks, especially during the very cold or hot parts of the year. A metal sculpture may not mind going from a controlled environment of 60° to 70°F to 35° or 90°F in a matter of minutes, but paintings, wood frames or furniture, and other items will.

Determine whose insurance will provide what type of coverage during which phase of the time your item is not at its home institution. Will the conservator provide coverage while your item is being worked on, or is it still under your coverage? If you have insurance and your policy needs to cover your item while it is away, you will need to notify the insurer where the piece will be and specify the period it will be at that location. If your piece is going on loan to another institution, it should provide the insurance. The status of the insurance should be addressed in the loan documents.

As with other contracts, be clear about what will or will not be provided by whom, what the fees are, and the payment method. Request notification when your piece arrives at its destination and provide the same courtesy when it returns. File shipping, loan, appraisal, and other important documents in the donor or control file for the piece or collection that is affected. These records document the history of the particular item and may be needed for future research or decisions relative to the piece.

A Word about Books

A number of specialists manage books. General librarians manage books that circulate in public, academic, school, or corporate libraries. Rare book librarians have special training in the identification and management of rare books. Rare books are often older books but can also be as young as the first edition of Stephen King's first novel, *Carrie*, before he became famous. Age does not guarantee rarity.[6] Archivists often manage rare books as one type of material in a Special Collections department. Care must be taken to distinguish between a book that is an information source for a patron and a book that is also an artifact. In the former case, the focus is on the content of the book. It may be repaired, rebound, or replaced if a specific copy is damaged or wears out. It is usually replaceable. When the value or significance of a specific book or specific copy of a book is also dependent on its appearance, the manner in which it was physically constructed, who previously owned it, or handwritten notations added after it was published, it cannot be repaired or handled in the same manner as an ordinary book. If it is, it will decrease not only in monetary value but also in value as an artifact, an object of cultural value.

There should be a clear distinction between books that are used by staff or researchers for their information content and those that also have *artifactual value*. Staff should clearly know which are which and handle them accordingly. Typical library book repair methods, including the use of tape and glue, should be avoided. Care must be given not to damage the spine during photocopying or when removing a book from the shelf. A conservator should be consulted for damage to books that have artifactual value or that are rare.

It is not easy for a novice to identify rare books. There are many variables for identifying or valuing them. If your institution owns or is offered a significant quantity of books that you suspect might include some rare ones, consider hiring a rare book specialist for a day or so, depending on the quantity of books. If it is a matter of a few volumes, start with some research as covered earlier in this chapter, or perhaps an antique book dealer will offer an opinion. If, however, there is a sizable quantity of books to evaluate, a consultation by a rare book appraiser or rare book librarian would be more helpful. If possible, try to eliminate books that are obviously not good candidates for the rare book category. An experienced librarian may be helpful for conducting a rough sort to make the best use of the consultant's time.

Vendors

Vendors sell all sorts of things: supplies, equipment, and services. Some try to sell the same product to everyone even though their needs and situation are not alike. Better vendors will try to develop the best fit from among the products they have to sell. The institution must decide from among the various vendors and products which best fits what they need, can afford, will be able to use, and will be able to maintain.

Archival supplies are best bought from vendors who specialize in archival products. They are not inexpensive when compared with office supplies and often have to meet specific standards for their chemical composition. Someone who sells primarily office supplies is unlikely to be familiar with the appropriate standards. It is unlikely that they would make a profit selling just one or two archival products, making it doubtful that their products truly meet archival standards. It would be wiser to deal with a vendor who self-identifies as specializing in archival products, will be able to answer questions about their composition, and is often willing to educate new people about what is an appropriate product for a particular use (names of some of the more well-known companies are included in appendix D.1). This list is not exhaustive but merely a starting point.

If the institution is considering specialized equipment, software, or a service with which it is unfamiliar or that is from an unfamiliar vendor, there are helpful resources available. Ask other institutions similar to yours whether they are familiar with the product, service, or vendor. These institutions may be local, state, or regional libraries; historical societies; archives; museums; historical properties; government; or civic or corporate organizations. Professionals who specialize in jobs using these products and services belong to professional associations at the metropolitan, state, regional, and national levels. Many of the associations have websites with resources available for use. The associations also tend to have listservs and discussion boards. While some of these are for members only, others are open to whoever would like to join the listserv. In some cases, it might be worthwhile to engage an outside consultant—someone who is experienced and doesn't have a product to sell you—to advise, help evaluate, and compare products or to help develop a work process for a new technology or function.

Sometimes an organization has a short-term need for a specialized skill or information that no one at the organization has. If the resources are available, consider temporarily hiring a qualified person who possesses the skills to address the need. Try to conduct some basic research to better evaluate potential specialists or to learn from them after they have been hired. If you don't know how to locate someone with the requisite skills, network. Ask others from an institution like yours or consult websites and listservs from professional associations.

Additional Reading/Resources

Appraisals

American Society of Appraisers. "Find an Appraiser." Accessed October 1, 2019. https://www.appraisers.org/find-an-appraiser. This international association educates, accredits appraisers, and helps consumers locate appraisers for the type of appraisal they need.

Appraisers Association of America. "Find an Appraiser." Accessed October 1, 2019. https://www.appraisersassociation.org/index.cfm?fuseaction=page.viewPage&pageID=741&nodeID=1. This web page provides assistance in locating an appraiser. Members appraise art, books, manuscript collections, objects/collectibles, and other materials.

Art Dealers Association of America. "Appraisal Service." Accessed October 1, 2020. https://www.artdealers.org/appraisal-service/. Members appraise only art. Provides help in locating an art appraiser.

International Society of Appraisers. "About Us." Accessed October 4, 2019. https://www.isa-appraisers.org/about. See also "Find an Appraiser." https://www.isa-appraisers.org/find-an-appraiser and "Questions to Ask an Appraiser" https://www.isa-appraisers.org/find-an-appraiser/questions-to-ask-an-appraiser. This association is for personal property appraisers only. Their website will help locate a qualified member for the type of appraisal desired.

About Conservation Treatment or to Locate a Conservator

American Institute for Conservation and the Foundation for Advancement in Conservation. "About Conservation" Accessed October 3, 2019. https://www.culturalheritage.org/about-conservation/what-is-conservation explains what conservation is, offers guides to care for some types of materials, and has a link to find a conservator. Their database identifies conservators by location, type of material in which they specialize, or service needed. "Resources": https://www.culturalheritage.org/resources. This web page provides many useful resources.

Conservation Center for Art and Historic Artifacts (CCAHA). "Services." Accessed October 4, 2019. https://ccaha.org/services. CCAHA provides a range of services and conserves a range of materials. "Education": https://ccaha.org/education provides links to workshops, guides, and fact sheets.

North Carolina Preservation Consortium (NCPC). "NCPC Preservation Grants" and "NCPC Resources." North Carolina Preservation Consortium. Accessed October 3, 2019 https://ncpreservation.org/programs/grants/ and https://ncpreservation.org/resources/. NCPC awards preservation grants to organizations in North Carolina for assessments, preservation, consultations, monitoring equipment, education, and more. The site also includes a bibliography and lists state, regional, national, and international preservation organizations. Follow the Programs link to Grants, and the Resources link to a list of topics.

Northeast Document Conservation Center (NEDCC). Accessed October 3, 2019. https://www.nedcc.org/. NEDCC specializes in preservation services for paper-based materials. The site has technical leaflets about how to work with a conservator and explanations of the conservation processes for some materials, including art and unbound paper items.

Do-It-Yourself Appraisal

Abe Books. Accessed October 5, 2019. https://www.abebooks.com/. You can buy, sell, or simply price new, used, and rare books at this website.

Antiquarian Booksellers' Association of America. Accessed October 5, 2019. https://www.abaa .org/. This association maintains databases of member booksellers (Find Member Booksellers), missing and stolen books (New Antiquarian Blog then Security), and antique and rare books for sale (Browse and Shop Books). All links are at the bottom of the page.

Bookfinder. Accessed October 5, 2019. https://www.bookfinder.com. This site can be used to check book prices.

Getty Research Institute. "Research Guides and Bibliographies." J. Paul Getty Trust. Accessed October 5, 2019. http://www.getty.edu/research/tools/guides_bibliographies/index.html. This page has an Appraisals Research Guide.

Rare Book Hub. Accessed September 27, 2019. https://www.rarebookhub.com/. Formerly the Americana Exchange, this site may also help with pricing books.

WGBH. "Antiques Roadshow Resources: Experts' Library." WGBH Educational Foundation. Public Broadcasting Service. Accessed October 5, 2019. https://www.pbs.org/wgbh/roadshow/ expertslibrary.html. This reference library about antiques and pricing has a bibliography of resources for art and collectible objects. Under "Appraisals Archive" is a series of search boxes. Pick a category and get a list of items with appraisal estimates. It may be possible to find something similar to an item you are researching.

Glossaries of Technical Language

American Institute for Conservation of Historic and Artistic Works. "Definitions of Conservation Terminology." Accessed October 7, 2019. https://www.culturalheritage.org/docs/ default-source/governance/definitions-of-conservation-terminology.pdf?sfvrsn=4. This web page defines common conservation terms.

Baldwin, Gordon, and Martin C. Jürgens. *Looking at Photographs: A Guide to Technical Terms*. Rev. ed. Los Angeles: J. Paul Getty Museum, 2009. This book defines and illustrates the vocabulary of photography from its earliest processes through today's digital photography.

Bookfinder. "Glossaries of Book Jargon." Accessed October 9, 2019. https://www.bookfinder .com/. The Glossary link at the page bottom goes to several English-language glossaries as well as several in foreign languages.

WGBH. "Antiques Roadshow Resources: Glossary." WGBH Educational Foundation. https:// www.pbs.org/wgbh/roadshow/glossary/.This glossary explains terms for art, antiques, and collectibles.

Notes

1. "Appraisal FAQ," American Society of Appraisers, accessed October 7, 2019, https://www.appraisers .org/all-about-appraisers-and-appraisals/appraisals-faq; "Find an Appraiser," https://www.appraisers.org/ find-an-appraiser; "Personal Property," https://www.appraisers.org/Disciplines/Personal-Property/pp-ap praiser-resources/definitions-of-value.

2. "Elements of a Correctly Prepared Appraisal," Appraisers Association of America, accessed October 7, 2019, https://www.appraisersassociation.org/index.cfm?fuseaction=document.viewDocument&documen tid=1187&documentFormatId=1958&vDocLinkOrigin=1&CFID=21507973&CFTOKEN=27bd18718951c29e -63EB3FBE-1C23-C8EB-80B8475A189F5FBA; "Areas of Specialization," https://www.appraisersassociation .org/index.cfm?fuseaction=Page.ViewPage&pageId=525; "Code of Ethics," https://www.appraisersassociation .org/index.cfm?fuseaction=document.viewDocument&documentid=720&documentFormatId=1353& vDocLinkOrigin=1&CFID=21507973&CFTOKEDN=27bd18718951c29e-63EB3FBE-1C23-C8EB-80B8

475A189F5FBA; "Find An Appraiser in Our Directory," https://www.appraisersassociation.org/index.cfm?fuseaction=Page.ViewPage&PageID=741; "Standards," https://www.appraisersassoc.org/index.cfm?fuseaction=Page.ViewPage&pageId=526; "Expert's Guide to Collecting," https://www.appraisersassociation.org/index.cfm?pageId=790.

3. Jan Paris, NEDCC Preservation Leaflets, 7.7: "Choosing and Working with a Conservator," accessed October 8, 2019, https://www.nedcc.org/free-resources/preservation-leaflets/overview.

4. Paris, "Choosing and Working with a Conservator."

5. E-mail correspondence with Wendy Partridge, paintings conservator at Intermuseum Conservation Association, Cleveland, Ohio, June 27, 2011; Paris, "Choosing and Working with a Conservator."

6. David Greenebaum, "Hidden Treasures: Rare Books in Your Library?" Lyrasis webinar, May 5–6, 2011.

Chapter 13

14

Additional Personnel

It would be the unusual institution that couldn't use more help of one nature or another to supplement its paid personnel or core volunteers. For the institution that has permanent full-time employees, additional help can include temporary employees who work full-time for a specified term or work part-time permanently or temporarily. Project personnel may be hired to accomplish a specific task, such as processing a large or significant collection, entering a backlog of records into a new or different software system, creating a permanent new exhibit, or moving. Sometimes project personnel are hired as part of a grant project that has fixed deadlines or involves something new the institution is trying to accomplish. Additional help can come from a variety of sources. There will be differences in knowledge, experience, skills, loyalty, motivation, and other qualities between permanent personnel and short-term, temporary, or volunteer help. This will be the challenge of managing and blending both groups.

Sources of Additional Personnel

Probably the first body of personnel people will think of, in contrast to paid employees, is volunteers. An organization may have an established program and actively recruit volunteers, deal with them on a case-by-case basis as they appear, or have a policy against volunteers. There may be organizations in your community that will recruit volunteers on your behalf. Volunteers can be retirees of the institution at which they volunteer or come from a different field entirely, with some surprisingly wonderful skills. People looking for work experience are encouraged to volunteer. They may be fresh out of school, changing occupations, or returning to the workforce after an absence.

Colleges and universities are a potential source of personnel for a variety of assistance. First, some college degree programs require their students to complete internships related to their future field of employment. Interns often have specific requirements for the tasks to perform or complete in order to get credit for the internship. Archives, library science, and public history fall into this category. These students may be studying archival arrangement and description, preservation tasks, web design, art, book cataloging, historical research, or any number of helpful topics. A frequently used number for a graduate-level internship is fifty hours of time spread over an academic semester, but this will vary by program.

Even if students don't need an internship, many are strongly encouraged to seek out volunteer opportunities related to their future field to gain work experience for their résumé. You can approach the program director or department chair for a program you think will be educating students with skills that would be a good match for you. Anthropology, museum studies, art, management, or technology students may not have internship requirements for their degree program but may be interested in work experience. A specific project of limited duration, such as researching an artist or painting, developing an exhibit, or expanding your website, may be an appealing opportunity. Students in some programs are required to complete a capstone project. This may be a research and writing project on a topic of interest, or it could be a more practical project that demonstrates use of a particular skill conducted at a host organization for their benefit. Some universities and colleges also have student chapters of professional associations. It may be possible to make connections with the chapter members. If you are unable to find a match for an ongoing volunteer commitment, the chapter might be interested in a service project that is small enough in scope for them to handle, perhaps a onetime event for which extra personnel are needed.

Not only are university students a potential source of additional personnel, but so are the faculty. In order for a faculty member to obtain tenure at most American colleges and universities, she must teach, produce scholarly research, and perform community service with the emphasis on the first two. She has five years to demonstrate her abilities before a decision is made to grant tenure. Even after obtaining tenure, faculty members are encouraged or required to varying degrees to perform community service. A junior faculty member (someone who is working to obtain tenure) may possess expertise that your institution desires. Depending on the size and specialty of the colleges in your region and the need of your institution, it is possible that you will locate someone who can assist you. The employment status of archivists and librarians varies by institution; some include them as faculty, and others do not.

A faculty member might catalog books; teach others to perform a task, such as how to physically handle or care for archival collections; identify art according to media type or differentiate reproductions from originals; design a brochure; classify anthropological objects; conduct oral history interviews; or countless other tasks requiring specialized knowledge or skills.

Institutions in the vicinity of approximately 361 colleges and universities from thirty-four states may be fortunate enough to engage the personnel of not only a professor but her entire class as well. The Carnegie Foundation for the Advancement of Teaching ranks American colleges and universities according to standardized criteria. In 2006, the Carnegie Foundation added a new elective category to evaluate the degree to which the faculty and students at a college or university participated in civic engagement with nearby communities. Faculty and their classes develop a collaborative relationship with local schools, government, or community organizations to solve community problems, apply knowledge or skills that the students are learning in a manner that benefits their community partner, or otherwise work together according to guidelines developed by each college. A public history class at Northern Kentucky University conducted research in area archives, historical societies, and libraries to identify archival records that documented the experiences of northern Kentucky in the Civil War. Students edited and annotated a selection of documents to create a booklet and DVD to be sold by the James A. Ramage Civil War Museum, their community partner. Students learned historical editing skills and about copyright, practiced reading English before standardized spelling and punctuation, and gained valuable pre-professional experience. The Ramage Museum benefited from the creation of a unique historical resource that they could sell as an additional source of revenue.[1] This is but one creative example of how a local historical society, public library local history room, museum, or cultural institution might engage with an entire class to accomplish something beyond the institution's ability relying solely on its own resources and skill sets.

Supplemental personnel are often hired temporarily to perform work that is funded by a grant. Their length of employment is frequently determined by the terms of the grant, as is the work to be completed, and the skills required of the grant personnel. Grants often run in one-year increments, with a maximum of three years unless renewed. Sometimes personnel hired by a grant will be hired as permanent employees after the grant expires. The opportunity to bring in this category of personnel is obviously contingent on writing and receiving grant money.

Another category of temporary employees is consultants. A consultant might work from several hours to a number of months, depending on the skills he provides to the institution. A trainer might work for only several hours to teach skills or information. Consultants who evaluate an aspect of the institution, such as processes, policies, or preservation, will require more time to complete their work. A consultant may be hired to perform tasks that only need to be done once, such as identifying or cataloging rare books. In essence, appraisers and conservators could also be considered consultants. Hiring consultants is a good way to obtain expert or specialized knowledge that is needed only infrequently. They can provide an unbiased opinion from a neutral party. Sometimes their opinion will carry more weight than an employee who says the same thing and can be effective in persuading a reluctant administrator.

A new, potential resource for a single day of professional assistance has begun emerging very recently. Local, regional, and national professional associations of archivists have begun conducting service days in the communities where the organization is based or the city where a regional or national conference is held. A session at the 2019 Midwest Archivists Conference saw presentations about service days by the Chicago Area archivists and St. Louis archivists.[2] The 2019 Society of American Archivists (SAA) conference program suggested there would be an opportunity to participate in (a) service project(s) before the conference in Austin, Texas.[3]

Such service days would provide a single day of assistance by a small number of professional archivists, possibly supplemented by graduate students in training to become archivists. Interested organizations would apply to the archival organization coordinating the project prior to a service day. They would need to describe the assistance they would like for a project of limited scope. There would be no guarantee that their project would be chosen; however, it would be a creative way to obtain some very limited assistance. Refer to the SAA website listing of local, state, and regional archival organizations for potential assistance in your area; see Additional Reading/Resources.

Managing Temporary Personnel

Having additional personnel is beneficial, but it comes with trade-offs that vary depending on the type of personnel. Issues can include the amount of turnover, time required to recruit and train, unevenness in skill levels, poor matches between skills and work to accomplish, reliability, and conditions on what is accomplished (in the case of interns or civic engagement). The question is whether the benefits outweigh the disadvantages. The answer to this question will vary by institution and perhaps by the individuals involved.

Temporary personnel have a limited or short-term commitment to the institution. Volunteers may stay only briefly or for many years, depending on a number of factors. Interns leave at the end of the semester. Grant personnel typically stay one to three years. As with permanent employees, temporary personnel need to be oriented to the organization, procedures, policies, and specific work that they will perform. Depending on their skills and experience and the work they will perform, training may also be required. Regular turnover or extensive orientation and training requirements will affect paid staff productivity. They can't perform other duties if they are orienting and training temporary personnel. If volunteers or interns are unreliable about showing up when scheduled, staff time can be lost preparing work for them or waiting to determine whether they will show up for their shift. If temporary personnel stay for only a short time, it is difficult to build up their skill level. This in turn is likely to limit the type of work they can perform, depending on the skills and knowledge they bring with them. A volunteer may have limited transferrable experience or may bring surprising depth in an area that matches an institutional need. He can be very dedicated and dependable and may stay for many years, helping to accomplish extra tasks that the staff would like to accomplish but never have sufficient time to do.

Temporary personnel can be outside the normal channels used to communicate information within an organization, whether staff meetings, e-mail, newsletters, or otherwise. Try to include them in those normal channels that make sense or to develop alternate methods of ensuring that they get pertinent information about what is going on within the organization. Not only will they be better informed for carrying out their duties, but they will also feel more a part of your organization, which will be good for morale.

If the institution would like to have volunteers to supplement paid staff or is a fully volunteer-run organization, a formal volunteer program would be the most effective method of obtaining volunteers who are a good match for the organization. Successfully run volunteer programs resemble paid employment in many ways. Each volunteer position should have a job description that clearly describes the duties, responsibilities, and qualifications for the position. Positions need to be marketed to target the best people for the job, not just warm bodies. Volunteers should be interviewed to determine why they wish to volunteer, why with your institution, and what their expectations are about the work they would perform if they volunteered with your institution. In screening volunteers to identify their strengths and weaknesses, it would also be appropriate to ask questions such as what types of jobs they have held and disliked (and why) and how would they describe their best supervisor.[4] This information is used to determine whether a potential volunteer is a good match for your institution and the work it does and the specific volunteer positions to be filled.

Once a volunteer has been recruited, matched with a position, oriented, and started volunteering, this doesn't signal the end of responsibility for whoever is managing the volunteer. The volunteer requires supervision—guidance and feedback on what he is doing to help him think, learn, and grow. He should follow standards for work performance and be evaluated. Detailed job descriptions, orientation, and supervision should clearly communicate expectations for volunteers and details of the evaluation process. In the words of Sue Vineyard, an expert in nonprofit management, "The goal of evaluation is to help people feel successful by specifically acknowledging their progress." Vineyard says that not evaluating volunteers actually implies that the work they have done is unimportant. Further, lack of evaluation implies that volunteers are different from paid staff, who are held accountable, and therefore are of lower status than paid personnel.[5] Volunteers also need to be appreciated and recognized, as do employees, but since they are not being paid for their services, their need for personal satisfaction is greater than for an employee in order to retain them.

Interns are among the most short-term of temporary help. They require supervision by someone who can teach them how to apply their classroom learning to a real-life experience. Normally, interns have conditions on the work they do for the organization where they are placed. They are expected to gain experience relevant to the course that requires the internship, frequently need to produce something that can be evaluated, and must complete everything by a set date. Interns may bring specialized sets of skills or knowledge, enthusiasm, energy, and a fresh perspective for the time they are available. Students frequently know if they are required to complete an internship and may start trying to identify a suitable organization the semester before they will complete the internship. Otherwise, they will scramble in the first several weeks of the semester to locate one for that semester. A program that regularly places interns may hold a recruitment fair for organizations seeking to host an intern, or the organization can simply contact the program director and express its desire to obtain an intern. It would likely go on a list until an intern became available. It can be challenging to develop a project that fits the requirements of an internship and matches the intern's strengths or interests. What constitutes a suitable internship project may not be high on the work priority list. There are advantages and disadvantages of supervising an intern.

College students or faculty who volunteer with an organization would be similar to a generic volunteer, except they should have a much stronger match in terms of skill sets, knowledge, and experience, particularly with the faculty member. If an organization desires additional personnel of this type, it should take the initiative and approach the college. Go to college websites and do some research. Look at their academic programs and try to identify those that most closely match the knowledge or skills your organization is seeking. Also try to determine whether there is a specific office that deals with community service or volunteer work. If no office can be readily identified, contact the chair of the department or departments that seem to be the best match. Identify your organization, indicate that you are seeking skilled assistance for a task or project, and ask whether the chair knows of a student or faculty member who might be able to help. Ask whether there are specific programs to help identify potential volunteers or what the college's preferred method would be to find a match. If the chair is unable to help, ask for a referral to someone who might be better able to assist you.

Department chairs are always busy because of all their responsibilities. The first few weeks of any semester are going to be hectic, as will the last several weeks, when exams are given and grades are calculated. Faculty teach about nine months of the year, so keep their schedule in mind when you try to contact them. The academic calendar will be available on the college's website. Be considerate of the chair's time. Be prepared to explain your request briefly but able to expand with some details if requested. Many faculty members have both a telephone number and e-mail contact information available on the college's website. Either method of communication should be acceptable.

Also, plan your request ahead of time. It may take time to identify a student who will be a good fit for your project, or a faculty member may be interested but need to complete other commitments before taking on a new one.

Recruiting a professor and her entire class may be somewhat similar to the above method of locating an individual professor. First, you should determine whether you are in the vicinity of a college or university that is involved in community service/civic engagement. The Carnegie Foundation's web page is listed in Additional Reading/Resources at the end of this chapter. Even if colleges in your area are not specifically listed on the Carnegie website, they may still perform civic engagement or community service activities. It would be worth a telephone call to find out. Once you know that the local college participates, the next step is to identify an academic department or program with whom to partner. You will need to identify a specific faculty member with whom to partner. There may be a central office on campus that coordinates community/civic/curricular engagement or partnerships. If they do, they should be able to help you locate a potential partner. If they don't, again, you may need to contact the potential department's chair and ask.

Once you have reached a specific faculty member, you will open discussion about what you might like to accomplish and what might be achievable. The professor will have to consider how this fits with the course objectives she must meet, what may be within the skill level of the students, and what can be accomplished in a semester. The professor also must have a way to measure each student's efforts to provide a course grade. Engaging the assistance of an entire class definitely will require planning. Faculty plan their course requirements by the start of the semester. Not all courses are taught every semester. Some sequential or specialized courses are taught only in the fall or spring of every other year. There may be additional research, coordination, or work that must be completed before the start of the semester in which a class is committed to your project. Anticipate at least a one-semester delay between the time you approach the college and the semester in which the class assists your organization. A project of this nature will require some time and planning but has the potential to produce work that the organization might not otherwise be able to accomplish.

Grant personnel are employees who are hired for a limited and specific duration. Frequently in cultural heritage organizations, grant positions are entry-level jobs. Grant personnel are similar to employees because they are paid yet dissimilar because they are not permanent. They undergo the recruitment, screening/hiring, orientation, and training process and are supervised as employees are. Depending on the length of their employment, they may be outside some of the routine communication channels, may have restricted access to workspaces, or may be excluded from activities in which permanent employees participate. Grant employees probably won't receive the same range of benefits as permanent full-time employees but may receive some benefits.

The shorter the term of employment, the more difficult it is to develop relationships between the grant personnel and the permanent employees because everyone knows that the grant personnel are leaving. In many ways, they are also excluded from the work experience of the permanent employees. The grant personnel can be less committed to the organization because they are not really part of it. A good supervisor will try to be as inclusive as possible to create an optimal work environment. If the possibility exists that at the end of the grant personnel might transition to permanent employment, there is incentive for both sides to work as if it will happen. As entry-level personnel, grant employees also seek to gain valuable work experience for their résumé and strong references to use when applying for future positions. Their goal will be to make the transition from temporary to permanent employee.

Depending on the service a consultant provides, he may work a few hours to several months. Sometimes the organization hires him to perform a clearly delineated task, such as training, conserving an item, or setting up and installing a system. Other times the organization knows it is having problems of some sort but isn't quite sure what is malfunctioning or what the remedy is: the temperature and humidity are erratic, or they have important records but have no idea what to do with them or how to start. For these types of concerns, the consultant may research, gather information, analyze, and produce a report with recommendations. Although a consultant works for the organization that hires his services, he is not its employee. He directs his own labors and works independently of other organizational personnel. He either is self-employed or works for a company other than the one he is assisting.

The one concern I would like to reiterate again here in regard to temporary personnel of all types is security. Temporary help is temporary. An organization has stronger ties with a full-time paid employee who risks losing his job and having difficulty securing his next position if he proves to be a security problem. The organization has less of a hold over a temporary person. Serious consideration needs to be given to the degree of access given to temporary help, especially if they are working alone. Volunteer-run local historical societies, public libraries managing local history rooms, and other small cultural heritage organizations fail to recognize the significant items in their holdings and, even worse, fail to take the security of those items seriously. As a result, they have had many things stolen that will never be recovered. When any rare, historical item is taken from the public collective through theft, it is a loss for all of us. Another piece of our common history is gone.

Additional Reading/Resources

Recruiting Volunteers

Fritz, Joanne. About.com. "Recruiting Volunteers—Three Approaches." Accessed October 13, 2019. http://nonprofit.about.com/od/volunteers/a/recruitvols.htm. An excellent article with tips for recruiting volunteers, recommendations of online volunteer matching sites, links to further reading on aspects of volunteering, and the author's newsletter.

Lynch, Rick. "Targeted Volunteer Recruiting." *Voluntary Action Leadership* (Fall 1990): 24–28. This is a good article on targeted recruitment of volunteers, although it may be a little difficult to locate. The publisher in 1990 was the National Volunteer Center. This was a quarterly journal. A library should be able to obtain a photocopy or electronic scan of the article for you through its interlibrary loan system. These library catalog codes may or may not help: ISSN: 0149-6492, OCLC: 3511276. For those who have access through a library to the electronic database called WorldCat, a search of the journal title will tell you all the libraries that own it, including whether a library near you does.

McCurley, Stephen, and Sue Vineyard. *101 Tips for Volunteer Recruitment*. Downers Grove, IL: Heritage Arts Publishing, 1988. This includes information on how to conduct the volunteer interview, questions to ask, and what to look for.

Managing Volunteers and Interns

Bastian, Jeannette A., and Donna Webber. *Archival Internships: A Guide for Faculty, Supervisors, and Students*. Chicago: Society of American Archivists, 2008.

Driggers, Preston F., and Eileen Dumas. *Managing Library Volunteers: A Practical Toolkit*. Chicago: American Library Association, 2002.

Fritz, Joanne. The Balance Small Business, "Essential Volunteer Management Strategies for Your Nonprofit." Accessed October 13, 2019. https://www.thebalancesmb.com/volunteer-management-strategies-for-your-nonprofit-4174396. This article provides a good overview of managing volunteers and provides links to other resources.

Journal of Volunteer Administration. This journal became the *International Journal of Volunteer Administration* in 2005 and has articles about working with and managing volunteers.

Reed, Sally Gardner. *Library Volunteer—Worth the Effort! A Program Manager's Guide*. Jefferson, NC: McFarland, 1994.

Society of American Archivists. "Best Practices for Volunteers in Archives." Accessed October 14, 2019. https://www2.archivists.org/standards/best-practices-for-volunteers-in-archives. This page explains the development of the Best Practices document. A PDF link at the bottom of the page goes to the document itself, which provides guidance and lists a number of web resources.

Vineyard, Sue. "Evaluating Volunteers, Programs and Events." *Voluntary Action Leadership* (Summer 1988): 25–26.

Training to Develop Volunteer Programs

American Association for State and Local History. This organization has online training regarding volunteers. Accessed October 24, 2019. https://aaslh.org/?s=training+volunteers.

Association for Volunteer Administrators. While the national association closed, many state and local branches still exist. A web search will quickly identify the one closest to your location.

Civic Engagement/Service Days

Brown University. Swearer Center. "CUEI: College & University Engagement Initiative, Previous Classifications." Accessed October 24, 2019. https://www.brown.edu//swearer/sites/swearer2/files/2010_and_2015_CE_Classified_Institutions.pdf. The Carnegie Foundation for the Advancement of Teaching has an optional elective classification for community engagement. The website for this classification is now being managed by Brown University. Download the full list of community engagement classified campuses to locate universities that met criteria for this rating. Since institutions nominated themselves for this rating category, there may be additional colleges and universities that practice community engagement but didn't apply to be evaluated.

Society of American Archivists. "Directory of Archival Organizations in the United States and Canada." Accessed October 14, 2019. https://www2.archivists.org/assoc-orgs/directory. This web page lists regional, state, and local professional archival organizations. It can be used to locate a professional organization near you for potential assistance.

Notes

1. "Carnegie Classification," CUEI: College & University Engagement Initiative, accessed October 24, 2019, https://www.brown.edu/swearer/carnegie. Select Previous Classifications. This page states that 361 institutions have obtained this classification; author's personal knowledge of how this is applied at Northern Kentucky University as she assisted and advised the class. See also Rebecca Bailey and Remington Leach, eds., *"With Every Consequence of War": The Civil War in Northern Kentucky Remembered* (Highland Heights: Northern Kentucky University, 2009), 1, 10, 117.

2. Session 803, "Transforming Outreach with Community Archives," Midwest Archives Conference, Detroit, Michigan, April 6, 2019, which the author attended.

3. Society of American Archivists, "2019 Annual Conference Program," accessed October 14, 2019, https://www2.archivists.org/am2019/attend/pre-conference-courses.

4. Stephen McCurley and Sue Vineyard, *101 Tips for Volunteer Recruitment* (Downers Grove, IL: Heritage Arts Publishers, 1988), 28-29.

5. Sue Vineyard, "Evaluating Volunteers, Programs and Events," *Voluntary Action Leadership* (Summer 1988): 25-26.

15

Disaster Preparedness

Preservation can be very broadly interpreted as any action that extends the usable life of historical records. This includes careful handling practices, rehousing in acid-free folders and boxes, using replicas in exhibits, practicing appropriate security measures, maintaining suitable environmental conditions, and applying good housekeeping practices. Preservation information has been woven into chapters throughout this book, just as their application should be integrated into all contact with collections, whether handling them directly or indirectly through proper management of the physical spaces in which they are stored and used. Note that *conservation* is a subspecialty of preservation that involves the physical or chemical treatment of documents.[1]

One aspect of preservation not mentioned so far is disaster planning. Large-scale events, such as hurricanes, floods, tornados, and earthquakes, are catastrophic and rightly qualify as disasters because of the degree and seriousness of their impact. Broken pipes and leaky roofs are minor when compared to a disaster, but they can still cause a lot of damage and are more common. It is more appropriate to classify them as emergencies. Institutions need to plan for both large disasters and smaller emergencies. Some authors use the term "disaster planning," while others use "emergency planning," but both are discussing the same topic.[2] Disaster preparedness provides two benefits. First, it does everything reasonable to prevent an emergency or minimize its impact. Second, it reduces response time if an emergency happens, in turn helping to minimize damage.

Steps for Disaster Preparedness[3]

Prepare

Conduct a thorough review of a wide range of aspects of the institution to identify and assess potential risks. The Northeast Document Conservation Center's (NEDCC's) Preservation Leaflet 3.3, "Disaster Planning," suggests starting with geographic and weather risks applicable to the region (see Additional Reading/Resources at the end of this chapter). Also, evaluate what is in the built environment around the institution. Are there businesses working with hazardous materials, transportation facilities, or controversial neighbors close by? Is your building near a lake or in a floodplain or built on top of subway lines? Consider the physical condition of your facility's exterior and interior. The NEDCC Risk Assessment Checklist (found in the Preservation 101 course) lists more general risks like these. Chapter 10 of the National Park Service (NPS) Handbook includes a thorough risk assessment worksheet. Although not all risks on the worksheet apply to all regions, it would be educational to review the entire list. The worksheet indicates the type of emergency to which each risk relates. Identify geographic and climatic risks first, then correlate them to the more detailed NPS worksheet. Note that the types of materials in NPS collections may differ somewhat from your institution, but additional research should suggest risks applicable to your materials/formats.

Prevent

The best way to prepare for a disaster is to prevent it or minimize its chances of happening. A regular program of building inspection and maintenance will go a long way toward preventing or reducing common emergencies. Once risks have been identified, they can be prioritized, and steps taken to address them. If one task on the list can't be addressed immediately, don't get stuck; move on to the next priority and come back to uncompleted items later.

The most common disaster is water related. Remove all collection materials from the floor. Use shelving that raises records at least three inches above the floor. Box as much of the collection as possible to provide protection against water and other types of damage. Try not to store records in basements or under pipes or leaky roofs. Water damage is sometimes a by-product of responding to fire. Potential fire hazards include materials blocking emergency exits, doors, or aisles; old electrical wiring; or overloaded electrical sockets. Establish and enforce a policy against smoking. Good housekeeping practices guard against inappropriate storage of flammable chemicals/supplies and accumulation of dust, debris, and broken-down junk that might contribute to a fire. Good security practices guard against theft.

Prevention includes the installation of systems that prevent, detect, or protect, such as smoke detectors, fire extinguishers, fire suppression systems (funds permitting), and security alarm systems for collection storage rooms.

Prioritize

Prioritization applies assessment information to make decisions that are recorded in the institution's disaster plan. Prioritization will determine what to quickly move to a safer location before disaster hits, what to salvage first from the disaster, and what will receive first priority during recovery for in-house treatment, professional services, or safe storage away from the disaster site. Disasters are stressful and not the best times for considered, clearheaded thinking. They do not allow time to consult professional conservators or others for advice. Decisions about priorities should be made before trouble strikes. This will enable quicker decisions during a crisis and potentially save more records.[4]

The safety of staff and patrons is the first priority. Once people are safe, the two main goals during initial response are to stabilize the condition of the collections to prevent any further damage and to salvage the greatest number of valuable materials possible. Time will be of the essence. If conditions are wet and warm, mold can develop in less than forty-eight hours. A mold outbreak will compromise successful recovery of collections materials and can pose serious health risks. Determine what has been damaged and apply the priorities to those materials. A simple system of high, medium, and low priority may work best. The priority level may be indicated by written lists of collection names and/or box numbers with location or a floor plan that uses a color-coding system. Be mindful that a list indicating the name and location of your most valuable materials is a grave security risk if it falls into the wrong hands. It would be wise to restrict access to this information to those who absolutely need to know to direct recovery efforts. This information may be one of those related organizational documents that is only referenced in the disaster plan and doesn't actually appear there.[5]

Actual criteria to consider in establishing priorities include *informational*, *evidential*, and *intrinsic* value; associational value (records directly linked to noteworthy people, groups, events, or activities); and monetary or administrative value (records crucial to the operation of the institution, such as finding aids, inventories, and donor/control files). Some of these same criteria were previously applied in chapter 2 to the evaluation of potential new acquisitions. Another consideration is how vulnerable materials are to a particular type of disaster and the likelihood of occurrence of that disaster type. This information may be more difficult to find. A conservator or other disaster consultant may be able to advise on this point. A third factor might be usage: how heavily is the collection, record, or item used by researchers? Of course, usage is often related to the informational, evidential, or intrinsic value of a collection.[6]

The NPS advises creating a table that measures the value, risk, and usage of each collection in order to prioritize it. Each of these three factors is given a point value for high, medium, and low ratings. The point values for each factor may be the same or different. The points for each collection are totaled, and the cumulative score is compared with a range of scores divided into ratings of high, medium, and low priority. If the point values are based on multiples of one-third (e.g., 9, 6, 3 or 6, 4, 2 or 3, 2, 1), cumulative scores in the top third equal the highest priority, those in the middle third equal medium priority, and those in the lowest third equal low priority. The NPS Conserv O Gram 19/10, "Reformatting for Preservation and Access: Prioritizing Materials for Duplication," gives an example of sample items, a scoring system, and a results table to illustrate how to apply this method.

Plan

Create an emergency response plan. Emergencies require a swift response to recover quickly and minimize damage and loss. Comprehensive planning and the creation of a written plan beforehand enable sound action during a crisis. An effective plan is comprehensive, simple, and flexible. It should do the following:[7]

State the purpose of the plan and the types of events addressed in the plan and refer to any other pertinent institutional documents.

Assign responsibilities. Designate a single person with overall authority to manage disaster recovery, specify methods for decision making, and indicate who will be responsible for specific aspects, such as preservation, the facility, and security.

Describe what actions to take if there is advance warning.

List disaster response activities. These are the first response/emergency/immediate actions, such as who to contact first, how to notify staff or emergency teams, contact the insurer, make sure the building is safe to enter, secure the site to authorized personnel only, determine the extent of the damage and document with photographs and/or lists, gather supplies, set up a work recovery space, and stabilize the damaged area (e.g., maintain temperature below 60°F, use dehumidifiers, and circulate air with fans). Make allowances for routine services that may be interrupted.

Debrief after the initial response phase about what worked and what didn't and revise the disaster plan accordingly later.

Describe recovery procedures. These are the longer-term/salvage/recovery responses that return the institution back to normal as much as possible. They include the removal of materials from the damaged area; discarding, drying, cleaning, and restoring damaged materials; repair work to the building or space itself; and return of both undamaged and restored materials once the space is ready. Catalog records and finding aids may need to be updated. Hypothesize potential disasters and specify in as much detail as possible what will be done, how, and in what sequence for each variation. Restored records will remain more vulnerable than other records. Plan to check them periodically, especially for mold and fungus if they suffered water damage.

Resources. Include contact information for staff or emergency response team members and their responsibilities, location of keys, procedures for fire and/or security alarm systems, outside people who have agreed to provide expertise or mutual aid, vendors previously identified to provide services or equipment, floor plans, forms to document materials moved to new locations for salvage, copies of mutual aid agreements/service contracts, or any other information that might be needed in case of a sudden emergency. Copies of the emergency plan need to be located both on- and off-site. Include information about these locations. NEDCC Leaflet 3.4, "Worksheet for Outlining a Disaster Plan," shows how to organize some of this information.

Practice

All personnel should be involved in disaster preparedness. At a minimum, they should be attentive to the identification and prevention of new risks. They should know how to implement the disaster plan, whether by reading and discussing key steps or possibly through mock drills. Contact information should be frequently updated, supplies checked, and the plan itself reviewed on a regular cycle for changes. Application of the activities described in this chapter, development of a written disaster plan, and practice should increase staff confidence in their ability to cope with unexpected events and provide a reasonable measure of safety for the institution's collections.

Additional Reading/Resources

American Institute for Conservation. "All Products." Accessed October 11, 2019. https://store.culturalheritage.org/site/. This organization sells an emergency response and salvage wheel that may be a useful tool to keep with your disaster response plan.

California Preservation Plan. "Emergency Preparedness & Response." Accessed October 11, 2019. http://calpreservation.org/disasters. This site includes a disaster plan workbook, template, resources (including video of a two-day workshop), and a mock exercise to test your institution's disaster response plan.

Conservation Center for Art and Historic Artifacts (CCAHA). "National Resource Guide for Disaster Preparedness." Accessed October 11, 2019. https://ccaha.org/sites/default/files/attachments/2019-04/National%20Resource%20Guide%20for%20Disaster%20Preparedness%202019.pdf. This extensive guide lists government agencies, vendors, and sources for emergency services, supplies, and equipment. While vendors may be based in the mid-Atlantic region, do not assume that they work only in this region. Damaged materials can be shipped to them, or they may consult or be able to recommend a business geographically closer to your institution. The CCAHA website also has guides and factsheets for salvaging art, photographs, books, photos, and more: https://ccaha.org/resources.

CoOL (Conservation OnLine). Foundation of the American Institute for Conservation. Accessed October 11, 2019. http://cool.conservation-us.org. From the CoOL home page, scroll down to the conservation topics for links to disaster planning and response, disaster mitigation advice, and mold. A number of links on the mold page are broken because pages have moved, but the Peter Waters article on salvaging water-damaged materials still works.

Fortson, Judith. *Disaster Planning and Recovery: A How-to-Do-It Manual for Librarians and Archivists.* How-to-Do-It Manuals for Libraries Series. New York: Neal-Schuman, 1992. Excellent, comprehensive guidance for emergency preparedness: risk prevention, response, and recovery. Includes resource lists, bibliography, and decision tree. The NEDCC recommends that if you can buy only one emergency planning guide, this should be it.

Halsted, Deborah, Richard Jasper, and Felicia Little. *Disaster Planning: A How-to-Do-It Manual for Librarians and Archivists.* How-to-Do-It Manuals for Libraries Series. New York: Neal-Schuman, 2005. This updated version of the Fortson book includes a CD with sample disaster plans, disaster plan templates, and resources.

Library of Congress. "Library of Congress, Preservation, Emergency Preparedness." Accessed October 11, 2019. https://www.loc.gov/preservation/emergprep. This page has links to various aspects of disaster planning, recovery, and resources.

Library of Congress Preservation Directorate, Center for Great Lakes Culture, and California Preservation Program. "Getting Your Feet Wet: Recovering Water-Damaged Collections Resource List." Accessed October 11, 2019. http://www.loc.gov/flicc/about/FLICC_WGs/diaster/FLICC_Disaster_Planning&Recovery_Resource%20List.pdf. This national resource list includes planning and recovery resources and other information.

Minnesota Historical Society. "Conservation, Salvage Procedures for Wet Items." Accessed October 11, 2019. https://www.mnhs.org/preserve/conservation/emergency.php. This site provides a list of resources for responding to a disaster (forms, guidance, and resources) and directions from the Minnesota Historical Society's emergency plan for salvaging specific formats.

National Archives. Preservation, Emergency Preparedness: "A Primer: Paper Based Materials." Accessed October 11, 2019. https://www.archives.gov/preservation/emergency-prep/disaster-prep-primer.html. This site brings together resources from the Smithsonian Institution, National Archives and Records Administration, Library of Congress, and National Park Service addressing more unusual risks and includes emergency responses for specific types of damaged materials and information on mold, drying procedures, and how to perform specific salvage activities. Some items like Peter Waters's work also appear under other links in this section.

———. "Preservation: Records Emergencies." Accessed October 11, 2019. https://www.archives.gov/preservation/records-emergency. This website has links to planning, recovery, and other resources, also guidance for contracting records recovery services and names of vendors that offer disaster recovery services.

National Park Service. "Museum Management Program. NPS Museum Handbook." Accessed October 11, 2019. https://www.nps.gov/museum/publications/MHI/mushbkl.html. The Museum Handbook (part 1, chapter 10, revised in 2019) focuses on disaster planning and writing a disaster response plan. The chapter is comprehensive and includes a detailed assessment checklist, information on which material types are most vulnerable to a particular disaster, guidelines for prioritizing collections for salvaging, glossary, and bibliography.

Northeast Document Conservation Center. Disaster Assistance. "dPlan: The Online Disaster-Planning Tool." Accessed October 11, 2019. https://www.nedcc.org/free-resources/dplan-the-online-disaster-planning-tool. This is a free online disaster planning tool developed by a leading conservation services provider specifically for small institutions without in-house preservation specialists. The dPlan walks you through planning by asking questions and providing blanks for your answers. One organization can keep a copy locally or on a secure server accessed through the dPlan. It is being upgraded in 2021.

_____. Free Resources, "Preservation 101." Accessed October 11, 2019. https://www.nedcc.org/free-resources/preservation-101. Follow the online textbook link at the bottom to the free self-guided course. Chapter 8 deals with disaster planning. Although creating a disaster plan is outside the scope of the chapter, it does lead the reader through tasks that prepare for writing a plan. There are links to a risk assessment exercise; checklists of preventive activities for water, fire, and security risks; tips for responding to various types of disasters; and a short list of resources. The Responding to Disaster—Initial Response and Assessment page might be a good resource to laminate and include in a disaster plan.

_____. "Preservation Leaflets." Accessed October 11, 2019. https://www.nedcc.org/free-re sources/preservation-leaflets/overview. Sections 1 and 3, on planning and prioritizing and emergency management, respectively, provide guidance on disaster planning and how to respond to a disaster. Note particularly Preservation Leaflet 3.4: Worksheet for Outlining a Disaster Plan, which illustrates one way to organize contact and other emergency information for a disaster plan.

Vogt-O'Connor, Diane. "Reformatting for Preservation and Access: Prioritizing Materials for Duplication." Conserv O Gram Number 19/10, 1995. Accessed October 11, 2019. https://www.nps.gov/museum/publications/conserveogram/19-10.pdf. This Conserv O Gram illustrates how to prioritize collections/materials according to a ranking system that could be applied to materials to set salvaging priorities in disaster planning.

Walsh, Betty. "Salvage Operations for Water Damaged Archival Collections: A Second Glance" and "Salvage at a Glance." *Western Association for Art Conservation Newsletter* 19, no. 2 (May 1997). Accessed October 11, 2019. http://cool.conservation-us.org/waac/wn/wn19/wn19-2/wn19-206.html and http://cool.conservation-us.org/waac/wn/wn19/wn19-2/wn19-207.html respectively. Excellent recovery guidelines based on the severity of the disaster. Both articles are heavily referenced resources. The second article is primarily a chart of how to salvage water-damaged records listed by the specific type of material. Consider laminating the chart and adding it to your disaster plan as a resource.

Notes

1. Bruce W. Dearstyne, *Managing Historical Records Programs: A Guide for Historical Agencies* (Walnut Creek, CA: AltaMira Press, 2000), 123.

2. Northeast Document Conservation Center (NEDCC), *Preservation 101*, ch. 12, "The Lesson," p. 1 of 6, accessed November 3, 2019, https://www.nedcc.org/preservation-training/preservation-101.

3. Dearstyne, *Managing Historical Records Programs*, 137–38.

4. NPS Museum Handbook, Part 1, ch. 10, 10:30–10:32, accessed November 3, 2019 , https://www.nps.gov/museum/publications/MHI/Chap10.pdf.

5. NEDCC, "Preservation 101, Session 8: Emergency Preparedness, Responding to Disaster, Initial Response and Assessment," https://www.nedcc.org/preservation101/session-8/8responding-to-disaster; NPS Museum Handbook, Part 1, ch. 10, 10:30–10:31.

6. NPS Museum Handbook, Part 1, ch. 10, 10:30–31; NEDCC, "Preservation Leaflet 3.3 Emergency Planning," 4, accessed April 4, 2020, https://www.nedcc.org/assets/media/documents/Preservation%20Leaflets/3_3_emergency_2017.pdf.

7. Dearstyne, *Managing Historical Records Programs*, 137–38; NEDCC, "Preservation Leaflet 3.3 Emergency Planning," 5–6; Gregory S. Hunter, *Developing and Maintaining Practical Archives: A How-to-Do-It Manual*, 2nd ed., How-to-Do-It Manuals for Librarians, no. 122 (New York: Neal-Schuman, 2003), 199–201.

List of Appendixes

Appendix C: Representative Examples

Appendix D: Vendors

Appendix A

Guidelines and Policies

Appendix A.1

Special Collections and University Archives
Northern Kentucky University

Guidelines for the Use of Archival Materials

The Northern Kentucky University's Special Collections and University Archives has a responsibility to maintain all material entrusted to its care in good condition. Researchers are asked to exercise the greatest care in handling documents and books and not mark them in any way. The Archives reserves the right to limit the use of restricted records as well as collections that are unprocessed or fragile. The following policies are intended to help preserve the university's collections.

1. Researchers are required to register on their first visit to the University Archives. Please sign in on each subsequent visit. Registration forms will become a permanent record of the department.

Explanation: *This is for security reasons, to document the identity of researchers and specific days when they used records.*

2. Collections are available to the public for the purpose of research. Persons under the age of sixteen, however, will not be permitted to use materials unless they are accompanied by adults who will take responsibility for the safe use of the materials.

Explanation: *Children may be unaware of the potential for permanent damage through careless handling.*

3. All packages, bags, and briefcases must be stored in the lockers outside of the Archives' Reading Room. The staff reserves the right to inspect all notebooks, laptops, and personal belongings prior to a researcher's departure from the Archives Reading Room.

Explanation: *This is for security and preservation reasons. It minimizes opportunities to steal material. It also removes potentially wet coats and bundles that crowd the workspace, might be put on top of archival materials, or otherwise cause physical damage to records.*

4. No food or beverages are allowed in the Archives Reading Room.

Explanation: *They can attract bugs that would eat the records. Sticky substances can cause records to stick against one another and tear. Grease can transfer to the records themselves, thus damaging them. These are all preservation concerns.*

5. In order not to disturb others, please silence all cell phones. Step outside the Reading Room to make telephone calls.

Explanation: *This is a courtesy to other researchers and department personnel.*

6. All material must be used in the Archives Reading Room.

Explanation: *If records leave the Reading Room, they may be handled improperly, causing physical damage, a preservation concern. If records leave, they may not return. Most are irreplaceable, causing a permanent loss of information/history. This is a security concern.*

7. Researchers must use pencil or laptop computer for note taking. Pens, markers, and scanners may not be used in the Archives Reading Room.

Explanation: *This is for preservation purposes. Pens and markers are not reversible and cause permanent damage. Many researchers do not know how to use scanners without causing physical damage, or when something can't physically undergo scanning. Almost none are knowledgeable enough to apply copyright or other restrictions. This is a legal concern.*

8. Care must be taken in handling all Special Collections and University Archives material. All items must lie flat on the tables. Nothing is to be placed on top of the material, excepting book snakes.

Explanation: *This is for preservation purposes. Some items are brittle and break easily. Bundles and other materials are placed in lockers to prevent accidental but possibly permanent damage.*

9. The original order of all collections must be maintained. Do not rearrange material. Please report any disarrangement to the staff.

Explanation: *During arrangement records are either left according to their original order, or intentionally put in a particular sequence. Most non-archivists are unaware of this and are unable to perform this work. Misfiling makes it difficult for others to locate information using these files and can create extra work for the staff.*

10. Limited photocopy services are available. Refer to the fee schedule for pricing. The Archives reserves the right to limit the number of copies made and to refuse to copy any item if such copying will damage the material. Copies of entire books, manuscript collections, or archival record groups will not be made. We reserve the right to refuse to copy material that in our judgment would violate copyright law.

Explanation: *This addresses concerns for the preservation of the records and copyright/legal issues.*

11. Researchers who wish to publish, reprint, or reproduce materials in the collection must request permission in writing from the university archivist.

Explanation: *This would also be a copyright concern.*

_____   _____

Name   Date

Appendix A.2

Special Collections and University Archives
Northern Kentucky University

Guidelines for the Safe Handling of Photo Collections

A. Clean Hands
1. Do not eat or drink while handling photographic materials (prints, negatives, slides, etc.).
2. Wash your hands before working with collections.

B. Plan
1. Make sure you have sufficient work space to accommodate the items with which you intend to work.
2. Make sure you have the tools you need for the job (pencils, paper, housing material).
3. Before moving items, especially oversize, check their condition. If damaged, seek advice before proceeding and use care.

C. Handle with Care
1. Do not lean on or set heavy objects on top of items, even if they are covered.
2. Do not write on paper, folders, or envelopes that contain photographic materials or are put on top of photographic materials.
3. Avoid touching the surface of images or dragging anything (jewelry, etc.) across images. Use care with negatives and slides not to drag them across surfaces that would damage the back of the negatives or slides.
4. Always keep photographic materials on a flat, well-supported surface. Do not place items on your lap or let them hang off the side of a table.
5. Support items carefully when moving them. Use two hands as necessary to prevent bending, tearing, or breaking. Use interleaving paper larger than the item to move large or damaged materials. When necessary, ask a second person for assistance to move oversize material.
6. Do not stack photographs or photograph boxes of widely varying sizes or weights.
7. Use pencils when working with or near collections, not pens. Ink is irreversible.
8. Treat housing materials with care to avoid scratched Mylar or misshapen paper.
9. Never attach paper clips to photographic materials. Use a folder or a piece of acid-free paper folded in half to keep information with a specific photograph.

D. Other Tips
1. Never use tape, staples, paper clips, rubber bands, or sticky notes on photographs.
2. Avoid removing photographs from their photo sleeves unless absolutely necessary.
3. Take your time and move with care.
4. Consult copies when available to conserve originals.

Based on: Library of Congress, Prints and Photographs Division, "Safe Handling Tips for Pictorial Collections," https://www.loc.gov/rr/print/tp/SafeHandlingTip.pdf (accessed November 19, 2005).

Appendix A.3

Copyright Warning Notice

The copyright law of the United States (Title 17, United States Code) governs the making of photocopies and other reproductions of copyrighted material.

Under certain conditions specified in the law, libraries and archives are authorized to furnish a photocopy or other reproduction. One of these specified conditions is that the photocopy or reproduction is not to be "used for any purpose other than private study, scholarship or research." If a user makes a request for or later uses a photocopy or reproduction for purposes in excess of "fair use," that user may be liable for copyright infringement.

The institution reserves the right to refuse to accept a photocopying order if, in its judgment, fulfillment of the order would involve violation of copyright law.

Appendix A.4

Special Collections and University Archives
Northern Kentucky University

Image Naming Conventions

Sequence of components for prints, slides, negatives:

Record Group or Collection name + series name + 3 digit sequential # + YYYY_MM_DD + insert tags below as applicable + adj (if applicable) + resolution + watermark (if applicable).

Examples: buildings_aerial_001_1999_10_1_600.tif
campus_life_concert_002_1992_11_ng_02_ext_2400.tif
academic_theater_as_you_like_it_001_1988_04_adj_2400.tif

Note: Use only lowercase letters (not capital letters); separate components with underscores.
Notes for athletic photographs:

Record Group or Collection name + series

m = mens
w = womens
players listed by gender, sport, last name, first initial   m_basketball_cousey_b_001
coaches listed as staff by last name, first initial   staff_admin_aker_w_001

Sequence:

Number images using three digits and include zeros as place holders; the first image is numbered "001" not left unnumbered; number images from the same record group, collection, series, or file name sequentially regardless of dates. Numbers are assigned sequentially as new items from that record group, collection, series, or file are scanned.

Examples: commencement_001_1979
commencement_002_2000
commencement_003_1968

Tags:

adj = adjusted (contrast, sharpness, color, cropped, etc. altered from original)
ng = scans from negatives
ngrp = batch scan of multiple negative strips
ds = descreened
ca = used for estimated time/date span
ext = exterior (use for building views only)
int = interior (use for building views only)
sl = scans from slides
yb = scans from yearbook
w = watermark added

image_naming_info.doc
1st ver: 2009/11/24,V.Cooper
last rev: 2018/01/31,VC

Appendix A.5

Scanning Resolutions for Preservation and Access Copies of Photographs[1]

Scanning Resolutions

Original Image Size	Preservation Cy dpi	Access Cy dpi
Slide	2400	1200
2" x 3"	2400	1200
3" x 5" or 4" x 6"	1200	600
5" x 7"	900	600
8" x 10"	600	300

Minimum settings:

B&W originals   8 bit grayscale

Color originals   24 bit RGB (32 if CMYK)

- Dots per inch (dpi) alone is not a sufficient measure of the quality of a scan; the resolution must be relative to the size of the original. If a 4" x 5" photo is scanned at 300 dpi but printed at 8" x 10," the resolution of the print will be less than the original 300 dpi. The size of the original (height x width) multiplied by the scanning resolution equals its resolution in pixels, so [4" x 5"] x 300 dpi = 1200 x 1500 pixels. When the pixel size is divided by the desired print size, 8" x 10," the resulting resolution for the print is only 150 dpi. This example illustrates that the final use of the digital image is important in determining the original scanning resolution.

- To calculate the file size of an 8-bit grayscale scan: multiply [the pixel height x pixel width] divide by 1,000,000 = __ approximate MB (megabytes).

- For a 24-bit RGB (red, green, blue) color scan: multiply [the pixel height x pixel width x 3] divide by 1,000,000 = __ approximate MB. The RGB color system has 3 channels (red, green, blue) each composed of 8 bits.

scan_resolution_chart.docx
1st ver: 2012/03/07, LH
last rev: 2017/11/07, LH

Note

1. See http://www.loc.gov/rr/print/tp/DgtlMastersSamplSpecsSelctdRcmndFinal7_2004.pdf.

Appendix B

Sample Forms and Workflows

Appendix B.1

Special Collections and University Archives
Northern Kentucky University

Deed of Gift

Northern Kentucky University's Special Collections and University Archives gratefully acknowledges receipt from:

Donor: _____

Address: _____

Telephone: _____ E-mail: _____

of the following materials: _____

_____

_____

_____

_____

I hereby make a gift of these materials to Northern Kentucky University. By making this gift, I assign and convey to Northern Kentucky University legal title and any and all copyrights and/or other intellectual property rights that I hold in these materials. The rights assigned include the right to create derivative works or compilations and to record or fix the materials in any tangible medium that currently exists or that may be developed. Title and rights shall pass to Northern Kentucky University at the time of transference of materials.

Northern Kentucky University will, at its discretion, dispose of materials not considered appropriate for retention in its collections. Suggestions for disposition, if any, may be detailed here:

_____

_____

NKU will make its best effort to fulfill these suggestions for deaccessioned materials to the extent it is able.

In the event that the Donor may from time to time hereafter give, donate, and convey additional historical materials, title to such materials shall pass to Northern Kentucky University upon their delivery, and all provisions of this instrument of gift shall be applicable to such additional materials. A description of the additional materials so donated and delivered shall be prepared and attached hereto.

I certify that I have read the terms of this deed and that I have absolute authority to donate this property.

_____   _____

Donor's Signature   Date

_____

Print Donor's Name

_____   _____

For NKU Special Collections & University Archives   Date

nku.donor.contract.doc
1st ver: 2008/05/09
last rev: 2009/05/04; legal rev: 2009/05/28, H. Jones

Appendix B.2a

Special Collections and University Archives
Northern Kentucky University

Processing Plan Form

Collection:

    Accession number:

    Donor:

    Creator:

    Span dates:

    Extent (before processing):

Potential research value: _____ High _____ Medium _____ Low

Restrictions (donor, copyright, privacy):

Background research resources used:

Collection description:

Current condition:

Current arrangement:

Proposed arrangement:

Proposed level of processing:

_____ Collection _____ Box _____ Series _____ Folder _____ Item

Special preservation or supply needs:

Proposed separations or discards:

Work assignment:

    Processing Archivist's tasks:

    Student tasks:

Other notes or decisions (date & name):

Recommendations for: _____ digitization _____ reformatting _____ exhibits

Projected processing time and completion date:

Recommended by: _____ Date: _____

Approved by: _____ Date: _____

NKU_processing_plan_form.docx
1st ver: 2011/01/07, A. Ryckbost
last rev: 2016/11/03, AR, header updated

Appendix B.2b

Special Collections and University Archives
Northern Kentucky University

Processing Checklist

Collection:

Accession Number: _____

Collection Number: RG #_____ (university records) or MS #_____ (Special Collections)

Span Dates: _____

Name: _____

Size (in lf):

before processing: _____ after processing: _____

Processing:

By (name[s]): _____

Started on (date): _____ Completed on: _____

CHECKLIST	DATE COMPLETED	INITIALS
☐ Donor/Control file setup	_____	_____
☐ Deed of gift/transfer form completed	_____	_____
☐ Thank-you sent	_____	_____
☐ Accession record completed	_____	_____
☐ Space and supplies for processing prepared	_____	_____
☐ Background research reviewed	_____	_____
☐ Brief Survey of collection conducted	_____	_____
☐ Arrangement completed	_____	_____
☐ Basic preservation performed (optional)	_____	_____
☐ Materials rehoused (optional)	_____	_____
☐ Folders labeled (RG and series)	_____	_____
☐ Is deaccessioning required? (complete form)	_____	_____
☐ Are restrictions required?	_____	_____
☐ Highest-value items photographed and inventoried	_____	_____
☐ Finding aid completed	_____	_____
☐ Folders and boxes labeled (box & folder #)	_____	_____
☐ Collection shelved	_____	_____

CHECKLIST	DATE COMPLETED	INITIALS
☐ Finding aid copy put into collection donor/control file	_____	_____
☐ Print copy of finding aid put into finding aids notebook	_____	_____
☐ Electronic copy of finding aid put on website	_____	_____
☐ Collection lists on website updated	_____	_____
☐ Processing checklist filed in donor/control file	_____	_____
☐ Publicity (optional)	_____	_____
☐ Adjustments made to insurance (if applicable)	_____	_____
☐ Evaluate secondary resources	_____	_____

Notes:

Appendix B.3a

Separation Sheet

Special Collections and Archives
Georgia State University Library

Separated item(s):

☐ Printed materials   ☐ Videotape (VHS, DVCAM, etc.)

☐ Three-dimensional objects   ☐ Audiotape or grooved disc (cassette, DAT, LP, etc.)

☐ Oversized materials   ☐ Restriction

☐ Photographs/negatives/film   ☐ Other _____

☐ Digital storage (disk, CD, DVD, flash drive, etc.)—assign item #(s), ex. Z2018-01_bd001,
    and list here: _____

_____

Number of items: _____ **Purpose of removal:** _____

Description of item(s):

Provide basic information below (ex. title of a printed object, topic of a group of photographs, description and size of an artifact, title/format for sound and AV recordings). Note if associated manuscript materials are also being separated. For born-digital items, identify media type, transcribe label, and provide brief physical description.

_____

_____

_____

_____

_____ ☐ Continued on back page

Original location:

Collection name/number: _____

Series:_____ Subseries:_____ Box/Folder#s:_____

Folder title: _____

For born-digital items, complete top portion of the Digital Media Processing Sheet. For other material, provide the new location below:

Collection name/number: _____

Series:_____ Subseries:_____ Box/Folder#s:_____

Folder title: _____

Date: _____ **Initials:** _____

Appendix B.3b

Digital Media Processing Sheet

Special Collections and Archives
Georgia State University Library

Date of removal: _____ **Removed by:** _____

Item number(s) (ex. Z2018-01_bd001): _____

Media type(s):

☐ CD   ☐ Hard drive

☐ DVD   ☐ Flash drive/thumb drive

☐ 3.5" floppy disk   ☐ Zip disk

☐ 5.25" floppy disk   ☐ Other: _____

Removed from:

Accession or MS # and title: _____

Series: _____ Subseries: _____

Box #: _____ Folder #/title: _____

Date of digital processing: _____

Original media retained:

☐ No

☐ Yes (new location, if applicable: _____)

Location of digital content:

☐ Files on preservation server; media discarded

☐ Files on preservation server

☐ Files on original media only; content accessible in reading room with digital archivist's
   assistance

☐ Other: _____

Please see Special Collections & Archives staff
for assistance in accessing content from this item.

Appendix B.4

Special Collections and University Archives
Northern Kentucky University

Permission to Publish Photographs Contract

1. Purchase of a photographic scan or print does not carry with it the right to publish or to make a reproduction in any form. Researchers may not reproduce or permit others to reproduce purchased photographic copies without written permission from the university archivist. Photographic images for personal use do not require a contract. Any other use, such as publication or exhibition, requires specific written permission from the university archivist.

2. Permission is for nonexclusive, onetime use only, with no other rights. Permission is limited to the use and format as indicated by the applicant only and excludes all other uses and formats. All subsequent use and reuse, in any form, must be applied for in writing.

3. Permission is valid only for the individual, company, or institution to whom it is specifically issued and may not be transferred, assigned, sold, or otherwise disposed of without prior written permission of the university archivist.

4. In authorizing the publication of a photographic copy, the university does not surrender its own right to use the image, or to grant that right to others.

5. A credit line must appear directly beneath the image published or reproduced. Video and film credits must appear in the section devoted to acknowledgments. The proper citation for each image should read: Photograph(s) courtesy of the Schlachter University Archives, W. Frank Steely Library, Northern Kentucky University, OR Photograph(s) courtesy of the Eva G. Farris Special Collections, W. Frank Steely Library, Northern Kentucky University as appropriate.

6. One complimentary copy of any publication in which images from the Eva G. Farris Special Collections and Schlachter University Archives appear shall be sent to the Eva G. Farris Special Collections and Schlachter University Archives. This includes books, brochures, pamphlets, periodicals, exhibition catalogues, and other media.

7. Responsibility for observance of copyright and other publication rights, including literary rights, as defined by the Copyright Act of 1998, rests with the applicant and not with Northern Kentucky University. The applicant shall indemnify and hold harmless Northern Kentucky University and the contributing organizations against any and all claims by third parties.

8. The Eva G. Farris Special Collections and Schlachter University Archives reserves the right to charge for the use of materials as it deems appropriate in any individual case.

I/We herewith agree to the conditions specified above:

Name (sign) _____ Name (print) _____

Date _____

Address _____

Telephone _____ E-mail _____

Publisher _____ Format & Title _____

Date of publication _____ Author(s) _____

Image description _____

nku_photo_publication_contract.doc
last rev: 2011/06/01
legal review: 2011/06/07, H. Jones

Appendix B.5

Special Collections and University Archives
Northern Kentucky University

Sample Pull Card

DATE OUT	INITIALS	ITEM TITLE & COLLECTION LOCATION	REASON FOR WITHDRAWAL	DATE REPLACED	INITIALS

Sample pull card. Special Collections and University Archives, Northern Kentucky University.

Appendix B.6

Special Collections and University Archives
Northern Kentucky University

Withdrawal Form

Withdrawal date _____

Type of materials: _____

_____

Title: _____

_____

_____

_____

_____

_____

_____

Sent to: _____

Reason: _____

Removed by: _____

Returned on: _____

Received by: _____

Appendix B.7

Special Collections and University Archives
Northern Kentucky University

Researcher Registration

Date: _____

Name (last, first, middle): _____

Permanent home address: _____

Home phone: _____

E-mail: _____

School or organization (if any) _____

Department (if any) _____

If unaffiliated, indicate best category:

☐ Genealogist   ☐ Journalist/Media   ☐ Author

☐ Other _____

I have read and agree to abide by the "Guidelines for the Use of Archival Material" (Appendix A.1), and any other applicable policies and guidelines. I understand that a current photo identification will be required.

Signature of researcher: _____

To be filled out by Special Collections staff:

Photo ID provided:
_____ NKU ID   Number: _____
_____ Student _____ Faculty _____ Staff
_____ Driver's license   Number: _____
_____ State ID   Number: _____
_____ Passport   Number: _____

nku_researcher_registration.doc last rev: 2007/10/29

Appendix B.8

Special Collections and University Archives
Northern Kentucky University

Missing Item Report

Date: _____

Reported by: _____

Verified by: _____

Accession/call number: _____

Book title: _____

Collection name: _____

Manuscript box number: _____ Folder number: _____

Does a copy of this document or book exist?

_____ Photocopy   Location: _____

_____ Microfilm   Location: _____

_____ Digital image   Location: _____

_____ Other   Explanation and location: _____

Report of searches: _____

_____

_____

Result of searches: _____

_____

_____

_____

Appendix B.9

Special Collections and University Archives
W. Frank Steely Library
Northern Kentucky University
Nunn Dr., Highland Heights, KY 41099 (859) 572-5863

Exhibit Loan Agreement

1. Exhibition

Title and dates: _____

2. Lender

Name: _____

Address: _____

Telephone: _____ Contact person: _____

Unless Steely Library, NKU is notified to the contrary before the close of the exhibition, works will be returned to the Lender's address as shown above.

_____

Exact form in which Lender's name should appear on labels, in print, or in online exhibit (please print).

3. Description of the object

Artist: _____

Title & date of work: _____

Museum, accession, or other identifying number: _____

Medium and support: _____

Size of painting, drawing, or prints:
(if object is framed, measure total visible area, label dimensions "Seen")

Inches

Framed: Height _____   Width _____

Unframed: Height _____   Width _____

Condition: _____

_____

_____

Special requirements: _____

_____

_____

Other inscriptions & location: _____

_____

_____

4. Publicity

Unless otherwise notified in writing, the loaned item(s) may be photographed and reproduced by Steely Library, NKU for educational, publicity, or catalog purposes connected with this exhibition. The Lender also authorizes Steely Library, NKU to display photographs of the loaned item(s) in an online web exhibit.

5. Shipping

Objects to be received by Steely Library, NKU no later than:

_____

Special instructions: _____

_____

6. Insurance

Insurance value: $ _____

Please check one of the following: NKU to insure wall-to-wall _____

Lender to provide own insurance _____

7. Conditions governing loan

Under the terms of this agreement, Steely Library, NKU will exercise the same care with respect to loaned items as it does in safeguarding its own property of the same or similar nature.

Evidence of damage at the time of receipt or while in the custody of Steely Library, NKU will be reported immediately to the Lender.

Loans shall remain in the possession of Steely Library, NKU for the time specified on the face of this loan agreement, but may be withdrawn from the exhibition at any time by the associate provost and dean of library services. Loans will be returned to the owner or Lender or to duly authorized agent or representative.

If the legal ownership of any object shall change during the period of the loan, whether by reason of death, sale, insolvency, gift, or otherwise, the new owner may, prior to its return, be required to establish his legal right to receive the object by proof satisfactory to NKU.

Unless the Lender expressly elects to maintain his own insurance coverage, NKU will insure this loan wall-to-wall under its fine arts insurance policy for the amount indicated above, against all risk of physical loss or damage from any external cause while in transit and on location during the period of this loan. The University's responsibility shall in no event exceed said specified amount. This policy contains the usual exclusions for damage due to such causes as gradual deterioration, inherent vice, war invasion, hostilities, rebellion, insurrections, confiscation by order of any government or public authority, risks of contraband, or illegal transportation and/or trade.

If the Lender elects to maintain his own insurance, NKU must be supplied with a certificate of insurance naming NKU as an additionally insured. The University can accept no responsibility for any error or deficiency in information furnished to the Lender's insurers or for lapses in coverage.

8. Signatures

Lender: Print name: _____ Date: _____

Signature: _____

Title: _____

Borrower: Print name: _____ Date: _____

Signature: _____

Title: _____

PLEASE COMPLETE ALL THREE PAGES.

One copy of agreement for Lender, one for Donor.

nku_loan_agreement.doc
1st ver: 2009/08/25
last rev: 2009/08/26
legal review: 2009/08/28

Appendix B.10

Special Collections and University Archives
W. Frank Steely Library
Northern Kentucky University
Nunn Dr., Highland Heights, KY 41099 (859) 572-5863

Condition Report

1. Exhibition title and dates: _____

2. Lender name: _____

Address: _____

_____

Telephone: _____

Contact person: _____

Object(s) Date in: _____ Date out: _____

Describe art item here in detail.

Examined and recorded by:

Signature: _____

Title: _____

nku_art_condition_report.doc
1st ver: 2009/08/27

Appendix B.11a

Sample Cover Letter for Community Member Digitization Agreement

BCPL
Boone County Public Library

Date:_____

To:_____
Re:_____

Dear _____,

Thank you for allowing Boone County Public Library to digitize _____.
If given permission by you, BCPL will place the image(s) in our catalog and store it/them
permanently within our digital archive.

Two copies of the scans have been burned to the enclosed CD. One is a low resolution file that can
be easily emailed to relatives or even placed on the Internet if you so choose. The second image is an
archival quality high resolution TIFF that your family will be able to store permanently or use to
make duplicates as needed. If for any reason you need a replacement copy of the images on the CD,
please submit a request in writing and BCPL will burn you a new CD of the images. Please note, the
low resolution file will be accessible to you for viewing via the BCPL catalog on the Internet.

Please sign and return the enclosed User Agreement Form giving BCPL permission to place the
images within our catalog and digital archive. Feel free to contact me at 859-342-2665 x8131 or
bstriker@bcpl.org if you have any questions or concerns regarding your donation.

Sincerely,

Bridget Striker

Bridget Striker
Local History Coordinator

BOONE COUNTY PUBLIC LIBRARY   **859-342-BOOK (2665)**   **www.bcpl.org**

Main Library	Florence Branch	Lents Branch	Scheben Branch	Walton Branch	Chapin Memorial Library
1786 Burlington Pike	7425 US 42	3215 Cougar Path	8899 US 42	21 S. Main Street	6517 Market Street
Burlington, KY 41005	Florence, KY 41042	Hebron, KY 41048	Union, KY 41091	Walton, KY 41094	Petersburg, KY 41080

Sample cover letter for community member digitization agreement. Used Courtesy of Boone
County Public Library, Burlington, Kentucky.

Appendix B.11b

Digitization Agreement for Community Member's Materials

 Digitization Agreement

This agreement is by and between:

_____

Printed Name ("Submitter")

_____

Street Address

_____

City, State, Zip

_____

Telephone

_____

Email

And
Boone County Public Library ("Library")
1786 Burlington Pike
Burlington, Kentucky 41005

The Library is engaged in the development, publication, promotion, and other activities related to the digital distribution of content via the Internet.

The Submitter owns the materials under this agreement and grants to the Library the right to digitally distribute the materials to the public via the Internet and to perform or display the materials. The Submitter grants to the Library the right to identify each person and use their likeness.

All original materials will be returned to the Submitter within two weeks of receipt of the material to the Library unless otherwise stated in writing.

Unless otherwise specified in writing: This agreement does not entitle the Submitter to any goods,

services, or other consideration in exchange for such agreement.

Submitter Signature/ Date: _____

Library Staff Signature/ Date: _____

Description of materials:

BOONE COUNTY PUBLIC LIBRARY   **859-342-BOOK (2665)**   **www.bcpl.org**

Main Library	Florence Branch	Lents Branch	Scheben Branch	Walton Branch	Chapin Memorial Library
1786 Burlington Pike	7425 US 42	3215 Cougar Path	8899 US 42	21 S. Main Street	6517 Market Street
Burlington, KY 41005	Florence, KY 41042	Hebron, KY 41048	Union, KY 41091	Walton, KY 41094	Petersburg, KY 41080

Digitization agreement for community member's materials. Used Courtesy of Boone County Public Library, Burlington, Kentucky.

Appendix B.12

Scanning Workflow for Photographs

1. Turn on computer.

2. Turn on flatbed photograph scanner (e.g., Epson Perfection V700).

3. Make sure the white cover is inserted into the lid to scan photos or paper. Remove white cover to scan negatives or slides.

4. Start SilverFast software.

5. Select Start button in lower right corner.

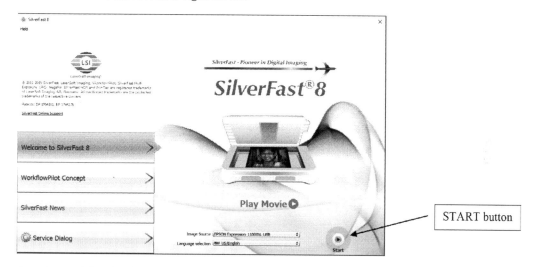

Scanning workflow for photographs. Courtesy of LaserSoft Imaging, Inc and LaserSoft Imaging, AG.

6. Select photograph to be scanned and measure size (8x10, 5x7, etc.) to determine the scanning resolution for a preservation copy of that size. Then refer to Appendix A.5: Scanning Resolutions for Preservation and Access Copies of Photographs. This separate document can be located in the same binder as these instructions or mounted somewhere near your scanner.

7. Place the photograph facedown on the scanner bed and gently close the lid so the photo doesn't move.

8. Next, set the appropriate settings on the SilverFast panel.

9. At the top of the panel:

Scanning workflow for photographs. Courtesy of LaserSoft Imaging, Inc and LaserSoft Imaging, AG.

Set the first icon from left to Reflective.

Set the second icon from the left at Positive, as shown. If the photo is a B&W, set the third icon at 16→8 bit as shown. For color, set it to 48→24 bit.

For negatives or slides:

Set the first icon to Transparency.

Set the second icon to Negative. If the photo is a B&W, set the third icon at 16→8 bit as shown. For color, set it to 48→24 bit.

10. In the Scan Dimensions box shown below:

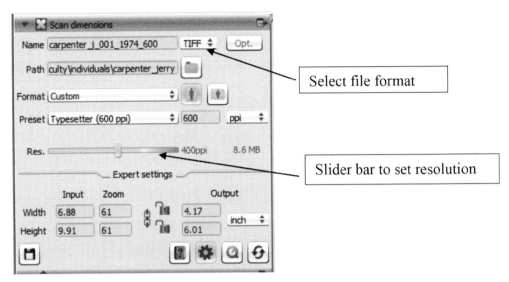

Scanning workflow for photographs. Courtesy of LaserSoft Imaging, Inc and LaserSoft Imaging, AG.

11. Create the file name for the scan you are about to make (see appendix A.4: Image Naming Conventions for how to correctly form the file name); enter it in the Name box. This is another handy document to locate in the same binder as these instructions or mount somewhere near your scanner.

12. Select the file format as TIFF for a preservation copy and JPG for an access copy. Other options might be used depending upon the final use of the scan.

13. In the Path box indicate where the image is to be saved. This will vary by project. Check with your supervisor if this information is not provided.

14. Use the slider bar to set the requisite resolution as determined in Step 6 above.

15. This should be the minimal settings required to scan.

16. On the top middle, there is another set of icons.

Scanning workflow for photographs. Courtesy of LaserSoft Imaging, Inc and LaserSoft Imaging, AG.

17. Use the Prescan button next. Once the photo image appears on the monitor screen, move the red border lines to the edge of the area you wish to scan. This may be the edge of the photo paper or a smaller area depending upon the purpose of the task.

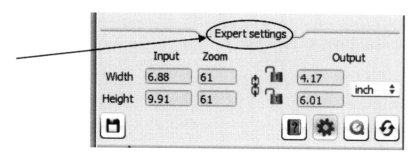

Scanning workflow for photographs. Courtesy of LaserSoft Imaging, Inc and LaserSoft Imaging, AG.

18. If the red box seems to be locked, check the Scan Dimensions box to see whether the Expert settings section is showing. If not, click on the second icon from the left at the bottom of this box to access these extra fields. This should allow you to move each of the four sides of the red box independently. Also, the field above labeled Format should read Custom.

19. Once the boundaries have been set for the scan and all other settings made or corrected, select the Scan button.

20. In order to get the optimal quality scan, do NOT use the computer for any other task while it is scanning.

21. After the scan has finished, you may need some of the icons on the vertical menu below the icons shown in Step 16 above. In particular, you may need the Rot/Flip icon to rotate the image from vertical to horizontal or vice versa.

Scanning workflow for photographs. Courtesy of LaserSoft Imaging, Inc and LaserSoft Imaging, AG.

22. Open Adobe Photoshop or similar software. Instructions below are for Adobe Photoshop CC 2017.

23. Use File→Open to locate and open the just-completed scan.

24. On the Image menu, select Image Size and confirm that the photo was scanned at the resolution you selected in Step 14. If it wasn't, troubleshoot. You will have to repeat your work until corrected. If you are unable to resolve, ask your supervisor for assistance.

25. You may need to use Image→Image Rotation here to further correct the skew of the image or crop if it was not printed level or the photo border is excessive.

26. After a preservation copy is made, if an access copy is required, use Photoshop to open the preservation copy.

27. Go to Image→Image Size and reset it using appendix A.5 to determine the appropriate access copy resolution based on the size of the original photo scanned.

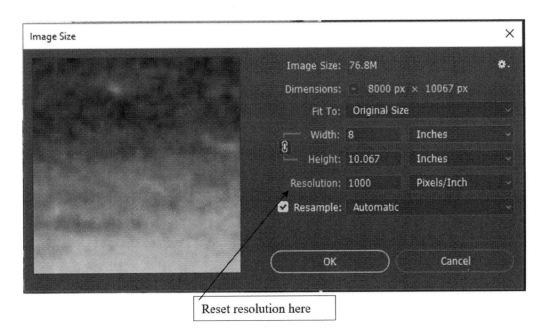

Scanning workflow for photographs. Courtesy of the author.

28. Select OK.

29. This will bring up the menu to save the image, be sure to Save As or you will destroy the preservation copy by saving the access copy over it. Change the file name to reflect the lower resolution of the access copy. Change the file format to jpeg (*.JPG, *.JPEG, *.JPE), not the other JPEG options.

30. Access copies are normally saved in a different location than preservation copies. Refer to project instructions for where to save them. The name of the preservation and access copies should be the same except for the file format (TIFF or JPG) and the scanning resolution, which forms part of the file name.

31. When the dialog box opens for saving:

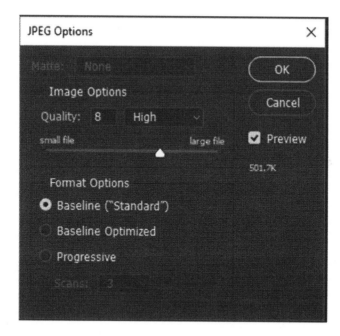

Scanning workflow for photographs. Courtesy of the author.

Select on the pulldown menu where High is shown in the example; this will change the Quality setting to 10. Use the slider bar to move it to the far right. The 10 should change to 12. Then select OK.

instructions_scan_photos.docx
1st ver: 2017/11/13, L. Hamill
last rev: 2019/11/02, LH

Appendix B.13

Scanning Workflow for Text Documents

1. **Purpose:** The purpose of this workflow is to create *access copies* of text information. Their delivery method will not affect this workflow. Decisions made in designing this workflow have been made based on access (i.e., speedy downloads), not to create preservation copies.

2. **Scanning Specifications:** Refer to appendix A.5 for scanning resolutions of access copies.

   Note: Black-and-white originals will be scanned as $16 \rightarrow 8$ bit grayscale.

   Color originals will be scanned as $48 \rightarrow 24$ bit color.

3. **File Names:** Refer to appendix A.4 for file naming guidance.

4. **Text Document Workflow and Settings**

1. Turn on computer, monitor, and flatbed scanner in that sequence.

2. Make sure the white cover is inserted into the lid to scan photos or paper.

3. Start SilverFast software.

4. Select Start button in lower right corner of opening software screen.

5. Open manuscript box; remove next file folder to scan and flag location of folder being removed from box.

6. Lay folder flat on table, open, remove first page to be scanned, and place on scanner, aligning with the appropriate corner of the scanner bed.

7. Gently close scanner lid so that the document doesn't move.

8. If scanning a page in a bound volume, be sure to support the half of the volume not being scanned. Try to raise the height of that half so it is level with the scanner bed to minimize damage to the spine and movement/misalignment of the side being scanned.

9. Next, set the appropriate settings on the scanning software.

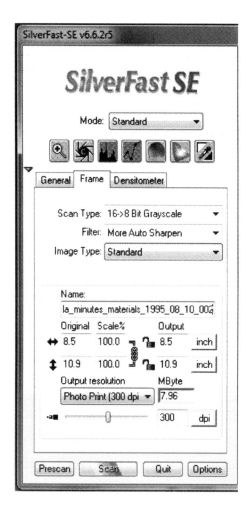

Select Frame tab:

Scan type: for B&W - 16 > 8 bit grayscale
                    For color - 48>24 bit color
Filter: more auto sharpen
Image type: standard [in other software it might be reflective + positive]

Name: see appendix A.4

Original & Output boxes: don't set here, set below

Output resolution: use slider bar and set to 300 dpi or type 300 in box between slider bar and dpi label

Scanning workflow for text documents. Courtesy of LaserSoft Imaging, Inc and LaserSoft Imaging, AG.

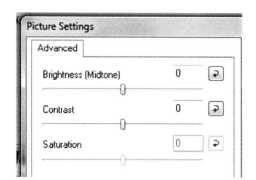

The base setting for Brightness, Contrast and Saturation is 0. In most cases, instructions will say when to adjust these. Selecting the boxes on the far right with the arrow will reset to 0.

Scanning workflow for text documents. Courtesy of LaserSoft Imaging, Inc and LaserSoft Imaging, AG.

10. After confirming settings, select Prescan button.

11. When document image appears on screen, set or confirm location of red box to ensure no parts of the document are cut off. Once set at the edges of the standard paper size, this shouldn't need resetting.

12. If the Prescan shows the document is positioned correctly, select Scan.

13. A new message box will ask for the file name, type, and location to save it.

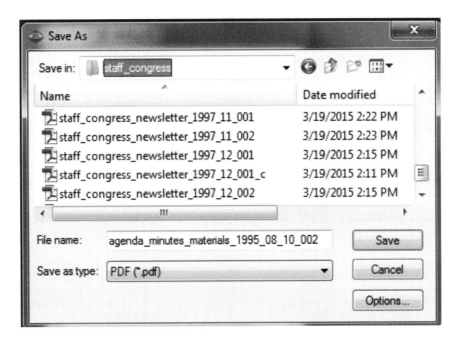

Scanning workflow for text documents. Courtesy of LaserSoft Imaging, Inc and LaserSoft Imaging, AG.

File Saving Settings

- Sequence of file name components: file name/record type + date (year, month, day) + page #.

- Use only lowercase letters (not capital letters); separate components with underscores.

- Item numbers go to three places (ex. 001, 002, 003. . .).

- File type: save as PDF.

- Location to save file: save all files to the Special Collections network in a folder labeled IR access as shown below. Staff Congress and Faculty Senate records will go into their respective folder, not in the combined documents subfolder.

▲ IR access cys	<Main folder
▲ faculty_senate	<Use this one for Faculty Senate
combined_documents	<Skip this one
▲ staff_congress	<Use this one for Staff Congress
combined_documents	<Skip this one

Scanning workflow for text documents. Courtesy of LaserSoft Imaging, Inc and LaserSoft Imaging, AG.

Once you have added an item to this folder, subsequent scans should automatically bring it back up unless you need to change locations.

14. Check the scan quality briefly when it comes up on the screen for correct orientation, legibility, that no parts are cut off, that no pages have been scanned twice or omitted.

15. Once all the pages for a document or file have been scanned, open or bring up Adobe Acrobat Pro on the screen.

16. Under Tools, select Combine Files to combine all the individual document pages/PDFs into a single combined PDF file.

17. In the Combine Files message box, select Add Files. This will open a new box that should show the file folder into which the just-completed scans were saved.

18. Highlight all the files for the pages of the document you just completed scanning. The files should all be adjacent to each other.

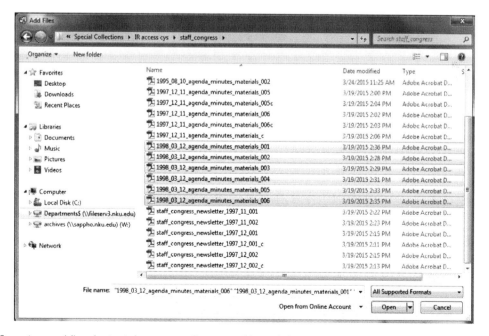

Scanning workflow for text documents. Courtesy of LaserSoft Imaging, Inc and LaserSoft Imaging, AG.

19. Select Open in the lower right-hand corner.

20. The files will show on the screen in the sequence they will be saved. Due to file name length, you will have to roll over each file in sequence to confirm they are in the correct numeric sequence. After performing this check, select the Combine Files button. See below.

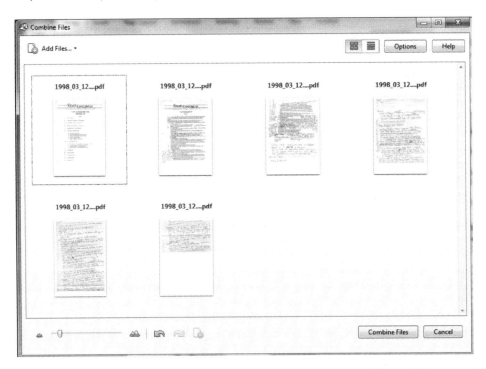

Scanning workflow for text documents. Courtesy of LaserSoft Imaging, Inc and LaserSoft Imaging, AG.

21. The combined file will open on the screen. Briefly conduct a visual check for page completeness (none missing, no duplicates), correct orientation.

22. If the document passes inspection, use the File menu in the upper left corner, select Save As to bring up the message box for the file name and location. Save the combined file in the same folder as the individual pages. Use the same file name as was used for the individual pages but **omit** the tag for the page numbers. Examples:

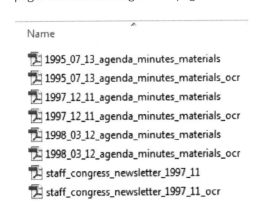

Scanning workflow for text documents. Courtesy of the author.

23. The final step will be to run the OCR process on the file that was just created—the combined PDF file.

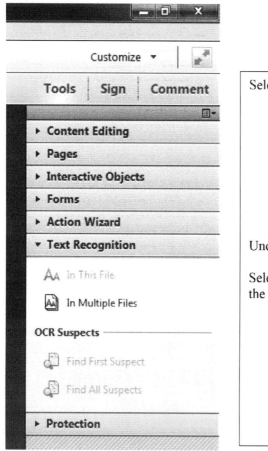

Select Tools if this menu isn't open.

Under Tools, open Text Recognition

Select AA in this file and let the software OCR the combined pdf file

Scanning workflow for text documents. Courtesy of the author.

24. Once the process has run, you will have to save the OCR version. Use the File menu in the upper left corner again, select Save As to bring up the message box for the file name and location. Save the new OCRed combined file in the same folder as before. Use the same file name as was used for the combined file but **add** the tag _ocr to distinguish it from the file in the last step.

25. Another staff member will spot check files, delete the working files created in the earlier stages (individual pages, combined file not read by OCR), review file names, and move them to another folder location.

Exceptions to "Standard" Scanning Settings Given Above

If the original paper is/has:

Red—leave the settings as given above.

Green—change Brightness to 13 and Contrast to 3.

Purple ink—leave Brightness on 0 and set Contrast to -45.

Legal size paper/too long—scan in two passes; make sure to overlap text on both so the reader can match them up; number the scans sequentially starting with the top of the page.

Light text is predominate—move the Contrast slider to the left (you will get negative numbers) until what appears on screen seems legible.

ir_technical_specs.docx
1st ver: 2015/03/19, L. Hamill
Last rev: 2015/05/05, L. Hamill

Appendix C

Representative Examples

Appendix C.1a

Special Collections and University Archives
Northern Kentucky University

Accession Record

Accession Number: NKU2008-020

Date: June 13, 2008

Title: Scrapbooks (three-ring binders)

Office of Origin or Donor's name:

This was brought in by retired professor George Jones, who got them from Linda Lane, who created them.

Quantity & Description:

- 1 three-ring binder with photographs, newspaper clippings, newsletters, etc. with publicity about her husband Thomas's term as acting president.

- 2 photo albums of materials for Thomas Lane's retirement May 1, 1989—includes correspondence, news clips, US Senate resolutions, greeting cards.

- NOTE—a letter from the White House with George Bush Sr.'s signature (hand signed or machine?)

Restrictions: normal copyright restrictions for published materials for newspapers, photographs

Record Group or Special Collection: RG-002 Presidents-Thomas Lane

Transfer Form: none

Inventories:

nku_accession_form.doc
1st ver: 2007/11/19
last rev: 2008/01/29

Appendix C.1b

Special Collections and University Archives
Northern Kentucky University

Accession Record

Accession Number: NKU2008-015

Date: July 2008

Title: Photographs

Office of Origin or Donor's name: Mary Jones, Steely Library staff

Quantity & Description:

- 1 CD of photographs taken by Mary Jones

o Archives Reading Room under construction	2006	5 color JPGs
o Archives Reading Room post construction	9/27/2007	48 color & B&W JPGs
o Farris Reading Room under construction	8/30/2007	8 color JPGs
o Farris Reading Room under construction	10/1/2007	4 color JPGs
o Farris Reading Room post construction	7/23/2008	15 color JPGs
o Bank of Kentucky Arena under construction	8/2007	7 color JPGs
o Harriet Tubman's nieces' event in the	7/15/2008	104 color and B&W JPGs

Archives Reading room

Restrictions: Donor Agreement on file

Record Group or Special Collection: RG-020 Buildings

RG 032 Events-Steely Library-Harriet Tubman's nieces

Transfer Form:

Inventories:

nku_accession_form.doc
1st ver: 2007/11/19
last rev: 2008/01/29

Appendix C.2

Generic File Structure

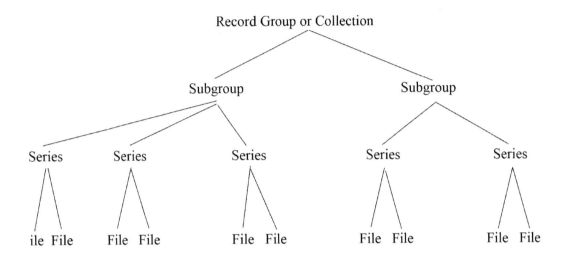

Generic file structure. Courtesy of the author.

Appendix C.3

Banks Family Papers File Structure

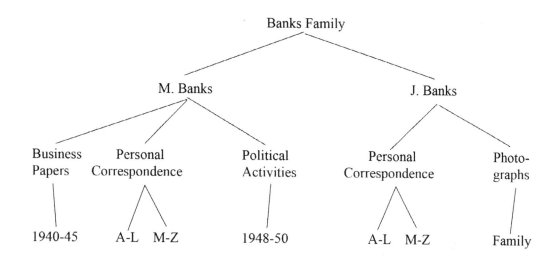

Banks Family Papers File Structure. Courtesy of the author.

Appendix C.4

Sample File Folder Headings

MS-409 Chelmsford Ginger Ale Co.	Employee Files - A-F	1902-1927	Box 1, Folder 1
MS-409 Chelmsford Ginger Ale Co.	Correspondence	1902-1904	Box 1, Folder 4
MS-409 Chelmsford Ginger Ale Co.	Photographs – Factory	early 20th c.	Box 3, Folder 1

MS-508 Banks Family Papers	Michael Banks	Business Correspondence	1940-1945	Box 1, Folder 1
MS-508 Banks Family Papers	Jennifer Banks	Family Photos	1938-1947	Box 3, Folder 1

Appendix C.5

Chelmsford Ginger Ale Company Records
MS-409

ABSTRACT

The collection contains a small amount of organizational records for the Chelmsford Ginger Ale Company, including employee files, correspondence, newspaper advertising, unidentified photographs, and two oversize financial ledgers documenting an early-twentieth-century family business in Chelmsford, MA.

SUMMARY INFORMATION

Creators: Henry Jones
Span Dates: 1902–1932, undated   **Bulk Dates:**
Extent: .694 cubic feet, two oversize boxes
Languages: English
Repository Location: Chelmsford Historical Society, 40 Byam Rd, Chelmsford, MA 01824

ACCESS POINTS

Subjects:
Names:
Places:
Formats:
Functions:
Occupations:

RELATED MATERIALS

Separated Materials:
Related Archival Materials: *A Chelmsford Sampler* by Aida Bacon includes an article on the Ginger Ale Company.
Existence and Location of Originals:
Existence and Location of Copies:
Publication Note:

ADMINISTRATIVE/BIOGRAPHICAL HISTORY

The Chelmsford Ginger Ale Company was founded in 1902 by local resident Henry Jones. Initially located at the Jones residence, the business was successful enough that Jones soon relocated to Acton Road, near the center of town. Henry's son George eventually joined him in the business. In 1931 a fire damaged a significant portion of the bottling and production rooms and the company never recovered financially, eventually closing the next year.

SCOPE AND CONTENT

The collection contains organizational records for the Chelmsford Ginger Ale Company. The records are organized into a single series, Business Records, which includes employee records, correspondence, newspaper clippings illustrating product ads, two oversized financial ledgers, and undated photographs of the exterior and interior of the factory. Interior photos illustrate the machinery used for manufacturing and bottling. Unidentified employees appear in some photographs.

SYSTEM OF ARRANGEMENT

This section is for the system of arrangement.

CONTAINER LISTING

Description	Date	Box	Folder
Series 1: Business Records			
Employee Files A-W		1	1-3
Correspondence	1902-1932, undated	1	4-14
News clippings	1902-1914, 1919-1929, undated	2	1-7
Photographs	Undated	3	1-5
Accounts Payable	1903	Oversize box 4	
Accounts Receivable	1904	Oversize box 5	

CONDITIONS GOVERNING ACCESS AND USE

Conditions Governing Access: This collection is open for research use.
Physical Access:
Technical Access:
Conditions Governing Reproduction and Use: The copyright law of the United States (Title 17, US Code) governs the reproduction of copyrighted material. The user assumes full responsibility and any attendant liability for the fair use of materials requested in total compliance with the copyright law of the United States (Title 17, US Code) that may arise through the use of any requested materials.
Preferred Citation: Box #, Folder #, MS-409, Chelmsford Ginger Ale Company Records, Chelmsford Historical Society, Chelmsford, MA.

ACQUISITION AND APPRAISAL

Immediate Source of Acquisition: Gift from George Jones
Custodial History: The records were donated by George Jones, son of the company founder Henry Jones.

NOTES

Processing Information: Processed by Chelmsford Historical Society volunteers, 1964.

Appendix C.6

Sample Electronic File Structure Trees

Arrangement for Digital Photographs

Photographs from a family/historical manuscript collection

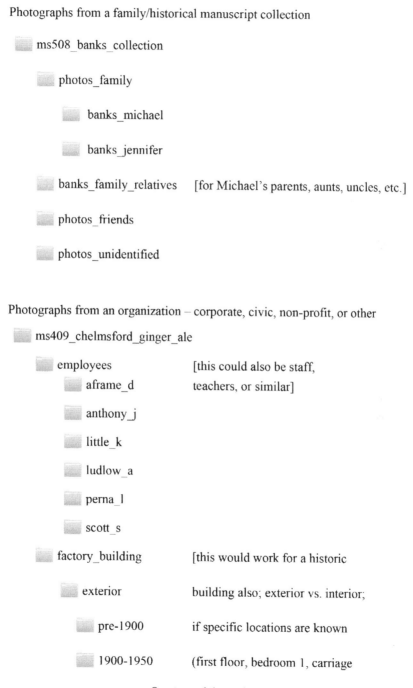

ms508_banks_collection

    photos_family

        banks_michael

        banks_jennifer

    banks_family_relatives   [for Michael's parents, aunts, uncles, etc.]

    photos_friends

    photos_unidentified

Photographs from an organization – corporate, civic, non-profit, or other

ms409_chelmsford_ginger_ale

    employees   [this could also be staff,

        aframe_d   teachers, or similar]

        anthony_j

        little_k

        ludlow_a

        perna_l

        scott_s

    factory_building   [this would work for a historic

        exterior   building also; exterior vs. interior;

            pre-1900   if specific locations are known

            1900-1950   (first floor, bedroom 1, carriage

Courtesy of the author.

undated	house) and there are enough
interior	photos, they can be further
undated	subdivided by location, then date]

School photographs – classes or individual photos, identified or unidentified

ms321_campbell_county_schools

    district_1

        1880_1900

        1901_1950

        1960s_1970s

            grade_1   [this would be all grade 1 except Mrs. Henderson because

                mrs_henderson   hers is the only identified class]

            grade 4

            grade_unidentified   [other grades are missing or unidentified]

    district_2

Photographs of property with multiple locations or buildings

elm_st	[sometimes historical societies
212	document sections of town to
214	show changes over time of key
1995	historic districts. Property is
2005	always best organized by location,
216	not owner; alphabetize by street
304	name, then by property number]

Courtesy of the author.

- laurel_st
- lee_st
- thomas_st

- founders_hall
  - exterior
    - subdivide by dates if necessary
  - interior
- nunn_hall

Sports photographs

- school_name
  - boy's or men's
    - list sport alphabetically
      - team [photos]
        - divide by date if necessary
      - individual
        - alphabetic by last name
        - unidentified
      - action/game
        - organize by season
  - girl's or women's

- recreation league
  - gender
    - sport
      - year/season

Courtesy of the author.

Appendix C.7

Sample Labels for Photographs that Were Scanned to Link Them to Digital Copy

A digital copy of this image exists.

File name: campus_life_orientation_001_300.jpg

Format: *Record Group name-Series name-image #-300 is the scanning resolution in dpi-file format*

Location: Z:\Special Collections\scanned_images_RG047_Campus_Life

This is the hard drive file location of the digital copy of the print which has this label

Scanned: 2 Nov 2009 at 300 dpi on Fujitsu 4340 color scanner

This is metadata about the scan made of the photo with this label

A digital copy of this image exists.

File name: extracurricular_dance_team_001_1999_300.jpg

Format: *1999 is what is known of the date for this photo*

Location: Z:\Special Collections\scanned_images_RG047_Extracurricular

Scanned: 3 Nov 2009 at 300 dpi on Fujitsu 4340 color scanner

A digital copy of this image exists.

File name: w_basketball_redmond_d_002_600_.tif

Format: *w designates women's-name of sport-name of individual in photo last name, first initial*

Location: computer NKU# 064621C:\archives_photos\athletics

Scanned: 1 Jul 2009 at 600 dpi on Fujitsu 4340 color scanner

Appendix C.8

Sample Fee Structure for Reproduction of Materials

Approved Fee Schedule (charged to patrons by Archives Department) for July 1, 2019–June 30, 2020

A. Reproduction
  1. Copying fee
     - Current NKU students/faculty/staff   1-20 cys $ .15 /cy
       21 and up cys $ .25/cy
     - All others $ .25/cy
  2. Photographic prints $10 each
  3. Scans $10 each
  4. Audiovisual originals $10 per physical piece

B. Other Fees
  1. Postage and Handling
     - First Class delivery $5 each
       (1 videocassette, 1 audiocassette, 1 CD/DVD, up to 8 oz paper copies)
     - "Overnight" delivery (USPS) $20 each
       (1 videocassette, 1 audiocassette, 1 CD/DVD, up to 8 oz paper copies)
  2. Burn a CD/DVD $5 each
  3. Commercial access/Publication fee $100 per image
     (book/journal/film)
  4. Archives Research fee (commercial use) $25/hr

Appendix C.9

Sample Labels for CDs and DVDs

MS-709	Spring Brook Dairy	CD-Data
Series 1	Correspondence	RHS2009-10
File 1	1993–2000	
Original files created with Microsoft Office Word		

MS-409	Chelmsford Ginger Ale	DVD-Data
Series 3	Photographs	CHS1963-052
File 1	Factory	
300 dpi JPEG scans of original B&W photos		
Copyright status—unknown		

MS-710	L. Doolittle Photo Studio	DVD-Data
Series 2	Photographs	
File 1	Graduation-Individuals—"A"	
41 300 dpi TIFF files (color)		
Copyright owned by Liza Doolittle		
Must call for permission to use		

MS-710	L. Doolittle Photo Studio	DVD-Video
Series 3	Videos	
File 1	Ames Wedding	
Name of file format		
Open with _____ [name software]		
Copyright owned by Liza Doolittle		

Appendix D

Vendors

Appendix D.1

Partial Vendors List

Vendors often include information about specific products to help you decide whether product A or B is better suited to your needs. Some offer newsletters or blogs to which you can subscribe. Often they include an educational component as well as new product information.

Archival Methods
235 Middle Rd., Henrietta, NY 14467
Phone: 1-866-877-7050
Fax: 1-585-334-7067
Website: https://archivalmethods.com
E-mail: mail@archivalmethods.com to subscribe to their newsletter and mailings.

This vendor focuses on photographic supplies. A recent blog post describes how to care for tintype photographs: https://www.archivalmethods.com/blog/tintypes-archival-preservation/.

Gaylord Archival
PO Box 4901, Syracuse, NY 13221-4901
Customer Service: 1-800-448-6160
Fax: 1-800-272-3412
Website: https://www.gaylord.com
E-mail: customerservice@gaylord.com

Gaylord sells archival supplies, including CD and DVD storage boxes, Tyvek sleeves, Pigma Micron pens, foil-back labels for electronic records, boxes specifically configured for video- and audiocassettes, and many other supplies appropriate for a wide range of archival records. Their Research Center (free resources) is rich with resources for organizations and individual on a wide range of topics (see bottom of their web page). They also have a glossary.

Hollinger/Metal Edge
9401 Northeast Dr., Fredericksburg, VA 22408
Phone: 1-800-634-0491 or 540-898-7300
Fax: 1-800-947-8814
Website: https://www.hollingermetaledge.com

Hollinger and Metal Edge were originally two separate companies until they merged some time ago. Hollinger focused on a wide variety of boxes and folders. Metal Edge carries a diverse range of archival products, including photographic supplies.

Rochester Institute of Technology/IPI
70 Lomb Memorial Dr., GAN-2000
Rochester, NY 14623-5604
Phone: 1-585-475-5199
Website: https://www.imagepermanenceinstitute.org
E-mail: ipiwww@rit.edu

The Image Permanence Institute (IPI) is a nonprofit research laboratory based at the Rochester Institute of Technology. IPI "is a recognized world leader in the development and deployment of sustainable practices for the preservation of images and cultural property."[1] They sell PEM environmental monitors (which are also available from several of the vendors listed here) and A-D strips to check the condition of film.

University Products, Inc.
517 Main St., Holyoke, MA 01040
Phone: 1-800-628-1912
Fax: 1-800-532-9281
Website: https://www.universityproducts.com
E-mail: info@universityproducts.com

University is another archival supplier with a broad range of supplies. At the bottom of the page on the right are links to another glossary and how-to tips and videos.

Note

1. Wikipedia, s.v. "Image Permanence Institute," accessed November 8, 2019, https://en.wikipedia.org/wiki/Image_Permanence_Institute.

Glossary

A Glossary of Archival & Records Terminology by Richard Pearce-Moses is available online at no charge from the Society of American Archivists at http://www2.archivists.org/glossary. It is also available in print.

access: The ability to use materials, inventories, or information. Access may require legal authorization, software, hardware, or retrieval from other physical locations.

access copy: A reproduction of an original archival document, photograph, illustration, or other record that is used by researchers in place of the original in order to better preserve or protect fragile or valuable originals from irreparable damage or theft. Also called a user copy or surrogate.

accession: The process by which an institution "takes physical custody and assumes legal and administrative control over a body of records." It includes documenting the transaction in a register, log, or database of the institution's holdings. An accession can also refer to the records themselves, as a group, that make up one accession.[1]

accession number: A unique number or code assigned to each new accession to link all parts of the accession to each other and to their associated documentation like the deed of gift.

access points: Or search terms, include names, places, subjects, formats (of the records), functions (of an office), and occupations according to DACS. They describe the substantive information in a set of records. This is an optional field in a DACS-compliant finding aid.

accretion: New material that is added to an existing collection or record group. Also called an accrual.

acquisition: New records that are obtained by donation, purchase, or records transfer. Can be an accretion or accrual.

administrative/biographical history: This field provides context for the records being described by providing essential information about the person, family, or organization that created or collected the records. This is an optional field in a DACS-compliant finding aid.

appraisal: The process of evaluating material offered to an archives or other historical organization to determine whether it has sufficient long-term research value to accept it as part of its holdings. The process involves the assessment of criteria and is different from a monetary appraisal of the fair market value of something.

archives: Materials created or received by a person, family, or organization (public or private) in the conduct of their affairs and preserved because of the enduring value of their informational content or as evidence of the functions or responsibilities of their creator.[2] The broadest, most general and inclusive term used to describe archival records. The organizational unit responsible for managing the institution's records of enduring value. The physical space that houses the archival records.

arrangement: A combination of intellectual and physical processes that organize records according to the two archival principles of provenance and original order in order to reveal their contents and significance. Arrangement intellectually identifies groupings within a collection or record group and physically places material in a particular sequence.[3]

artifactual value: The value of an item based upon its physical form versus its intellectual content. Artifactual value is the prime component of intrinsic value. See intrinsic value.

base layer: One of two layers in magnetic media, the base layer provides structural support.

binder layer: One of two layers in magnetic media, the binder layer contains the magnetic particles that translate into audio or video information. It is also thinner and more fragile than the base layer.[4]

bit depth: The number of bits used to represent each pixel in an image. Sometimes the term is used to represent bits per pixel and at other times, the total number of bits used multiplied by the number of total channels.[5]

bulk dates: The oldest and most recent dates for the majority of the records being described. See span dates.

call slip: A form typically used in an archives research room used to call for or request records to be retrieved from storage for use.

cased photographs: A category of photographs common in the mid-nineteenth century. Due to their fragile nature, they were mounted in shallow hinged boxes made of wood. Some cases were elaborately carved, others covered in leather, paper, or cloth. Typically daguerreotypes and ambrotypes were cased because the images were on glass, but some tintypes were cased to protect from scratching the image.[6]

closed records: A group of records that will have no new records added to it, usually because the records creator is either deceased or the organization is defunct. See open records.

closed stacks: A storage system for archival records, rare books, and historical or cultural objects that does not permit access or browsing by researchers. Staff members retrieve material requested by patrons. See open stacks.

collection: An aggregate term used to describe "a group of materials with some unifying characteristic." It can be an artificial collection of materials collected by the same individual or about the same subject.[7] See papers and records.

collection policy: An important document that details what the organization will and won't collect. It may identify records creators, subjects, formats, or geographic locations of the records it will accept.[8] It should be sufficiently specific to answer the question of whether a particular set of records falls within the scope of the policy yet allow some leeway for the acceptance of unexpected but suitable records.

collective description: The practice of describing related records as a unified group or unit in finding aids or catalog records. Collective description is contrasted with item-level description. Collective description starts with the general and proceeds to the specific; collection or record group, series, and folder level.[9]

conservation: A professional specialty requiring specialized training to perform physical or chemical treatments to repair damage to records, materials, or objects.[10] See preservation.

control file: The function of a control file and a donor file are the same: to collect important documentation about a body of records for the purpose of managing the same. Examples include the transfer form, accession record, processing plan, and loan or conservation documents. The method of acquiring the material in question is different. An institution may obtain new records by transfer of its own inactive records from an office. Since these records are not donated, the term donor file would be inaccurate. See donor file.

controlled vocabulary: A limited set of terms or phrases used as access points or subject terms in an index, catalog record, or software database. Only one term represents a concept so all material related to that concept can be retrieved using that term.[11]

data content standard: A set of formal rules that specify the information within a field and how to format it. Examples include DACS.

deaccession: The process of reevaluating items already in the collection and removing them if they no longer fit the collection policy, are too badly damaged to use, or have marginal research value.

deed of gift: Also called a donor agreement. A legal document transferring physical and intellectual property rights, like copyright, in the material being given by a donor to the organization. The document may contain restrictions on access or use of the donated materials. An artist may retain the copyright to his art, or a collection may be closed for a period.

description: The written record of the physical organization of a body of records. The process of creating a finding aid or other access tool that provides context for and helps researchers locate information in a set of records.

documentary form: Terms that describe the documentary form or intellectual characteristics of records being described (minutes, diaries, reports, maps).[12]

donor agreement: See deed of gift.

donor file: The purpose of a donor file is to assemble the documentation needed to manage the collection, object, or items given. Examples include the deed of gift, donor correspondence, an appraisal, and conservation or loan documents. Everything important to know about the donation is located in one spot, making it easier to answer questions about the donation. The file holds information *about* the donation, not items *from* the donation. See control file.

evidential value: Some institutional records have evidential value in the historical sense, meaning they document the structure, functions, and activities of the institution that created them. Examples include annual reports and meeting minutes.[13] See informational value.

eye readable records: Records that can be read by the human eye without the use of a machine. Examples include paper records and microfilm or microfiche. Contrast with machine-dependent records.

file: "A group of documents related by use or topic, typically stored in a folder" (or group of folders if the file is large). Examples include all the correspondence for 1981, all the correspondence with a specific person or business, or all the correspondence on a specific topic.[14]

finding aid: A "written" document that includes a generally agreed-upon set of information about a collection or record group that provides context and is used by researchers to discover information in the body of records. Finding aids provide intellectual control over the institution's records, come in many formats and can exist electronically rather than on paper. See inventory.

form or format: "Terms that indicate the documentary form(s) or intellectual characteristics of the records being described" (e.g., minutes, diaries, reports, etc.) "provide the user with an indication of the content of the materials based on an understanding of the common properties of particular document types."[15] PastPerfect uses "medium" to mean format.

foxing: Small brown disfiguring spots on paper probably caused by the presence of tiny metal particles in the paper, triggered by the combination of high humidity and temperature.[16]

holdings: The sum total of all the historical or archival or cultural items owned by an institution, archives, or manuscript repository regardless of the format: records, photographs, objects, books, film, maps, etc.

housing: A general term used to describe all the various types of archivally safe containers and products used to store archival records and materials of all formats. To house or rehouse records is to put or transfer them into acid free, archival folders, envelopes, photo sleeves, boxes, or other housing appropriate for their size and format.

inclusive dates: See span dates.

informational value: The degree of usefulness a set of records is judged to have based on its information content. The more ways in which a set of records can be used to provide information, the higher its informational value. See evidential value.

institutional archives: Records created by businesses, organizations, or institutions that are maintained by the body that created them because the records document information of permanent value about the institution, its activities, and its transactions.

institutional knowledge: Knowledge acquired over time by people who work or volunteer at an institution about the institution's collections and their informational content as well as the specific guidelines, policies, and practices of the institution.

intellectual control: To gain control over the contents of a collection by knowing what is in a collection including its size, information content or significance, and the dates of the material. This information is initially recorded in various internal forms and eventually in finding aids to make it available to researchers.[17]

intrinsic value: All types of records can have intrinsic value. This is their monetary value due to age; content; the circumstances under which they were created; someone's signature; seals, stamps, or attachments; illustrations; or uniqueness. See artifactual value.

inventory: A document that includes a generally agreed-upon set of information about a collection or record group that is used by researchers to discover information in the body of records it describes. A type of finding aid. See finding aid.

item: The smallest archival unit or lowest hierarchical level for arrangement or description purposes. It is something that can be distinguished from a group and is complete in itself. An item is not the same as one piece of paper. It may consist of one physical item, such as a photograph, but can consist of more in the case of a [multi-page] letter or a report [of pages bound together].[18]

levels of control: The practical implementation of provenance and original order. Five hierarchical levels: the repository, record group or collection, series, file, and item, which progressively group and describe records from the most general to the most specific.[19]

lignin: "A complex polymer that makes cell walls in plants strong and rigid."[20]

lignin free: "Lignin-free paper is produced from cotton or linen, or other materials from which the lignin, a natural component of wood that darkens when exposed to light, has been chemically removed."[21]

linked (open) data: Technology that links related items across the internet. Hyperlinks require a person to know about related items to create a link between them. The use of linked open data technology enables computers to locate related items across the internet that are unknown to the person encoding names, concepts, subjects, and other search terms.

machine-dependent records: Records that require a specific type of machine to access the information recorded therein. Examples include phonograph recordings, reel-to-reel tapes, compact discs, and other computer formats. Contrast with eye-readable records.

manuscript collection: Unpublished papers created, received, or acquired by an individual or family during their private life (as opposed to during "official" hours when they are employed by someone). This may include photographs, diaries, scrapbooks, financial or legal records, and other types of unpublished materials. Also called papers or personal papers. Contrast with record.

manuscript repository: A type of archives that collects archival records of permanent enduring value created by private individuals, other institutions, businesses, or government.

master copy: A duplicate of a digital or microform preservation copy, stored separately from the preservation copy, that is used to make new access copies when needed.

migration: The "process of converting records to newer formats in order to maintain their compatibility with a newer generation of hardware and/or software computer technology" in order to retain the ability to "read" (interpret and understand) a digital file.[22]

MS: abbreviation for manuscript as in manuscript collection.

name authority file: A list of the preferred form of names used in finding aids, catalog records, or other descriptive systems. These lists include possible variations for each name, which refer the user back to the preferred form.[23]

open records: A group of records that is expected to receive new additions as more records are created, that will require integration with the existing records already in the archives. See closed records.

open stacks: A storage system that typically allows users to access and browse materials for themselves. Typically used for books in a library. See closed stacks.

original order: "The second fundamental principle of archival arrangement" states that records should be kept in the same order in which they were kept, filed, or maintained by their creator in order to provide evidence of how the records were used by their creator. Although this is a goal, it is not always possible. In the case of personal papers, original order may be completely lost. "Provenance and original order provide information *about* a group of records which is not *in* those records, but which is essential to understanding them."[24]

orphan work: A copyright-protected work for which the rights holder is unidentified or if known, for whom there is insufficient information to locate to request permission to use the protected work.

papers: A group of materials created, received, or acquired by the same person or family in the course of their affairs "of a purely private or non-public character," not official records of a business, organization, or governmental unit. Papers includes materials in a variety of formats.[25] See collection and record.

personal papers: See manuscript collection and papers.

photographic activity test (PAT): An international standard that "predicts possible [chemical] interactions between photographic images and the enclosures in which they are stored." PAT is an international standard test (ISO18916) for evaluating photo storage and display products developed by the Image Permanence Institute (IPI). Enclosures for photographic materials should pass the PAT (this should be noted in the supplier catalog); those that pass would be appropriate for other types of collection materials as well.[26]

preservation: Activities or actions such as rehousing or relative humidity and temperature regulation that protect "materials by minimizing chemical and physical deterioration and damage to minimize the loss of information and extend the life of cultural" records, materials, and objects.[27]

preservation copy: A copy of an original analog record that is in poor or fragile physical condition or created when an original made by an obsolete machine-readable format is **migrated** to a new format. A digital preservation copy is not normally used except to create **master copies**, which are used to create access copies. Once created, digital preservation copies are put away in safe storage under environmentally stable conditions to greatly extend its life until a new master copy is required.

processing: An inclusive term that describes work done on a new **acquisition** to prepare it for research use and establish intellectual control of the records. It includes physically **arranging** the records, followed by **description** of the arrangement in a fixed format such as a word document (finding aid or inventory) available in print or on the web, a software program (collection management or database), a library catalog record, or a similar equivalent. Processing normally also includes **rehousing** in appropriate archival containers (folders and/or boxes), labeling, and possibly minor **preservation** work.

provenance: The fundamental archival principle that requires that the records of one records creator be kept separate from the records of all other records creators in order to preserve their context. Museums interpret provenance as information about the chain of custody or ownership for an object or item.

public archives: The body of records created or received by a government agency during the course of its business, which it preserves, and which is available to the public.

pull card: A card placed on the collections storage shelf when a container is removed from the shelf for any reason. The pull card records who removed the container, when, and for what purpose. When the container is returned, the card is removed and annotated with the return date and name of person reshelving the container.

record: Any type of recorded information, regardless of physical form or characteristics, created, received, or maintained by an institution or organization and preserved as evidence of an activity or function. Not all records have sufficient value to merit preservation. Records are often unique. The term implies documents as opposed to objects or published material.[28]

record copy: The single copy of a document designated as the official copy for purposes of duplication, reference, or preservation, often the first or original copy.[29]

record group: A body of records that have the same **provenance**, meaning they are created by the same organizational unit (the same person, office, department, or other group) and are of a convenient size to manage. This term does not apply to manuscripts or personal papers.

reference code: According to DACS 2.1, this is a required field in a finding aid. It is a unique number assigned to a manuscript collection or record group. Per DACS, it is comprised of a country code + a repository code + a unique local identifier for the specific materials being described, which could be the MS or RG number.[30]

refolder: To transfer the contents of each non-archival folder to an acid-free archival one. One step in **processing** a new acquisition. See housing.

refresh: The process of copying digital content from one digital medium to the same medium or another without any alteration to ensure continued access as the storage medium becomes obsolete or degrades.[31] See migration.

rehouse: To transfer archival materials into archival containers appropriate for their size and format. See housing.

repository: Any type of organization, business, institution, or government unit that keeps documents regardless of format. Repository or repository level refers to all the collections or records held by a single organization, that is, its holdings.[32] See levels of control.

RG: abbreviation for record group.

scope and content: Generally, this section of an inventory or finding aid summarizes the contents of the collection at the series level, describing the format and functions of series records, dates, creators, strengths, and weaknesses (such as significant chronological weaknesses, missing records). It is one of the most important parts of a finding aid.

secondary value: When records have information that can be used for a different purpose from the one for which they were originally created. Informational and evidential values are examples of secondary value.

separation sheet: A form that is filed in the original location of an item that is removed. It describes the item that has been removed and tells where to find it. Items are often removed because they are dissimilar to surrounding records (photographs, CDs, audio or video cassettes) and/or to protect fragile, damaged, or oversized items.

series: A group of similar records organized according to some filing system (in the original office) that are related because they were created as a result of the same function, activity, or process; or because they have a particular form; or because of some other relationship pertaining to their creation or use. The series is the most common unit in archival description. Correspondence, applications, licenses, publicity, and theatrical programs are all examples of a series.[33]

shelf list: A listing of the archives holdings organized in the same order as the materials are physically stored. Staff uses shelf lists to manage the collections for various purposes such as locating all the electronic records to monitor them for obsolescence.

span dates: The dates of the oldest and most recent material in a collection or record group, series, or folder, also known as inclusive dates.[34] See bulk dates.

Special Collections: An institutional archives that collects the same type of materials as a manuscript repository in addition to the records of its own organization. The term *Special Collections* is used to describe their historical or manuscript holdings. Colleges and universities are the most common examples of institutions with Special Collections.

standards: A national, international, or industry-wide agreement that establishes practices or qualities to achieve common goals.[35]

surrogate copy: See access copy.

thesaurus (singular), thesauri (plural): A specialized vocabulary list of preferred words and phrases commonly used for indexing, subject terms in catalog records, or other types of description.[36]

transfer form: A form used to document the transfer of managerial responsibility and physical custody of permanent institutional records from their office of origin to the institution's archives.

type: The nature or genre of the material being described. Examples include text, still image, sound, image, moving image, collection, software.[37]

union catalog: A single catalog that includes descriptive records of the holdings of more than one institution. A union catalog can exist in print or electronically.

user copy: See access copy.

Notes

1. Fredric M. Miller, *Arranging and Describing Archives and Manuscripts*, Archival Fundamental Series (Chicago: Society of American Archivists, 1990), 5.

2. Pierce-Moses, *Glossary*, s.v. "archives."

3. Gregory S. Hunter, *Developing and Maintaining Practical Archives: A How-to-Do-It Manual*, 2nd ed., How-to-Do-It Manuals for Librarians, no. 122 (New York: Neal-Schuman, 2003), 113; Pierce-Moses, *Glossary*, s.v. "Describing Archives: A Content Standard."

4. Dan Riss, "Preservation of Magnetic Media," Conserv O Gram Number 19/8, 2, 1993, National Park Service, accessed January 28, 2020, https://www.nps.gov/museum/publications/conserveogram/19-08.pdf.

5. Federal Agencies Digitization Guidelines Initiative, *Glossary*, s.v. "bit depth (image)," accessed January 3, 2020, http://www.digitizationguidelines.gov/glossary.php?alpha=B.

6. Pierce-Moses, *Glossary*, s.v. "cased photographs"; also e-mail with Mark Savolis, September 28, 2010.

7. Pierce-Moses, *Glossary*, s.v. "collection"; Society of American Archivists, *Describing Archives A Content Standard [DACS]*, 2nd ed. (Chicago: Society of American Archivists, 2013), 2.3.19 "collection," 21.

8. Pierce-Moses, *Glossary*, s.v. "collection development."

9. Pierce-Moses, *Glossary*, s.v. "collective description."

10. Bruce W. Dearstyne, *Managing Historical Records Programs: A Guide for Historical Agencies* (Walnut Creek, CA: AltaMira Press, 2000), 123.

11. Pierce-Moses, *Glossary*, s.v. "controlled vocabulary."

12. Society of American Archivists, *DACS*, "Documentary Forms," xxiv.

13. F. Gerald Ham, *Selecting and Appraising Archives and Manuscripts*, Archival Fundamentals Series (Chicago: Society of American Archivists, 1993), 8.

14. Pierce-Moses, *Glossary*, s.v. "file."

15. Society of American Archivists, *DACS*, "Documentary Forms," xxiv.

16. Northeast Documentation Center, Preservation 101 Course, Session 4: Caring for Paper Collections, accessed January 21, 2020, https://www.nedcc.org/preservation101/session-4/4evaluating-your-collections.

17. Hunter, *Developing and Maintaining Practical Archives*, 1108, 131–33.

18. Pierce-Moses, *Glossary*, s.v. "item."

19. Miller, *Arranging and Describing Archives*, 28.

20. Pierce-Moses, *Glossary*, s.v. "lignin."

21. Northeast Document Conservation Center, Preservation Leaflet 5.5: "Storage Enclosures for Photographic Materials," 5, updated 2018, https://www.nedcc.org/free-resources/preservation-leaflets/overview.

22. AIMS Workgroup, Appendix A, Glossary, s.v. "migration," in *AIMS Born Digital Collections*, accessed January 31, 2020, https://dcs.library.virginia.edu/files/2013/02/AIMS_final_appA.pdf.

23. Pierce-Moses, *Glossary*, s.v. "name authority file."

24. Hunter, *Developing and Maintaining Practical Archives*, 114; Miller, *Arranging and Describing Archives*, 20.

25. Pierce-Moses, *Glossary*, s.v. "papers" and "personal papers."

26. Northeast Document Conservation Center, Preservation Leaflet 5.5.

27. Pierce-Moses, *Glossary*, s.v. "preservation."

28. Pierce-Moses, *Glossary*, s.v. "record"; Society of American Archivists, *DACS*, 2.3.19, 21.

29. Pierce-Moses, *Glossary*, s.v. "record copy."

30. Society of American Archivists, *Describing Archives*, 39–40.

31. InterPARES 2 Project, Glossary, s.v. "refreshing" and "refreshing of records." http://interpares.org/ip2/display_file.cfm?doc=ip2_glossary.pdf&CFID=22752451&CFTOKEN=33719892.

32. Pierce-Moses, *Glossary*, s.v. "repository."

33. Pierce-Moses, *Glossary*, s.v. "series."

34. Pierce-Moses, *Glossary*, s.v. "span dates."

35. Pierce-Moses, *Glossary*, s.v. "standard."

36. Pierce-Moses, *Glossary*, s.v. "thesaurus."

37. Dublin Core Metadata Initiative, "DCMI Metadata Terms," accessed February 6, 2020, https://www.dublincore.org/specifications/dublin-core/dcmi-terms/.

Bibliography

Aber, Hal. Smithsonian Institution. "Guidelines for Universal Design of Exhibits." Accessed April 22, 2020. https://airandspace.si.edu/rfp/exhibitions/files/j1-exhibition-guidelines/4/SI%20 Guidelines%20for%20Universal%20Design%20of%20Exhibits.pdf.

American Society of Appraisers. "Personal Property." Accessed October 7, 2019. https://www .appraisers.org/Disciplines/Personal-Property.

Appraisers Association of America. "Elements of a Correctly Prepared Appraisal." Accessed October 7, 2019. https://www.appraisersassociation.org/index.cfm?fuseaction=document .viewDocument&documentid=1187&documentFormatId=1958&vDocLinkOrigin=1&CFID =21507973&CFTOKEN=27bd18718951c29e-63EB3FBE-1C23-C8EB-80B8475A189F5FBA; "Areas of Specialization." https://www.appraisersassoc.org/index.cfm?fuseaction=Page .ViewPage&pageId=525; "Code of Ethics." https://www.appraisersassociation.org/index.cfm? fuseaction=document.viewDocument&documentid=720&documentFormatId=1353& vDocLinkOrigin=1&CFID=21507973&CFTOKEDN=27bd18718951c29e-63EB3FBE-1C23 -C8EB-80B8475A189F5FBA; "Find An Appraiser in Our Directory," https://www.appraisersas sociation.org/index.cfm?fuseaction=Page.ViewPage&PageID=741; "Standards." https://www .appraisersassoc.org/index.cfm?fuseaction=Page.ViewPage&pageId=526; "Expert's Guide to Collecting." https://www.appraisersassociation.org/index.cfm?pageId=790.

Association of College and Research Libraries. "ACRL/RBMS Guidelines for Interlibrary and Exhibition Loan of Special Collections Materials." Accessed August 30, 2019. http://www.ala.org/ acrl/standards/specialcollections.

———. "ACRL/RBMS Guidelines Regarding Security and Theft in Special Collections." Accessed August 23, 2019. http://www.ala.org/acrl/standards/security_theft.

Bailey, Rebecca, and Remington Leach, eds. *"With Every Consequence of War": The Civil War in Northern Kentucky Remembered.* Highland Heights: Northern Kentucky University, 2009.

Bellardo, Lewis J., and Lynn Lady Bellardo, comps. *A Glossary for Archivists, Manuscript Curators, and Records Managers.* Archival Fundamentals Series. Chicago: Society of American Archivists, 1992.

Blauvelt, Angela. "How to . . . Properly Store Your Negatives?" *Archival Methods Newsletter* no. 3 (December 10, 2009). https://www.archivalmethods.com/newsletters/issue3.

Bowling, Mimi, and Richard Strassberg. "Security in Archives and Manuscript Repositories." Society of American Archivists Workshop, Louisville, KY, June 26–27, 2008.

Brown, Karen E., and Beth Lindblom Patkus. "Emergency Management 3.11 Collections Security: Planning and Prevention for Libraries and Archives." Accessed August 23, 2019. https://www .nedcc.org/free-resources/preservation-leaflets/overview.

Buck, Solon J. "Essentials in Training for Work with Public Archives and Historical Manuscript Collections." In *Archives and Libraries*, edited by A. F. Kuhlman, 114–22. Chicago: American Library Association, 1940. This is the published proceedings of the American Library Association's annual meeting for 1940.

Byers, Fred R. *Care and Handling of CDs and DVDs—A Guide for Librarians and Archivists.* Washington, DC: Council on Library and Information Resources and Gaithersburg, MD: National Institute of Standards and Technology, 2003. Accessed September 9, 2019. https://clir.wordpress.clir.org/wp-content/uploads/sites/6/pub121.pdf.

Campbell, Tony. "E. Forbes Smiley III Map Thefts: Reports and News Stories." Accessed August 23, 2019. http://www.maphistory.info/smileynews.html.

Carlisle, Stephen. "The Music Modernization Act: What's In It, Why Is It In There, and Is It a Good Thing?" Accessed August 3, 2019. http://copyright.nova.edu/music-modernization-act/.

Carmicheal, David W. *Organizing Archival Records: A Practical Method of Arrangement and Description for Small Archives.* 4th ed. Lanham, MD: Rowman & Littlefield, 2019.

Code Sector. "TeraCopy for Windows." Accessed June 28, 2019. http://www.codesector.com/teracopy.

CUEI: College & University Engagement Initiative. "Carnegie Classification." Accessed October 24, 2019. https://www.brown.edu/swearer/carnegie. Select Previous Classifications.

Darrah, William C. *Cartes de Visite in Nineteenth Century Photography.* Gettysburg, PA: W. C. Darrah, 1981.

Dearstyne, Bruce W. *Managing Historical Records Programs: A Guide for Historical Agencies.* Walnut Creek, CA: AltaMira Press, 2000.

Denver Public Library. "Recovered James Lyman Brubaker Photographs: Are They Part of Your Institution?" Accessed August 23, 2019. https://www.flickr.com/photos/dplwesternhistory/sets/72157623286262023.

Eastman Museum. "Glossary." Accessed July 19, 2011.

Farr, Gail. *Archives & Manuscripts: Exhibits.* Basic Manual Series. Chicago: Society of American Archivists, 1980.

Gaylord Archival. "Archival Environmental Control." https://www.gaylord.com/listing.asp?H=3&PCI=128038.

Greenebaum, David. "Hidden Treasures: Rare Books in Your Library?" Lyrasis webinar, May 5–6, 2011.

Haider, Salman. "Anglo-American Cataloging Rules (AACR, AACR2, AACR2R)." Librarianship Studies and Information Technology. Accessed June 15, 2019. https://www.librarianshipstudies.com/2018/12/anglo-american-cataloguing-rules-aacr.html.

Ham, F. Gerald. *Selecting and Appraising Archives and Manuscripts.* Archival Fundamentals Series. Chicago: Society of American Archivists, 1993.

Hamill, Lois D. "Provenance and Original Order: The Evolution of Their Acceptance as Principles of Arrangement and Description." Master's thesis, University of Massachusetts–Boston, 1997. Ann Arbor, MI: UMI, 1997.

Hollister, Sean, "The Incandescent Light Bulb Isn't Dead," *The Verge*. Accessed August 30, 2019, https://www.theverge.com/2014/1/1/5263826/the-incandescent-light-bulb-isnt-dead.

Hunter, Gregory S. *Developing and Maintaining Practical Archives: A How-to-Do-It Manual*. 2nd ed. How-to-Do-It Manuals for Librarians, no. 122. New York: Neal-Schuman, 2003.

Image Permanence Institute. *The Archival Advisor, Photography Timeline*. Accessed July 19, 2011. https://www.archivaladvisor.org/index.shtml.

———. "Photographic Activity Test (PAT)." Rochester Institute of Technology. Accessed July 19, 2011. https://www.imagepermanenceinstitute.org/shtml_sub/srv_pat.asp.

Joint Steering Committee for the Development of RDA. *Resource Description and Access (RDA)*. Chicago: American Library Association, 2010.

Knapp, Tony, and Diane Vogt-O'Connor. "Caring for Cellulose Nitrate Film." Conserv O Gram Number 14/8. National Park Service. Accessed September 9, 2019. https://www.nps.gov/museum/publications/conserveogram/14-08.pdf.

Lee, Timothy, B., "Mickey Mouse Will Be Public Domain Soon—Here's What That Means." *Ars Technica*, copyright by Conde Nast, January 1, 2019. Accessed August 3, 2019. https://arstechnica.com/tech-policy/2019/01/a-whole-years-worth-of-works-just-fell-into-the-public-domain/.

Lewis, Alan. "Archives Basic Film Workshop." Association of Moving Image Archivists, Boston, November 19, 2002.

Library of Congress. "Care, Handling, and Storage of Works on Paper." Accessed August 31, 2019. https://www.loc.gov/preservation/care/paper.html.

———. "Preservation—Collections Care—Limiting Light Damage from Display/Exhibition." Accessed August 30, 2019. https://www.loc.gov/preservation/care/light.html.

Linden, Jeremy. "Environmental Data Analysis—Tips and Tricks." Image Permanence Institute Webinar in Sustainable Preservation Practices series, Rochester Institute of Technology, Rochester, NY, March 23, 2011.

———. "Sustainable Preservation Practices." Image Permanence Institute Webinar in Sustainable Preservation Practices series, Rochester Institute of Technology, Rochester, NY, May 25, 2011.

McCurley, Stephen, and Sue Vineyard. *101 Tips for Volunteer Recruitment*. Downers Grove, IL: Heritage Arts Publishers, 1988.

Midwest Archives Conference, Session 803. "Transforming Outreach with Community Archives." Detroit, Michigan, April 6, 2019.

Miller, Fredric M. *Arranging and Describing Archives and Manuscripts*. Archival Fundamental Series. Chicago: Society of American Archivists, 1990.

National Institute of Standards and Technology and Library of Congress, *Final Report: NIST/Library of Congress (LOC) Optical Disc Longevity Study*. Washington, DC, 2007. Accessed April 20, 2020. https://www.loc.gov/preservation/resources/rt/NIST_LC_OpticalDiscLongevity.pdf.

National Park Service. Museum Management Program: "NPS Museum Handbook, Part 1: Museum Collections." Accessed September 9, 2019. https://www.nps.gov/museum/publications/MHI/mushbkl.html.

Nolo. "Stanford University Libraries Copyright and Fair Use Website." Board of Trustees, Leland Stanford Junior University. Accessed July 4, 2019. http://fairuse.stanford.edu/Copyright_and_Fair_Use_Overview/index.html.

Northeast Document Conservation Center. *Preservation 101*. Accessed November 3, 2019. https://www.nedcc.org/preservation-training/preservation-101.

——. Preservation Leaflet 3.3 Emergency Planning. Accessed April 4, 2020. https://www.nedcc.org/assets/media/documents/Preservation%20Leaflets/3_3_emergency_2017.pdf.

Northeast Historic Film. *How Do I Identify Film?* Bucksport, ME: Northeast Historic Film, 1994.

O'Toole, James M. *Understanding Archives and Manuscripts*. Archival Fundamentals Series. Chicago: Society of American Archivists, 1990.

Paris, Jan. NEDCC Preservation Leaflets, 7.7: "Choosing and Working with a Conservator," https://www.nedcc.org/resources/leaflets/7Conservation_Procedures/07ChoosingAConservator.php.

Partridge, Wendy, painting conservator at Inter-museum Conservation Association, Cleveland, OH, June 27, 2011 e-mail correspondence with author.

Pearce-Moses, Richard. *A Glossary of Archival and Records Terminology*. Archival Fundamentals Series II. Chicago: Society of American Archivists, 2005.

Peterson, Kit A., comp. "Digital Master Images—Sample Technical Specifications for Photograph Collections." Washington, DC: Library of Congress, 2004. http://www.loc.gov/rr/print/tp/DgtlMastersSamplSpecsSelctdRcmndFinal7_2004.pdf.

——. "Introduction to Basic Measures of a Digital Image for Pictorial Collections." Washington, DC: Library of Congress. Accessed August 17, 2019. https://www.loc.gov/rr/print/tp/IntroDgtlImage.pdf.

——. "What to Look for in a Scanner." Washington, DC: Library of Congress. Accessed August 17, 2019. https://www.loc.gov/rr/print/tp/LookForAScanner.pdf.

Prints and Photographs Division, Library of Congress. "Safe Handling Tips for Pictorial Collections." Library of Congress. Accessed July 9, 2019. https://www.loc.gov/rr/print/tp/SafeHandlingTip.pdf.

Riss, Dan. "Preservation of Magnetic Media." National Park Service. Conserv O Gram Number 19/8. Accessed September 9, 2019. https://www.nps.gov/museum/publications/conserveogram/19-08.pdf.

Ritzenthaler, Mary Lynn. *Preserving Archives and Manuscripts*. Archival Fundamentals Series. Chicago: Society of American Archivists, 1993.

Ritzenthaler, Mary Lynn, Diane Vogt-O'Connor, Helena Zinkham, Brett Carnell, and Kit Peterson. *Photographs: Archival Care and Management*. Chicago: Society of American Archivists, 2006.

Schlipp, John. *Intellectual Property and Information Rights for Librarians*. Santa Barbara: ABC-CLIO, 2019.

Serrell, Beverly. *Exhibit Labels*. Walnut Creek, CA: AltaMira Press, 1996.

Shaw, Seth E. "Arrangement and Description of Electronic Records, Part 1." Society of American Archivists Digital Archives Specialist workshop, Chapel Hill, NC, June 11, 2015, course booklet.

Slattery, Oliver T., and Jian Zheng. *Final Report: NIST/Library of Congress (LOC) Optical Disc Longevity Study*. Washington, DC: Library of Congress and Gaithersburg, MD: National Institute of Standards and Technology, 2007. Accessed September 9, 2019. http://www.loc.gov/preservation/resources/rt/NIST_LC_OpticalDiscLongevity.pdf.

Society of American Archivists. "ALA/SAA Joint Statement on Access to Research Materials in Archives and Special Collections Libraries, Section 4 Policies." Accessed August 23, 2019. https://www2.archivists.org/statements/alasaa-joint-statement-on-access-to-research-materials-in-archives-and-special-collection.

———. *Describing Archives: A Content Standard [DACS]*. 2nd ed. Chicago: Society of American Archivists, 2013.

———. 2019 Annual Conference Program. Accessed October 14, 2019. https://www2.archivists.org/am2019/attend/pre-conference-courses.

Strassberg, Richard. "Security in Archives and Manuscript Repositories." Society of American Archivists workshop, Louisville, KY, June 26–27, 2008, handout and course booklet.

Suits, Linda Norbut. "Hazardous Materials in Your Collection." Conserv O Gram Number 2/10. National Park Service. Accessed September 9, 2019. https://www.nps.gov/museum/publications/conserveogram/02-10.pdf.

Trinkaus-Randall, Gregor. *Protecting Your Collections: A Manual of Archival Security*. Chicago: Society of American Archivists, 1995.

Twomey, Steve. "To Catch a Thief." *Smithsonian*, April 2008.

University Products. "Equipment & Tools, Temperature & Humidity Monitoring." University Products, Inc. https://www.universityproducts.com/equipment-tools/temperature-and-humidity-monitoring-equipment.

US Copyright Office. "Circular 40: Copyright Registration for Works of the Visual Arts." Accessed September 4, 2019. http://www.tabberone.com/Trademarks/defs/legal/CopyrightOffice/circ40_VisualArts.pdf.

US Department of the Interior. National Park Service. "Museum Management Program, NPS Museum Handbook." National Park Service. Accessed April 4, 2020. https://www.nps.gov/museum/publications/handbook.html.

Vineyard, Sue. "Evaluating Volunteers, Programs and Events." *Voluntary Action Leadership* (Summer 1988): 25–26.

Vogt-O'Connor, Diane. "Care of Archival Digital and Magnetic Media." Conserv O Gram Number 19/20. National Park Service. Accessed September 9, 2019. https://www.nps.gov/museum/publications/conserveogram/19-20.pdf.

Watkin, Kathleen. "What is 'Universal Design?'" Museum Association of Saskatchewan (blog), December 18, 2017. https://saskmuseums.org/blog/entry/what-is-universal-design.

Wikipedia, s.v. "cloud storage." Accessed October 21, 2019. https://en.wikipedia.org/wiki/Cloud_storage.

———, s.v. "file hosting service." Accessed October 21, 2019. https://en.wikipedia.org/wiki/File_hosting_service.

———, s.v. "halogen lamp." Accessed August 30, 2019. https://en.wikipedia.org/wiki/Halogen_lamp.

———, s.v. "U-Matic." Accessed September 19, 2019. http://en.wikipedia.org/wiki/U-matic.

———, s.v. "universal design." Accessed April 22, 2020. https://en.wikipedia.org/wiki/Universal_design.

———, s.v. "xerography." Accessed July 24, 2019. http://en.wikipedia.org/wiki/Xerography.

Wilsted, Thomas P. *Planning New and Remodeled Archival Facilities*. Chicago: Society of American Archivists, 2007.

Witt, Betsy S., Jennifer C. Whitfield, and Adam J. Stepansky. *PastPerfect Software for Museum Collections: Version 5 User's Guide*. Exton, PA: PastPerfect Software, Inc., 2010.

Yakel, Elizabeth. *Starting an Archives*. Lanham, MD: Society of American Archivists, 1994.

Index

digital records: appraisal, 169; arrangement and description of, 170; CD/DVD care and handling, 171–72; digital file migration, 169; format for maintaining digital files, 169; migration defined, 272; opening digital files, 169; refreshing defined, 273; refreshing digital files, 169; sample arrangements for digital records, 252–53, 257–59. *See also* description

digitization: access copy, 100–103, 163; delivery systems impact technical decisions, 106; equipment selection, 96–97; examples of delivery methods, 107–8; file copying, 100; file naming, 74–75, 98–100, 102, 214; file naming examples, 99; file size calculation, 98; file storage, 102–4; file structure/organization, 100–102, 103; labels linking photos to digital scans, 260; master copy, 98, 100–103, 163; master copy defined, 271; preservation copy, 97–98, 100–103, 163; preservation copy defined, 272–73; scanning specifications, 97–98, 215; selecting records to digitize, 104; workflow for multi-page text documents, 105–6, 242; workflow for photographs 105, 237

disaster preparedness: emergency response plan, 203–4; prepare for, 201–2; prioritize collections, 202–3; scope, 201

donation. *See* accession; acquisition

donor: interview, 7; document, 7

donor agreement. *See* deed of gift

donor file: contents of, 8; defined, 269–70. *See also* control file

electronic records. *See* digital records

emergency planning. *See* disaster preparedness

evidential value: defined, 270 ; examples, 6

exhibits: alternative exhibits, 144–46; archival versus museum, 135–36; display methods, 141–42; exhibit documentation, 140–41; labels, 143–44; loan documents, 139–40; publicity, 144; purpose, 135; sample exhibit loan documents, 231–34; selection of materials, 137; topic selection, 136–37; universal design, 141; virtual exhibits, 145–46. *See also* preservation; security

fair use. *See* copyright

finding aid: defined, 270; sample finding aid, 255. *See also* inventory

foxing, 152; defined, 270

government records. *See* public archives; records

gunsmiths, 187

hierarchical levels. *See* levels of control

housing: bound volumes/books, 20; defined, 270; labeling boxes, 21; refoldering, 19; refoldering defined, 273

informational value: defined, 270; examples, 6

institutional archives: defined, 1–2, 270; transfer form, 275

insurance: during shipping, 187–88; and exhibits, 140, 143, 232–33

intellectual control: defined, 25, 271

intrinsic value: defined, 271; examples, 6

inventory: application guide for DACS fields in template, 29–36; DACS compliant template, 27–29; defined, 271; goal of, 26; table format of DACS fields application, 37–42; writing process, 26. *See also* description; finding aid

levels of control: defined, 13, 271

light. *See* preservation

linked open data: defined, 271; linking records across institutions, 44; and Omeka S software, 146

machine dependent: audio records, 163–64; defined, 271; digital records, 168–69

manuscript collection: defined, 2, 271; naming, 10. *See also* arrangement

manuscript repository: defined, 2, 271

moving film. *See* projected film

name authority file: application of, 43–44; defined, 43, 272; in PastPerfect, 44, 47

National Union Catalog of Manuscripts (NUCMC), 44

objects: replacing plaques with photographs, 176; storage, 175–76

Omeka software, 146

original order: defined, 13, 272; replacement during arrangement, 18–19. *See also* provenance

PastPerfect software: access points, 53–55; collection level records, 51–53; completing common fields in catalog records, 49; creating description/catalog records, 46–47; describing photographs, 76–78; identifying records for research question, 121; virtual exhibits, 145

personal papers. *See* manuscript collection; papers

personnel: college/university faculty, 194, 197; consultants, 195; consultants for projected film care, 168; grant employees, 194–95, 198;

management of, 195–99; professional service days, 195; student interns, 193-94, 196–97; volunteers, 193, 196. *See also* civic engagement

photograph: handling, 59–61, 212; housing, 68-71; identification based on format, 63-65; identification based on image information, 66–68; identifying information from photographs as objects, 65–66; processes compared to formats, 76; publication contract, 90-91, 225; publication fee, 89-90, 261; storing photographs, 70-72; use on the internet, 88. *See also* arrangement; copyright; description

Photographic Activity Test (PAT): defined, 272; and photographic supplies, 68

preservation: book storage, 158-59; book tying, 158; defined, 272; during arrangement, 20; fire and water protection, 155; good housekeeping, 154-55; implications for exhibits, 137-39; lighting, 138-39, 154; recommended settings for relative humidity and temperature, 152-53; relative humidity and temperature for collections storage, 152-53; relative humidity and temperature for exhibits, 139; relative humidity and temperature monitors, 153. *See also* art; audio records; disaster preparedness; housing

processing: defined, 273; goal, 13; processing plan, 17; sample processing plan form, 220; sample processing checklist, 221. *See also* arrangement; description

projected film: care, 168; cellulose ester, 167; deterioration, 166-67; identification, 167-68; nitrate, 166; polyester, 167; reformatting, 168

provenance: defined, 13, 273. *See also* original order

public archives: defined, 1-2, 273

pull cards, 119-20, 142; defined, 273; sample, 227

rare books. *See* books

record: defined, 1, 273

record group: defined, 14, 273; naming, 10. *See also* accession; arrangement

reference process, 115-18; assessment of research use, 122; call slips, 128; fees, 117, 119, 261; identifying records for research question, 121; inexperienced researchers, 115-16; records retrieval, 117; reference interview, 115-16; researcher registration, 128, 229; role of staff, 115-19; safe handling of materials, 117, 119-20, 210-12; use of surrogate copies, 119. *See also* security

rehousing. *See* housing

relative humidity. *See* preservation

scanning. *See* digitization

scope and content: defined, 274; scope and content field in inventory, 33

secondary value: defined, 274; examples, 6

security: in collections storage space, 151-52; documents that aid security, 128, 131, 230; during exhibits, 120, 130-31, 139, 142-43; during processing, 130; good practices, 126-27; notorious thieves, 125; people's honesty level, 126; and researchers, 117, 119, 127-29; and temporary personnel, 198-99; withdrawal log, 121, 228

shipping companies, 187-88

Silverfast software, 105, 237-39, 242-45

special collections, 2, 274

standards: *DACS*, 25-27, 37-42; defined, 42, 274; *Standardized Statistical Measures and Metrics for Public Service Areas in Archival Repositories and Special Collections Libraries*, 122

surrogate copies, 119

temperature. *See* preservation

TeraCopy software, 100

value of archives, 122

vendors: archival supplies, 264-65; services, 189

Visual Artists Rights Act (VARA). *See* copyright

women's names: formation of, 42-43

About the Author

Photo by Adam Henry.

Lois Hamill is head of the Special Collections and University Archives department and a professor at Northern Kentucky University's Steely Library. A practicing archivist for more than twenty years, she holds master's degrees in history/archival methods and library and information science; and is both a certified archivist and a digital archives specialist. She has been professionally active in New England and the Midwest, holding board positions and serving on committees. Ms. Hamill presented at the first Global Conference on Digital Memories in Salzburg, Austria; has spoken at national and regional conferences on diverse history, archival, and library topics; and is a successful grant writer. She is the award-winning author of two books: *Archives for the Lay Person: A Guide to Managing Cultural Collections* and *Archival Arrangement and Description: Analog to Digital*.